THE COURT MASQUE

WITHDRAWN
NDSU

W9-BAS-237

33 1161

PLATE I

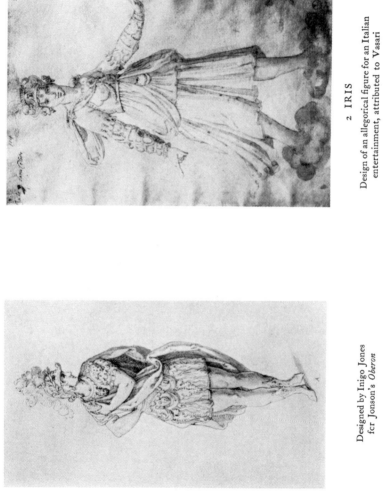

Designed by Inigo Jones
for Jonson's *Oberon*

Copyright of His Grace the Duke of Devonshire.

2 IRIS

Design of an allegorical figure for an Italian
entertainment, attributed to Vasari

Foto Garberini

THE COURT MASQUE

A STUDY IN
THE RELATIONSHIP BETWEEN
POETRY & THE REVELS

BY

ENID WELSFORD

SOMETIME FELLOW OF NEWNHAM
COLLEGE

NEW YORK / RUSSELL & RUSSELL

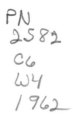

PN
2582
C6
W4
1962

FIRST PUBLISHED IN 1927
REISSUED, 1962, BY RUSSELL & RUSSELL
A DIVISION OF ATHENEUM PUBLISHERS, INC.
WITH THE PERMISSION OF CAMBRIDGE UNIVERSITY PRESS
L. C. CATALOG CARD NO: 62-13854
ISBN: 0-8462-0294-8
PRINTED IN THE UNITED STATES OF AMERICA

To
MY BROTHER

PREFACE

THE English Court Masque is not an unexplored subject, and anyone venturing to follow in the wake of Professor Brotanek, M. Reyher, Sir E. K. Chambers, Mr W. J. Lawrence, and the learned editors of *Designs by Inigo Jones* is almost bound to offer a preliminary word of excuse and explanation. This book, however, is not intended as an exhaustive treatise on the masque. My chief aim has been to interpret and to coordinate rather than to accumulate facts, and consequently it has not been my primary object to add to the great wealth of detailed information collected in *Les Masques anglais* and *The Elizabethan Stage*, although I have tried to trace the foreign sources of our Court entertainments in order to retell the story in the light of this new evidence, and to set the English revels against their proper background of European folk-custom and Court pageantry.

My central theme is the English Court masque of the seventeenth century—that elaborate form of entertainment in which all the skill of all the best artists, poets, and musicians of the day was required for the purpose of introducing a band of masked noblemen to an expectant assembly. This is the central theme, but not the whole scope of the book.

My attention was first drawn to the masque when, in preparing some lectures on Shakespeare, I had to consider the relationship between *A Midsummer Night's Dream* and the Elizabethan revels. First of all it was necessary to find an answer to the question what is a masque; and the answer proved of an unexpected interest and complexity. The masque, I began to realise, had no modern parallel; and yet for several centuries it had been inseparably bound up with social life, and had had an incalculable influence on art and literature. I wondered why it had disappeared so completely, and whether its loss was to be regretted. My curiosity moreover was whetted by something paradoxical in the very essence of the masque. It was exclusive and aristocratic, yet popular; it was artificial and sophisticated, yet primitive—so primitive indeed that it was strangely like those pantomimic ritual dances of which we hear so much from the students of comparative religion. All this I could see would carry me far beyond the scope of an hour's lecture; and moreover, before I could begin to answer my original question about *A Midsummer Night's Dream*, I had to satisfy my mind upon a further point. Was it part of my business to put labels upon Shakespeare's plays? Yet I soon discovered that it was not a matter of attaching a label, or even of tracing an influence: it was a matter of understanding a creative process and the nature of the individual poet's debt to his environment. It was in a word a question not of classification but of interpretation.

I have therefore been chiefly pre-occupied with the significance of the masque, and this has determined the arrangement of the book. In the first part I have dealt with its origin and history; in the second part I have tried to show its influence upon art and poetry; in the third part I have discussed certain aspects of the masque, which do, I believe, throw some light upon the nature of art, and particularly upon its social value.

My obligations are many. In the first place, I have to thank Newnham College for the generous gift of a Fellowship. His Grace the Duke of Devonshire very kindly allowed me to study his collection of the designs of Inigo Jones at Chatsworth, and also gave me permission to reproduce some of them in this book. I have pleasant recollections of courtesy shown to me in libraries in Paris and Florence, and I am grateful for permission to reproduce designs from collections in the Uffizi Gallery, the Louvre, and the Bibliothèque Nationale.

This book would hardly have been written had it not been for the unfailing interest and encouragement of both Professor and Mrs Chadwick, and to Professor Chadwick I am also deeply indebted for a long and delightful initiation into research. Mr E. J. Thomas of the Cambridge University Library I thank for the unremitting patience with which he has read my proofs discussed my problems, made valuable suggestions, and in par ticular I thank him for indispensable help given to me in certain philological difficulties. To Miss Jane Harrison I owe gratitude not only for the stimulus of her writings, but also for most welcome personal encouragement.

The Index is the work of Miss M. H. James, to whom my thanks are due for the expert care which she has bestowed upon the somewhat intractable subject-matter.

Finally it is a pleasure to record my indebtedness to the authorities and officials of the Cambridge University Press.

E. W.

March 1927

CONTENTS

PART THREE

THE SIGNIFICANCE OF THE REVELS

LIST OF ILLUSTRATIONS

Note: The figure on the title-page and cover is a design by Inigo Jones for 'Entheus or Poeticke Furie'; see p. 256 and *Designs*, p. 48, No. 56. Copyright of His Grace the Duke of Devonshire.

PART ONE: *The Origin &*
History of the Masque

✳✳✳✳✳✳✳✳✳✳✳✳✳✳✳✳✳✳✳✳✳✳✳✳✳✳✳✳

CHAPTER I

The Origin of the Masque

'Who lists may in their mumming see
Traces of ancient mystery.' SCOTT.

THE story of the Masque begins with the dance of the seasonal festivals. Curiously enough, the Court masquerade, that very sophisticated amusement of Renaissance society, was more primitive than the drama of the rough Elizabethan playhouses. From the beginning to the end of its history, the essence of the masque was the arrival of certain persons vizored and disguised to dance a dance or present an offering. This brings us very close indeed to ancient and almost world-wide ritual.

At critical seasons of the year, spring, harvest, the winter solstice, there are strange doings among undeveloped races and superstitious peasants all the world over. At these times, when the fate of the food supply hangs in the balance, the mummers make their appearance. Dressed in leaves or flowers or beasts' skins, sometimes masked, sometimes with blackened or whitened faces, they parade the streets and fields, leaping and shouting, clashing swords and staves, sprinkling water, waving torches, ringing bells, all this to the accompaniment of much horseplay and many indecent jokes and gestures. But in spite of the noise and buffoonery, there is rhythm and purpose in the movements of the mummers. They arrive in procession, pass in and out of the houses, gather together to dance round the sacred tree or Maypole. They drive out into the woods some grotesque person or effigy, they bring back from the woods flowers, budding branches, and one of their number dressed up as a Jack-in-the-Green. They chase and kill an animal. They choose a sovereign to rule over them. They dance out a mimic battle in which their grotesque leader is supposed to be slain—this sham fight sometimes taking the form of a drama in which the hero is married, killed and brought to life again.

But who are the mummers? As a rule the term is used very loosely[1], but I think that it will always be found to imply a set

---

[1] It has, as I shall try to show, a more definite meaning, but at first I am using the word in the usual vague way.

of disguised persons who perform some action which is of ritual origin but has little or no connection with the great historical and official religions, although it is still performed as a good custom rather than as a mere game. In England the mummers are familiar to us as villagers who disguise themselves at Christmas time and act a traditional play involving, among other things, a fight, the death of the hero, his revival by the doctor, and a final quête or money collection[1]. This Christmas mummers' play is substantially identical with the Plough Monday play and the Pace-eggers' play which is performed at Easter; it has points of resemblance with the folk-plays of countries as far removed as Scandinavia and Thrace; its main action is paralleled not only by European folk-customs but by the Old Comedy of the Greeks, by various myths and rites recorded of ancient peoples and modern savages in every part of the world[2]. Without knowing it, the Christmas village actor is keeping up practices proper to that early stratum of religion which persists unchanged while higher creeds and philosophies rise and fall. The same can be said of all other mummers, including the masquers of Whitehall. For the masque, as we shall see, is a sophisticated mumming.

Simple-minded and uncivilised people are apt to believe in the efficacy of magic and the existence of spirits. Volumes have been written on the nature of magic and its relation to religion; here it must suffice to remark that both religious ritual and the magic art consist chiefly in the performance of imitative acts, but that the doings of the priest appear to refer to powers outside himself; whereas the magician seems to be acting on the principle that 'like produces like' and that 'things which have once been in contact continue to act on each other even after the contact has been severed.'[3]

[1] For a typical mummers' play cf. E. K. Chambers, *The Medieval Stage* (Oxford, 1903), vol. II, p. 276, appendix K; R. J. E. Tiddy, *The Mummers' Play* (Oxford, 1923).
[2] Cf. *Med. Stage*, vol. I, chap. X; T. F. Ordish, *Folk-Drama*, in *Folk-Lore*, vol. II, pp. 314 ff., vol. IV, pp. 149 ff.; F. M. Cornford, *The Origin of Attic Comedy* (London, 1914), especially chap. IV; Sir William Ridgeway, *Dramas and Dramatic Dances of non-European Races* (Cambridge, 1915); and *The Origin of Tragedy* (Cambridge, 1910), pp. 16–24 (Sir W. Ridgeway does not believe in the ritual origin of Greek comedy); B. S. Phillpotts, *The Elder Edda* (Cambridge, 1920), chap. XI ff. especially p. 126.
[3] Sir J. G. Frazer, *Lectures on the Early History of the Kingship* (London, 1905), p. 37.

Judging from known practices, it seems that part at least of the effectiveness of a magic act depends upon the purpose behind it, the chief function of the spell being to formulate the intention of the act[1].

There is then method in the madness of the mummers. They come leaping and dancing that the crops may grow, they perform sword-dances and dramas of death and resurrection to help on by imitative magic the eternal struggle between summer and winter, darkness and light, life and death.

Some of the mummers' doings are more difficult to explain. The folk-plays, May games, and sword-dances of European peasants probably preserve fragments of an old, widespread, and cruel ritual, in which at certain seasons of the year some poor wretch was chosen as a mock priest-king, was united in sacred marriage with a priestess, was allowed a short life of regal luxury, and finally was put to death for the sake of the god, whom, in some curious kind of way, he was supposed to represent. This tragedy is the main theme of *The Golden Bough*, yet nobody really knows why the periodic death of the king or his substitute was regarded as essential to the well-being of the community[2].

[1] R. R. Marett in art. *Magic* in *E.R.E.* outlines the most representative views as to the nature of magic and its relation to religion. The most familiar theory of magic is that which Sir J. G. Frazer expounds in *The Golden Bough*; cf. *The Magic Art*, vol. I, pp. 52 ff. Marett disagrees with Frazer' conclusions. His own theory is developed in the aforesaid article and more convincingly in 'From Spell to Prayer' in *The Threshold of Religion*[2] (London, 1914), pp. 29 ff. For the view that magic is a religious activity (i.e. an expression of group consciousness) cf. É. Durkheim, *Les formes élémentaires de la vie religieuse* (Paris, 1912), bk III, chap. III, pp. 501 ff., 'Les rites mimétiques et le principe de causalité.' He regards mimetic magic as an expression of the desires of the social group; and belief in its practical utility as due to experience of its psychological efficacity. This idea is the basis of Miss Jane Harrison's lucid and beautiful book on *Ancient Art and Ritual* (Home University Library), where she expounds the doctrine that art and religion both spring from magical ritual but that religion errs in attributing objective reality to its subject-matter.

[2] A vast amount of evidence on all these points is collected in the variou' volumes of *The Golden Bough*[3]; cf. vol. XII, Bibliography and General Index pp. 332–335 under *King, Kings* and *Kingship*. Cf. also A. B. Cook, *The European Sky-God*, in *Folk-Lore*, vols. XV, XVI, XVII, XVIII, esp. XV, pp. 299 ff., 369 ff., XVI, pp. 299 ff.; and *Zeus* (Cambridge, 1914), esp. vol. I, pp. 11–14, 70–81, 644–715, and references given in vol. II, pt II, Index II, s.v. *King*.

The facts that bear on the sacrifice of the king are brought together

The mock king was not the only being to perish in reality or pretence at the festivals. Some of our village customs make it evident that there was a time when an important action of the mummers was the killing of the sacred animal. After the death, the worshippers clothed themselves in the hide and horns of their victim, they sprinkled his blood over themselves, their fruit trees and their crops, they buried portions of his flesh in the fields, they all partook of a sacrificial banquet. This rite, also, has its obscure side (i.e. the relationship between god and victim) but the sequel to the slaughter shows that it rests chiefly on the principles of contagious magic[1]. Many of the sacrificial acts are only explicable on the assumption that the animal was full of contagious virtue, so that one at least of the motives leading to his death was the desire of the worshippers to shed his blood (i.e. his life) over themselves and their belongings, and to strengthen themselves and their crops by partaking of his fertilising flesh. Whatever else it may be, sacramental sacrifice is, at least, a means of establishing physical contact with a source of life and power, and the ceremonial procession which follows it, and which survives in the mummers' quêtes and processional dances, is an attempt to spread the infection of holiness through the whole community[2]. This quickening property was found in the sacred tree as well as in the sacred animal; so that it is not surprising to find that both tree worship and animal worship were practised at agricultural festivals, that both animal and vegetable offerings were acceptable to the gods, and that both skins and leaves were used as mumming disguises[3].

It is useless to re-invigorate crops and cattle if they are to be

with copious notes and references by Frazer in *Lectures on the Early History of the Kingship*, and more fully still in *The Dying God*. There is a brief discussion of Frazer's interpretation of these facts in *Med. Stage*, vol. I, pp. 133 ff.

[1] *Med. Stage*, vol. I, pp. 130–131.

[2] W. Robertson Smith, *Lectures on the Religion of the Semites* (London, 1894), pp. 312–352; *Med. Stage*, vol. I, chap. VI (where further references are given); J. Harrison, *Ancient Art and Ritual*, pp. 87–99; *E.R.E.* art. *Sacrifice*, 'Introductory and Primitive.'

[3] The wild man, who appears so frequently in the art and literature of the later Middle Ages and the Renaissance, seems to be a descendant of the worshipper who has made 'a garment of his god.' Both the hairy and the

left unprotected against their ghostly enemies. The lives of un-civilised people are profoundly affected by their belief that the world is swarming with spirits and souls of the dead[1]. Their attitude to these ghosts is ambiguous. Dead relatives are honoured, and there is some desire to keep in touch with them and to go on enjoying their help in war, agriculture, etc., and it is the main duty of some tribal medicine-men to invoke the dead or to become possessed by them[2]. The best way of keeping the dead in good temper is to supply them with plenty of food—particu-larly, it would seem, with beans or peas, which is interesting in view of the Twelfth Night custom of choosing a King of the Bean and Queen of the Pea[3]. Some peoples celebrate funerals and anniversaries by inviting the dead to a banquet, which is often eaten in silence—a fact worth recalling in view of the proverbial silence of the mediaeval mummers[4]. On the other hand, there is a strong feeling that the dead should not encroach too much on the sphere of the living, and steps are taken to keep them at a distance. One simple method of getting rid of ghosts is to sweep them out of the house[5]. Both attitudes are exemplified in the Balto-Slavonic festivals:

'One account describes the mourners at the funeral banquet inviting in the departed....What lay on the ground was not picked up, but was

leafy variety of wild man occur in the revels. He has possibly penetrated into Arthurian romance as 'the Grene Knyghte,' whose story looks like an account of an agricultural rite that has been misunderstood. Cf. *Med. Stage*, vol. I, p. 186, note 1.

[1] E. B. Tylor, *Primitive Culture* (London, 1913), vol. I, chap. XI; *E.R.E.* arts. *Aryan Religion, Animism*; Frazer, *Belief in Immortality* (London, 1913, 1922), *The Scape-Goat*, esp. chap. II; L. R. Farnell, *Greek Hero Cults and Ideas of Immortality* (Oxford, 1921), esp. chap. XII; E. Rohde, *Psyche*, English tr. of eighth ed. (London, 1925).

[2] W. W. Skeat, *Malay Magic* (London, 1900), pp. 59 ff.; G. Brown, *Melanesians and Polynesians* (London, 1910), p. 209; J. Roscoe, *The Baganda* (London, 1911), pp. 273, 275, 283 ff.; C. G. Seligmann, *The Veddas* (Cambridge, 1911), pp. 128 ff.; *E.R.E.* art. *Shamanism*.

[3] W. Warde Fowler, *The Roman Festivals* (London, 1899), pp. 109, 110; Frazer, *The Scape-Goat*, pp. 143-155; *E.R.E.* art. *Aryan Religion*, section entitled 'The food of the dead,' p. 27.

[4] For silence in chthonic ritual see Frazer, *Folklore of the Old Testament*, vol. III, pt III, chap. XVII, 'The Silent Widow.'

[5] Cf. Tylor, *op. cit.* vol. II, pp. 25 ff.; *E.R.E.* arts. *Death and Disposal of the Dead*, p. 440; *Carnival*, pp. 227-228.

left for friendless and kinless souls. When the meal was over, the priest rose from table, swept out the house, and hunted out the souls of the dead "like fleas," with these words, "Ye have eaten and drunken, souls, now go, now go!"[1]

Rites of this kind have points in common with scape-goat ceremonies and with the popular customs of sweeping away evil spirits and witches with brooms[2]; for in certain moods all spirits are dreaded, irrespective of their origin or character. So the mummers shout, ring bells, brandish swords and brooms, to scare away hostile influences of all kinds; they drive them off with whips, they burn them by lighting bonfires and running about the fields with flaming torches. Sometimes it is difficult to distinguish between expulsory rites and imitative magic. Bonfires have been explained as sun charms, and the shouting and bell-ringing may be interpreted as either an attempt to frighten away ghosts or as a method of arousing the vitality of the crops. Very likely both motives are at work[3].

Magical and religious ritual is practised chiefly at times which are felt to be turning-points in the life of men and of nature, such as the attainment of puberty, marriage, burial, spring, harvest, mid-winter, etc.

The history of European masques and mummings is bound up chiefly with the history of the agricultural festivals. It is difficult, however, to give a clear account of the customs belonging to the various feast days, because identical rites may be performed at any critical time of year and, moreover, the festivals have been dislocated and confused by the clash of different civilisations. In Europe we have to reckon with at least Christian, Roman and Celto-Teutonic calendars.

---

[1] Tylor, *Primitive Culture*, vol. II, p. 40.

[2] Broom-sweeping occurs in certain mummers' plays. 'Thus at Leigh the performance is begun by Little Devil Doubt, who enters with his broom and sweeps a "room" or "hall" for the actors....In the Midlands this is the task of the woman....' The broom is also used at the quête with which the plays end. 'In a considerable number of cases, however, the *quête* is preceded by a singular action on the part of Little Devil Dout. He enters with his broom, and threatens to sweep the whole party out, or "into their graves" if money is not given.' *Med. Stage*, vol. I, pp. 216–217.

[3] Cf. *The Scape-Goat*, especially chaps. III–VI.

In Western Europe, mumming took place at Christmas and Epiphany, Shrove Tuesday, Candlemas, May Day, St John's Eve, and many other festivals. For the history of the masque the most important mumming seasons are the Carnival and the Twelve Days of Christmas.

The name for a division of the year lasting from about mid-November to mid-January was derived from Yule[1], a mid-winter festival of the Teutonic peoples, about which we know little or nothing. For the Celts and Teutons the beginning of winter was the beginning of the year, when probably magical acts were performed to ensure the prosperity of the coming time. The feast at the beginning of winter was probably also a festival of the dead, and this aspect of it has survived in All Saints' Day and All Souls' Day. But above all, winter was a time of animal sacrifice and of great sacrificial banquets, for which there was an economic as well as a religious reason, for, since it was impossible to feed large numbers of cattle during the cold months, a great slaughter at the beginning of winter was a practical necessity. Bede tells us that the Anglo-Saxons called November 'blot-monath,' or the month of immolations, because it was then that they devoted to the gods the cattle that were to be killed[2].

The Kalends of January was a New Year festival which spread all over the Roman Empire. It was celebrated by the relaxation of all ordinary rules of conduct, and the inversion of customary social status. Masters and slaves changed places, feasted and played at dice together[3].

Christian ecclesiastics were unsparing in their denunciation of the Kalends. Peculiarly hateful to them was the custom of the perambulation of the streets by mummers dressed in skins, beast-masks or women's clothes, carrying with them the *cervulus*, a kind of hobby-horse which was probably a survival of the sacrificial victim.

---

[1] On the Christmas festival see A. Tille, *Yule and Christmas* (London, 1899).
[2] Bede, *De temporum ratione*, chap. xv.
[3] The ceremonial game of dice survived in mediaeval and Renaissance mummings; cf. *infra*, pp. 30, 32, 36, 37, 39–41.

'These miserable men and, still worse, some baptized Christians take on false likenesses and monstrous faces, of which people should rather be ashamed and sad....Others dress themselves up in the hides of their cattle; others put on the heads of animals....How horrible is it, further, that those who have been born men take on women's dresses, and effeminate their manhood by girls' dresses in an abominable masquerade!'[1]...'Therefore he who gives to anyone of those miserable men any human requirement in the Calends of January, when in the sacrilegious rite they rather rage than play, shall know he does not give it to men but to demons. Therefore, if you do not want to participate in their sins, do not permit that the stag or the cow or any such portent come before your house.'[2]

This cervulus procession seems to be a forerunner of the masque.

The Kalends, being a celebration of the New Year, was, like Yuletide, a time for prognostication and magic. Everything that happened on that day was ominous. People feared to carry fire or iron outside their houses, they offered presents to one another and to the Emperor, they decorated their houses with greenery to ensure a year of wealth and fertility. The same motive may lie behind the practice of setting out at night a 'Table of Fortune' loaded with food and drink; but there is some evidence that this was done partly at least for the sake of wandering spirits. The two ideas are not necessarily mutually exclusive[3]. In the eleventh century Burchard of Worms explained the custom as an offering to the goddesses of fate:

'You do what some women at certain seasons of the year are accustomed to do, in that you prepare a table in your house, and you place upon it food and drink, together with three knives, so that if those three sisters—whom antiquity and ancient folly call Parcae—should arrive, they might be refreshed there....You believe that those whom you call sisters may prove useful to you now or in the future.'[4]

In mediaeval times these Tables of Fortune were sometimes

---

[1] In the original *demutatione*; I should prefer to translate it 'transformation.'

[2] Caesarius of Arles?, *Sermo Pseud.-Augustin.* CXXIX, *de Kal. Jan.* in P.L. XXXIX, 2001; CXXX in P.L. XXXIX, 2003. Quoted in *Med. Stage*, vol. II, pp. 297–299, and in (English translation) Tille, *op. cit.* pp. 97, 98.

[3] Cf. Tille, *op. cit.* pp. 108–111.

[4] *Decreta* (Coloniae, 1548), 198 *d*. Quoted by Tille (original Latin), *op. cit.* p. 108, note 7; and in *Med. Stage*, vol. II, pp. 305, 306.

set out at Christmas and Epiphany as well as on New Year's Day. In the fifteenth century it was a custom in Bohemia to eat a lengthy roll on Christmas Eve.

'I am sorry to say that in that custom, as in the rest, the devil has invented a great illusion in his own favour; for, as I was told, in some regions the Christians put the rolls and knives on the tables and dishes, not for the praise of the childhood of Christ, but in order that in the night the gods might come and eat them.'[1]

In England also the 'Table of Fortune' was intended as a spirit banquet. In 1493 mention is made of 'alle that take hede to dysmal dayes, or use nyce observaunces in the newe moone, or in the new yere, as setting of mete or drynke, by nighte on the benche, to fede Alholde or Gobelyn.'[2] This food was sometimes eaten by maskers, who impersonated the spirits[3].

Whether popular survivals of these and other chthonic rites go back to the Kalends[4] or the Teutonic Yule feast is uncertain and from our point of view unimportant. Undoubtedly there are Christmas traditions which witness to a belief in the presence of ghosts and the advisability of propitiating them with food offerings, and that is all that really concerns the history of the masque.

Many legends and superstitions cling about the Twelve Days of Christmas which have nothing to do with the Gospel story[5]. Most of these customs—the election of the mock king, the lighting of bonfires, the wassailing of fruit trees, etc.—are Christmas observances derived from Yule or the Kalends, even from the ritual of spring and summer festivals[6]. Frazer has sug-

---

[1] Tille, op. cit. p. 110.

[2] Dives and Pauper (Pynson, 1493) quoted in John Brand, Observations on the Popular Antiquities of Great Britain, revised by Sir Henry Ellis (London, 1849), vol. I, p. 9, and cf. Med. Stage, vol. I, pp. 265 ff.

[3] Cf. infra, pp. 14, 15; Med. Stage, vol. I, pp. 266–268.

[4] For the Kalends cf. Ducange, s.v. Kalendae; Med. Stage, vol. I, chap. XI, 'The beginning of winter,' chap. XII, 'New Year Customs,' which gives further references. Cf. also particularly vol. II, appendix N, 'Winter Prohibitions,' which gives a whole series of adverse references to the Kalends, from the second to the eleventh centuries.

[5] Cf. Frazer, The Scape-Goat, pp. 313–345; Brand, op. cit. vol. I, pp. 21 ff.; Med. Stage, vol. I, pp. 243–244, 267, 269 (and note 2).

[6] There is a racy account of Twelfth Night customs in 'The Popish Kingdome or reigne of Antichrist, written in Latine verse by Thomas Naogeorgus (or Kirchmaier), and englyshed by Barnabe Googe...Anno 1570,'

gested that the Twelve Days represent an ancient intercalary period, which was once inserted to bridge the gap between the lunar and solar years[1]. The prevalence of superstition, the buffoonery and licentiousness, may have been due to the feeling that it was an anomalous period, falling outside the regular order of things and yet giving its character to the year that was to follow[2]. It is in favour of this view that the Twelve Days separating the two disputed anniversaries of our Lord's birth necessarily occupy a somewhat ambiguous position in the Church's calendar[3] and might well attract customs belonging to an ancient intercalary period. All this, however, is mere conjecture. In England Twelfth Night was the most important of all the masquing seasons.

The Christmas festival is elastic. Properly speaking, it ends with Epiphany or Plough Monday (i.e. the first Monday after Twelfth Night), but sometimes it is taken as extending from All Souls' Day to Candlemas, and according to some reckonings it merges into the Carnival[4].

Shrovetide or Carnival is ostensibly a time when Christian people permit themselves a final outburst of riotous merrymaking before submitting to the discipline of Lent; but since the chief Carnival customs, masquerades, broom-sweepings, the burial of the Carnival fool, are probably much older than the Christian religion, it has been suggested that it is a revival of the Saturnalia, a Roman festival of ploughing and sowing[5], which was very

4th Book printed in *Abuses in England,* ed. Furnivall (N.S.S. London, 1877–9), pt I, p. 326.

[1] Frazer, *The Scape-Goat,* p. 325.

[2] '...And in these dayes beside,
    They iudge what weather all the yeare shall happen and betide:
    Ascribing to ech day a month...' Googe, *op. cit.* p. 327.

[3] Cf. *Med. Stage,* vol. I, pp. 238–244.

[4] Cf. Records of City of Norwich cited in *Med. Stage,* vol. I, pp. 261–262, note 4 to p. 261; 'Gesta Grayorum,' p. 49, published by John Nichols in *The Progresses and Public Processions of Queen Elizabeth* (London, 1823), vol. III, pp. 262 ff.

[5] Warde Fowler, *op. cit.* pp. 269–273; Frazer, *The Scape-Goat,* chap. VIII, 'The Saturnalia and Kindred Festivals'; *E.R.E.* art. *Carnival.*

There is a very amusing and vigorous onslaught on the carnival customs of the sixteenth century in *Popish Kingdome,* p. 329. This attack is invaluable to the student of folk-custom.

similar in character to the Kalends, and was marked by the waiving of all ordinary rules of rank and conduct, and by the supposed presence and unusual activities of ghosts and spirits. A mock monarch was chosen by lot to preside over the Saturnalian revels.

The word 'Carnival' is of uncertain origin. Possibly the name is connected with the Christian aspect of the festival and is to be derived from *carne vale*, farewell flesh, or from *dominica ad carnes levandas*, a title given by Pope Gregory to the last Sunday before Lent. Usener derives 'carnival' from *currus navalis*, the ship car, and finds its origin in some ship procession similar to that which figured in the cult of the goddess Isis. Certainly in the Middle Ages ship processions were held as spring celebrations in England, Germany and the South of Europe, sometimes a plough taking the place of the ship[1].

The plough procession may take place either at Christmas or at the beginning of Lent; for the resemblance between the Kalends and the Saturnalia is paralleled by the resemblance between the Twelve Days and the Carnival. In England the Monday after Twelfth Night is called Plough Monday. On this day the Fool Plough is dragged about by young men dressed in white shirts, who are known as plough bullocks, boggons, or stots.

'They sometimes dance a morris- or sword-dance, or act a play. At Haxey, they take a leading part in the Twelfth Day "Hood-game." In Northants their faces are blackened or reddled.' The plough is accompanied by music and by one or more grotesques; the Bessy, a man dressed as a woman, and the Fool, a man adorned with skins, hairy cap and animal's tail[2].

It is worth noticing that the word 'boggon'[3] is a dialect word, meaning 'ghost, bug-a-bear, or terrifying spirit.' The white

---

[1] Chadwick, *The Origin of the English Nation* (Cambridge, 1909), chap. x, 'The Cult of Nerthus'; *E.R.E.* art. *Carnival*; *Folk-Lore*, vol. xvi, pp. 247–248, 257–259; J. Grimm, *Deutsche Mythologie*[4], vol. I, pp. 213 ff.

[2] *Med. Stage*, vol. I, p. 208, note 4; Brand, *op. cit.* vol. I, pp. 505–511.

[3] Cf. J. und W. Grimm, *Deutsches Wörterbuch*, s.vv. *Bögge, Bögke*: 'larva, terraculamentum,…vermummte gestalt.' The word seems also to have meant 'a spirit, a bugbear.' Cf. Grimm, *Myth.* vol. III, p. 146.

shirts may have originally represented dead-clothes[1]. Barnaby Googe describes a similar performance on Ash Wednesday[2].

In *Dives and Pauper* one of the New Year superstitions is 'ledyng of the ploughe aboute the fire as for gode begynnyng of the yere, that they shulde fare the better alle the yere followyng.'[3]

Other rites, besides the plough procession, belong both to Christmas and the Carnival, for instance, the mummings connected with the mythical being Perchta, which are very interesting to students of the masquerade.

Perchten-running was a name given to processions of masked mummers in the Alpine regions of Germany, who rushed along the streets, leaping and dancing, blowing ashes and soot in people's faces, cracking whips, ringing bells, and accompanied in their wild progress from village to village by a crowd of lads bearing torches and lanterns, and also (in Salzburg) by two fools, a man, and a man in woman's clothing. The mummers were divided into two bands known as the Beautiful Perchten and the Ugly Perchten. In the Tyrol all of them wore masks and tall pointed caps with bells attached, but the Beautiful ones were decorated with ribbons, the Ugly ones hung about with mice, rats, chains and bells. In Salzburg 'the Ugly Perchten are properly speaking twelve young men dressed in black sheepskins and wearing hoods of badger-skins and grotesque wooden masks, which represent either coarse human features with long teeth and horns, or else the features of fabulous animals....They all carry bells....From time to time they stopped at a farm, danced...before the house, for which they were rewarded by presents of food....' Their procession took place by night. The beautiful Perchten, on the other hand, wear no masks and always appear by day. Perchten-leaping is supposed to have a good influence on the harvest. 'The appropriate season for the celebration of the rite was Perchta's day, that is Twelfth Night...but in some places it was held on Shrove Tuesday, the last day of the Carnival, the very day when many farmers of Central Europe jump to make the crops grow tall.'[4]

---

[1] The traditional white smock of mummers and morris-dancers, the white dresses and the white faces of carnival clowns such as Pierrot, are also possibly connected with chthonic ritual. White clothes are thought of as dead-clothes, for instance the ghost is still popularly regarded as an insubstantial form clothed in a white sheet. For white in connection with death cf. Ridgeway, *The Origin of Tragedy* (London, 1908), p. 89; Webster, *Primitive Secret Societies*, p. 44, note 2, which gives many further references. For white in connection with the Wild Hunt, Perchta, Holda, etc., cf. Grimm, *Myth.* vol. I, pp. 222, 232, vol. II, pp. 777 ff., 803 ff.

[2] *Popish Kingdome*, p. 331. Quoted in Brand, *op. cit.* vol. I, p. 97.

[3] *Ibid.* vol. I, p. 506.   [4] Frazer, *The Scape-Goat*, pp. 240–252.

Perchta, who is looked upon as a fierce ogress with a long iron nose, seems to have been at one time a goddess of the earth and of the dead. It is interesting that the name 'Perchten,' like the name 'boggons,' was sometimes given to evil spirits. Perchta was supposed to come with a troop of subordinate female spirits to eat the food on the Table of Fortune[1]. She was also said to lead the Wild Hunt[2]. For the dead grow restless and walk abroad both at Carnival time and during the Twelve Days of Christmas. They are also apt to bestir themselves at the beginning of spring.

In ancient Rome, the first of May was connected with the cult of the Bona Dea, a somewhat vaguely conceived earth-mother, from whose ritual all men were excluded[3]. On the 9th and 11th and 13th days of May, the Roman paterfamilias expelled the Lemures and Larvae (i.e. malignant ghosts) by walking through his house at midnight and spitting out black beans, and, at the end of the month animals were sacrificed to Mars on behalf of the growing crops. 'It was considered ill-omened to marry in May, as it still is in many parts of Europe.'[4] The uncanny side of the May festival still makes itself felt in the great precautions that have to be taken against ghosts and witches and fairies on May Day and May Day Eve[5]. There is also a living superstition that it is unlucky to bring hawthorn (the typical May blossom) into a house[6].

[1] Cf. *Med. Stage*, vol. I, pp. 265 ff., and footnotes where are quoted interesting references to the practice in the thirteenth and fifteenth centuries. For instance, in the thirteenth century, Martin of Amberg tells us that the food was left for 'Percht mit der eisnen nasen,' and in the fifteenth century (*Thes. Paup.* s.v. *Superstitio*) we learn that during the Twelve Days food was left for Perchta and her company of women, in the hope that she would bring good luck to the house. There is some evidence that the food was sometimes taken by masqueraders. Cf. *supra*, p. 14, *infra*, pp. 35, note 6, 97 and note 3.

[2] Grimm, *Myth*. vol. II, pp. 777, 778.

[3] *Med. Stage*, vol. I, p. 144. Warde Fowler, *op. cit.* pp. 100–106. Traces of this old sex festival remain in the traditional freedom of women in the month of May. Cf. *Med. Stage*, vol. I, p. 170.

[4] Warde Fowler, *op. cit.* p. 100.   [5] *The Scape-Goat*, pp. 158 ff.

[6] On the May festival see Philip Stubbes, *The Anatomie of Abuses* (N.S.S. ed. F. J. Furnivall, 1877–9), pt I, p. 149; Warde Fowler, *op. cit.* pp. 98–128; *Med. Stage*, vol. I, chap. VIII, 'The May-Game'; Brand, *op. cit.* vol. I, pp. 212–270; *The Magic Art*, vol. II, chap. X.

On the whole, however, the joyful aspect of the feast predominated in mediaeval times. May was the merry month which marks the beginning of summer, and May Day was devoted to the cult of the sacred tree or Maypole, and to the simplest kind of fertility ritual and magic.

The May Day ritual is so beautiful in itself, it has borne such fair fruit of mediaeval carol and lyric, it has been so etherealised by the poets, that it is hard to sympathise with iconoclasts. Nevertheless, the angry Protestants were perfectly right in regarding May Day as an essentially heathen institution and comparing the Maypole to a pagan idol whereof it is the 'perfect pattern, or rather the thing it self.'[1] The graver charges they brought against it, though exaggerated, were not altogether unfounded.

Mumming seasons are almost invariably times of lawlessness, buffoonery and licentiousness, and this fact is emphasised in various names that have been applied to folk-festivals and mock kings. One of the days of Carnival is known as Senseless Thursday, and in Germany the popular name for the Carnival itself is *Fasnacht*, which is probably derived from *faseln*, to talk nonsense[2].

It is hard to track the religious motive behind behaviour of this kind, which is the result of many varied, even contradictory thoughts and emotions. Any kind of religious excitement is apt to break bounds and end in hysterical or improper conduct especially among those who feel—as simple people often do—that frenzy or even madness is a sign of inspiration or possession[3]. The part played by the clown in the village festivals suggests that the village idiot[4] was sometimes chosen as mock king, and

---

[1] Stubbes, *loc. cit.*   [2] Cf. *E.R.E.* art. *Carnival* in vol. III, p. 225.

[3] Russian peasants credit idiots with special powers of divination; cf. *E.R.E.* art. *Divination* (Litu-Slavic), vol. IV, p. 816. Cf. also *E.R.E.* arts. *Possession* and *Shamanism*; *The Scape-Goat*, pp. 217 ff.; and *Adonis, Attis and Osiris*, vol. I, pp. 72 ff.

[4] Cf.   'In comes I, Big Head and Little Wits,
My head's so big, and my wits so small,
I'll sing a song to please you all.'
                                        Folk-Lore, vol. X, p. 193.
Cf. similarities in the costume of festival 'fools,' court jesters and real lunatics; and traces of the sacrificial exuviae in all these costumes. *Med.*

probably both he and to a lesser extent all the mummers were regarded as 'fools,' that is to say, people beside themselves, god-intoxicated, possessed by spirits. The wild character of the mumming may be partly due to the idea that licentiousness promotes the growth of the crops[1], but I imagine it is mostly a kind of epidemic of inspiration.

The idea of 'possession' may well lie behind the masking as well as behind the 'folly' of the mummers; for according to the laws of magic the wearing of a mask is a sure way to get into the closest possible touch with the being in whose image the mask is made. Among savage tribes the masquerade is very often a means of becoming identified with ancestral spirits, totem animals, etc., and it is not unreasonable to suppose that a similar idea underlies the use of masks in European theatres and folk-festivals[2]. We know that maskers represented the dead at Roman funerals[3]; that Boggons and Perchten are names applied both to maskers and to ghosts or demons; that *larva*, *masca*, and perhaps the root of 'mumming,' are all words whose meanings waver between 'face-mask,' and 'demon, ghost or witch.' Also it must be remembered that spirits are supposed to be particularly active on the festivals which play most part in the history of the masquerade, and that the dead are often connected with the fertility of the earth and worshipped at agricultural festivals[4].

The mummers, still more the maskers, are men who, having

Stage, vol. I, pp. 142–143 (especially p. 142, notes 2 and 3), 150, 192 and note 1, 196–198 (especially pp. 196, note 2, 197, notes 2, 3, 4, 198, note 1), 214, 386–388.

[1] *Magic Art*, vol. II, chap. XI, 'The Influence of the Sexes on Vegetation.'
[2] The wealth of material is so great that it is difficult to give references, but for masqueraders as spirits cf. Frazer, *The Belief in Immortality*, vol. I, pp. 176, 179–183, vol. II, p. 306; *The Scape-Goat*, pp. 382–383; *Spirits of the Corn and Wild*, vol. I, pp. 95 ff., 186 ff.; H. Webster, *Primitive Secret Societies* (New York, 1908), pp. 76 and note, 100–105 (and p. 105, notes 1–3), 149, 157–159.
[3] Ridgeway, *Dramas and Dramatic Dances*, p. 7.
[4] Cf. *E.R.E.* art. *Serpent-Worship*, particularly 'Introductory,' 'Teutonic and Balto-Slavic'; *Adonis, Attis, Osiris*, vol. II, pp. 65–68; *E.R.E.* art. *Egyptian Religion*, 'Festivals of Fertility and Harvest' and 'The Kingdom of Osiris,' 'Human Gods, Osiris cycle'; H. Munro Chadwick, *The Origin of the English Nation* (Cambridge, 1907), chap. X, 'The Cult of Nerthus,' especially pp. 261–264.

put themselves in close contact with spirits or divine beings greater than themselves, are in a state of enhanced vitality, and are therefore able to perform with peculiar effectiveness ritual actions which promote the growth of vegetation, the productiveness of the family and the general luck and well-being of the whole community. The story of the masque is the tale of how the magic of the mummers was transformed into a noble pastime and only just failed to become an enduring form of art.

CHAPTER II

The Later Middle Ages: the rise of the Momerie

'Let us play and dance and sing,
Let us now turn every sort
Of the pleasures of the spring
To the graces of a court.'   *The Vision of Delight.*

ELIGIOUS systems rise and fall, while the lower strata
of ritual and belief persist almost unchanged. It is, therefore, not surprising that the Christian Church found it
easier to establish ecclesiastical discipline than to uproot paganism
in Europe. In the early centuries of our era, the divines were for
ever denouncing the Kalends and other heathen customs, but
the penitentiaries show that only too often those denunciations
fell upon deaf ears[1].

Popular custom is not easily broken. As time went on the
Church was obliged to modify her attitude, though not without
protest from the more zealous ecclesiastics. Much of the pagan
ritual she absorbed into her own system, the rest she tolerated as
a permissible recreation for the red-letter days of her own
calendar. This was the more possible because gradually as
Christian ideas filtered through into all sections of society the
old rites lost their religious significance and became mere *ludi*;
although the peasants never quite lost their belief that the games
were lucky and brought good years[2]. Still, though superstition
lingered on, the agricultural rites dwindled more and more into

---

[1] Cf. *Med. Stage*, vol. II, appendix N, 'Winter Prohibitions,' where extracts
are given from sermons, penitentials, etc., forbidding Kalends celebrations,
and ranging from the second to the eleventh century. Some of these extracts
are accompanied by Dr Chambers' critical comments on the character of
the documents cited. In bk II, 'Folk Drama' (especially chaps. V to VIII),
Dr Chambers deals with the pagan origin of European folk-customs, and
gives numerous references to quotations from original authorities on the
attitude of the Church to these things. For the *carole* in the churchyard,
cf. *Med. Stage*, vol. I, p. 93, note 1, pp. 161–163 and footnotes.

[2] Cf. Googe, trans. of Naogeorgus, *Popish Kingdome*:

'An other takes the loafe, whom all the reast do follow here,
And round about the house they go, with torch or taper clere,
That neither bread nor meat do want, nor witch with dreadful charme,
Haue powre to hurt their children, or to do their cattell harme.
There are that three nightes onely do perfourme this foolish geare,
To this intent, and thinke themselues in safetie all the yeare.' (ll. 169–174.)

Quoted by Brand, *op. cit.* vol. I, p. 28. Cf. also *supra*, p. 14.

mere meaningless acts accompanied by meaningless jargon, and then in the later Middle Ages their downward course was arrested, and they took on a fresh lease of life not as ritual, but as a form of art.

This new development was due to the fact that the traditional games were played not only by peasants, but by courtiers, clerks, and the bourgeoisie of the great towns which at that time were becoming more and more important. The more educated classes valued the ludi not so much because they were lucky, as because they could be made amusing and afforded a fine opportunity for making a display of wit and wealth and bodily gracefulness, and also for expressing the civic consciousness. In this chapter we shall see how in their hands the traditional ludi were transformed into the various kinds of aesthetic play or revelling, out of which at last grew the Italian opera, the French ballet, and the English masque.

The folk-customs which concern the history of the masque may be roughly divided into three groups: (1) the king-game, a convenient and ancient name for the ceremonies connected with the election of a mock ruler; (2) the sword-dance, a mimic rhythmic combat, often accompanied by song or dialogue; and (3) the mumming[1], a procession of people disguised by masks, beast-heads, or discoloured faces, who enter into their neighbours' houses to dance or play at dice—often in complete silence. All three types of ludi are intimately connected and sometimes indistinguishable, and it may be added that it is not always easy to distinguish between the peasant, bourgeois, and courtly form of the traditional games.

The customs which the authorities tried so hard to suppress eventually penetrated into churches and monasteries and flourished exceedingly under priestly patronage. The Feast of Fools[2],

---

[1] The question of nomenclature is particularly difficult, because we are dealing with revels which are popular and constantly changing, and those who have recorded them have not taken them seriously enough to worry about exact definition. For the sake of clearness I use the term 'mumming' in a vague sense; but the term 'momerie' always for a particular kind of entertainment which will be discussed later. There is no historical justification for this distinction—I adopt it as a matter of convenience.

[2] Cf. *Med. Stage*, vol. I, chaps. XIII, XIV, 'The Feast of Fools,' and the authorities in the bibliographical note appended to chap. XIII.

which is first heard of in France[1] in the twelfth century, though no doubt it existed before then, was a New Year's festival of the inferior clergy, who for the time being took precedence over their superiors, elected one of their number as Bishop or Pope or Abbot of Fools and celebrated the occasion by drinking bouts, riotous masquerading in beast-heads or women's clothes through church and street, and by burlesque celebrations of the Divine Office when the censing was done with pudding and sausages, and the priests played dice upon the altar. All these practices have their equivalents in the folk-festivals, and no doubt the hostile theologians were right in regarding the feast as a survival of the pagan Kalends[2]. Only there was, as was natural, more deliberate parody and satire and less superstitious conservatism than in the true folk-festivals. 'The ruling idea of the feast is the inversion of status, and the performance, inevitably burlesque, by the inferior clergy of functions properly belonging to their betters.'[3]

Late in the fifteenth century the voice of authority began to take effect; but the Feast of Fools did not wholly die. The annual riot was appreciated by the ordinary citizens as well as by clergy, and when the former were deprived of their expected amusement they took the matter into their own hands, and all over France there sprang into being *sociétés joyeuses*, guilds formed to continue the tradition of the Feast of Fools, to celebrate with mock

---

[1] The festival was not confined to France. Traces of it are found in England, especially at Beverley and Lincoln. Cf. *Med. Stage*, vol. I, pp. 321 ff.

[2] In pp. 325–335 Dr Chambers discusses the origin of the Feast of Fools, its probable connection with the Kalends, its possible Byzantine origin. In the twelfth century the clergy of Saint Sophia *masqueraded* at Christmas and at Candlemas, kept up an ancient custom of wearing masks, and disguised themselves as women or four-footed beasts. This is particularly interesting in view of the fact that the word 'momerie' is possibly derived from the Greek Μορμώ (cf. *infra*, pp. 34 ff.). It would be in accordance with other aspects of the history of European civilisation, if the masquerades of Mediaeval Europe and also Renaissance Italy came from Byzantium. Very interesting in this connection is the Γοτθικόν, the game that was played in Byzantium in the tenth century. It was a New Year's game in which the Emperor was greeted by a ring dance performed by two parties of men, headed by 'Goths' masked and dressed in skins. This game, however, seems to be of Teutonic origin. Cf. *Med. Stage*, vol. I, p. 273, and B. S. Phillpotts, *The Elder Edda*, p. 187.

[3] Cf. *Med. Stage*, vol. I, p. 325.

solemnity the annual election of a leader known as *Prince des Sots, Abbé des Fous, Mère Folle*, etc., and to avenge by satirical verse and drama and pageantry any offence against the social or fashionable code of the time[1]. The members of these guilds wore the fool's dress[2], their main business was parody and burlesque, though they were sometimes called upon to celebrate civic functions by pageantry, plays or *mystères mimés*, and out of their dramatic activities rose the *sotie*, a type of comedy inspired by the idea of the universal domination of folly. Like the ecclesiastical fools, they amused themselves and their neighbours by *larvales et theatrales jocos*, and one such society actually had a monopoly of the masquerade and could sell to non-members the right to disguise themselves and to take part in the public merrymakings of Carnival[3]. Members of schools, colleges, etc., were frequently organised into 'kingdoms' very similar to the sociétés joyeuses. For instance, the Basochiens, young law-clerks of the Parlement, were closely allied with the Enfants-sans-souci of Paris, were noted for masquerading and acting, and were often used as public entertainers. In 1532 the 'Emperor' of 'Galilee' was employed by Francis I to entertain the Queen with 'danses, morisques, momeries.'[4]

The société joyeuse was an institution more adapted to the French than to the English temperament. We do, however, know of one such society in England in the fourteenth century, the 'Order of Brothelyngham,' whose members chose an abbot, disguised themselves as monks, captured people in the streets and extorted ransom 'instead of a sacrifice.'[5] In the sixteenth

---

[1] Cf. *Med. Stage*, vol. I, chap. XVI, 'Guild Fools and Court Fools,' and appended bibliographical note. For discussion of relation between the Feast of Fools and the sociétés joyeuses, see Petit de Julleville, *Les Comédiens en France au moyen âge* (Paris, 1885), pp. 29–41, and C. Leber, *Collection des meilleurs dissertations, notices, et traités particuliers, relatifs à l'histoire de France* (Paris, 1838), vol. IX, p. 150, for a charivari at Lyons.

[2] 'Le sot avait son costume traditionnel et consacré, assez semblable au costume des fous de cour à la même époque....Mais la pièce essentielle du costume était le chaperon, muni d'oreilles d'ânes et de grelots....Le jaune et le vert étaient les deux couleurs affectées au costume des sots et des fous.' Julleville, *op. cit.* pp. 146–147.

[3] Julleville, *op. cit.* pp. 247–248.

[4] Julleville, *op. cit.* p. 94.

[5] Cf. *Med. Stage*, vol. I, pp. 383–384, 383, note 2.

century, Philip Stubbes described how 'the wilde-heds of the Parish,' dressed in 'liueries of green, yellow, or some other light wanton colour,' accompanied by hobby-horses, pipers, etc., led by a 'Lord of Mis-rule,' would disturb the parson and amuse the congregation by dancing through and around the church, 'their bels iynglyng...and swinging their hand-kercheifs ouer their heds.' This seems to be a rustic form of société joyeuse[1]. Another survival of the vanished feast was the 'Christmas Lord' (known in England as Lord of Misrule, in Scotland as Abbot of Unreason), who flourished at Court, in the households of noblemen, mayors, sheriffs, etc., and in schools and colleges; and was closely related to, and sometimes identical with, the Twelfth Night King of the Bean[2]. The ceremonial of the mock king—called the Constable-Marshal or Lord of Misrule—who presided over the Grand Christmasses of the Inns of Court, contained some interesting ritual survivals, particularly the solemn entry upon a mule, the march three times round the fire, the hunting and killing of a fox and cat, which preserved the ancient sacrifice more nearly intact than did the rites of the Order of Brothelyngham[3].

The Lords of Misrule at Court and in great houses were temporary officials appointed to provide amusement for the Christmas holidays, and so were rather different from the French Abbés des Fous and Princes des Sots, who were the elected heads of societies composed chiefly of young men with a taste for drama and satire. The king-game of the Inns of Court, however, was more like that of the French sociétés

---

[1] Stubbes, *op. cit.* pp. 146 ff.

[2] Stow, *A Survey of London*, ed. C. L. Kingsford (Oxford, 1908), vol. I, p. 97, quoted in *Med. Stage*, vol. I, p. 403, note 3; *Med. Stage*, vol. I, pp. 403–419; *The Diary of Henry Machyn*, ed. J. G. Nichols (London, 1848), pp. 28, 29: 'The sam day affor non landyd at the Towre w[harf] the Kynges lord of myssrulle...and a-bowt ym syngers...ys trumpeters, taburs, drumes, and flutes and fulles (i.e. fools) and ys mores dansse'; A. Feuillerat, *Documents relating to the Revels at Court in the time of King Edward VI and Queen Mary*, in Bang, *Materialien zur Kunde des älteren Englischen Dramas*, vol. XLIV (Louvain, 1914), pp. 56–61, 89–94, 117–125.

[3] John Nichols, *The Progresses and Public Processions of Queen Elizabeth* (London, 1823), vol. I, pp. 131–141, vol. III, pp. 262 ff.

joyeuses and particularly that of the Basoche; there was the same mock ceremonial of the pretended king and kingdom, the same stimulation of dramatic production, the same half-serious, half-mocking concern with the maintenance of social order, and, what interests us chiefly, the same pre-occupation with morris-dances, mummings, and masquerades. As the French Court looked to the Basochiens[1] and the Enfants-sans-souci, so the English Court looked to the Inns of Court for the provision of merrymaking at the seasonal festivals and at times of public rejoicing.

Unlike the sociétés joyeuses, the English law clerks and students never produced any special form of comedy comparable to the French sotie; that particular vein of ironic comedy and light raillery at the whole of society was not for them. On the other hand, they seem to have played a greater part in the development of the masquerade than did their French brethren. The first developed English masque was closely connected with the solemn foolery of the 'Prince of Purpoole,' and the tradition of the mock king and his masquerades was not altogether lost even during the Puritan Revolution.

In Germany, as well as in France and England, the king-game and the masquerade were closely associated[2].

The king-game cannot be neglected in the history of the revels, but it is not one of the direct forerunners of the masque. Our other two folk-customs, however, the sword-dance and the mumming, were not mere opportunities of masquerading; under certain conditions among certain classes of the community they actually developed into the Court masque.

In the fifteenth and sixteenth centuries the sword-dance was danced all over Western Europe. The main movements of the sword-dance consisted in the arrival of grotesque dancers, one by one or in couples, the combat, the interlacing of the swords, sometimes over the head of one of the performers. In Scan-

---

[1] Julleville, *op. cit.* chap. v, 'Les Basochiens,' and chap. vi, 'Les Enfants-sans-souci.'

[2] Cf. Bartholomew Sastrow's account of a king-game in which he himself played the principal rôle, *Social Germany in Luther's Time* (London, 1902), pp. 273-275.

dinavia, the Isle of Man and elsewhere, the sword-dance is thought of as a fight between summer and winter.

The dance is often accompanied by cantilenae: that is to say, one of the characters acts as presenter to the rest, introducing each dancer with descriptive verses; or sometimes there may even be rough dialogue, and then the performance merges insensibly into that kind of folk-drama which survives in our St George and mummers' plays. This folk-drama has already been described; it preserved the ritual form with some fidelity, but it had little or no influence on the Court masque[1].

More important for our purpose is a dance known as the morris or morisco[2], which was very popular in all the chief European countries in the fifteenth, sixteenth and seventeenth centuries. From the time when we first hear of it, it appears both as a folk-dance and a favourite dance at Court theatricals, but never as a purely social dance[3]. As a rule it was danced by people of one sex and usually by men: sometimes, however, one woman or man in woman's clothes danced in the morris[4].

[1] Cf. *Med. Stage*, vol. I, chaps. IX, X, vol. II, appendix J; P. Reyher, *Les Masques anglais* (Paris, 1909), pp. 458–459; Tiddy, *The Mummers' Play.*

[2] F. Douce, *Illustrations of Shakspeare* (London, 1807), vol. II, pp. 431 ff.; *Med. Stage*, vol. I, chap. IX, especially pp. 195 ff., with references in notes; Reyher, *op. cit.* pp. 454–459; H. Prunières, *Le Ballet de Cour en France avant Benserade et Lulli* (Paris, 1914), p. 8; *N.E.D.* s.vv. *Morris, Morris-dance*; F. Kidson and M. Neal, *Folk-Song and Dance* (Cambridge, 1915), a good account of modern survivals of morris-dances, but remarks on origins are unreliable.

[3] '...he maye...daunce the morisco and braulles (It. *brando*), yet not openlye onlesse he were in a maske.' *The Book of the Courtier,* translated by Sir Thomas Hoby (The Tudor Translations, XXIII), p. 116; *Cortegiano,* bk II, chap. XI, cited Prunières, *op. cit.* p. 54, note 1.

[4] The man disguised as a woman was a familiar figure in folk-festivals. Cf. *Med. Stage,* vol. I, p. 144, and references; Ducange, s.v. *Robinetus*: Larvatorum ludicra caterva, sub appellatione *Robin et Marion,* memoratur in *Lit. remiss.* ann. 1392. ex Reg. 142. Chartoph. reg. ch. 309: 'Jehan le Begue et cinq ou six autres escoliers ses compaignons s'en alerent jouer par la ville d'Angiers desguisiez à un jeu, que l'en dit Robin et Marion, ainsi qu'il est accoustumé de faire chascun an les foiriez de Penthecouste en laditte ville d'Angiers par les gens du pays, tant par les escoliers et filz de bourgeois comme autres; en compaignie duquel Jehan le Begue et de ses compaignons avoit une fillette desguisée.' Douce, *op. cit.* vol. II, p. 446, reproduces an engraving of a Flemish morisco executed by von Mecheln in the fifteenth century, which shows male dancers encircling a woman, who holds out an apple (?) in her right hand. Creizenach, *Geschichte des neueren Dramas* (Halle, 1911), vol. I, p. 414, and note 1, speaking of the

A dance with so long a history has naturally varied very much at different times and places. The most constant features are: a mock combat, the wearing of bells round knees and ankles, the disguising, which was usually accompanied by masking or blacking the face, the clashing of sticks and waving of handkerchiefs in time to the music, also it seems always to have been a step-dance, danced on the heels or ball of the foot. Tabourot describes it in his *Orchésographie*:

'De mon jeusne aage, iay veu qu'és bonnes compagnies, aprez le soupper entroit en la salle, un garçonnet machuré & noircy, le front bandé d'un taffetats blanc ou jaulne, lequel auec des jambieres de sonnettes dançoit la dance des Morisques, & marchant du long de la salle, faisoit vne sorte de passage, puis retrogradant, reuenoit au lieu ou il auoit commencé, & faisoit vn aultre passage nouueau, & ainsi continuant, faisoit diuers passages bien aggreables aux assistans....Les Morisques se dancent par mesure binaire: Du commencement on y alloit par tappements de pieds, & par ce que les danceurs les treuuoient trop penibles, il y ont mis des tappements des talons seullement, en tenãt les arteils des pieds fermes.'

Tabourot adds that the dance had gone out of fashion because it caused gout[1]. The steps and costume described by him are very much like those of our surviving morris-dances, and I think it is clear that the morisco is essentially a dance in which progress is made by means of a peculiar kind of marching step.

Though the morisco could be a solo, it was usually danced by six or eight persons, who in England—where the dance was especially connected with May and Whitsun customs—were often disguised as characters of the Robin Hood legend. At the French and Tudor Courts the dancers sometimes appeared as 'fools' or 'wild men,' i.e. sophisticated versions of the village

Nuremberg Fool Plays, says, 'Im vierzehnten Spiel tritt eine Frau mit einem Apfel auf, wohl Frau Venus; der Apfel soll demjenigen gehören, der die gröszte Narrheit begangen hat. Hierauf erzählt ein Narr nach dem andern, zu was für wunderlichen Streichen ihn die Liebe verführt habe, bis endlich der zehnte den Preis erhält. Dieses Spiel wird in der Überschrift als "Morischgentanz" bezeichnet, ein Tanz, der mit dem Schwerttanz nahe verwandt ist und gleichfalls im späteren Mittelalter in ganz Westeuropa verbreitet war....An das oben erwähnte Spiel erinnert es, wenn Celtes in seinem Epigramm lib. v, 14 die Planeten, die den Erdball umkreisen und die Maurisci, die um ein schönes Weib herumtanzen, miteinander vergleicht.'

[1] Thoinot Arbeau (pseudonym for Tabourot), *Orchésographie* (Lengres, 1588), p. 94.

grotesques[1]. In Renaissance Italy the performers were often dressed as mythical personages of Greece and Rome. In 1509, for instance, when Ariosto's comedy, *I Suppositi*, was performed at Ferrara:

'Li intermeci furono tuti canti et musiche, et in fine de la comedia, Vulcano cum Ciclopi baterno saete a sono de piffari, battendo il tempo cum martelli et cum sonagli che tenivano a le gambe, et facto questo acto de le saette col menar de' mantici, fecero una morescha cum dicti martelli.'[2]

Castiglione has furnished us with a good example of the developed Italian morisco in a letter describing the performance of Cardinal Bibbiena's comedy, *Calandra*, at the Court of Urbino in the Carnival of 1513.

The 'intromesse'[3] were as follows: the first was a moresca of Jason ...who came in dancing, dressed as a warrior of antiquity, and in a series of rhythmic movements yoked the fire-breathing bulls, ploughed the ground and sowed the dragon's teeth, which quickly sprang up as armed men, who danced a proud moresca. The second intermezzo consisted of the car of Venus, drawn by doves and accompanied by Cupids who danced a moresca beating time with their lighted torches. Other cars of Neptune and Juno, other dances of moresche and brandi followed; and at the end of the comedy appeared the God of Love[4].

In 1542 a very elaborate morisco was designed by Giulio Romano.

In this dance eight shepherds, all dressed alike, were led in by their God Pan. Pan had a harp in his hand and he came into the hall in the manner of the moresca (*uscì in modo di moresca*) and was followed by the others, who came in one by one performing the same moresca (*facendo la medesima moresca*) as their god had done. When they had all entered and joined up in a circle they did certain dance-turns (*contrapassi*) round the hall, and then four of them who had musical

---

[1] Cf. the tragic French dance of 1393 (*infra*, p. 43), which was probably a morisco, for it was accompanied by 'choreas saracenicas.' Cf. also for French entertainment of 1457 Prunières, *op. cit.* p. 9, and the English translation of A. Favine, *The Theater of Honour and Knighthood* (London, 1623), p. 345. For England cf. *Accounts of Performances and Revels at Court in the reign of Henry VIII* in Sh. Soc. Papers, vol. III, pp. 87 ff. For further references to Court moriscos in France and England cf. Lobineau, *Hist. de Bretagne*, vol. II, p. 1069; Prunières, *op. cit.* p. 8.

[2] Bernardino Prosperi to Isabella Gonzaga, quoted in D'Ancona, *Origin del Teatro Italiano*[2] (Torino, 1891), vol. II, p. 394, note 2.

[3] On the word *intromesse* cf. *infra*, pp. 44 ff.

[4] Quoted D'Ancona, *op. cit.* vol. II, p. 103.

instruments, began to play and sing, while the other four, who held spears, together with Pan put themselves in a listening attitude[1].

In spite of appearances, there is a connection between the courtly Italian moriscos and the 'morises and syk riot' of the English countryside: the Italian dancers, for instance, wear bells, they often fight a mock battle, and even in this morisco of Pan it is possible to trace the equivalent of our English 'morris-on' and 'morris-off.' The Cupids brandishing their torches, Vulcan and his Cyclops beating time with their hammers, are not so very far removed, after all, from the villagers beating time with their sticks in 'Bean-setting' or 'Rigs-o'-Marlowe.' According to M. Prunières, the Italian morisco differed from the Italian brando in having no set forms and in lending itself to pantomimic rather than to figured dancing[2]. In England there is a similar difference between the morris and the country dance; the most characteristic movement of the latter being the formation of geometrical patterns. This fact tells in favour of the hypothesis that the morisco is essentially a march and is differentiated from other dances not by figure but by step.

The question of origin is difficult[3]. The word 'morisco' means 'Moorish,' and there was a strong and persistent tradition that it was a dance of Moorish origin. Dr Chambers, however, points out that it is very strange to find an oriental dance so intimately bound up with the most conservative aspects of English village life, and adduces convincing evidence to prove that the morris is merely a variant of the sword-dance[4]. In Spain and elsewhere the morisco was sometimes represented as a struggle between Christians and Mohammedans; Gregorovius considers the dance to have been originally a mock fight between Moors and Christians, and the name may have been introduced as a sub-title for this particular type of sword-dance[5].

---

[1] D'Ancona, vol. II, p. 438.   [2] *Op. cit.* pp. 9, 54.

[3] The tradition that the morris-dance was brought to England from Spain in the reign of Edward III, I cannot trace further back than to F. Peck, *Memoirs of Milton* (London, 1740), p. 135, cited by Douce; Peck gives no evidence.

[4] *Med. Stage*, vol. I, pp. 198 ff.

[5] Cf. Gregorovius, *Lucretia Borgia*, tr. from third German edition by J. L. Garner (London, 1904), p. 255. Gregorovius gives no evidence, but

I would suggest that the morisco was originally a Moorish dance, which was introduced into Spanish and Italian Courts, and was characterised by a peculiar step and possibly also by the jangling of bells. A new step could be introduced into many different kinds of dances without seriously disturbing the traditional costumes and figures, and a new Moorish step would be most naturally introduced into those folk-games and dances at which the villagers already blackened their faces, and so resembled Moors, or into those sword-dances where the opposing parties were known as Saracens and Christians. This is pure hypothesis, but a hypothesis that does account for all the facts.

The village morris-dance is still living, but the Court morisco died out, or rather was absorbed[1]. It was often inserted into plays and other revels and in its developed form it closely resembled the momerie or disguising; and it was inevitable that sooner or later the two kinds of entertainments should be identified with each other, and both together be merged into the new and popular masquerade.

In England we may perhaps trace the morisco in the anti-masque or grotesque dance which preceded the entry of the courtly masquers. It is worth noting that the connection between masque and village morris was still felt, if not understood, in the seventeenth century. In Ben Jonson's entertainment, *The Satyr*, 1603, the amusement appointed for Monday afternoon was a morris-dance, and the introductory speech was to have been delivered by Nobody:

> 'We are the huisher to a morris,
> A kind of masque, whereof good store is
> In the country hereabout,
>
> .   .   .   .   .   .

D'Ancona gives instances of mock fights between Christians and Saracens which were still performed in the nineteenth century in Corsica, Elba and the Abruzzi. 'Il Pitrè (p. 63) ricorda in proposito la *Moresca* di san Pietro e sant' Ilario nell' Isola dell' Elba, dove soleano sfidarsi due schiere di Cristiani e Turchi, forse per qualche commemorazione storica: e similmente lo spettacolo carnevalesco di Capoliveri. Il Valery (*Voyage en Corse, à l'Ile d'Elbe et en Sardaigne*, Bruxelles, 1838, vol. i, p. 45) ricorda una *Moresca* corsa, danzata da 160 attori divisi in due schiere, rappresentanti Côrsi e Saraceni, ormai passata d'uso da una cinquantina d'anni.' D'Ancona, *op. cit.* vol. ii, p. 200, note 5.

[1] Cf. *infra*, pp. 85 ff.

But see, the hobby-horse is forgot.
Fool, it must be your lot,
To supply his want with faces,
And some other buffoon graces.'[1]

In the fifteenth century the morisco was sometimes combined
with a ludus called the momerie. The guests of Gaston de Foix,
for instance, were entertained with 'moresques, momeries,' and
according to the author of *Mistére du viel Testament*[2] the
very same amusements were enjoyed by the Jewish Court in
the time of King David:

> 'HELIAB.   Trompettes, sonnez haultement,
>   Pour resjouir la seigneurie.
> *Icy sonnent les trompetes. On met les tables.*
> DAVID.   Faictes venir la momerie
>   Qui est dedens le char enclose;
>
> .   .   .   .   .   .
>
>   Entendez a vostre morisque;
>   Vous en sçavez bien la pratique.'

The Court momerie was a sophistication of a popular custom,
probably of ritual origin. It consisted of a procession of masked
persons, who paraded the streets and entered their neighbours'
houses to dance or play a game of dice called mumchance[3]. It
was a popular mode of celebrating winter festivals[4], and it looks
as if it were the old procession of the Kalends, which was so
hateful to the Church, so dear to the lay and clerical 'Fools' of
the Middle Ages.

It is, however, difficult to discover the precise nature of the
momerie, and unfortunately the root meaning of the word is
uncertain. It has been suggested that it belongs to the group of

---

[1] J. Nichols, *The Progresses of King James I* (London, 1828), vol. I,
pp. 184–186.

[2] *Le Mistére du viel Testament*, ed. James de Rothschild (and Émile
Picot), Paris, 1882, t. IV, p. 143.

[3] E.g. in 1405 'une vespree les barons, prinches, contes et dus s'avisont
qu'ilh yroient momeir et joueir aux dees al hosteit de monsangneur de Lyge.'
Chronique de Jean de Stavelot (ed. Borguet), p. 95. Quoted by Reyher,
op. cit. p. 16, note 5.

[4] 'Icellui suppliant...partist de l'ostel de son maistre...en entention de
aler *mommer*; et de fait y ala desguisé, ainsi que l'on a accoustumé faire au
pais (Therouenne) en temps d'iver' (1454, *Arch. J.J.* 184, pièce 515). Cf.
Godefroy, *Dictionnaire de l'ancienne Langue française*, s.v. *Momer.*

onomatopoeic words mumble, mutter, mute, etc., meaning 'to be silent, to murmur indistinctly,'[1] etc. Certainly the silence of the mummers was proverbial, the game of mumchance was often used as a metaphor for silence or secrecy[2], and although it cannot be proved that silence was invariable, and examples have been brought forward to show that it was not[3], yet it must be remembered that literary remains of the mumming, like those of the masque, are deceptive and often turn out to be mere descriptive programmes or speeches to be made by a presenter, not by the mummers themselves.

It is worth noticing that the word 'momerie,' like the later word 'masque,' is applied primarily to the masked cortège rather than to the semi-dramatic business accompanying it. In the example quoted from the *Mistère du viel Testament* the momerie is the collection of morris-dancers who are enclosed in the chariot. So that a momerie might involve much song and dialogue and yet be itself a procession or dance of silent people. Of course in time the word was bound to enlarge its meaning to include the drama as well as the silent procession; but although this did happen (cf. our English mummers' play) yet the real nature of the performance was never quite forgotten[4].

[1] 'The origin is imitative, from the sound *mum* or *mom*, used by nurses to frighten children, like the E. *bo!* See Wedgwood, who refers to the habit of nurses who wish to frighten or amuse children, and for this purpose cover their faces and say *mum!* or *bo!* whence the notion of masking to give amusement. Cf. G. *mummel*, a bugbear. Thus the origin is much the same as in the case of *mum*, *mumble*.' Skeat, *Etymological Dictionary of English Language*[4], s.v. *Mummer*. Cf. also *N.E.D.* s.vv. *Mumchance, Mummer*. Kluge in the 1st ed. of his *Etym. Wtb.* s.v. *Mumme*, connects this and cognate words with 'einem alten Verbalstamm *mum* "brummen,"' and appears to be merely following Diez, who in *Wörterbuch der Romanischen Sprachen*, 5th ed. (Bonn, 1887), II, c. s.v. *Momer* derives the OFr. *momer* 'vom dtschen *mummen, mummerei*, eigentlich nachahmung des vom dumpfen laute so benannten gespenstes *mumel*,' and he refers to Grimm, *Mythol.* p. 473. In later editions of his *Etym. Wtb.* Kluge discards Diez's view and connects *mumme*[2] with OFr. *momon*, Span. *momo* ('wohl eigentlich Kinderwort der Ammen'). OFr. *môme* meant 'slanderer' and in popular parlance, 'little child, idiot' (cf. Godefroy, s.v. *Môme*). Meyer-Lübke, *Romanisches Etymologisches Wörterbuch*, 5653, connects the Spanish, German, French words with *momo*, an onomatopoeic word meaning 'grimace,' rejects a German origin, but regards the derivation from Greek *momos*, mockery, as questionable.

[2] Reyher, *op. cit.* p. 20 and note 6; Prunières, *op. cit.* p. 5, note 5; *N.E.D.* s.vv. *Mumchance, Mummer*.

[3] Prunières, *op. cit.* pp. 5, 6.   [4] Prunières, *op. cit.* p. 6, note 1.

Nevertheless, I am by no means convinced that the word 'momme,' 'momerie,' had originally anything to do with silence; for it usually has (together with its cognates and derivatives) a very positive concrete meaning. OFr. *momon* meant 'a mummer, a face-mask and a ring or sum of money carried in a cup as a prize for the game of mumchance.'[1] The expression *momer à quelqu'un* surely means 'to play at dice with someone,' not 'to be silent with someone.'[2] German *mumme* means 'a mask, or a masked visage.'[3]

Of course, the meaning 'face-mask, dicing stake,' etc., may have arisen from the fact that the mummers, 'the silent ones,' did wear masks and did play at dice, but it seems remarkable that it is the meaning of 'face-mask' that is most persistent, and it is difficult to see how the word could be commonly used in this sense until its root meaning began to be forgotten; for the change of meaning from 'silence' to 'face-mask' is not an easy or natural transition. Yet the silence of the mummers was so

---

[1] Godefroy, *Dictionnaire de l'ancienne Langue française* (1888), s.vv. *mome* (*momme*), *momeor, momerie, momon, momer.*

[2] 'Comme plusieurs bourgeois de la ville d'Aire feussent alez esbatre a un esbatement, que on dit *momme*...lesquels demanderent ausdiz serviteurs dudit Sohier, s'ilz estoient mommeurs, lesquelz respondirent oïl; et lors ledit Coustant leur dist qu'ilz momassent a lui, et ledit Simmonnet respondi qu'ilz n'avoient point de clarté, car leur torche estoit faillie, et ne vouloient mommer a lui, ne a autre' (quoted in Godefroy, s.v. *Mome*).

[3] Grimm, *Wörterbuch*, MUMME, f. *larve, verlarvte person*, Frisch, I, 673a; mummen laufen, *larvis incedere*, das mumen gehen *wird in der straszburgischen policeiordnung verboten, ebenda.*; *mittellat.* muma, Schm. I, 1598 *Fromm.*; *niederl.* momme, vermomt, *personatus, larvatus, mommius, larva velatus, persona indutus*, momme, mom-aensicht, *larva, persona, ora corticibus horrenda cavatis*, Kilian.

MUMMEL, m. 1. *vermummte gestalt, schreckgestalt, popanz* (=old bogy, bugbear), *maniae* sive *maniolae*, ungestaltige bildnussen, butzenböck, auf die man den kindern trawet, die mûmel, Dasyp....ein mummel, *sive* mummelmann, *manducus* (= a grotesque, masked puppet, with huge teeth), *personatus*, Stieler 1305; mummelspiel, *spiel mit larven*, mummelthier, *monstrum*, Keisersberg *bei* Frisch, I, 673a.

MUMMEL, f. 1. *hülle, weiszes leintuch, womit in Ulm die trauermägde noch am ende des 18. jahrh. das gesicht bis über die nase verhüllten*, Schmid, 394... 3. MUMMEL, *altes zahnloses gesicht, mund, maul*, Schm. I, 1598 *Fromm.*; *in Tirol* mumel, *maul der thiere und verächtlich der menschen*, Fromm. 5, 332.

MUMMELESSER, m. *verhüllte schreckgestalt und kinderfresser*....

MUMMELSPIELEN, n. *sich als popanz verkleiden*, mummelspilen, Garg. 68a.

far from being forgotten that it passed into a proverb. But if *momme* originally meant 'a face-mask,' and this mask was worn by silent and grotesque mummers, it is very easy to understand how the word could be confused both with the onomatopoeic word 'mum' (cf. mumble, mutter, mute, etc.), and also in Spain and Italy with Grk. μῶμος, mockery, and the God Momus, a personification of mockery[1].

In view of the persistent use of the word in the sense of face-mask (or in a sense which might be easily derived from face-mask) it seems unwise to disregard the conclusions of those French scholars who in the sixteenth and seventeenth centuries derived *mommon, mommerie*, from the Greek word *mommo*, meaning 'a mask.'[2]

[1] For the momerie in Spain and Portugal see Don Emilio Cotarelo y Mori, *Colección de Entremeses* (Madrid, 1911), tom. I, vol. I, pp. lvi ff. The Span. *momo* seems to have been recognised as a game of foreign origin, and to have been connected with masquerading. In a sixteenth century play, a man is said to have seen at a Corpus Christi festival

'las carátulas, visiones,
los juegos y personajes,
los *momos* y los visajes,
los respingos á montones.' Cotarelo, *op. cit.* p. lvii.

'Paralelamente á estos *entremeses*, y aun confundiéndose con ellos, hubo en la Edad Media otra clase de divertimientos llamados *momos*, introducidos en Castilla antes de mediar el siglo XV, como demuestra el siguiente pasaje del ya citado D. Alonso de Cartagena. En su *Glosa* al capítulo XIII, libro 2º *de Providentia*, dice: "El juego que *nuevamente agora* se usa de los *momos*, aunque dentro dél esté onestat é maduretat é gravedat entera, pero escandalízase quien ve fijosdalgo de estado con visages ajenos. E creo que non lo usarían si supiesen de quál vocablo latino desciende esta palabra *momo*."
'En la *Crónica del Condestable Miguel Lucas* también se mencionan con frecuencia:
'1461: "Y después de cenar vinieron *momos* mandados; la mitad brocados de plata y la mitad dorados con cortapisas; en las partes izquierdas sendas feridas; sombreros de Bretaña, é en ellos peñas y veneras y con sus bordones; y danzaron por gran pieza." (p. 57.)
'1463: "Y fecha la colación vinieron dos órdenes de *momos* con falsos visajes, unos después de otros; los primeros, vestidos unas ropas de fino paño blanco bien fechas, todas entretalladas de llamas de fuego; é los segundos traían unos mantos cortos de bocarán negro bordados de marros y compases, y danzaron muy gentilmente gran rato."' (p. 117.) Cotarelo, *op. cit.* pp. lvi, lvii.

[2] *Traitté contre les Masques par M. Jean Savaron, sieur de Villars* (Paris, 1608), 'La preuve que le Diable est autheur des Masques et mommeries se tire de la propriété et origine de ces mots de Mommon et de Masque; *Mommo* en grec, *Masca* en toscan et lombard et en latin *Larva* signifient un démon et un masque.' Quoted by Prunières, *op. cit.* p. 2, note 2.

The word *mommo* occurs in the glossary of Hesychius, who equates it with *mormo*: 'what we call *mormo*, a thing that frightens children.'[1]

The Greek word Μορμώ means 'a child's bug-bear, a frightening mask, and an ugly female spirit' (sometimes identified with the child-slaughtering ogress Lamia[2]), and according to Roscher[3] is merely a shortened form of Μορμολυκεία, Μορμολυκεῖον, which has similar meanings, and is to be derived from Μορμολύκη[4], a female spirit connected with the underworld and described by Strabo as 'the nurse of Acheron.' Rohde produces a good deal of evidence to prove that Mormo was one of

J. Morelli, *Operette*, vol. I (Venice, 1820), p. 160, 'Non sembri qui strana la voce di *Momaria*, la quale bene vi sta, tuttochè andata sia ella in disuso; nè altro significa, se non mascherata, o giullería. Ad intenderne il significato ci guida Giovachino Perionio nei Dialogi *de Linguae Gallicae origine eiusque cum Graeca cognatione* [pag. 105. Ed. Paris. 1555] scrivendo cosí: *Inter coenam nonnulli intervenire solent ludendi caussa, quos nostro sermone* mommons *vocamus. Ita est, atque hoc verbum totum graecum est;* μομμὼ *enim larvae appellantur a Graecis.* E il di Caseneuve aggiunge: "Le Lexicon Longolii: μομμὼ, *larvae, terriculamenta puerorum.*...Je puis ajouter que peut-être nous avons fait ce mot de Momus, qui etoit le Dieu des moqueries" [*Origines de la Langue Franc.* à Paris, 1694, pag. 79].'

[1] Hesychius, *Lexicon* (Jena, 1861).
Μομβρώ· ἡ Μορμώ. καὶ φόβητρον. μομοκύκια· τῶν τραγῳδῶν τὰ προσωπεῖα (Suid. μορμολύκεια).
Μομμώ· ὃ ἡμεῖς Μορμώ φαμεν, τὸ φόβητρον τοῖς παιδίοις.
μορμολυκεῖα· τὰ τῶν τραγῳδῶν προσωπεῖα.

[2] Cf. Schol. on Theocr. 15. 40, where a mother uses the word *mormo* to frighten a child, '*Mormo:* Lamia queen of the Lastrygons who was also called Gelo, wretched about the death of her children, wished to kill also those that were left.' *Mormolukia* was also identified with Lamia: 'In order that you may know what I say, your excellent bride is one of the Empousai, which the multitude reckon as Lamias and Mormolukias.' Philostratos, *Vit. Apoll. Tyan.* 4, 25.

Plato (*Phaid.* 77 e) compares the fear of death with the fear of the μορμολυκεῖον and in *Timaios lex.* this word is interpreted as a face-mask for frightening children. In *Etym. Magn.* μορμολυκεῖον = a frightening face-mask. Cf. German *mummelesser*, a devourer of children; *mummel*, f. an ugly toothless face; *mummelmann*, manducus personatus (i.e. a glutton and also a masked, wooden figure carried in procession); *mummel*, m. a covered face, a horrible bugbear.

[3] *Lex. Griech. und Röm. Myth.* (Leipzig, 1890–1897), s.v. *Mormo, Mormolyke.* My interpretation of the Greek Μορμώ is based upon Roscher, who gives the evidence in full.

[4] In Roscher's view the later, shortened form survived among the people; and with the loss of the termination -*luke*, the ogress lost her wolfish nature. Apparently, however, she continued to share with Lamia an unpleasant habit of devouring children.

many underworld spirits or ogresses (Gorgo, Lamia, Empusa, etc.) who were all variants of Hecate, an underworld goddess, who appears, preferably by night, at the cross-roads, accompanied by her 'schwarm,' her troop of handmaidens. These are the souls of the untimely dead, who, finding no rest in the grave, have to travel in the wind accompanied by Hecate and her demon dogs[1]. Mormo, in fact, belongs like Perchta to the Wild Hunt. Although it cannot perhaps be proved, it seems to me probable that this Mormo, Mommo lies behind the momerie[2].

Mormo seems to have been a well-established figure in Greek folk-belief, and the use of her name as a term for 'mask' suggests that she was often impersonated. She may easily have reached Italy and become one of the spirits imitated by maskers at Kalends and Saturnalia, have travelled to other European countries with the rest of the Kalends customs, and then have become identified with similar beings already found in the rest of Europe. There is, for instance, a striking resemblance between Perchta and Mormo[3], and it is certainly remarkable that the Germ. *mummel*[4] should mean (among other things) 'frightening face-mask, female bogy, ugly face,' and even 'devourer of children,'[5] and that, apparently, she should have been impersonated[6].

---

[1] Rohde, *Psyche* (Leipzig, 1894), pp. 371 ff. and footnotes; English tr. App. VI. The form μορμών is used in the same sense of bugbear, Hesych. μορμόνας· πλανῆτας δαίμονας; Xenophon says that the Lacedemonians despised their allies because they feared the peltasts ὥσπερ μορμόνας παιδάρια. *Hell.* IV, 4. 17.

[2] If the form *mommo* survived in Latin and was combined with the romance suffix *-arius*, it could give the French forms *mommerie, momerie*, It. *momaria*, while the form without suffix would give French *mommon*, *momon*, Low Germ. *mumme*, Sp. *momo*.

[3] Perchta is impersonated, is connected with the Wild Hunt, visits houses during the Twelve Days, etc., eats food on the Table of Fortune, leads a band of female spirits, is an ugly ogress. Her 'maskers' wear animal masks; cf. the wolfish nature of *mormoluke, supra*, p. 34.

[4] Cf. Grimm, s.v. *Mummel*.

[5] Cf. Grimm, *Myth.*4 vol. III, p. 146, 'die mutter spricht: "nit gang hinusz, der *mummel* (auch 'der man') ist dusz." denn das kind vörcht den *mummel* (man). Keisersb. bilgr. 166c.'

[6] Googe records of maskers in the Carnival:

'Both men and women chaunge their weede, the men in maydes aray,
And wanton wenches drest like men, doe trauell by the way,
And to their neighbours houses go, or where it likes them best,
Perhaps vnto some auncient friend or olde acquainted ghest,

If the mummers are impersonators of an underworld spirit Mormo, their silence is very easy to interpret, for it is often a part of chthonic cult[1]. (It is interesting that in Ulm, *mummal* was used for the white linen cloth with which mourning girls covered their faces.) 'Mumchance' looks like a continuation[2] of the dice play at the Kalends and Saturnalia, it may possibly be connected in some obscure way with the Tables of Fortune[3]. I suggest then that the momerie (and also perhaps, as we shall see, the masquerade) was a winter celebration, especially connected with Christmas and Shrovetide, in which maskers impersonated underworld spirits, and possibly mimed the Wild Hunt led by a female spectre.

The difficulty, of course, is that the Greek *mommo* cannot be traced later than the fourth century, and the momerie does not appear until the thirteenth century and only comes into prominence in the fourteenth and fifteenth centuries[4]. The difficulty is grave but not insuperable. The argument from silence is admittedly dubious, and *all* the folk-customs with which we are dealing in this book seem to have remained more or less obscure for several centuries and then to have taken on a fresh lease of life in the later Middle Ages and early Renaissance. We know that in the early Middle Ages mummings and masqueradings took place at the Byzantine Court and in St Sophia[5], and the connection between the culture of Italy and the culture of Byzantium is an historical commonplace. It is interesting that in Italy the *momaria* seems to be especially associated with Venice[6].

Unknowne, and speaking but fewe wordes, the meate deuour they vp,
That is before them set, and cleane they swinge of euery cup.'
(*Popish Kingdome*, ll. 303–308.)
This is an interesting passage, for it suggests a connection between the masking and the Tables of Fortune. Are not the maskers coming to the house as impersonators of the spirits?

[1] Cf. *supra*, p. 7.   [2] Cf. *supra*, p. 9.   [3] Cf. *supra*, pp. 10, 11.
[4] In the earliest MS (eleventh century) of Commodianus, *Instructiones*, ed. Dombart (1887), bk XI, no. XVIII, l. 17, occurs the phrase 'Das tibi momerium.' This does not make good sense and has been emended to 'Dat tibi momentum,' but it suggests that a word 'momerium' existed at the time when this MS was written.
[5] Cf. Diehl, *Manuel d'Art byzantin* (Paris, 1910), p. 484, and *supra*, p. 21, note 2.
[6] I have not, however, a sufficient knowledge of Italian diaries, chronicles,

Whatever its origin, in the thirteenth century the mumming was a popular amusement which was looked at askance by the authorities. It is prohibited in an edict of Troyes in 1263: 'Et ne doit on point recevoir gens qui momment,' and again in an edict passed at Lille in 1395: 'Defense de mommer de nuit a tout faulx visage ou le visage couvert de mascarure ou autrement.' In 1450 it was once again sternly decreed: 'Qu'il ne soit personne...qui le jour d'huy voist armez par la ville juer, mommer, le visaghe deghisé.'[1]

Similar edicts were issued in England.

'Orders of the city of London in 1334, 1393, 1405, forbid a practice of going about the streets at Christmas *ove visere ne faux visage* and entering the houses of citizens to play at dice therein. In 1417 "mummyng" is specifically included in a similar prohibition.'[2]

In the popular mummings, the dice was loaded to the advantage of the mummers, but probably it was the vagrancy and incognito rather than the dishonesty of the mummers to which the authorities objected. In 1418 it was proclaimed

etc., to be able to make this statement with any confidence; but D'Ancona seems to associate the 'momaria' with Venice, and the instances he gives of Florentine momeries were performed at Venice and Constantinople and in close conjunction with Venetians.

'Anche a' 14 febbrajo del 1498 furono fatte feste e *momarìe* in Venezia, ma nulla vi si trova di recitato o parlato, e le fecero i fiorentini, o per dimostrar l' allegria della tregua fra Francia e Spagna o per la speranza di riaver Pisa, ovvero per farsi nominar dicendo: *fiorentini fanno tal cosse*. La *momarìa*, di uomini vestiti da cavalli marini con *volti inargentadi*, e altri mascherati da mori, corse una giostra nella corte del Palazzo, ma la cosa *non reuscite come si credeva, et dirò cussì, fo una zanza fiorentina. Il principe era a li balconi et tutta la corte piena di populo, ma presto sono saciati di veder tal favola*: così il SANUTO, *Diarj*, I, 873.' D'Ancona, *op. cit.* vol. II, p. 113, note 1.

Cf. also a festival of 1512 described in Sanuto's Diary:

'A Muran in cà Lippomano fu recitato una Comedia,...et era assa' persone ad udirla, et veder la festa i feno: li quali feno redur numero 12 done scosagne di la terra, vestite però onoratamente di seta...Et poi feno una sontuosa cena, poi una colation con spongade, et poi una mumarìa bufonesca, et balando con dite done tuta la note.' Quoted from Sanuto's Diary by D'Ancona, vol. II, p. 115.

Could the momerie have travelled from Greece via Venice and the Tyrol to Germany? It is only a suggestion, but it might be worth working out in future.

[1] Godefroy, s.v. *momer*; Prunières, *op. cit.* p. 5.

[2] *Med. Stage*, vol. I, pp. 393, 394 and note 1, where authorities are cited. Cf. H. T. Riley, *Liber Albus* (R.S. 12), vol. I, pp. 644, 645, 647, 673, 676; *Memorials of London and London Life* (London, 1868), pp. 193, 534, 561, 658.

'that no manere persone, of what astate, degre, or condicioun that euere he be, duryng this holy tyme of Cristemes be so hardy in eny wyse to walk by nyght in any manere mommyng, playes, enterludes, or eny other disgisynges with eny feynyd berdis, peyntid visers, diffourmyd or colourid visages in eny wise.'[1]

In the third year of Henry VIII's reign there was passed an

'*Acte against disguysed persons and Wearing of Visours*...lately wythin this realme dyvers persons have disgysed and appareld theym, and covert theyr fayces with Vysours and other thynge in such manner that they sholde nott be knowen and divers of theym in a Companye togeder namyng them selfe Mummers have commyn to the dwellyng place of divers men of honor and other substanciall persones; and so departed unknowen.'[2]

It is obvious that such a custom could very easily be abused. It was said that in 1414 'Lollers hadde caste to have made a mommynge at Eltham, and undyr coloure of the mommynge to have destryte the Kyng and Hooly Chyrche.'[3]

There seems to have been no objection made to elaborate mummings organised by noblemen or prominent citizens. In 1377 the Commons of London paid a complimentary visit to Richard II disguised as mummers. This mumming is important because it is the first English *ludus* about which we have any detailed information.

'At ye same tyme ye Comons of London made great sporte and solemnity to ye yong prince: for upon ye monday next before ye purification of our lady at night and in ye night were 130 men disguizedly aparailed and well mounted on horsebacke to goe on mumming to ye said prince, riding from Newgate through Cheape whear many people saw them with great noyse of minstralsye, trumpets, cornets and shawmes and great plenty of waxe torches lighted and in the beginning they rid 48 after ye maner of esquiers two and two together clothed in cotes and clokes of red say or sendall and their faces covered with vizards well and handsomely made: after these esquiers came 48 like knightes well arayed after ye same maner: after ye knightes came one excellent arrayed and well mounted as he had bene an emperor: after him some 100 yards came one nobly arayed as a pope and after him came

---

[1] Riley, *Memorials*, p. 669. Quoted in *Med. Stage*, vol. I, p. 394, note 3.
[2] Quoted in *Med. Stage*, vol. I, p. 396, note 1.
[3] *Gregory's Chronicle* in *Hist. Collections of a Citizen of London*. Quoted in *Med. Stage*, p. 395, note 3.

24 arayed like cardinals and after ye cardinals came 8 or 10 arayed and with black vizardes like deuils appearing nothing amiable seeming like legates, riding through London and ouer London bridge towards Kenyton wher ye yong prince made his aboad with his mother and the D. of Lancaster and ye Earles of Cambridge, Hertford Warrick and Suffolk and many other lordes which were with him to hould the solemnity, and when they were come before ye mansion they alighted on foot and entered into ye haule and sone after ye prince and his mother and ye other lordes came out of ye chamber into ye haule, and ye said mummers saluted them, shewing a pair of dice upon a table to play with ye prince, which dice were subtilly made that when ye prince shold cast he shold winne and ye said players and mummers set before ye prince three jewels each after other: and first a balle of gould, then a cupp of gould, then a gould ring, ye which ye said prince wonne at thre castes as before it was appointed, and after that they set before the prince's mother, the D. of Lancaster, and ye other earles euery one a gould ringe and ye mother and ye lordes wonne them. And then ye prince caused to bring ye wyne and they dronk with great joye, commanding ye minstrels to play and ye trompets began to sound and other instruments to pipe &c. And ye prince and ye lordes dansed on ye one syde, and ye mummers on ye other a great while and then they drank and tooke their leaue and so departed toward London.'[1]

This was a sophisticated mumming; yet it differs from the folk-mumming only by its scale and magnificence. This mumming has been taken as a proof that the mummers—like the later masquers—were accustomed to dance with the spectators. The actual words of the chronicle will hardly bear this interpretation: 'And ye prince and ye lordes dansed on ye one syde, and ye mummers on ye other a great while.' This surely means that when the minstrels played dancing became general; only the mummers danced with each other in one group, and the noblemen did the same in another group: the two groups keeping to opposite sides of the hall. Even the other early source, where it is stated that the 'lordes daunced one the one parte wth the mummers' and Stow's paraphrase: 'and Lords daunced on the one part with the mummers, which did also daunce', can be interpreted in this way (why, otherwise, should

---

[1] *Harleian MS.* 247. The passage is taken from a collection of historical fragments formerly in Stow's possession, and is printed in *The Appendix to the Introduction* to the *Chronicon Angliae*, ed. E. M. Thompson (London, 1874), pp. lxxxii, lxxxiii; also in *Med. Stage*, vol. I, p. 394, note 4.

the expression 'daunced with the mummers' be expanded at all?) and moreover Stow's interpretation of his text would be influenced by his knowledge of the later masque, see for instance, his anachronistic use of the term 'maskers.'[1]

Another point worth noting is that apparently this mumming was not accompanied by set speeches. The words 'and ye said mummers saluted them, shewing a pair of dice upon a table to play with ye prince,' though they are not explicit, yet suggest that the game was played in silence, and that the mummers expressed themselves by gestures and dumb show.

In the fifteenth century poets began to write verses for momeries. We have several libretti for mummings, composed by John Lydgate; and both the verse libretto and a detailed description of the performance of a momerie at the Court of Philip the Good, Duke of Burgundy. The verses, however, do not seem to have been recited by the mummers themselves, so that no real change had taken place in the form of the mumming, which was still a cortège of maskers who came to dice, or to dance or to act a rough play or pantomime.

When the Renaissance reached France in the sixteenth century, the term 'momerie' came to be used in a more restricted sense, and was almost exclusively applied to the dice-playing processions; the dancing and dramatic momerie being absorbed into the fashionable Italian masquerade, which closely resembled it and was probably of very similar origin. As a result of this, the momerie went down in the world. In the middle of the sixteenth century Martial d'Auvergne forbade merchants and people of low condition to take part in masquerades but allowed them to go mumming: 'Et n'entend-on par ce les priver d'aller en momon, en robbes retournées, barbouillés de farine ou de charbon, faulx visaiges de papier, portant argent à la mode an-

---

[1] Stow, *A Survey of London* ed. Kingsford, vol. I, pp. 96–97. It is odd that Dr Chambers (both in *Med. Stage*, vol. I, p. 401, and in *Eliz. Stage*, vol. I, p. 153) should have followed Brotanek's interpretation of this passage, which is based not upon the earlier version, but upon Stow's paraphrase, and possibly upon the other early description (*Harleian MS.* 247, pr. in *Introd. Chron. Angl.* p. lxvii), which is only an incomplete fragment of a few lines, and which apparently misdates the performance. (Cf. R. Brotanek, *Die Englischen Maskenspiele*, p. 7, note I.)

cienne.'[1] Even in the sixteenth century, however, the French momerie was not entirely in the hands of the bourgeoisie, for when the King was in Paris in 1516 'il alloit quasi tous les jours faire des mommons en masque et habitz dissimulez et incognuz.'[2]

The same kind of thing took place in England. In that country the momerie was called 'a mummery, mumming, or disguising.' The latter term (in its adjectival form) first occurs at the beginning of the fourteenth century, in the English translation of the romance of *William of Palerne*, where the meeting of the Roman and Greek Emperors is described:

> '& eche a strete was striked · & strawed with floures
> & realy railled · with wel riche clothes,
> & alle maner menstracie · maked him a-ʒens;
> and also daunces disgisi · redi diʒt were,
> & selcouth songes · to solas here hertes.'[3]

The words 'daunces disgisi' were added by the English translator, but the expression is obviously the French *dances déguisées*[3].

In the fifteenth century the terms 'mumming' and 'disguising' are apparently used indiscriminately, but in the Tudor period the disguising generally corresponded to the more dramatic momerie (though it could sometimes be used for any kind of dressing up), and the word 'mumming' was limited in meaning to the cortège of masked and silent dice-players.

This kind of mumming was played by Henry VIII, as it was by Francis I, even after the introduction of the Italian masquerade. Gradually, however, its vogue ceased, it lost its special significance, it became once more a purely popular amusement. So the term 'mummers' became again just one among many names given to the disguised country folk who went about at Christmas time, May Day, etc., playing their age-long games for the sake of lucky years.

---

[1] Cf. Prunières, *op. cit.* p. 37, note 4, and *infra*, p. 136.
[2] Quoted by Prunières, *op. cit.* p. 36, note 1.
[3] *The Romance of William of Palerne*, ed. Skeat, E.E.T.S., E.S. 1. ll. 1617–1621. Quoted by Brotanek, *op. cit.* p. 6. The name of the Cornish 'goosey dance' would seem to be derived from 'dance déguisée.'

CHAPTER III

The Later Middle Ages: the literary and aesthetic development of the Momerie

'Is it not fine to dance and sing
While the bells of death do ring?' ANON.

THE rise of the Court momerie was one of the results of the gradual transformation of folk-games surviving from primitive ritual into bourgeois, scholastic, and aristocratic revellings; the literary and aesthetic development of the Court momerie was due to the absorption of various characteristics of the religious drama, the civic pageant, and the institutions of chivalry. To this development, which took place chiefly in the later half of the fourteenth and in the fifteenth centuries, we must now turn our attention.

The history of Court disguising in England begins in the reign of Edward III. In 1347 the King held a solemn Christmas at Guildford, and we can form some idea of how he amused himself from the accounts of the expenses of the Great Wardrobe. The maskers were divided into six groups of fourteen persons; all the members of a group being dressed alike; the members of the first three groups represented women, men, and angels, and wore face-masks. The members of the other groups wore, not masks but whole heads, representing dragons, peacocks, and swans. This entertainment is described in the account books as 'ludi domini regis.'[1]

The next year there were similar ludi at Otford. In these games apparently every one wore a head and not a mask, and most of the groups were composed of twelve performers, figuring men, animals, and wild men[2].

In 1349 the Court kept Epiphany at Merton, but the records are not very illuminating. Money was spent on 'heads of dragons and heads of men with diadems.'[3]

The accounts of expenditure naturally throw no light on the movements of the disguised persons, for knowledge of which we

---

[1] 'Accounts of the expenses of the great wardrobe of King Edward III,' *Archaeologia*, vol. XXXI, pp. 37 ff., and given in R. Brotanek, *Die Englischen Maskenspiele* (Wien und Leipzig, 1902), p. 2.

[2] *Arch.* vol. XXXI, p. 43; Brotanek, *op. cit.* p. 3. Cf. *supra*, p. 6.

[3] *Arch.* vol. XXXI, p. 43; Brotanek, *op. cit.* p. 3.

PLATE II

THE CAR OF THE DRYADS

Design for the *Ballet comique de la Reine* (1581). See p. 107

must look elsewhere. A manuscript in the Bodleian Library contains miniatures made in 1344 by Jehan de Grise, depicting groups of ladies, of fools, and of men wearing animal heads, who are clasping hands and are apparently engaged in some kind of rhythmic movement. The ladies are perhaps engaged in the *carole*, the fools are performing a vigorous step-dance that may well have been a kind of morisco[1]. These pictures do not, however, give any very clear idea of the nature of Court ludi in the reign of Edward III, and we can only guess what the games were like from what we know of Court entertainments held somewhat later in France and England.

The mumming which the Londoners brought to the young prince Richard in 1377 has already been described[2].

Sixteen years later, at the French Court, a ludus was performed with tragic consequences[3]. On the 29th of January, 1393, Charles VI and five of his lords prepared a surprise for the guests at a fashionable wedding. They masked themselves, covered their garments with pitch, on to which was stuck frayed linen, so that they appeared as *hommes sauvages* covered with hair from head to foot, and in this guise they rushed into the hall holding hands, making queer gestures, uttering horrible wolfish cries, and performing a mad dance. The end was tragic. The Duke of Orleans, anxious to discover their identity, approached too near with a torch in his hand. In a moment they were in flames. Two died on the spot, two succumbed after two days' agony, and the King, although his life was saved, never recovered from the shock. This dreadful performance is sometimes spoken of as a momerie, but as a matter of fact the chroniclers do not use the word. Froissart calls it an 'ébattement,' Juvenal des Ursins 'une feste...d'hommes sauvages enchaisnés, tous velus.' In *Religieux de Saint Denis* the King and his companions are said to have danced to the accompaniment

---

[1] Some of these have been reproduced as a frontispiece to *Med. Stage*, vol. I.

[2] *Supra*, pp. 38 ff.

[3] Cf. Prunières, *op. cit.* p. 3 and footnotes, where he cites *Religieux de Saint Denis*, t. II, chap. XVI, p. 65; *Les Chroniques de Sire Jean Froissart*, bk IV, chap. XXXII, ed. Buchon (Panthéon Littéraire), vol. III, pp. 177 ff.; Juvenal des Ursins, *Histoire de Charles VI, Roi de France*, ed. Buchon, *Choix de Chroniques et Mémoires*, pp. 378 ff.

of 'choreas saracenicas,' which is simply a Latin translation of
'Moorish dances.' The bride was a widow, and the impromptu dance was evidently a charivari, a ludus which Ducange
defines as 'a game in which those who involve themselves in
second nuptials are mocked with vile tinklings and varied
clamours.'[1]

Besides the mumming proper, the morris-dance or the charivari, there is still another form which the Christmas ludi of
Edward III may have taken. Christine de Pisan has described
an entertainment given during the course of a great banquet by
King Charles V to the Emperor of the Romans in 1377:

'Deux entremés y ot: l'un, comme Godefroy de Buillion conquist
Jherusalem, laquelle histoire ramentevoir estoit pertinent pour exemples
donner à telz princes; estoit la cité grande et belle, de bois painte à
panonceaulx et armes des Sarrazins, moult bien faicte, qui fu menée
devant le doiz; et puis la nef où Godefroy de Buillon estoit; et puis
l'assault comencié et la cité prise: qui fu bonne chose à veoir.'[2]

This kind of entertainment (which is called a momerie in the
Mistére du viel Testament) is very important in the history of
the revels. It may or may not have been known at the Court
of Edward III, but we find it fully developed at the Court of
the first Tudors, where it was generally known as a disguising,
or pageant. In France it was usually called an *entremets*.

The word 'entremets' (Sp. *entremes*, It. *tramesso, intromesso*)
is apparently derived from Low Latin *intromissum*, meaning 'the
third or middle course of a banquet,' the original sense evidently
being 'something inserted into something else,' and so any course
which was served by the aristocratic on especially important
occasions[3]. Then by a natural extension of meaning the word
'entremets' came to signify not only an extra course, but any
extra dish or ornament which diversified a banquet, including
the ingeniously wrought cakes, pies, or meats, which were as

---

[1] Ducange, s.v. *Charivarium*.

[2] *Le Livre des fais et bonnes mœurs du sage roy Charles*, pt 3, chap. XL, ed.
Buchon, *Choix de Chroniques et Mémoires*, p. 301.

[3] Cf. Ducange, *Glossarium*, s.v. *Intromissum*, Medium seu tertium convivii
ferculum, Italis *Tramesso*, Gallis *Entremets*. Gesta Innocentii III, PP. pag.
76: *Nisi forsan Comitibus, Baronibus, et aliis nobilibus, tertium ferculum, quod
vulgo dicitur Intromissum, ultra id, quod exhibetur familiae, apponatur.*

ornamental as they were delicious, and also the elaborate structures which were used as table decorations, or placed in the hall
for the entertainment of the guests, and even the music or
dancing, etc., that amused the guests between the courses[1].
Sometimes these entremets were decorated with wooden figures,
sometimes with living, disguised people. At intervals during the
course of the banquet fresh entremets might be drawn into the
hall, and often these entremets contained people who danced,
sang, or acted in dumb show. The history of the word 'entremets' is just the history of the ever-increasing splendour and
luxury of the great Court banquets in Spain and Italy, France
and Burgundy.

In Italy *tramesso* came to be used for the spectacular or
musical shows which were inserted into plays as well as into
feasts[2]. This kind of theatrical interlude was often called an

---

[1] At a banquet given in 1308 by Cardinal Pelagru to Pope Clement V,
there were numerous courses diversified by music and entremets and mock
fights and dances.

'Dopo le tre vivande de le nove, venne un castello, per tramessa, grandissimo, dove furono salvaggine solamente di bestie; cioè, un grandissimo cerbio
che pareva vivo, ed era cotto, un cinghiale, cavriuoli, lievri, conigli; che
tutti parevano vivi ed erano cotti: fu guidato e recato dagli scudieri ed
accompagnato da' cavalieri cogli stromenti di diverse maniere.'

After the fifth course a great fountain was brought in: 'Questo venne,
come il primo tramesso, accompagnato col mescolato romore de le genti e
degli stromenti.'

The ninth course arrived 'e per tramessa fu udito un cantare di cherici,
ma no' veduti; di boci d' ogni maniera, grosse, men grosse, mezzane, picciole
e puerili, con una dolcezza soavissima, che rendarono cheta tutta la sala,
perchè gli attenti orecchi tutti feciono tacere le parlanti lingue, per la soavità
de la dolce melodia. Chetato il canto e levata l' ultima vivanda, vennono le
frutta...' According to D'Ancona, this description was written by an eye-
witness, a Florentine resident at the Papal Court of Avignon.

I due sontuosissimi conviti fatti a papa Clemente V nel MCCC VIII ec.,
pubblicato da G. Milanesi, Firenze, Successori Le Monnier, 1868, quoted
in D'Ancona e Bacci, *Manuale della Letteratura Italiana* (Firenze, 1906),
vol. I, pp. 232–233.

A banquet given in Rome in 1513 to Lorenzo and Giuliano de' Medici
was enlivened by 'homini, quali da intramesso ad intramesso, dilettarono li
convitati e circostanti di qualche dolce e faceta inventione.' Quoted from a
contemporary account by D'Ancona, *Origini*, vol. II, p. 85.

[2] Cf. *infra*, pp. 85 ff. A letter written by Isabella d' Este shows how the
word could come to acquire theatrical significance: 'A le ventitre hore et
meza si principiò la comedia de la *Bachide*, quale fu tanto longa et fastidiosa et
senza balli intramezzi....Due moresche solamente furono tramezate.' Cf.
D'Ancona, *op. cit.* vol. II, p. 385.

intermedio, intermezzo, a word which, I imagine, was coined or adopted by men of the Renaissance because they wanted a term with a learned sound and purely literary associations. The earlier word, however, continued in use, although both in France and Italy it gradually lost its dramatic sense and was confined to the menu. In Spain, on the other hand, the word *entremes* came to mean 'a short comedy or farce.'

The entremets was sometimes combined with the momerie. At the Court of Don Juan II (1481–1495), for instance, the Count of Vimioso had a 'Momo...no quall levava por antremes huum anjo e um diabo.' The angel presented to the Count's wife a letter in prose and a poem in octosyllabic verse[1]. It was natural that the entremets machine should sometimes be used to convey a momerie into the hall, especially as the wagon, the ship, and the plough had formed part of ritual and folk mumming from very early times. The words might be used loosely enough at times, but the distinction between them was never lost; the momerie meant primarily 'the masked procession,' the entremets, 'the elaborate machine, the apparatus, the grouping of the various figures'; as distinct from the music and movement which might also be part of the entertainment. Christine de Pisan, for instance, applies the term entremets not to the whole performance but to the respective machines which were drawn up in front of the dais, one figuring the town of Jerusalem, the other the ship of Godfrey of Boulogne[2].

The different kinds of entremets are found in England as well as in the romance countries, although the word itself does not occur there[3]. The elaborately dressed dish, or table decora-

---

[1] Don Emilio Cotarelo y Mori, *Colección de Entremeses* (Nueva Biblioteca de Autores Españoles, Madrid, 1911), tom. I, vol. I, p. lvii. See also his remarks on pp. liv–lvi; he equates the Spanish word with the French and Italian forms and derives them all from *intromissum.*

[2] Cf. *supra,* p. 44.

[3] It is curious that the rise of the entremets on the Continent should have been more or less coincident with the rise of the interlude in England, and that recent research should have 'rehabilitated the old explanation of an Interlude as a play interposed in the pauses of some other entertainment, in opposition to the meaning assigned to it by Mr E. K. Chambers (*The Mediaeval Stage,* vol. II, pp. 181 f.) of a play carried on between two or more performers.' A. W. Pollard, *English Miracle Plays,* 7th ed. (Oxford,

tion, was called a 'subtilty' or 'soteltie,' the larger machine, stationary or moving, in the body of the hall, was called a 'pageant,' a word derived from Latin *pagina*, a plank, and applied in the first place to the wheeled stage of the religious plays, then also to the fixed stages and decorative structures that were set up at various prominent parts of the town during civic shows, and finally to the play, show, or procession itself[1]. Hence our use of the term 'pageantry.'

The association of the momerie with the entremets of the banqueting hall (also perhaps with the plough- or ship-car of seasonal ritual) meant that it was bound to be affected by the development of the pageant.

The fourteenth century is an important time in the history of pageantry. At the beginning of that period in England the Crafts celebrated royal events by functions which were—as Dr Chambers points out—little more than 'masked ridings' of folk-origin[2]; towards the end of the century the Goldsmiths honoured the coronation of Richard II by the erection of a very ingenious structure in Cheapside[3], and when in 1392 the peace made between the King and the rebellious Londoners was celebrated by civic pageantry, speech and song and music played an important part in the proceedings, and the subject-matter of the shows was obviously influenced by the religious drama[4].

Whether the foundation of the Feast of Corpus Christi (1264, 1311) was a cause or an early symptom of the growing

1923), Introd. p. lii. The interlude was often closely associated with the Tudor disguising, which did correspond in many ways to the entremets. But a reference in Robert Manning of Brunne, 'Interludes and somour games Of suich things came many shames,' suggests that the interlude came from the village green rather than from the aristocratic banqueting table. But the English interlude and the Continental entremets are both symptoms of the elaboration of courtly life and the rise of the courtly Renaissance drama. Our interlude is part of 'the movement of the drama during this period, from the publicity of the street to the halls of large houses, or in fine weather to a stage in a garden ' (*loc. cit.*).

[1] Cf. *Med. Stage*, vol. II, p. 137, note 4.

[2] *Med. Stage*, vol. II, pp. 167, 172 f., and *Annales Londonienses (Chron. of Ed. I and Ed. II*, R.S.), vol. I, p. 221; H. T. Riley, *Memorials of London*, p. 107.

[3] T. Walsingham, *Hist. Anglica* (R.S.), vol. I, pp. 331, 332.

[4] Fabyan, *The New Chronicles of England and France*, ed. H. Ellis (London, 1811), p. 538; *Richardi Maydiston de concordia inter regem Ric. II. et civitatem London (Political Poems and Songs*, R.S. vol. I, pp. 291 ff.).

popularity of pageantry, it certainly encouraged the development of this aspect of civic life and helped to establish contact between the different types of ludi. Secular festivities had a similar effect, and in particular the solemn entries of princes into their cities were occasions which called out all the resources and artistic talent of the community: knights, priests, burghers, even cooks, all had their contribution to make to these great solemnities. One such royal entry is described in detail by Froissart[1]. The chronicler was an eye-witness of the events he relates, and his account of the festival gives a very good idea of the conditions under which the momerie grew up, and the stage of development which had been reached by the revels at the end of the fourteenth century.

On Sunday, the 20th of August, 1389, when Isabella, Queen of France, arrived in Paris, pageants and tableaux had been arranged at all the more prominent parts of the city through which she was to pass. At the first gate of St Denis there was a starry heaven with a golden sun radiating light (the symbolical device of the King), and full of children dressed as angels, who sang sweetly; there was also an image of the Madonna and Child.

Round the fountain of St Denis young girls sang sweetly as they offered wine to all the passers-by. A little further on a stage was erected in the street, on which was performed a combat between Christians and Saracens[2]. At the second gate of St Denis, God the Holy Trinity was seated in majesty surrounded by choir-boys dressed as angels, and as the Queen passed by, the gate of Paradise opened, and two singing angels placed a golden crown upon her head.

At the gate of the Chatelet of Paris there was a wooden castle, on which was a bed curtained and adorned as though for the King's chamber. 'Et étoit appelé ce lit le lit de justice; et là en ce lit, par figure et par personnage, gissoit madame sainte Anne.' The castle also contained quite a large enclosure full of trees,

---

[1] *Op. cit.* book IV, chap. I, vol. III, pp. 3 ff.
[2] This is interesting in view of the possible meaning of the words morris-dance, morisco; cf. *supra*, pp. 28, 29.

with birds and hares and conies flying and running in and out. From this thicket there issued a white stag and approached the bed of justice, while from the other side of the thicket came a lion and an eagle 'faits très proprement,' who proudly walked up to the stag and the bed of justice. At this, twelve young girls, holding naked swords in their hands, came out of the wood and put themselves in position to protect the stag and the bed of justice, 'laquelle ordonnance la roine et les dames et les seigneurs virent moult volontiers.'[1]

On Monday the King gave a dinner-party to the ladies in the Palace. We can see the scene. The great marble table was reinforced with a thick oaken plank and laid for dinner; above it was the King's dresser, filled with gold plate, in front of it a barrier guarded by sergeants-at-arms to prevent the intrusion of unauthorised persons. There were quantities of minstrels and so many people present that it was hardly possible to turn round. Down the length of the hall there were two other tables at which more than five hundred young ladies were seated, but they could scarcely be served, the crowd was so great. The entremets, we are told, were very well planned, and would have given great pleasure if it had been possible to perform them properly.

The first was a wooden castle forty feet in height, twenty feet in length and breadth, representing the city of Troy, the second was a pavilion and the third a ship which could hold a hundred soldiers. The Greeks of the pavilion and the ship assaulted Troy, but the fight could not last long because of the press of people. The heat and confusion grew so great—a table where many ladies were sitting was overturned and the Queen was nearly fainting—that the King broke up the assembly[2].

Next day a number of notable bourgeois of Paris arrived at the Hôtel Saint-Pol to present wedding presents to the Queen. They were divided into several groups, each group bringing a wedding present in a litter carried by men disguised as *hommes sauvages*, animals and Moors.

On the same day at three o'clock the company repaired to the field of St Catherine, where elaborate preparations had been

<hr>

[1] *Op. cit.* p. 5.   [2] *Op. cit.* p. 7.

made for a great tournament. The knights in the lists bore the device of the King, and were called the Knights of the Golden Sun.

For three more days there were nightly supper-parties and dancing, and on Friday the King gave a dinner, at which there was jousting performed inside the hall for the amusement of the ladies. After this the festival came to an end.

This example, I think, shows very well how Court ludi, civic pageants, and the institutions of chivalry had so great an influence on one another. The episode of the twelve young girls, who guarded the stag and the bed of justice from the lion and the eagle, was a crude attempt at the symbolical action which became more common in the next century and was a characteristic of later masques and ballets.

In the fifteenth century allegory and symbolism pervaded all art and literature; moralities rivalled miracle plays in popularity, vices and virtues jostled Biblical, historical, and contemporary characters both in pageantry and the drama. As a necessary result of this mummings and pageants gradually became more literary. Already in the fourteenth century princes were welcomed into their cities by the singing of young virgins and choir-boys dressed as angels. In the fifteenth century something more was required. There is little reason for the introduction of abstract personages into an entertainment unless they are meant to illustrate some definite idea; and moreover descriptive speeches are needed to make their identity obvious. This means that the poet must be called in. During the fifteenth century pageantry began to acquire plot, design and poetry[1].

When Henry VI made his entry into Paris to be crowned King of France in 1431, he was met by 'the ix worthies, sittyng richely on horsebacke,...and euery cōpany, as their course came, saluted the kyng, with eloquent oracions, and heroicall verses.' There were also pageants 'of greate shewe and small coste,' and 'mystères mimés' or plays acted in pantomime[2].

[1] Cf. R. Withington, *English Pageantry* (Cambridge, Mass. 1918, 1920), vol. I, chap. III, 'The Royal Entry.'
[2] Hall's *Chronicle* (London, 1809), p. 161; *Chroniques d'Enguerrand de Monstrelet*, ed. Buchon, *Choix de Chroniques et Mémoires*, book II, chap. CIX, p. 652.

When Henry returned from France, he was given a most magnificent reception.

On entering the capital, the King found on the drawbridge a goodly tower, out of which issued Dame Nature, Dame Grace, and Dame Fortune, all of whom addressed to him poetical speeches. At the right hand of these three ladies stood seven virgins who presented the King with the seven gifts of the Holy Ghost; and on the left hand were another seven virgins who gave him the seven gifts of grace. After this salutation they sang a 'roundell with an heuynly melodye.' At the entry of Cornhill there was 'ordeyned a tabernacle of curyous werke, in the whiche stode dame Sapyence, and aboute her the vii artes or scyences lyberall. As first, grāmer, logyke, rethoryke, musyke, arsmetryke, gemetry, and astronomye, eueryche of theym exercisynge theyr connynge and facultie.' At the conduit in Cornhill there was set 'a pagent made cercle wyse, and in the summet or toppe thereof was sette a childe of wonderfull beaute, apparaylled lyke a kynge: vpon whose right hande satte lady Mercy, and vpon the lefte hande lady Trouth, and ouer them stode dame Clennesse enbrasynge ye kynges trone. Then before the kynge stode .ii. juges & .viii. sergeauntes of the coyfe; and dame Clennesse had this speche to the vi Henry the kynge....' At the conduit in Cheap 'were ordeyned dyuers wellys, as the welle of mercy, the welle of grace, & the welle of pyte: and at euery welle a lady standynge, that mynystered the water of euery welle to suche as wolde aske it, and that water was turnyd into good wyne. Aboute thyse welles were also sette dyuerse tryes with florysshynge leuys and fruytes...the whiche were so cunnyngly wrought, that to many they apperyd naturall trees growynge. In the bordour of this dilicious place, which was named Paradyse, stode ii forgrowen faders, reasemblyng Ennok and Hely.' These fathers made a speech. A little further on there was a wonderful tower which by means of artificial trees showed the title of Henry to the throne of France. At the conduit at Paul's Gate 'was pyght a celestyall trone, and therin was sette a personage of the Trinite, with a multytude of aungellys playinge and syngynge vpon all instrumentes of musyk; and upon ye front of the sayd crowne was wryten thyse verses or balades folowynge, the whiche were spoken by the fader vnto the kynge.'[1]

This London show marks an epoch in English pageantry. As far as we know, it is the first instance of the use of well-thought-out symbolism and allegory and of the recitation of poetic

[1] Fabyan, *Chronicles*, pp. 603 ff. The word *bagina* is here used for the first time in connection with these London shows. Cf. the contemporary description by John Carpenter, the town clerk, printed by H. T. Riley, *Liber Albus* (R.S.), vol. III, p. 457. Cf. *Med. Stage*, vol. II, p. 169 and note 5.

speeches by performers stationed on all the various pageants. Again, each pageant contributes to the idea that Henry VI was endowed with all the gifts and graces proper to a monarch; and the presence of this real, though slight, thread of unity is an advance on anything of the kind that had gone before.

This English pageant does not seem to have had any influence in France. In 1437 Charles VII was welcomed into Paris with much the same kind of show as had been used for the entertainment of Henry VI a few years earlier. In the procession went the Provost of Paris, and other dignitaries, among whom rode the Seven Deadly Sins, and the Seven Virtues 'all clothed according to their characteristics.'[1] Besides this there were performances of mimed mysteries. On the whole, in France and the Low Countries silent dramas seem to have been more popular than the symbolic tableaux which became so elaborate in England. Leaving Italy out of account, the pomp and splendour of pageantry was most highly developed in the rich towns of the Low Countries—Bruges, Ghent, Lille and Ypres—where commerce flourished, and where there was a strong sense of corporate life and civic liberty. It is however beside our purpose to pursue further the history of European pageantry, which had already by the middle of the fifteenth century contributed scenery, symbolism and poetry to the Court momerie.

The first literary momeries which have come down to us are the work of John Lydgate, and were probably written during the years 1427–1430[2]. Lydgate seems to have been much concerned with the pageantry of his day. He has left verse descriptions of a Corpus Christi procession, and of the entry of Henry VI into London; it is probable that he was the author of the verses which were spoken to the King on that occasion, and he may well be responsible for the attempt to give a rational design and unity to the pageantry. It has been maintained that the introduction of learned allegories into town pageantry and Court

---

[1] Monstrelet, *op. cit.* bk II, chap. CCXIX, p. 756.
[2] These momeries of Lydgate are printed in Brotanek, *op. cit.* pp. 305–325, and discussed by him, pp. 9–15.

entertainment was due to Lydgate[1]. Symbolical figures, however, appeared in Continental pageants before his time, and the taste for allegory was in Lydgate's day affecting all European literature and drama. Lydgate followed the general tendency, but no doubt he did much to make the allegories more purposeful, consistent, and learned.

Whether allegory made its way first into the religious play or the town pageant or the Court momerie is uncertain and unimportant. On the whole it is fairly safe to say that all the aesthetic improvements acquired by the ludi during the fifteenth century (introduction of speech, symbolism, plot, ingenious scenic devices) appeared first on the Continent and then in England, first in the civic shows and then in the courtly momerie; this generalisation, however, is more certainly true in the case of the introduction of speech and scenery than in the case of the introduction of symbolical figures. Lydgate's momeries, for instance, probably belong to an earlier date than Henry VI's entry into London.

When we turn to examine the form taken by the momerie after it had absorbed the influence of pageantry, we are at once met by a difficulty. Unfortunately, Lydgate's momeries are mere libretti, with few stage directions, and it is impossible to gather from them for what precise kind of entertainments they were intended. We cannot even tell how far speech had by this time become a recognised part of the momerie. With one possible exception there is nothing in these pieces to suggest that the mummers themselves broke silence.

The exception is the disguising which was performed before the Court at Hertford, and which seems to have been a kind of cross between a débat and a farce. Six countrymen hand in by letter a complaint against their wives, and their letter is read out by the King's secretary. The wives reply to the accusation, apparently by one of their number who acts as spokesman. The matter is determined by the secretary, who makes a satirica speech on behalf of the King. It is not certain, to my mind,

[1] Cf. Withington, *op. cit.* vol. I, pp. 141 ff. and footnotes. He discusses the question at length and cites the opinions of other scholars.

that one of the wives actually spoke; they may have had an interpreter with them (a familiar figure in the mumming) who spoke in their name. It is possible that the form of the disguising was a mock fight or burlesque dance between the husbands and the wives[1].

The 'balade made by daun John Lidegate at Eltham in Cristmasse, for a momyng tofore the kyng & the Qwene' seems to have been an explanatory speech introducing some mummers who, in the persons of Bacchus, Juno and Ceres, brought wine, wheat, and oil to the sovereigns as a token of peace, plenty, and gladness.

The next mumming is more difficult to interpret:

'And nowe filowethe a *lett*re made in wyse of balade by daun Johan, brought by a poursuyaunt in wyse of Mommers desguysed to fore the Mayre of London, Eestfeld, vpon the twelffethe night of Cristmasse, ordeyned Ryallych by the worthy Merciers, Citeseyns of london.' This balade tells how Jupiter sent out a poursuivant with letters, who having passed out of Egypt came down by the river Jordan:

> 'And sayled forthe soo all the Ryver of Geene,
> In which see regnethe the mighty qweene,
> Called Cyrses....
> And ther he saughe, as he gan approche,
> with Inne a boote a fissher drawe his nette
> On the right syde of a crystal Rooche;
> Ffishe was ther noon, for the draught was lette,
> And on thoon syde ther were *lett*res sette
> That sayde in frenshe this Raysoun: *Grande travayle.*
> This aunswere next in ordre: *Nulle avayle.*'

He then goes through the Straits of Morocco, and passing by Spain comes into England.

> 'And in a ffeeld, that droughe in to the Eest,
> Besyde an ylande he saughe a shippe vnlade
> which hade sayled ful fer toward the west;
> The Caban peynted with floures fresshe and glaade,
> And lettres frenshe, that feynt nyl ne faade:
> *Taunt haut e bas que homme soyt,*
> *Touz Joures regracyer dieux doyt.*

---

[1] *Mumming at Hertford*, ed. E. P. Hammond, *Anglia*, vol. XXII, pp. 364–374.

And in a boote on that other syde
Another fissher droughe his nette also,
fful of gret fisshe (Neptunus was his guyde)
with so gret plentee, he nyst what til do.
And ther were lettres embrouded not fer froo,
fful fresshly wryten this worde: *grande peyne*;
A[nd] cloos according with this resoun: *grande gayne*.'

The poursuivant came to the banks of Thames and landed hastily:

'where certayne vesselles now by the anker ryde.
hem to refresshe and to taken ayr,
Certein estates, wheche *pur*veye and provyde
ffor to vysyte and seen the noble Mayr
Of this cytee and maken theyre repayr
To his presence, or that they firther flitte,
Vnder supporte, that he wol hem admytte.'

The meaning of all this is obscure. No doubt it has reference to contemporary events, possibly some commercial transactions for which the Mayor Eastfield was responsible. It is impossible to say whether the three boats described by the poursuivant existed only in his imagination or were ship-pageants stationed in the hall. Nor can it be decided whether the poursuivant had come to announce the arrival of a water-pageant on the Thames, or whether he came to introduce mummers who were drawn into the hall on ship-pageants. On the whole, the latter explanation seems most probable, as a water-pageant would hardly have been called a mumming. If the mummers did come in in ship-pageants the mumming may be compared with French and Burgundian entremets such as those described by Froissart and Christine de Pisan.

The next mumming is much easier to understand:

'And nowe folowethe a *lett*re made in wyse of balade by ledegate daun Johan, of a mo*m*mynge, whiche the Goldesmythes of the Cite of London mo*m*med in Right fresshe and costele welych desguysing to theyre Mayre Eestfeld, vpon Candelmasse day at nyght, affter souper; brought & presented vn to the Mayre by an heraude, cleped ffortune.'

In this case David and the Twelve Tribes brought to the Mayor the Ark, which was carried by Levites.

> 'Of purpoos put this Aark to youre depoos,
> with good entent, to make youre hert light;
> And thoo three thinges, which ther Inne beo cloos,
> Shal gif to yowe konnyng, grace and myght,
> ffor to gouuerne with wisdome, pees and Right
> This noble Cytee, and lawes suche ordeyne,
> That no man shal haue cause for to compleyne.
> A wrytt with Inn shal vn to you declare
> And in effect pleynly specefye,
> where yee shal punyshe and where as ye shal spare,
> And howe that Mercy shal Rygour modefye.
> And youre estate al so to magnefye,
> This Aark of god, to make you gracyous,
> Shal stille abyde with you in youre hous.'

In all three mummings the object of the cortège is the presentation of gifts; it may or may not be significant that the pieces of Lydgate's which are called disguisings are pieces in which the performers come to dance or debate, and apparently not to bring presents:

'Lo here filowethe the deuyse of a desguysing to fore the gret estates of this lande, thane being at London, made by Lidegate daun Johan, the Munk of Bury. of dame fortune, dame prudence, dame Rightwysnesse and dame ffortitudo. beholdethe, for it is moral, plesaunt and notable.'

The libretto is evidently a speech made by a presenter who describes each lady as she comes forward, and in the end exhorts them to the dance:

> 'And yee foure susters, gladde of cheer,
> Shoule abyde here all this yeer
> In this housholde at libertee;
> And Joye and al prosparytee
> with yowe to housholde yee shoule bring.
> And yee all foure shal nowe sing
> with all youre hoole hert entiere
> Some nuwe songe about the fuyre,
> Such oon as you lykethe best;
> Lat ffortune go pley hir wher hir list.'

In Italy and Spain the momerie seems to have taken much the same form as in France and England, and to have consisted primarily of a masked cortège, and to have acquired a dramatic character through the custom of introducing the mummers by means of a letter, or a presenter's speech. Morelli tells us that

certain Venetian guilds[1] were obliged on pain of a fine to celebrate
their weddings by 'una Festa, Commedia ovver Momaria,' and
he illustrates the nature of a momaria by quoting a description
of a wedding, written in Latin verse by an anonymous author
of the year 1497. The Latin is bombastic and difficult to interpret, but it would seem that first there were grotesque dances,
then various gods, etc., came in, performing characteristic
actions, then Saturn and the rest produced a display of fireworks,
by lighting a machine set up in the hall, and Venus made a final
speech of eulogy[2].

The mumming performed at Windsor stands apart from the
rest and is related to the religious drama:

'Nowe folowethe next the devyse of a momyng to fore the kyng

[1] For Spain and Portugal cf. Cotarelo, *op. cit.* pp. lvi, lvii. 'Se conservan
unos *momos* hechos en Arévalo, en 1467, ante Doña Isabel la Católica. Figura
esta composición en el *Cancionero de Gómez Manrique* (Madrid, 1885, tomo II,
p. 122), y fué representada en 14 de Noviembre de dicho año, cumpleaños
del príncipe D. Alfonso, hermano de Enrique IV, y á quien la revoltosa
nobleza castellana de entonces había declarado rey después de la burlesca
deposición de Avila. Supone el poeta que las nueve Musas bajan del Helicón,
ocho de ellas vestidas ó cubiertas de plumas, y la novena, que era la misma
infanta Isabel, con una esclavina de pieles. Dirige cada una su correspondi-
ente copla al príncipe, fingiendo concederle ó *fadarle* un don ó cualidad,
que habrían de hacerle el hombre más dichoso de la tierra.'

[2] 'Post epulas pulsant citharas, et tecta resultant
Concita cuncta iocis. Illic spectacula cernes
Saltantum iuvenum, ut lascivaque sumeret ore
Forma Lupercalis illic praebentia cuique
Agmina spectanti nebulonum scenica risum.
Illic Enceladus, et bello fictus Echion
Saeva giganteo torquebat pectora Divis.
Illic Tymbraeo similem, similemque putares
Ignivomum Pythona illi qui corruit arcu.
Iuppiter astabat crinito fulmine comptus,
Caede cruentato radiabat cuspide Mavors,
Hastigeramque sua rutilantem Gorgone cernes
Pallada, Daphneis Phoebum portare sagittas,
Falcifer ac ignem manibus Saturnus habebat,
Unde Dei accenso solvebant lampade turrim,
In nihilum tanquam tempus compelleret orbem.
Tunc Venus ingenium risit, sumptusque profusos
Admirata, procul vix estque credere mille
Aurea sufficiant tantisque nomismata rebus,' etc.
Morelli tells us that the poet has written in the margin of the MS *Ludicra
spectacula, quae Bombariam vulgus appellat.* I suppose (as he gives us this as
an example of a momerie) he thinks *Bombariam* a mis-spelling of Momariam.
Cf. *Operette*, vol. I, pp. 162, 163.

henry the sixte...howe thampull and the floure delys came first to the Kynges of ffraunce by myrakle at Reynes.'

Lydgate's verses were meant either for recital as a preliminary speech, or else to be set up on a roll, that all might read the explanation of the ensuing performance:

'Nowe, Royal braunche, O blood of saint lowys,
So lyke it nowe to thy magnyfycence,
That the story of the flour delys
May here be shewed in thyne heghe presence,...
Lyst to supporte, here sitting in thy see,
Right as it fell this myracle to see.'

The entertainment probably corresponds to the mystères which were popular at that time in France and Burgundy, and not always sharply distinguished from momeries. Both terms, for instance, are applied to the mumming of Grace-Dieu; and the performance of the wild men who jumped out of a rock and danced a morisco before Gaston de Foix is called a 'mystère d'enfans sauvages.'[1] The rise of the mystery is indeed so marked a feature of the period which saw the literary development of the momerie that it is worth while to give a little attention to this phenomenon. First, however, we may notice a possible link between Lydgate's momeries and the popular religious drama of Brittany.

Commentators have been puzzled by the insertion of the letter M in the margin of Lydgate's mummings. Luzel records a similar usage in manuscripts of the plays of the Breton peasants:

'Toute représentation...commence ordinairement par une invocation à l'Esprit-Saint; puis un des acteurs, le plus habile et le mieux au fait des usages et des vieilles traditions, s'avance seul sur la scène, salue profondément, et, d'un ton lent et grave, moitié chantant, moitié déclamant, il récite une sorte de discours rimé, où il réclame d'abord le silence et l'attention de l'auditoire....Ensuite il donne le résumé de ce que contient l'acte qui va être représenté. C'est ce qu'on nomme le *Prologue*. Ces morceaux sont jugés importants et indispensables, pour que l'auditoire prévenu, ne soit pas surpris et dérouté par les mouvements trop brusques de la scène.... Tous les manuscrits que j'ai consultés portent à la marge des prologues, à tous les quatre vers, un M ou le mot *Marche*. C'est qu'en effet un usage bizarre, et dont nous ignorons le

---

[1] Prunières, *op. cit.* p. 9.

motif et l'origine, voulait que l'auteur qui récitait le *Prologue* fît, de quatre vers en quatre vers, une évolution autour du théâtre, suivi de tous ses compagnons. C'est ce qu'on appelait la *Marche*.'[1]

M. Luzel[2] acquired his MSS of old Breton mysteries with great difficulty, because the peasants who possessed them regarded them with an almost superstitious awe, and believed that the family luck depended on their safe preservation. In 1878 he attended a revival of the ancient mystery of St Tryphine[3] in Pluzunet in the canton of Plouaret, where a tradition of acting seems to have been preserved, in spite of the suppression of the plays in the eighteenth century. Before each act the Prologue entered accompanied by two attendants, who followed all his movements. After saluting the audience the Prologue chanted four verses at the extreme left of the stage, then four verses in the centre of the scene, then four verses to the right of the scene and so on, backwards and forwards. Between each recitation he and his companions saluted the audience. In his recitation he related the action that was about to follow. This account of the Prologue is interesting because it not only throws light on the meaning of the letter M, but it shows that description of the action by a Prologue does not necessarily imply that the action is in dumb show.

Evidence drawn from the behaviour of the Breton Prologue must however be used with caution. The peasants are conservative, it is true, but M. Luzel gives an amusing example of the way they could misinterpret their MSS. Apparently they were accustomed to continuous acting and could not understand why the word 'scene' occurred in some of their plays, and at Pluzunet it was traditional that wherever the prompter came across the word he should cry in a loud voice *Scene!* and instantly all the actors would rush on to the stage, holding hands, dancing a round dance with great vigour and merriment. The custom

[1] *Sainte Tryphine et le roi Arthur*, Mystère Breton (Quimperlé, 1863), p. xxiv. Quoted in D'Ancona, *op. cit.* vol. II, p. 273, note 2. The last two sentences are quoted by Luzel from E. Souvestre, *Les Derniers Bretons* (Paris, 1836), vol. III, p. 82.
[2] Cf. *Une Représentation de Sainte Tryphine*, in *Revue Celtique*, 1876–1878, t. III, pp. 386 ff.
[3] Probably of the sixteenth century.

proved so useful and popular, that apparently it was extended, and if an actor was not ready, or something had gone wrong, the prompter would shout *Scene!* the hurly-burly would begin, and the audience would be fully appeased. Immense satisfaction was caused by the sight of God the Father, the Virgin Mary, devils, angels, ruffians, etc., all taking hands and joining in the frolic.

The March of the Prologue, both in the traditional Breton plays and in Lydgate's momeries, is probably connected with customs of the religious drama; and I cannot help wondering (although it is nothing but a suggestion) whether that queer sideways march at Pluzunet is a survival from the liturgical drama, for the movements of the Prologue and his two attendants are oddly reminiscent of the movements of priests and acolytes in front of the altar. But, however that may be, I do not think that the letter M in Lydgate's MSS denotes a sideways movement, but a march round the hall, and the words of E. Souvestre, quoted by Luzel, suggests that something of the kind may have taken place in the performance of Breton plays. No doubt, however, Lydgate[1] modified customs inherited from the popular religious drama, in accordance with what he supposed to be classical dramatic method. The idea that classical plays were originally recited by one man, while another actor or actors performed them in dumb show, was a common mediaeval misconception, and Lydgate gives a very detailed reconstruction of one of these performances in his *Troy Book.*

'*Of a Theatyre stondynge in þe princypale paleys of Troye, declarenge the falle of Pryncys and othere....*
> In þe theatre þer was a smal auter
> Amyddes set, þat was half circuler,
> Whiche in-to þe Est of custom was directe;
> Vp-on þe whiche a pulpet was erecte,
> And þer-in stod an aw[n]cien poete,
> For to reherse by rethorikes swete
> Þe noble dedis, þat wer historial,
> Of kynges, princes for a memorial...

[1] I have not sufficient evidence to assert that Lydgate was the first to shape the literary momerie, but it is possible that this is the case. Cf. Withington, *loc. cit.*

And how Fortune was to hem vnswete—
Al þis was tolde and rad of þe poete.
And whil þat he in þe pulpit stood,
With dedly face al devoide of blood,
Singinge his dites, with muses al to-rent,
Amydde þe theatre schrowdid in a tent,
Þer cam out men gastful of her cheris,
Disfigurid her facis with viseris,
Pleying by signes in þe peples siȝt,
Þat þe poete songon hath on hiȝt;
So þat þer was no maner discordaunce
Atwen his dites and her contenaunce:
For lik as he aloft[e] dide expresse
Wordes of Ioye or of heuynes,
Meving and cher, byneþe of hem pleying,
From point to point was alwey answering....
And þis was doon in April and in May,
Whan blosmys new, boþe on busche and hay,
And flouris fresche gynne for to springe;
And þe briddis in þe wode synge
With lust supprised of þe somer sonne,
When þe[se] pleies in Troye wer begonne....'[1]

This is not a description of a Trojan tragedy, but it is a very good description of a fifteenth-century momerie or mystère mimé, and it would be interesting if we had here an earlier parallel to the work of Beaujoyeulx and Rinuccini, who in the next century in trying to revive, not merely the literary forms of Greek and Latin drama, but the classical method of performance, succeeded in shaping the traditional entertainments into the new genres of opera and ballet[2].

The word 'mystery' is so often treated as a synonym for religious play, that it is difficult to remember that at first a mystery was not necessarily a religious, or even in the full sense of the word, a dramatic performance at all. The first instance of the use of the word in connection with drama occurs in 1402, when King Charles VI sent letters to the Confrères de la Passion, permitting them 'jouer quelque Misterre que ce soit, soit de la dicte Passion, et Résurreccion, ou autre quelconque tant de saincts

[1] Quoted in J. W. Cunliffe, *Early English Classical Tragedies* (Oxford, 1912), pp. xvii, xviii.
[2] Cf. *infra*, pp. 104 ff.

comme de sainctes....'[1] There is no indication in this passage that *mystère* had a more precise meaning than had *action*, *représentation* or *histoire*, and other vague words of the kind. 'Mystery,' coming from Latin *ministerium*, meant 'action, office, function'; mysteries or actions of the saints were performed dramatically just as the mysteries of Hercules (i.e. his twelve labours) were both acted and woven into tapestry[2].

In the fifteenth century French chroniclers use the word *mystère* with many subtle variations of meaning, impossible to translate into English, but very illuminating for the historian of the revels. The root significance of the word (as used by them) seems to be public action, solemn ceremonial, any kind of proceeding that has a touch of ritual or of etiquette or of make-believe about it. For instance, Olivier de la Marche witnessed the ceremonial meeting of the Duke of Burgundy and the King of the Romans, but could not—so he tells us—understand 'pourquoy ne à quelle raison se faisoient les misteres ne les honneurs'[3]; and again on one occasion a pantomimic fight was performed so well 'que ce ne sembloit pas mistere, ains sembloit trop mieulx une très aigre et mortelle bataille.'[4]

Sometimes the word is used in connection with great tournaments, and then it refers not so much to the actual contests, the athletic part of the business, as to the accessories, the pageants and disguisings, and all that made the tournament a grand public spectacle: 'Or est bien temps que je me passe des preparatoires et misteres de cestuy hault et noble pas, et que je viengne à l'execution et effect de la matiere commencée.'[5] Mystery in this sense

---

[1] Quoted by Julleville, *Les Mystères*, vol. I, p. 417.

[2] I follow Julleville's derivation of the word from *ministerium* rather than from *mysterium* because the chroniclers do not seem to regard it as implying anything especially mysterious or religious, and for similar reasons given below. Cf. Julleville, *op. cit.* pp. 188 ff. and *Le Théâtre en France*, chap. I, 'Les Mystères,' p. 18.

Cf. G. Cohen, *Histoire de la Mise-en-Scène dans la Théâtre Religieux Français du Moyen Age* (Paris, 1906). He deals only with the spoken drama, not with the mystère mimé.

[3] Olivier de la Marche, *Mémoires*, ed. H. Beaune, J. d'Arbeaumont (Paris, 1883), vol. I, bk I, chap. VII, p. 277.

[4] *Ibid.* vol. II, bk I, chap. XXIX, p. 360.

[5] *Ibid.* vol. I, bk I, ch. IX, p. 295.

becomes almost equivalent to entremets or pageant. The figures of the Lady of Tears and the Fountain of Tears which decorated the lists of a tournament held at Chalon-sur-Saône in 1449 were called mysteries: 'Et depuis furent portez iceulx misteres à Nostre Dame de Boulongne, où l'on les peult encoires veoir et trouver en l'eglise, sur l'oratoire du duc de Bourgoingne.'[1]

Then, again, the word 'mystery' is often used with special reference to the *symbolical meaning* or *dramatic design* of pageants and disguisings. At the Feast of the Pheasant in 1454 there was a famous momerie of Grace-Dieu and the Twelve Virtues, in which Grace-Dieu the presenter introduced each of the mummers in turn to the Duke, and afterwards 'pource que le mystère estoit parachevé, leur furent ostés les brevets qu'elles portoient sur leurs espaules; et commencèrent à danser en guise de mommeries.'[2] A letter was handed to the Duke containing verse descriptions of the mummers and explanations of their names, and of the meaning of their disguise. These verses were called mysteries: 'Le brief de Foy contenoit les misteres qui s'ensuyvent.'[3] Again on another occasion, the word was used for the *allegorical significance* of certain disguised characters appearing at a tournament in Bruges[4].

Mystery became a dramatic term through the custom of using religious plays as part of the solemn celebration of royal entries and progresses. In 1420 Henry V was entertained in Paris by 'un moult piteux mystere de la passion Nostre Seigneur, au vif, selon que elle est figurée autour du cueur de Nostre-Dame de Paris.'[5] Mystery here need not mean religious

[1] *Ibid.* vol. II, bk I, chap. XXI, p. 202. Cf. also 'ung cerf volant bien et somptueusement fait, lequel *par mistère* s'agenouilla devant le roy quand il passa par là...estoient aux fenestres la femme du conte de Dunois et celle du duc de Sombrecet pour voir le dit *mystère*.' Cf. Jean Chartier, *Chronique de Charles VII*, chap. 209 (Bibl. Elzévir.), t. II, p. 169. Quoted by Julleville, *Les Mystères*, vol. I, p. 193.

[2] *Chroniques de Mathieu de Coussy* (usually spelt d'Escouchy), ed. Buchon, *Choix de Chroniques et Mémoires*, chap. LXXXVIII, p. 175.

[3] Olivier de la Marche, *op. cit.* vol. II, bk I, chap. XXIX, p. 374.

[4] Cf. *ibid.* vol. III, bk II, chap. IV, p. 175, and *infra*, p. 70.

[5] Julleville, *Les Mystères*, vol. I, p. 192. Cf. also Enguerrand de Monstrelet, *Chroniques*, ed. Buchon, *op. cit.* bk II, chap. CIX, p. 652, and *Journal d'un Bourgeois de Paris*, ed. Michaud et Poujoulat (Paris, 1854), in *Mémoires relatifs à l'Histoire de France*, vol. III, p. 243.

drama; it is merely equivalent to representation, action, etc.; indeed when the word is used with a special meaning, it refers to the manner of performance rather than to the subject-matter. 'Devant la Trinité étoit la passion, c'est à savoir comment Notre-Seigneur fut pris....Et ne parloient rien ceux qui ce faisoient, *mais le montrèrent par jeux de mystère.*'[1] These dumb shows were not necessarily religious. At the Burgundian Court in 1453 the story of Jason was enacted as a mystère mimé[2]. It was only in the later half of the fifteenth century (particularly after the Church drama had become popularised by printing) that the word 'mystery' came to be used chiefly in the sense to which we are accustomed, and was the regular term for a religious play[3].

In England the word 'mystery' is not used of religious drama before the eighteenth century, and we do not know whether or not the thing itself was ever an item in the Court programme. Lydgate's mystery (which he calls a mumming) may be an isolated imitation of a French fashion.

But although the mystery may have had little or no direct influence on English mumming, it does illustrate very well certain tendencies of the time which had a great effect on the revels of England, as of all other European countries. The primary meaning of the word, as we have seen, was function; but it came to be used for dumb show, as distinct from spoken drama; for the more dramatic and symbolical part of an entertainment, as distinct from the traditional dancing; for the disguised personages, and even the decorations and pageants which graced the lists, as distinct from the trial of strength which originally was the essential part of the tournament; last of all, mystery became equivalent to religious drama. In fact, the use of the word 'mystery' in the fifteenth century is a symptom of the meeting and interaction of traditional games, civic functions, and Church drama, and of the tendency of all public activities

---

[1] Monstrelet, *op. cit.* bk II, chap. CCXIX, p. 756.

[2] Olivier de la Marche, *op. cit.* vol. II, bk I, chap. XXIX, p. 357. He calls the performance of 'l'ystoire de Jason,' which was acted in dumb show, both a 'mistere' and an 'entremectz.'

[3] Cf. Julleville, *Les Mystères*, vol. I, p. 196.

to become symbolical and spectacular, and possibly of a dawning interest in the Theatre of the Ancients.

The traditional mumming enlarged its scope and subject-matter by contact, not only with civic pageantry and religious drama, but also with the dying institutions of chivalry.

During the fifteenth century, while feudalism and the true spirit of chivalry declined, the knightly institutions were becoming ever more resplendent and self-conscious. The tournament, in particular, was turning into a grand public mummery; knights came to the lists in all kinds of fantastic disguises; the challenges were couched in terms of romantic gallantry, which furnished suggestions for the plots of many later French and English masquerades.

In England the aesthetic development of the tournament was beginning already in Edward III's reign. On one occasion the King and the Court rode to the lists masked as Tartars, on another occasion the knights jousted disguised as the Pope and the twelve Cardinals. In 1375 'rood dame Alice Perrers, as lady of the sune, fro the tour of London thorugh Chepe; and alwey a lady ledynge a lordys brydell. And thanne begun the grete justes in Smythefeld.'[1]

The spectacular development of the institutions of chivalry is seen at its height in the Court of Burgundy, during the period when Philip the Good and Charles the Bold were trying to build up for themselves a kingdom made out of the most heterogeneous and incompatible materials[2].

Duke Philip was conservative in temperament, and a great lover of magnificence. He patronised the ancient Feast of Fools, which the more zealous churchmen were trying to abolish, dallied with the idea of a crusade, founded the Order of the Golden Fleece, and promoted tournaments and banquets and every kind of expensive ceremonial that could shed a glamour on his Court.

It was, however, the external form rather than the soul of chivalry that Duke Philip valued. He lowered the ideal of

[1] *London Chronicle*, 70. Quoted in *Med. Stage*, vol. i, p. 392, note 4.
[2] Cf. De Laborde, *Les Ducs de Bourgogne* (Paris, 1849–1852), 3 vols.

knighthood by bestowing the honour upon mere babes in arms, and it seems that his real motive in founding the Order of the Golden Fleece was to create a Burgundian aristocracy, for the Knights of the Fleece were bound to resign their membership of all other orders of chivalry. It is possible, too, that the name of the Order was expressive of the Duke's design to encourage the woollen industry of Flanders.

The development of Burgundian art and pageantry was promoted not only by Duke Philip's deliberate fostering of aristocratic and chivalrous customs; but also by his connection as overlord with the wealthy commercial cities of the Low Countries where there were flourishing schools of art, and where the civic sense was peculiarly keen. Some of these Flemish towns, Bruges and Lille, for instance, had their annual festivals, which were great occasions for the practice both of folk-customs and of chivalrous exercises. Particularly famous was the feast of the Roi de l'Épinette, which was held on the first Sunday in Lent. This festivity was a form of the king-game, of uncertain but ancient origin. Each year a monarch known as *Syre de la Joye* or a *Roi de l'Épinette* was elected and his reign was celebrated by banquets, dances, mysteries, and above all, by a great tournament which was attended by contingents of jousters from other cities and also by other mock monarchs, the Abbé de Liesse from Arras, the Prince de Plaisance from Valenciennes, the Prince d'Amour from Tournoi, etc. In 1438 the jousters and their friends from Valenciennes arrived at Lille disguised as wild men[1].

The kings of France and the dukes of Burgundy took a surprising interest in these games, and people of the most exalted rank did not disdain to take part in them; the Roi de l'Épinette himself was, however, more often than not, chosen from the merchant class, and afterwards ennobled as the reward for his services during his short, but ruinously expensive, reign. This, of course, was a method of encouraging industry and commerce by the bestowal of honours, but it also led to a rapid widening

---

[1] Cf. L. de Rosny, *L'Épervier d'Or, ou description historique des Joûtes et des Tournois qui, sous le titre des Nobles Rois de l'Épinette, se célébrèrent à Lille au Moyen-Âge* (Paris, 1839).

of the ranks of the aristocracy, and probably was one of the causes which led at last to the abolition of the tournament.

Chivalric customs, however, lingered long in the town of Lille, and it was there that Duke Philip held his famous Feast of the Pheasant, a most interesting ceremony, which illustrates very well the way in which the momerie was influenced by chivalric customs, and the stage of development reached by the revels of the Burgundian Court in the latter half of the fifteenth century.

The Lille festivities were held for the ostensible purpose of giving the great noblemen there assembled an opportunity of solemnly and publicly devoting themselves to warfare against the conquerors of Constantinople. Vows were made, but not kept, the splendour of the ceremony was most impressive, but it was devoid of serious political or religious purport. The day of the Crusades was over. It was, however, not inappropriate that one of the most striking manifestations of the final phase of mediaevalism should take place in connection with an event which is sometimes taken as the starting-point of the Renaissance.

The proceedings[1] began with the banquet given by the Duke of Cleves, at which was cried a great tournament to take place in about eighteen days' time. The prize of the tournament was to be a golden swan, and 'as far as I can see,' adds the chronicler, 'this cry was made apropos of an entremets which was fashioned for the said banquet and occupied the greater part of the principal table.'

That same night the chaplet was presented to the Count of Estampes, who would therefore, according to the prevalent fashion, be expected to provide the next great feast. This he did in ten days' time. His banquet also was abundant, 'and richly garnished with many new entremets,' but the most important function was the solemn presentation of the chaplet to the Duke of Burgundy, by the Princesse de Joye, a beautiful lady, twelve years old, riding on a palfrey led in by three men singing songs made for the occasion.

---

[1] I follow the account of Mathieu d'Escouchy (*op. cit.* chap. LXXXVII, pp. 145 ff.), which seems to me to be the original. It is fuller than that of Olivier de la Marche and contains expressions which seem to suggest *personal* comment.

On the 18th of February, 1454, Duke Philip of Burgundy gave his famous banquet. The day began with the Tournament of the Swan, Adolf of Cleves appearing as Knight of the Swan. Before the end of the tournament our chronicler, Mathieu d'Escouchy, hurried away to the great hall where the banquet was to be held. In this hall there were three raised and covered tables, loaded with most elaborate entremets, the chief of which was a church with a sounding bell and four people inside it who were to sing and play upon the organ. There was also a huge pie, containing twenty-eight people, who were to play on different musical instruments, each when his turn came. In the middle of the hall, the statue of a naked woman, draped with a veil worked with Greek characters, was set up on a pillar, and this statue served as a fountain which poured out hippocras as long as the supper lasted. Near this there was another pillar, to which was attached a fine living lion, as though he were defender and guardian of the image, and over his pillar was the inscription: 'Ne touchez pas à ma dame.'

Our chronicler had hardly had time to inspect all these entremets before the Duke and Duchess of Burgundy came in, with a great multitude of noble people, most of whom were distinguished strangers, who had come from afar to be present at the famous banquet.

As soon as the guests were seated a bell sounded from the entremets of the church, and three little choir-boys and a tenor voice sang a very sweet song, which the chronicler thought was a kind of grace before meat. When that was done, a shepherd played on a musette from inside the pie; and here it may be added that this singing and playing by the musicians in the church, answered by one or more of the musicians inside the pie, was repeated between each item in the programme.

Immediately after this musical prologue began 'the living and moving entremets,' which came in by the great entrance door of the hall, accompanied by fifteen or sixteen knights, clothed in robes of the livery. The most noteworthy of these entremets (which for the most part suggest the circus rather than the Court) was the appearance of a fiery dragon, who descended from the roof, flew the length of the hall, and disappeared, and the mystère mimé of Jason, which was performed in three acts, on a platform placed at the end of the hall and covered by a curtain. With the last act of this mystery the worldly entremets and pastimes came to an end, and then the central event of the evening took place.

There came in a gigantic man, disguised as a Saracen of Granada, leading an elephant with a castle on its back, the castle containing a lady disguised as a nun or devotee. As soon as this strange cortège arrived, the lady looked round the assembly and said to her companion:

> 'Géant, je veux ci arrester;
> Car je voy noble compagnie....'

The giant having obediently led her in front of the Duke, she recited a long verse lament, the gist of which was that she, Holy Church, after making the round of all European courts, had come to appeal to the Duke of Burgundy for help against the Saracens. Her lament finished, Toison-d'Or, king of arms, brought in a living pheasant, upon which the Duke and other nobles made their crusading vows.

With this ceremony the banquet came to an end, the tables were cleared to make room for the performance of a momerie. First came torch-bearers and musicians; then a lady, dressed as a nun, with her name, 'Grace-Dieu,' inscribed on her shoulder in letters of gold; then twelve masked knights, each of whom held a torch and led in a lady. The ladies had their faces covered with transparent veils, and each had her name (which was that of a virtue) inscribed on a roll fastened to her left shoulder. And so Grace-Dieu, followed by the twelve ladies and their knights, paced the hall, stopped before the Duke and recited some verses saying that she was come to introduce to him the twelve virtues and to hand him a letter. This letter was accepted by the Duke, and handed to the Seigneur de Créquy, who read it aloud. Its purport was that on hearing the vows made by Duke Philip and other good Christians, God had sent Grace-Dieu to present to him and others the twelve virtues, who would assist him in his enterprise. This letter read, Grace-Dieu announced that 'Ces hautes dames bailleront par escript leurs parfaits noms, lesquels je vous liray.' Then each lady came up in turn, and handed a letter to Grace-Dieu, who presented her to the Duke and read out her letter which consisted of a verse stanza describing the virtue in question. When the twelve virtues had all been intro-duced, Grace-Dieu bade the Duke farewell and departed; whereupon the brevets were taken off the ladies' shoulders, and they began to dance 'en guise de momeries.' Whilst the dancing was going on, the kings of arms and the heralds consulted the ladies as to who deserved the prize for the Tournament of the Swan. Two princesses presented the prize to the Count of Charolais, and with that the festivity ended between two and three o'clock in the morning.

In 1468[1] Duke Charles the Bold married Margaret of York, and the wedding ceremonies which took place at Bruges mark an advance on the mysteries and entremets of the Feast of the Pheasant.

The bride made a solemn entry into the city of Bruges, the streets being hung with rich tapestries, and adorned at intervals by various *histoires* or *personnaiges*, that is to say, dramatic scenes or tableaux.

In the market place there was set up a great gilded tree, which was guarded by a giant and a dwarf, and was the scene of the magnificent tournament which was fought out day after day, and formed the chief entertainment of the wedding festivities. This jousting had a certain semi-dramatic element, and was concerned with the imprisonment of a giant by a dwarf and the 'dame de l'Isle celée.' A few of the lords came in fancy dress. On one day the Count of Roussy came on horseback enclosed in a four-towered castle, with a great door that could shut and open of itself, and despatched his dwarf, 'Petit Espoir,' to plead for his freedom. When the ladies gave orders for his release, the door of the castle opened, and the knight on his horse leapt out, and entered the lists.

The wedding festival was also celebrated by a succession of luxurious banquets. Three moving entremets were presented;

---

[1] Olivier de la Marche, *op. cit.* vol. III, bk II, ch. IV, pp. 101 ff.

first, a unicorn as big as a horse, with a leopard on top of him, bearing a marguerite and the flag of England. The marguerite was taken from the leopard, and presented to the Duke of Burgundy with the announcement that the proud leopard of England had come to visit the noble company, bringing with him the gift of a noble marguerite. Next came a great golden lion, covered with the arms of Burgundy, and carrying on his back the female dwarf of Madame of Burgundy, dressed as a shepherdess. The lion sang a song, and the shepherdess was placed on the table, and received very humanely by Madame. For the third entremets there was a dromedary.

Other banquets were very similar to this, but always they were increasing in extravagance day by day. On one occasion the high table was decorated with a marvellous edifice:

'moult soubtivement faict, car il y avoit ung palais, et ung hault mirouer où se veoit personnaiges incongneuz. Il y avoit personnaiges et morisques mouvans, moult bien et soubtivement faictz, roches, arbres, fuilles, et fleurs; et devant icelluy palais avoit une petite fontaine qui sourdoit du doit d'un petit sainct Jehan...et sembloit que celle fontaine arrosast les arbres et jardins d'icelluy bancquet....'[1]

During the course of the banquets the Twelve Labours of Hercules were represented. The form of the representation was similar to that of the mystery of Jason, which had been performed at the Feast of the Pheasant; but Olivier de la Marche does not use the word *mystère* in connection with it, and 'Hercules' was a longer and more elaborate performance than the Jason mystery.

Some of the entremets resembled Italian moriscos, and one in particular would seem to have been suggested by a morisco of dancers issuing from a golden wolf, which had graced a banquet in Siena a few years earlier[2]. The Burgundian entremets[3] began with the arrival of two giants, who entered the hall armed with sticks, dragging after them a great whale, sixty feet long, moving his fins and body and tail, as if alive. 'Ses deux yeulx estoient des deux plus grans mirouers que l'on avoit sceu trouver.' It was 'la plus grande et la plus grosse qui fut jamais veue par nulz

<hr>

[1] *Ibid.* p. 197. [2] Cf. *infra*, p. 86. [3] De la Marche, *loc. cit.* pp. 197 ff.

entremectz et presens en ung personnaige.' When the whale
had made the round of the hall to the sound of trumpets, it
stopped opposite the high table and opened its throat to disgorge
two sirens, who jumped out,

'ayant pignes et mirouers à leurs mains, qui commencerent une chanson
estrange...et au son de celle chanson saillirent l'ung après l'aultre, en
maniere de morisque, jusqu'au nombre de douze chevaliers de mer,
ayans en l'une des mains talloches, et en l'aultre bastons deffensables. Et
tantost après commença un tabourin à jouer dedans le ventre de la
balaine, et à tant cesserent les seraines de chanter, et commencerent à
danser avecques les chevaliers de mer; mais entre eux se meust une
amoureuse jalousie, tellement que le debat et tournoy commença entre
les chevalliers, qui dura assez longuement; mais les geans, à tout leurs
grans bastons, les vindrent deppartir; et les rechasserent dedans le
ventre de la balaine, et pareillement les seraines, et puis recloyt la balaine
la gorge, et en la conduicte des deux geans reprint son chemin....Et
certes ce fut un moult bel entremectz; car il y avoit dedans plus de
quarante personnes. Sur ce point furent les tables levées et commencerent les danses.'

A curious but rather tasteless entremets was the high tower
placed in the middle of the hall, which was a model of a tower
that Duke Charles had begun to build in one of his Dutch
towns, while he was still Comte de Charolais. On the top of
this tower stood a watchman, who sounded his horn several
times, and each blast was the signal for an odd entremets first
of bears, then of wolves, then of asses looking out of the windows
and singing songs, and so on. For the fifth and last entremets,
the watchman blew his horn, and called for a morisco to amuse
the company, and in response to his summons there issued from
the tower a monkey followed by six others, all made to appear
as if they were really alive, who went round the tower and stole
the wares of a merchant who was lying asleep. 'Et le cinge, qui
avoit le tabourin, commença à jouer une morisque,...firent le tour
autour de la tour, et, après plusieurs habiletez de cinges, s'en
retournerent par où ilz estoient venuz.'[1]

Such were the ingenious, bizarre, and very expensive entertainments which delighted our forefathers in the later Middle

[1] De la Marche, *loc. cit.* p. 154.

Ages; and one cannot help wondering why this taste for gorgeous, highly coloured revels was so very strong in the fifteenth century, particularly in the Court of Burgundy. The same question presented itself to contemporaries.

Towards the end of the Feast of the Pheasant, there was a pause in the proceedings. The tables were cleared away, the great entremets removed, and to Mathieu d'Escouchy the splendour seemed suddenly to have vanished like a dream. Looking round for fresh amusements, and finding none, he was thrown back upon his own thoughts.

'Premièrement, je pensay en moy-même le très outrageux excès, et la grande despense qui, pour l'occasion et la cause de ces banquets, ont esté faits depuis peu de temps; car ceste manière de chappelets avoit desjà très longuement duré; et sur cela chacun s'efforçoit à son ordre, et mettoit peine, à son tour, de recevoir la compagnée le plus hautement qu'il se pouvoit, ledit duc, principalement, qui avoit fait un si grand appareil, coust et assemblée, sans que ce fust au sujet de faire nopces ou alliance d'autres princes, ou bien des festoyements d'estrangers. Pour dire le vray, je disois et nommois ceste chose là outrageuse et desraisonnable despense, sans y sçavoir ne trouver entendement de vertu, fors volonté de prince, sinon touchant l'entremets de l'église, et les voeux ensuivis en conséquence de cela; et encore me sembloit si haute entreprinse trop soudainement et trop précipitamment commencée. Or, en ceste pensée et imagination je demeuray fort longuement....'[1]

D'Escouchy put his difficulties before a Lord Chamberlain who was in the confidence of the Duke of Burgundy, who affirmed on his knightly honour that the prime cause of all these festivities was Duke Philip's desire to undertake a crusade.

This did not really meet the difficulty. Why could not Duke Philip show his zeal for Holy Church without all this pomp and circumstance? How was it that although the knightly crusading spirit was quite obviously dead, the forms and trappings of chivalry were ever increasing in splendour and costliness, and how was it that a banquet like the Feast of the Pheasant could be prepared when no useful diplomatic purpose was served thereby? It was because pageantry was the fashion of the day. But that only suggests a further question. What hidden cause

[1] *Op. cit.* p. 172.

was at work in the fifteenth[1] century to stimulate people's instinct for pageantry and every kind of semi-dramatic activity, and why was it that then at last the old traditional ludi, which had endured for so long, fruitless and almost unchanging, awoke to life, had a considerable aesthetic development, played a great part in social life, and coloured much of the literature and the drama of the time?

For that was what happened. As soon as French and English literary historians reach the fifteenth century, they complain of dullness, sterility. But the student of pageantry and dramatic activity has quite a different experience. His investigations, whether they be concerned with disguisings, morris-dance, danse macabre, guild plays, formation of dramatic troupes, or varieties of sociétés joyeuses, all alike take him back to the fifteenth and later half of the fourteenth centuries. In the religious drama certain innovations appear in this century, 'a tendency to substitute mere spectacular pageantry for the spoken drama, and a tendency to add to the visible presentment of the Scriptural history an allegorical exposition of theological and moral doctrine,'—tendencies which are not unrelated, for the simplest and most obvious way of lending meaning to a dance or procession is by making it symbolical, and moreover mediaeval allegory is perhaps due less to the love of abstract thinking than to the childlike habit of personification. At any rate these two tendencies—to pageantry and to symbolism—coloured not only the drama, but a great deal of the non-dramatic literature of the time. Sometimes fifteenth-century poets see nature through the medium of Court pageantry, and think in terms of disguise and dance.

William Dunbar is a case in point.

> 'Quhat throw the mirry fowlis armony,
> And throw the reveris sound that ran me by,
> On Florayis mantill I sleipit quhair I lay,

> Quhair sone vnto my dremis fantesy
> I saw approche agane the orient sky
> Ane saill, as quhite as blosome upon spray,
> With mast of gold, bricht as the sterne of day,
> Quhilk tendit to the land full lustely,
> As falcoun swift desyrouse of hir pray.
> ...quhairfro annon thair landis,
> Ane hundreth ladeis, lustie intill weidis;
> Als fresche as flouris that in the May vpspreidis,
> In kirtillis grene....'[1]

It might well be an idealisation of the ship-pageant wheeled into the banqueting-hall, and there discharging its burden of disguised ladies. Similarly, in the *Dance of the Sevin Deidly Synnis*, the ground of the poet's imagination is a wild mumming or morisco.

The effect of courtly revels on the poetic imagination is still more strikingly illustrated by Christine de Pisan in *Le Dit de la Rose*[2], a very charming contribution to the controversy which had been stirred up by Jean de Meung's attack on women. The poetess describes how in the month of January, 1401, a courteous and gentle company assembled together for supper in the house of the Duke of Orleans. There was much laughter, much pleasant talk of books and of 'balades' and of love 'Senz diffamer grant ne menour,' when suddenly, in spite of barred doors and closed windows,

> 'Une dame de grant noblesse
> Qui s'appella dame et deesse
> De Loyauté, et trop belle yere.
> La descendi a grant lumiere
> Si que toute en resplent la sale.
>
> .   .   .   .   .
>
> Si fu entour avironnée
> De nymphes et de pucelletes,
> Atout chappelles de fleurettes,
> Qui chantoient par grant revel
> Hault et cler un motet nouvel....'[3]

They approached the tables, bearing golden cups, while the goddess recited certain ballads, announcing the foundation of

---

[1] *The Goldin Terge*, VI, 46 ff.
[2] *Œuvres poétiques de Christine de Pisan*, ed. M. Roy (Paris, 1891), vol. II, pp. 29 ff.   [3] *Ibid.* ll. 89 ff.

the Order of the Rose, to which only those might belong who would vow never to defame women. The goddess then took some fresh roses from the cups, and distributed them to the company, who all enrolled themselves into the Order of the Rose. Her task accomplished, the goddess disappeared, but the nymphs remained behind, singing such sweet melodies:

> 'Que il sembloit a leur doulz chant
> Qu'angelz feussent ou droit enchant.'[1]

That night, when Christine was in bed, she was startled by the appearance of a luminous cloud, out of which came a voice that made a long discourse to her about true love and loyalty, and entrusted to her the establishment of the new Order.

The *Life of Blessed Henry Suso*[2] offers many illuminating examples of the way in which pageantry and revellings coloured the poetic imagination in the later Middle Ages, and it is interesting that Suso by his horrible asceticism is akin to the Flagellants, whose religious frenzy was *possibly* one of the springs of Italian drama, and that he is also one of those German mystics who are often regarded as forerunners of the Reformation. But above all, Suso was a poet, and a poet in whom the tendency to think by means of sound and vision was almost dangerously developed—and very often his visions came to him as an idealised presentment of the revellings and folk-customs practised by the people around him. He fights a spiritual tourney, he celebrates May Day, New Year, the Carnival, but he does so in spiritual poetic fashion:

'It is the custom in certain parts of Swabia, his native country, for the young men to go out in their folly on New Year's Night, and beg for May wreaths: that is to say, they sing ditties and recite pretty verses, and do all they can, with such-like courtesies, to make their sweethearts give them garlands. Now, when he heard of this, the thought came at once to his young and loving heart, that he too would go on that same night to his Eternal Love, and beg a May wreath. Accordingly, before break of day he went to the image of the most pure Mother which

---

[1] *Ibid.* ll. 246, 247.
[2] Trans. by the Rev. T. F. Knox (London, 1913), chaps. VII, X, XIII, XIV. The introduction by Dean Inge gives a good account of Suso's temperament and its connection with his environment.

represents her holding in her arms, and pressing to her heart, the gentle Child, the beautiful Eternal Wisdom; and, kneeling down before it, he began with the sweet voiceless melody of his soul to sing a sequence to the Mother, praying her leave to beg a garland from her Child....'

When his sufferings are at their worst he is comforted by a celestial momerie or carole.

'At another time, on the same festival, after he had spent many hours in contemplating the joys of the angels, and daybreak was at hand, there came to him a youth, who bore himself as though he were a heavenly musician sent to him by God; and with the youth there came many other noble youths, in manner and bearing like the first, save only that he seemed to have some pre-eminence above the rest, as if he were a prince-angel....Then they drew the Servitor by the hand into the dance, and the youth began a joyous ditty about the infant Jesus, which runs thus:—"In dulci jubilo," etc....It was a joy to him to see how exceeding loftily and freely they bounded in the dance. The leader of the song knew right well how to guide them, and he sang first, and they sang after him in the jubilee of their hearts. Thrice the leader repeated the burden of the song, "Ergo merito," etc. This dance was not of a kind like those danced in this world; but it was a heavenly movement, swelling up and falling back again into the wild abyss of God's hiddenness.'

The fifteenth century, then, was a time when literature felt the influence of pageantry and revellings. It was also a time when certain vague emotions and sentiments (sometimes directly connected with the ludi) emerged out of the sub-consciousness of the people, and took the form of a criticism of life cast in dramatic or semi-dramatic shape. For instance, the figure of the Fool comes from the ancient ritual. He is the frenzied worshipper, clothed in the sacrificial exuviae; his grotesque appearance and wild behaviour made him a very popular character indeed; he appeared in almost all forms of English drama; he (or a close relation of his) was a valued Court official; he survives to this day in folk-customs. There are innumerable varieties of him; the wild man, the Captain Caufstail, the Vice, the comic devil, the jester, the sword-dancer, all differed greatly in behaviour and appearance, but in the fourteenth and fifteenth centuries appeared what one might call the idea of the Fool. He became generalised in costume and psychology, he caused the dramatic activities of the Fool societies, he appeared frequently in art, he inspired a whole section of literature which was little else but an exceedingly simple and direct criticism of life, namely, *Numerus stultorum est infinitus.*

Another exceedingly simple and sweeping criticism of life which took concrete form in the fifteenth century was the idea of the power of death.

And so took shape that strange Danse Macabre, the dance in which pope and emperor, bishop and king, monk and merchant, clerk and labourer, lover and child, are each in turn led off by a grinning skeleton.

M. Lanson[1] sets down the prevalence of the danse macabre to the troubled state of the times, to the prevailing unrest and gloom. This is not altogether satisfying. This might account for the danse macabre, and even the fool dance, but not for the development of pageantry, for the beginnings of the French mystère, for the development of the great comprehensive religious cycles; and certainly it does not account for the development of the mummings and disguisings which were in origin and always in essence fertility dances, dances of life, joy, good luck, the very opposite of the danse macabre.

The real cause for the taste for dramatic dancing and pageantry, indeed the cause of all the literary and dramatic tendencies of which we have been speaking, is to be found in the social and economic changes which were taking place in the later Middle Ages.

When society rests on generally accepted principles, these principles can be taken for granted, and the poetic mind is set free to build up tales of heroism and adventure, dramas con-cerned with the struggles, the successes and failures of great individuals. But when society is changing noticeably and rapidly, when the theoretical authority is not the real power in the state; then, just as the sick person becomes conscious of his bodily organism, so the attention of all thoughtful men is directed to institutions, and the state of the body politic, and to the ethical ideas on which society is founded. This is a mental atmosphere,

[1] G. Lanson, *Histoire de la Littérature française* (Paris, 1909), p. 173.

very favourable to the production of sotie and morality play, of processional pageants and danses macabres, of Langland's *Piers Plowman,* of Chaucer's Prologue to the *Canterbury Tales* and of all those late mediaeval writings and works of art which in one way or another make a great roll-call of the different estates of men, all of them foolish and all pitiably mortal.

Mental unrest is not an agreeable sensation, but it is not necessarily synonymous with gloom. We have already seen how the decaying institutions of chivalry furnished fresh fuel for the blaze of pageantry and Court entertainment, the real history of which was only just beginning.

From the social point of view, the fifteenth century was a time of birth as well as of death. Chivalry and feudalism were dying, because nationality and the power of the bourgeoisie were being born. The organisation of the middle classes had been going on for several centuries, and by the fourteenth and fifteenth centuries, particularly in France, the guild or confrérie which was largely bound up with this movement had come to play a very important part in city life. Guilds, temporary or permanent, serious or burlesque, were formed for every conceivable purpose, and with the most varying constitutions. This guild movement naturally strengthened the taste for pageantry and mumming. Groups of people, unless they are united for purely utilitarian or combative objects, find procession and pageant, etc., their most natural mode of artistic expression; it is the easiest kind of art for amateurs to produce, and it is most expressive of the social sense.

The history of English pageantry, as everyone knows, is closely bound up with the history of trade guilds and great city companies. In France the arrangement of pageants and masquerades was one of the chief functions of the Basochiens and the sociétés joyeuses; the guild movement was also mainly responsible for the spread of religious drama outside the churches. In England this process was brought about mainly by trade and parish guilds, in France it was the work more especially of literary societies and guilds of amateur actors. But, in both cases, the result was much the same. The religious drama, through its popularity with the laity, was brought into close contact with the traditional ludi of the middle and lower classes, and both stimulated the literary and dramatic development of the folk-customs, and also gained for itself fresh vigour and vitality, a phase which is marked by the rise of the mystère.

There has been a distinct tendency of late to look for the origin of drama, romance, and much else, in folk-custom and pagan ritual. It is a tendency which has perhaps been allowed to go too far. For several centuries it seems that the mumming, as a survival of forgotten ritual, remained merely a riotous kind of game which roused the hostility of the authorities, and it only began to develop after it had come into contact with drama and literature, springing from the genuine faith of the more educated sections of the community. This contact was made possible by the education of the laity and the growth and organisation of the middle classes.

The chief lack was noble theme and artistic unity. That was to be supplied in the next century, when the Renaissance had reached France and England, and when the centralising policy of the kings had triumphed. It was the national sentiment supporting the centralising policy of the kings; it was the desire to revive an ancient loveliness inspiring Italian artists, which raised the ephemeral Court revels into a beautiful, though still ephemeral form of art.

CHAPTER IV

The Renaissance

'New pleasures press into this place
Full of beauty and of grace.' CAMPION.

IN the last chapter the story of the momerie in the fourteenth
and fifteenth centuries was told without any reference to
Italy. The omission was deliberate. In the fifteenth century,
in spite of new influences which were already making themselves
felt, the culture of France and England was still mediaeval; in
Italy, on the other hand, it was in the fifteenth century that the
Renaissance reached its zenith, and effected a transformation in
revelry and pageantry, as it did in all other departments of Italian
life and thought. The cultivated groups of poets, artists and
Platonists that gathered round Lorenzo de' Medici and other
Italian despots were not to be contented with the glorified cir-
cuses and variety entertainments which amused the Court of
Philip of Burgundy. At Florence and Ferrara, at Venice and
Rome, even ephemeral shows had to satisfy the Italian love of
beauty and taste for classical culture.

The Italian revels are of the highest importance in the history
of European mumming and masquerading. From the time of
Henry VIII to the outbreak of the Civil War, the history of
our English masque is the history of the absorption (and modification) of influences coming from Italy, either directly or by
way of France. It seems convenient, therefore, at this point, to
take a survey of the development of Italian revels and their
French imitations from the fifteenth to the seventeenth century;
although this will involve stepping backward a century when
we take up our particular subject, the development of the
English masque.

Italy had the same traditional games and festivities as other
European nations. There, as elsewhere, the king-game, the
morris-dance, the momerie were practised[1]; the wild man was
a familiar figure in the revels[2]; bands of young people celebrated

---

[1] Cf. *supra*, pp. 27, 36, note 6; *infra*, p. 86.
[2] In the thirteenth century great festivals were held at Prato della Valle,
a suburb of Padua. At one of these festivals, held in 1208, there was a

May Day by bringing flowers and foliage from the woods, by
music, dancing and feasting, by the election of a Lord of Love,
or May Countess[1]. Another traditional summer festival, the
Feast of St John the Baptist, was even more important than
May Day in the history of the revels; chiefly because St John
was patron saint of the city of Florence.

In Italy, as in other countries, the cult of the Baptist was very
largely a mere continuation of the old nature worship, and folk-
custom had a considerable place in the celebrations. On St
John's Day in Florence there were races, fireworks, bonfires,
processions in which giants and *spiritelli* jostled the more orthodox
saintly figures, and of course there was the king-game[2].

For us, however, the interest of the Florentine festival lies,
not in its links with paganism, but in those civic and ecclesiastical celebrations which, through their connection with
religious drama, had considerable influence on the evolution of
pastoral, ballet and opera. The central event of St John's Day
in Florence was a procession of ecclesiastics, civic authorities and
trade guilds, bearing wax offerings for the shrines of their patron
saints, and accompanied by *edifizi* (structures corresponding
roughly to our pageants) which in the fifteenth century carried
actors and represented various episodes drawn from Scripture or
the lives of the Saints, to be enacted in dumb show as each
edifizio arrived at the Piazza Signoria, the chief square of the
city. In all this there was nothing new; it was just a typical
mediaeval show; although in artistic merit the Italian festivities
may have excelled those of other countries[3]. One of the first to
improve the national celebrations was the artist Cecca[4], who was

'magnus Ludus de quodam homine salvatico,' *Chronicon Patavinum*, in
Muratori, *Antiquit. Ital.* vol. IV, col. 1126. Cf. Alessandro D'Ancona,
Origini del Teatro Italiano, vol. I, p. 89.

[1] D'Ancona, *op. cit.* vol. II, pp. 246 ff.

[2] *Ibid.* vol. I, p. 219. Descriptions of the St John's Day festival in the
fifteenth century are cited by D'Ancona, vol. I, pp. 228 ff.

[3] On this point cf. *The Renaissance in Italy*, Jacob Burckhardt, trans. by
S. G. C. Middlemore (London, 1878), vol. II, pt V, chap. VIII, 'The Festivals.'

[4] Cf. D'Ancona, *op. cit.* vol. I, pp. 232, 233; *Opere* di Giorgio Vasari
(Biblioteca Classica Italiana, No. 10, Trieste, 1862), pp. 339 ff.; *Lives of the
most eminent Painters*, trans. by Mrs J. Foster (Bohn's Popular Library,
London, 1850), vol. II, pp. 179–186.

said to have invented the *nuvole*, or clouds, that were borne in the procession and shaped according to various fanciful devices, suitable to the guilds to which they belonged; he also designed the figures of saints for the same purpose, and in his time the custom of painting the wax tapers in all sorts of fanciful ways went out of fashion, and instead of this it was determined that a splendid triumphal chariot should be made for every part of the city that offered a wax light. The plan was not completely carried out, but the first chariot of the Mint was made under Cecca's direction by the best wood-carvers to be found in Florence.

Cecca did not confine himself to improving the St John's Day pageants; he was much in request for the preparations of entertainments given by the guilds and fraternities and by gentlepeople in their own houses; he also helped to arrange the four great public shows, which were given every year, one for each quarter of the city. Of these four shows, that of the Ascension was surpassingly beautiful, on account of the device of our Lord's ascent into Heaven in a cloud, which was worked by an ingenious arrangement of vast wheels moving ten circles representing the ten heavens, and glittering with innumerable lights. In these and other similar inventions, Cecca was improving on the Paradises which had been constructed by Brunelleschi at the beginning of the century for the representation of the Ascension in San Felice in Piazza[1]. These inventions were possibly the fruit of Brunelleschi's study of the machines and scenery belonging to the ancient theatres of Greece and Rome[2]. However this may be, the innovations or revivals of Brunelleschi and Cecca are of great interest to us, for the ascent and descent of celestial beings in clouds and glory always remained a most popular scenic device in later masques, ballets and intermezzi.

The influence of Lorenzo the Magnificent made itself felt in pageantry, as in all other aspects of Florentine life. The enthusiasm of the humanists for everything Greek or Roman led,

[1] Vasari, *Opere*, p. 227; *Lives*, vol. I, p. 457.
[2] Symonds, *Italian Literature*, vol. I, pp. 319–328; L. B. Campbell, *Scenes and Machines on the English Stage* (Cambridge, 1923), which gives further references.

among other things, to a revival of the 'Triumphs' with which Roman generals had celebrated their victories. Sometimes Italian princes actually celebrated their military successes in this way; more often, the triumphs formed part of the pageantry at peaceful civic festivals[1]. Lorenzo de' Medici combined the Roman triumph with the St John's Day procession, and in his time the number of religious edifizi was limited to ten, and four solemn triumphs were added, that is to say, four chariots illustrating some episode of Roman history to which a symbolical meaning was applied: the triumph of Caesar signifying mercy, the triumph of Pompey, liberality, the triumph of Octavian, peace, and the triumph of Trajan, justice. These chariots were surrounded by mounted knights and all the accompaniments of a tournament. The spiritelli were also classicised[2].

The same influences which affected seasonal festivals naturally affected the religious drama, which was closely associated with them. The Italian Representation, like the French Mystery, seems to have been primarily a dumb show[3], but in Florence, in the fifteenth century, there existed a more literary type of religious drama, known as the *sacre rappresentazioni*, which were distinguished from the religious dramas of other countries by their musical and scenic excellence. Lorenzo de' Medici partially secularised the religious plays, as he did the St John's Day pageants, and his innovations were justified in 1471, when Politian, one of the most famous members of his literary circle, produced *Orfeo*, a drama, which although in its first form nothing more than a sacra rappresentazione on a secular theme, was nevertheless the first pastoral play and the forerunner of the opera[4]. It concerns us, particularly, because of the close connection which existed later between masque, ballet and pastoral. The revival of classical methods of staging, the invention of complicated stage mechanism, the introduction of classical and pastoral subjects, were the most important contributions made

[1] Burckhardt, *op. cit.* vol. II, pp. 196 ff.
[2] D'Ancona, *op. cit.* vol. I, pp. 255, 256.
[3] Cf. *ibid.* vol. I, pp. 223 ff.
[4] Cf. *ibid.* vol. I, pp. 217 ff.; vol. II, pp. 1 ff.; and Rolland, *L'Opéra avant l'opéra* in *Musiciens d'autrefois* (Paris, 1908), pp. 19 ff.

PLATE III

Foto *Garberini*

THE CAR OF MERCURY
Design for a triumphal chariot. attributed to Parigi. See p. 158.

by Italian artists and princes to the development of European revels.

The pastoral, however, is not the only link between the masque and the religious drama of Italy. The Italian dramatists, besides developing, in their own way, the spectacular and musical elements found in the religious plays of all European countries, made also a particularly effective use of the custom of inserting episodes of dance, song or light entertainment into the sacred action—a custom which, again, was not peculiar to Italy. Gradually from the occasional and sporadic insertions of dance or song, mock fight or banquet, there grew up a habit of inserting at regular intervals intermezzi of dancing, music or symbolical pantomimes, and soon these intermezzi came to be regarded as the necessary ornaments of every drama, sacred or secular, Latin or vernacular[1]. The age of the despots was as favourable to the development of the intermezzo as it was to the development of the pastoral drama, and for the same reason. The unscrupulous Renaissance princes drugged their subjects with sensuous pleasures of dance and music, and with alluring daydreams of a golden age, that they might the more easily distract their attention from the real deeds and motives of men, the proper subject-matter of tragedy and serious comedy. So the intermezzi became ever more popular and more complicated, while the complaints of the poets that they were killing drama went unheeded[2].

Neither the history of the intermezzo nor the history of the masque can be wholly dissociated from the history of the morisco; for in the fifteenth and sixteenth centuries the morisco and the brando were favourite forms of the intermezzo, and by the sixteenth century the morisco—whether as an interlude or as an independent entertainment—had itself developed into a kind of *ballet d'action*. Again the development of the intermezzo and of the morisco is bound up with the social development of the time, and particularly with the growth of a luxurious Court life.

[1] Cf. D'Ancona, *op. cit.* vol. I, pp. 515 ff., 'Intermezzi e Pompe sceniche.' On the connection between the intermezzo and the entremets, cf. *supra*, pp. 45, 46.　　　[2] Cf. Burckhardt, *op. cit.* vol. II, pp. 48 ff.

Contemporary diarists and chroniclers give us many vivid pictures of banquets, royal entries, and highly coloured tournaments, held from time to time at the different Italian courts, and their descriptions enable us to watch the morisco changing from a simple traditional dance into an elaborate and often beautiful performance requiring the co-operation of painters, musicians, poets and choreographers for its successful production.

At a ball held in Siena in 1465, the chief attraction was a great gilded wolf, out of which issued a morisco of twelve persons, one of them dressed as a nun, who danced to the sound of singing[1]. A few years later, a more developed form of the morisco is found at Rome. In 1473 Cardinal Pietro Riario, nephew of Pope Sixtus IV, gave a sumptuous carnival banquet.

The festival 'king' who had been chosen for the occasion entered into the hall, accompanied by more than a hundred torches. After supper there was a 'worthy morisco.' A Turkish ambassador arrived, complaining of the coronation of the 'king of Macedonia,' which would certainly, he said, lead to war. This pronouncement made, there entered into the hall a troop of Turks who had been captured by Christians. After some reasoning they became converted, singing:

> 'Viva la fede de Jesu Christo
> Cum il Papa e il Cardinal San Sisto.'

Later on a triumphal chariot was displayed in the courtyard and out of it issued morris-dancers, one by one. Next day the Turk and the King of Macedonia appeared in two chariots, and their followers engaged in a mock battle, after which the Macedonian led the Turk captive through Rome[2].

In the same year, 1473, the Cardinal gave a magnificent banquet in honour of Leonora of Aragon, the espoused wife of Ercole d'Este, Duke of Ferrara. The tables were loaded with elaborately wrought dishes, in which Greek fables were represented in foodstuffs. At the end of the feast, dances were performed by eight pairs of the famous lovers of antiquity. Hercules fought 'una bella scaramuccia' with eight centaurs who came to steal away the nymphs, and finally there was a representation of Bacchus and Ariadne[3].

[1] Muratori, *Rer. Ital. Script.* vol. XXIII, col. 772.
[2] D'Ancona, *op. cit.* vol. II, pp. 66 ff.
[3] Burckhardt, *op. cit.* vol. II, p. 190; Corio, *Storia di Milano* (Milan, 1857), vol. III, pt VI, chap. II, pp. 267–275.

The logical conclusion of this aesthetic development of the banquet was reached in 1489, when Gian Galeazzo, Duke of Milan, and his newly wedded wife, Isabella of Aragon, were entertained at Tortona by Bergonzio di Botta. At the banquet given in their honour it was no longer a matter of entremets and occasional moriscos, the feast itself was turned into a grand spectacular ballet, each course being introduced by some suitable divinity[1]. When the young couple reached Milan, they were welcomed by a wonderful festival which was known as *Il Paradiso*, on account of the gorgeous Paradise made by Leonardo da Vinci. This Paradise was a whirling heaven, set with the seven planets, which were represented by men dressed according to the descriptions of the poets. Jove from his heavenly throne ordered each planet in turn to descend from its sphere and offer praises to the Duchess Isabella on behalf of the deity[2]. The great Florentine painter was evidently improving on the scenic devices which had been well known in his native city since the days of Brunelleschi and Cecca.

Under the rule of Duke Ercole d' Este, the city of Ferrara became as important a centre of revelling and Renaissance culture as was Florence itself. In particular, Duke Ercole was passionately devoted to the theatre, and the year 1486, when the *Menoechmi* of Plautus was produced under his direction, is an important date in the history of the revival of classical drama. This venture was followed next year by the production of the *Favola di Cefolo*, an original pastoral play by Nicolà da Correggio, written on the lines of Politian's *Orfeo*, which had been produced at Mantua in 1471. From this time onwards, every festive occasion was marked by the production of Latin and Italian comedies at the Court of the House of Este[3]. The fashion

---

1 Cf. Cartwright, *Beatrice d' Este*, p. 46; Calchi, *Nuptiae Mediolanensium Ducum*, in Graevius, *Thes. Ant. Hist. Ital.* tom. II, pt I, coll. 508, 509.

2 Burckhardt, *op. cit.* vol. II, p. 192. Cf. *supra*, pp. 82 and note 4, 83 and note I. The cult of spectacular pomp was carried to its utmost limit in Venice, where there were special societies for promoting these entertainments. Cf. Julia Cartwright, *Beatrice d' Este* (London, 1903), pp. 200–202; L. Burckhardt, *op. cit.* vol. II, pp. 203, 204.

3 E. G. Gardner, *Dukes and Poets in Ferrara*, gives a good account of the social and artistic life of Ferrara in the Renaissance period and a valuable list of authorities. Cf. also the monographs on Beatrice and Isabella d' Este by Julia Cartwright.

soon spread to other Italian cities, particularly to states such as Milan, Urbino and Mantua, whose reigning families were bound to Duke Ercole by special ties of friendship and relationship. The Duke took special personal pains to introduce classical comedy into Milan, the home of his daughter Beatrice. It is unlikely that these plays would have been so well received if they had not been varied by elaborate intermezzi and moriscos. Isabella d' Este—a typical great lady of the Renaissance—was extremely bored when on one occasion the comic part of the performance was insufficiently relieved by music and dancing[1]. Luckily, there are full descriptions of many of these intermezzi in the diaries and correspondence of the time[2].

One of the most celebrated social events of the time was the betrothal and marriage of Lucrezia Borgia to Alfonso, eldest son of Duke Ercole d' Este, in 1502. On New Year's Day triumphs of various heroes of antiquity were performed in the streets of Rome, and comedies were acted in the Vatican. A morisco was performed in the Pope's chamber upon a stage decorated with foliage and lighted by torches. After a short eclogue, a jongleur dressed as a woman danced the morisco to the accompaniment of tambourines; Caesar Borgia himself took part in the performance, and was recognised in spite of his disguise. Trumpets announced a second performance, and a tree appeared with a Genius sitting on top of it reciting verses. His recitations over, he dropped down the ends of nine silk ribbons, which were taken by nine masked persons, who danced about the tree. This morisco was loudly applauded. In conclusion, the Pope asked his daughter to dance, which she did with one of her women, a native of Valencia, and they were followed by all the men and women who had taken part in the performance. The Ferrarese ambassador at Rome sent to his master an account of the acting of the *Menaechmi* on this occasion, and

---

[1] D'Ancona, *op. cit.* vol. II, p. 385.

[2] In 1491, for instance, the Milanese ambassador described a performance of the *Menaechmi* at Ferrara: 'Se fecino dentro tre intermesse molto belle: la prima fu de certi che feceno una moresca con le torcie in mano: la seconda fu Apollo...dreto lui erano le nove Muse....' *Arch. Stor. Lomb.* anno XI (1884), p. 752. Quoted by D'Ancona, *op. cit.* vol. II, p. 130, note 1.

described an allegorical and spectacular performance, referring
to the marriage alliance between Rome and Ferrara, which
served as a kind of curtain-raiser before the acting of the comedy.
This performance had much in common with some of the
political disguisings which, a few years later, were to be acted
at the Court of Henry VIII of England[1].

Every kind of delight was prepared for Lucrezia on her
triumphal progress from Rome to Ferrara, and a no less splendid
welcome greeted her arrival at her destination. Duke Ercole, as
usual, arranged a nightly performance of classical comedies,
with intermezzi of music and moriscos. There were moriscos
of armed gladiators, of horned shepherds, of Moors with burning
tapers in their mouths, of satyrs dancing to the sound of a
musical box inside an ass's head, of peasants performing the
whole round of their agricultural labour. One morisco was led
by a young woman riding upon a car drawn by a unicorn. On
the car appeared several persons bound to the trunk of a tree,
and four lute players seated under the bushes. The captives,
having been freed by the young woman, descended from the car,
and danced while the lute players sang beautiful canzoni. The
last play was followed by

'a dance of savages contending for the possession of a beautiful woman.
Suddenly the god of love appeared, accompanied by musicians, and
set her free. Hereupon the spectators discovered a great globe which
suddenly split in halves and began to give forth beautiful strains. In conclusion twelve Swiss armed with halberds and wearing their national
colors entered, and executed an artistic dance, fencing the while.'[2]

It is worth noticing that the Ferrarese diarist mentions that
on this occasion *balletti* were danced in the great hall[3]. The
word *balletto* is a diminutive of *ballo*, a dance, and at the outset
it had no kind of dramatic significance, but simply denoted
figured dancing, an amusement which was much cultivated in
Milan, and had a great vogue among fashionable people of the
time. The balletto only became dramatic after it had been im-

[1] Ferdinand Gregorovius, *Lucretia Borgia*, trans. from 3rd German
ed. by John Leslie Garner (London, 1904), pp. 218–221.
[2] Gregorovius, *op. cit.* pp. 256–264.
[3] *Diario Ferrarese*, in Muratori, *Rer. Ital. Script.* vol. XXIV, col. 404.

ported into France. The morisco, on the other hand, was a stage-dance, and although it is usually quite easy to recognise the original traditional dance with its processional entry, jingling of bells, etc. [1], it sometimes, in the sixteenth century, had a more dramatic character. Castiglione describes the Roman Carnival of 1521 in a letter addressed to Federico Gonzago[2]. He tells how Pope Leo X was always in his castle watching 'maschere musiche et moresche.' One Sunday evening eight Siennese, accompanied by about fifty torch-bearers, performed a fine morisco in the palace courtyard. The Pope with his courtiers watched the show from a window:

A woman entered and in *ottave rime* prayed Venus to give her a worthy lover. Thereupon to the sound of drums a morisco of eight hermits came out of a pavilion, attacked and surrounded an unfortunate Cupid, and took from him his bow and arrows. Venus, in response to Cupid's appeal, gave a magical potion to the hermits and restored to Cupid his weapons, with which he promptly shot his adversaries. At this the wretched hermits uttered dolorous laments, danced round Cupid and began to make amorous speeches to the lady who had invoked Venus. She bade them give her some proof of their valour. Obediently they threw off their religious habits and showed themselves to be gallant gentlemen, ready to fall upon each other in a frenzy of courage and jealousy. The lady obtained as her lover the sole survivor of this furious combat.

In France and Burgundy, as we have seen, the morisco was often closely associated with the momerie, and this appears sometimes to have been the case in Italy. In 1524 the Carnival was celebrated by Florentine and Venetian merchants residing in Constantinople.

The Florentine nation gave a banquet with music and dancing, and young Turkish women performed a dance with many playful gestures and agile movements. Then there came in a *momaria*, which consisted of a young maiden splendidly dressed, accompanied by two old men and two shepherds, who began to sing a lamentation by which it appeared that the young girl was kept in constraint by the old men, and that she would die unless she could have some taste of worldly delights. After that the girl herself danced and expressed the same thing by her gestures, until at last a 'Death' came in, seized her in the middle of her dancing, despoiled her of her finery and left her naked and dead. There

[1] Cf. *supra*, pp. 27, 28.   [2] Quoted in D'Ancona, *op. cit.* vol. II, p. 92.

then came in an ambassador from the King of Portugal with a giant who held two Saracens in chains, and they performed first a *moresca*, then a jousting[1].

The momerie in this case seems to have been much the same sort of entertainment as the morisco witnessed by the Pope in 1521. Very little change would have been needed to turn either of them into a real ballet d'action.

The development of the morisco in a dramatic direction naturally strengthened the tendency to turn the intermezzo into a miniature drama or operetta. Italian artists, such as Peruzzi, Aristotile di San Gallo, etc., were also bringing about the same result by their success in devising magnificent stage effects. The regular Italian drama was a Court product, and had its abode in the great hall, or palace courtyard. In the fifteenth, and early sixteenth century, there were no permanent public theatres in Italy, but many of the best architects of the time were employed in erecting very imposing temporary structures, modelled on the theatres of antiquity, for use during Court festivities. For their ingenious machines and sceneries the architects were also indebted to the descriptions of Vitruvius and other classical authorities. Some time towards the end of the fifteenth century the picture stage was substituted for the mediaeval system of dispersed decorations, and the various houses or mansions were arranged according to the principles of perspective, so as to form a single picture. Both secular plays and the intermezzi were also adorned by the various machines which were employed at religious festivals to produce Paradises, drifting clouds, flying deities, the rising and setting of the sun, devices which also were probably of classical origin. For the classical tragedy or comedy one scene sufficed. But for the intermezzi more variety was needed, and the Renaissance artists were not slow to adopt and improve on the Roman methods of scene-changing, the *scena ductilis*, which consisted of painted side wings, sliding in grooves, and the *scena versatilis*, which was a system of revolving prisms[2].

This perfecting of scene-painting and stage mechanism led to

[1] D'Ancona, *op. cit.* vol. II, p. 125 (i.e. note 1 to p. 123).

[2] Cf. L. B. Campbell, *Scenes and Machines on the English Stage*, pt I, 'The Classical Revival of Stage Decoration in Italy.'

an alteration in the character of the intermezzi. Just as the interludes of music and dancing had tended to swamp the dramatic action, so in the intermezzi themselves even music and dancing tended to become subordinate to the grand pictorial effects which served as their background. It is worth bearing in mind that the architects meant their scenes to have an intrinsic beauty, and did not design them to add to the verisimilitude of the dramatic action. To these spectacular intermezzi we shall have to return, for they became important at a later stage of the Renaissance when the revels of Italy, France and England had been influenced by the invention of the opera and the ballet de Cour.

The Italian intermezzo made a deep and lasting impression on the theatrical art of Europe. During the sixteenth and seventeenth centuries it was almost equalled in influence and popularity by the Italian Masquerade.

On May Day, New Year, and at Carnival times, it was customary for bands of masked and disguised persons to parade the streets of Rome and Florence, Venice and Ferrara, and other Italian cities[1]. It is not possible to give a date for the beginning of this custom. No doubt it goes back to those traditional celebrations of pagan festivals which gave rise to the morris-dance and the momerie. It is indeed difficult to draw any clear distinction between the masquerade and the mumming in their more primitive forms. The descriptions we possess of the two kinds of entertainment hardly clear up the difficulty, and the etymology of the two words is obscure and doubtful.

The Italian word *mascherata* comes from Italian *maschera* (Sp. *máscara*), which denotes 'a face-mask or a person wearing a face-mask.' The ultimate derivation of the word is uncertain[2].

---

[1] 'In hoc carnisprivio (A.D. 1498)...non facte maschare.' *Burchardi Diarium*, ed. L. Thuasne, vol. II, p. 433. Cf. Ducange, s.vv. *Mascara, Mascarata.*

[2] F. Diez, *Wörterbuch der Romanischen Sprachen* (Bonn, 1887), pp. 206–207. Mahn regards Fr. *masque* as shortened from *máscara* through the influence of *masca*, witch. Diez suggests that It. *maschera* might come from *masca* through the insertion of *r* (cf. Piedm. *mascra* = mask, and compare Spanish *cascaro* from *casco*). He also suggests that *maschera* is connected with a group of words OE. *mæscre*, a spot, OFr. *mascurer*, MFr. *mâchurer*, to blacken, Ptg. *mascárra*, Cat. *mascára*, a black spot on the face, Ptg. vb. *mascarrar*; but there seems no reason to connect these words which are unlike both in form

PLATE IV

MERCURY AND OTHER ALLEGORICAL FIGURES SEATED IN CLOUDS

Design for an Italian entertainment, attributed to Parigi but more probably by Buontalenti

The usual view is that it is derived from Arabic *maskhara*, mockery, a laughing-stock, a buffoon, a jester (from the verb *sakhira*, to ridicule), a word which in the form of 'buffoon, comic actor,' is given by Dozy as occurring in a twelfth-century Spanish glossary (*Gl. Esp.* 304, 305)[1]. If this derivation is correct, it would seem that either the masquerade must have come to Italy from the Moors or Arabs, or else that the masquerade was a special kind of performance in which the actors personated Arabian buffoons, and indeed I do not think that the last word has yet been said on the subject of a possible Moorish origin of this or of the morisco.

The difficulty to my mind is that the root meaning of the Arabic word is 'mockery,' while *máscara* always means either 'a mask' or 'the wearer of a mask.'[2]

A. Horning has conjectured that *máscara* may be derived from *marásca*, a man-woman (by metathesis and influence of *másculus*), and *marásca* may be derived from *mas, maris*, a male, plus the derogatory suffix -asca.

Körting mentions this as an ingenious but improbable suggestion, and indeed it does seem rather unnecessary to resort to a hypothetical form when an existing Arabic word can serve the purpose. In favour of Horning's idea, however, is the fact that according to Il Lasca the Florentine masquerade was developed out of a popular Carnival show, in which masked men assumed

and meaning. Brotanek, *op. cit.* p. 119, note 1; *N.E.D.*s.v. *Mask, Masquerade*; A. Horning, *Zur Wortgeschichte des Ostfranzösischen*, in *Ztr. für Romanisch. Philologie*, 1894, Band XVIII, 223, 224. Cf. Dozy et Engelmann, *Glossaire des mots espagnols et portugais dérivés de l'arabe*[2] (1869), pp. 304 ff.; K. A. F. Mahn, *Etymologische Untersuchungen auf dem Gebiete der Romanischen Sprachen* (Berlin, 1863), p. 60; Körting, *Lateinisch-romanisches Wörterbuch* (Paderborn, 1907), s.vv. *Mas, Marem*, 5986 and *Masq*, 5990; Meyer-Lübke, *Romanisches Etymologisches Wörterbuch*, 5390, 5393, 5394.

[1] Dozy, *Supplément aux dictionnaires arabes*, vol. I, pp. 637, 638.

[2] Dozy (who argues for the Arabic derivation) admits that *maskhara*, in the sense of 'masker,' is late and may be explained as being derived from the use of *maschera*, with the meaning of 'mask,' in the Romance tongues. Meyer-Lübke, however, regards this as most improbable.

It may be worth mentioning that Peter of Alcalá, in his *Spanish-Arabic Glossary* of the sixteenth century, does not appear to recognise any connection between the Spanish and Arabic words, for he translates *mascara caratula* by two Arabic words meaning 'false face.' *Petri Hispani De Lingua Arabica Libri Duo*, ed. P. de Lagarde (1883), p. 308.

a feminine disguise and parodied the rites performed by women on the Kalends of May. That last remark may seem to bring us back to the Arabic 'mockery,' but to me it sounds like the invented explanation of an obscure misunderstood custom. We have already met with the man disguised as a woman in morris-dances, and in the clerical Feast of Fools, and in the sixteenth-century May games, etc., and in this case the explanation may be that, originally at any rate, the masquerades were impersonating female spirits. There is some evidence for this in the history of the Low Latin *mascus, masca*, witch, face-mask, and its possible connection with the puzzling French form *masque*.

The French word *masque* appears first in the sixteenth century, when the Italian masquerade was being introduced into France, and it means a 'face-mask' and the 'wearer of a face-mask.' Meyer-Lübke derives it from the Spanish and Italian forms *máscara, maschera* (which he regards as unquestionably Arabic in origin), but does not explain the loss of *r*. Perhaps this loss might be explained by the influence of the word *masca* which was similar in sound and sense. The editors of the *N.E.D.* believe in a connection between *masca* and *masque*, which possibly 'survived in some French dialect, and was thence taken into literary use as the equivalent of the like-sounding Spanish *máscara*.' In this case, I suppose, the retention of the *s* in *masque* must be explained by the influence of *mascara*, which was similar both in sound and meaning. It is philologically impossible to derive It. *maschera* from Low Latin *masca*, but I do not think that the latter form can be left out of account. The two words were connected in the mind of the twelfth-century scholar Ugutio; and the meaning of the terms does suggest that though they are phonetically unrelated there was some historical connection or confusion between them.

Low Latin *masca* is an interesting word. In the *Corpus Glossary*[1] *masca* is glossed *grima* (i.e. terror) and in the same glossary *larva* is interpreted in a very similar way. In the *Lombard Laws*[2] (*c.* 800) *masca* is equated with *striga* and means

[1] Ed. J. H. Hessels, M. 33, L. 69.
[2] *Mon. Germ. Hist.*, Legum, vol. IV, pp. 48, 394.

'a witch.' In the seventh century we find Aldhelm[1] connecting the words *larva* and *masca*, and although the passage in which these words occur is not easy to interpret, it would seem that to him *larva* certainly and *masca* probably denoted (1) a nocturnal female spectre and (2) a face-mask by means of which such a spectre was impersonated[2]. Gervais of Tilbury[3] (thirteenth century) speaks of 'Lamias quas vulgo mascas aut in Gallica lingua strias nominant, physici dicunt, nocturnas esse imaginationes,' which *lamiae* or nightmares he connects with nocturnal *larvae*, and goes on to say that these creatures go about places at night, enter houses, oppress sleepers, drink human blood and move children from place to place. This equating of *masca* and *larva* is interesting in view of the connection between *larva* and *Mormo, Mormolyke*, the female phantom, who seems to have given her name to face-masks and to the momerie[4].

Ducange (s.v. *Mascha*) quoting from the MS twelfth-century glossary of Ugutio, Bishop of Ferrara, which is unfortunately unpublished, defines *mascha* as 'Larva, Simulacrum quod terret, quod vulgo dicitur Mascarel, quod apponitur faciei ad terrendos

---

[1] Aldhelmus, *De Virginitate, Opera*, ed. R. Ehwald (Berlin, 1919):

'Nam tremulos terret nocturnis larba latebris,
Quae solet in furvis semper garrire tenebris;
Sic quoque mascarum facies cristata facessit,
Cum larbam et mascam miles non horreat audax....' (ll. 2856–2859.)

'For the "larva" who is wont to howl ever in furtive darkness terrifies the timid in nocturnal coverts, and so also does the crested face of masks when the bold soldier does not fear the "larva" and the "masca."'

Again: 'Linquentes larvam furvum fantasma putabant.' (l. 2244.) 'Leaving the "larva" they thought it a furtive phantasm.'

Again: they smite: 'Ut procul effugeret facies larvata nefandi.' (l. 2252.) 'That the masked face of the unspeakable one may flee far away.'

[2] Horning (*loc. cit.*) derives *masca* from *marásca, a man-woman and so an evil woman, a witch.

[3] Gervasius von Tilbury, *Otia Imperialia*, ed. Felix Liebrecht (Hanover, 1856), LXXXVI, pp. 39–40.

[4] We may also compare with 'larva' and 'masca' the word 'telemascha,' which would seem to be connected with the latter word, and is used in the early Middle Ages with the meaning of 'mask,' and apparently a mask representing some supernatural being. Ducange, s.v. *Talamasca*, quotes Burchardus of Worms, *Coll. Decretorum*, bk II (before 1024), chap. 161, 'nec larvas Dæmonum, quas vulgo Talamascas dicunt, ibi ante se ferri consentiat,' and adds: 'Apud Kilianum *Talmasche*, est larva, ut *Talmaschen*, larvam induere.'

parvos.' In the thirteenth century John of Genoa[1] compiled a
glossary founded on the work of Ugutio but with many additions
of his own, and in the corresponding passage he has, 'Larua...
est simulacrum quod terret, quod vulgo solet dici mascara, quia
apponitur faciei ad terrendum pueros.'

These two passages are evidence for the early interpretation of
mascara as 'face-mask' and as a synonym for *larva*, which John
of Genoa regards as meaning 'a demon,' and then a 'face-mask,'
which latter meaning is acquired through the idea of impersonating demons[2].

It would seem that in the thirteenth century *mascara* was a
popular word meaning 'face-mask' and possibly also 'spirit,' and
that it was not necessarily associated with the idea of 'buffoon.'
To Ugutio in the previous century the form *mascarel* (i.e.
diminutive from *mascara*) was merely a popular form of *masca*.

The word *masca* taken by itself implies the existence of a
masquerade in the Middle Ages. How else explain the two
meanings 'female spirit' and 'face-mask'? I would suggest then
that originally the masquerade went back to the same order of
ideas as did possibly the momerie and the Perchten-running.
That is to say, it was originally a dance or procession in which
bands of maskers impersonated a female spectre, and her attendant
spirits. If the maskers were disguised as women (as we know
that they often were) they might be nicknamed 'marascas,'
effeminate men, and the word *marasca* might change to *mascara*
through the influence of *masca* as well as of *mascula*, and finally
supersede the earlier word *masca*, or perhaps the Arabic word
may have been introduced into Italy possibly via Sicily and
applied as a nickname to the masquers[3], who probably did affect
folly as part of the proper Carnival behaviour, and the similarity
of sound would make the application of the nickname all the
more natural. In either case 'face-mask' would be the secondary

[1] Johannes Balbus, *Catholicon* (Strasburg, about 1470), s.v. *Larva*.
[2] 'Et inde tractum est illud quod apponitur faciei ne quis cognoscatur.
Vel ad terrorem dicitur larua, quia videtur esse imago demonis...et hinc
laruatus...id est larua indutus, vel a demone possessus.' His remark that the
larvae are said 'to howl in dark corners' ('angulis garrire tenebrosis') suggests
that he had the poem of Aldhelm in his mind.
[3] I think the Arabic derivation is much the more probable.

not the primary sense of the word *maschera*. Some scholars indeed suggest that Low Latin *masca* goes back to a German root **mask*, meaning a 'net,' but whatever be its ultimate origin I should incline to think that it was used as a name for a class of mythical beings, for all the references suggest that 'spirit, witch,' was the root meaning of the word, and it is the meaning which has to a certain extent survived in the modern word 'mascot.'[1] But in all these matters no certainty can be reached, and any suggestions as to the ultimate meaning and origin of the Italic masquerade must unfortunately remain as pure conjecture. Very interesting, however, in this connection is a practice that was initiated (or, I should say, revived) by Duke Ercole d' Este in the year 1473. At Carnival time, during a terrible tempest of wind and snow, the Duke and others went about the streets of Ferrara masked, accompanied by music and singing and 'cercando la sua Ventura,' seeking fortune, that is to say, calling unexpectedly at various houses and taking away gifts of food and other things[2]. Part of the proceeds went to the poor, part was used for supplying a great banquet and ball. A similar folk-custom is found among peasants in Brittany[3]. It looks like a continuation of customs which arose in connection with Tables of Fortune[4].

The ultimate origin of the masquerade may be obscure, but there is little doubt about its nature. The masquerade was a band of masked people who paraded the streets at Carnival time, May Day, etc., singing and dancing, making all kinds of verbal and

[1] Cf. *N.E.D.* s.v. *Mascot*.

[2] Cf. E. G. Gardner, *Dukes and Poets in Ferrara*, p. 129; *Diario Ferrarese*, in Muratori, *Rer. Ital. Script.* vol. XXIV, col. 243.

[3] M. le Braz in his preface to *Chansons Populaires de la Basse-Bretagne*, recueillies et traduites par F. M. Luzel (Paris, 1890), p. xxxii, describes certain local customs to which allusion is made in the folk-songs. 'La chanson du *Guidonné*, par exemple, met en scène les troupes de jeunes garçons et de jeunes filles qu'on voyait jadis errer de ferme en ferme, de maison en maison, aux approches de l'année nouvelle. Ils pénétraient dans les cuisines, en chantant, et sollicitaient la générosité des ménagères.... "Eguinannê!" criaient-ils, ou encore "Donné, ar Guidonné!" La formule variait, suivant les pays. Ils repartaient, comblés de cadeaux en nature....Enfant, j'ai accompagné bien des fois ces "théories" paysannes....' The *Guidonné* poem expresses much the same ideas as do our wassailing songs. Cf. *ibid.* vol. II, p. 171.

[4] Perchta and her troop of female spirits were supposed to come and eat the food on the Tables of Fortune, cf. *supra*, p. 15

practical jokes, dressed up as women, or decked out in other fantastic disguises. It seems to have been a popular but very insignificant form of amusement until Lorenzo de' Medici deliberately undertook its transformation. His idea was that each masquerade should have a definite subject, and should be accompanied by musicians singing Carnival songs explaining the symbolism of the costumes and the meaning of the whole performance. He also encouraged poets and artists to draw their masquerade themes from classical mythology rather than from Christian and romantic literature. In this Lorenzo was simply doing for the masquerade what he did for the St John's Day pageants and the sacre rappresentazioni, and he was helped in his work of transformation by the artists of the time, some of whom, if we may trust Vasari, increased their reputation by their work on masquerades[1]. Lorenzo also paid considerable attention to the composition of the music and songs, and this part of his work was recognised as so important that Florentine masquerades were often known as *canti* from the Carnival songs that accompanied them[2].

It was pointed out in the first chapter that there are two main types of ritual mummings, the simple procession of maskers, or the solemn progress of a car, ship or waggon, sometimes containing an image of a god, and accompanied by a crowd of worshippers. The distinction seems to have held good in the case of the early masquerade; at any rate from the time of Lorenzo de' Medici onward we find masquerades of two distinct types: (1) the procession of masquers on foot, (2) the arrival of masquers in a car, surrounded by a crowd of musicians and torchbearers. This latter kind of masquerade was often known as a *Trionfo* from the fact that Lorenzo transformed the masquers' car, as he transformed the edifizio of the religious processions, into a grand triumphal chariot fashioned after the Roman style[3].

Il Lasca, a poet who was one of the last to compose Carnival

[1] Cf. Vasari, *Opere*, pp. 494, 495, 720, 824; *Lives*, vol. II, pp. 415, 416; III, 453, 454; IV, 207.
[2] Cf. *Tutti i trionfi, carri, mascherate o canti carnascialeschi andati per Firenze dal tempo del Magnifico Lorenzo de' Medici, fino all' anno* 1559 (Florence, 1750).   [3] Cf. *supra*, p. 84.

songs, has described Lorenzo's influence on the development of the masquerade:

'Questo modo di festeggiare fu trovato dal Magnifico Lorenzo... perciocchè prima gli uomini di quei tempi usavano il carnevale, immascherandosi, contraffare le Maddonne, solite andar per lo calendimaggio; e così travestiti ad uso di donne e di fanciulle cantavano Canzoni a ballo: la qual maniera di cantare, considerato il Magnifico esser sempre la medesima, pensò di variare non solamente il canto, ma le invenzioni e il modo di comporre le parole, facendo Canzoni con altri piedi varj, e la musica fevvi poi comporre con nuove e diverse arie: e il primo canto o mascherata che si cantasse in questa guisa fu d' uomini che vendavano berriquocoli e confortini, composto a tre voci da un certo Arrigo Tedesco, maestro della Cappella di San Giovanni e musico in que' tempi riputatissimo. Ma doppo non molto ne fecero poi a quattro; e così di mano in mano vennero crescendo i compositori così di note come di parole.'[1]

It would seem from this that the original distinction between masquerade and momerie may have been that the masquerade was a kind of parody of mummings and other traditional customs[2].

After the time of Lorenzo de' Medici and Pope Leo X the masquerade gradually altered its character. Spectacle was developed at the expense of music and poetry, and the masquerade became a procession of chariots and groups of masquers, representing some mythological subject. The procession would file past the throne of state and each chariot in turn would pause, while the masquers declaimed some complimentary speech or sang together or descended to perform a dance. Afterwards, perhaps, all the masquers from all the chariots might join together in one great figured dance. Very often verses were printed and circulated among the audience describing the chariots and masquers and explaining the symbolism[3]. This latter practice was inherited by the later *ballet de Cour*[4].

[1] *Tutti i trionfi*, pp. xl, xli; also quoted by D'Ancona, *op. cit.* vol. I, p. 255, note I.

[2] Further research might show that the masquerade was at first a kind of momerie in which the actors wore some kind of Moslem costume.

[3] For examples of this type of masquerade, cf. *Discorso sopra la Mascherata della Geneologia degl' Iddei de' Gentili* (Florence, 1565); *Descrizione dell' Apparato fatto in Firenze per le nozze dell' Illustrissimo ed Eccellentissimo Don Francesco de' Medici, principe di Firenze e di Siena e della Serenissima Regina Giovanna d' Austria*, in Vasari, *Opere*, pp. 1199 ff.

[4] Cf. Prunières, *op. cit.* pp. 198 ff.

The masquerade was very adaptable, and was associated with various Florentine pastimes, such as the game of *calcio* (a kind of football), the *bufolata* (a buffalo-race)[1], and the tournament which became little more than a succession of *trionfi*. For such performances it was customary to erect a great theatre (a circular or oval space surrounded by raised seats) in a public square or in a palace courtyard. The French engraver, Jacques Callot, has done a number of engravings of tourneys, etc., held in the theatre of the Piazza Santa Croce, Florence, in the early years of the seventeenth century[2], and these tourneys are particularly interesting to us because they have furnished a few hints to some of our Stuart masque-writers. Ben Jonson himself took some ideas from a tournament held in October, 1579, in the Pitti Palace, Florence[3].

In Renaissance Italy masking was a favourite form of amusement which was not confined to those taking part in a regular masquerade. In the fifteenth century a custom grew up, first of all among the young men of Modena and Ferrara, of going about the streets at night masked or disguised in a particular hooded cloak or domino and of penetrating unasked into supper-parties and balls and inviting the guests to dance. For instance, during a banquet given at Ferrara during the Carnival of 1473,

'ballato il Signore, eccote venire grande multitudine di mascare, e quì si cominciò a ballare a suono di Piffari infino appresso le septe hore di nocte in grande triumpho, e piacere, cenando in dicta Sala la dicta Brigata.'[4]

And during that same festival,

'Da principio di Zenaro per tutto dui giorni di Marzo durò il Carnevale, e si andò in mascara per la Cittade di Ferrara, e Burgi con grande triumpho, e feste; e ge andette il prefacto Duca con tutta la Casa da Este; dove per li Cittadini fu facto festa in le loro Case con Damiselle e Balli.'[5]

---

[1] Cf. *Descrittione della Mascherata della Bufola* (Florence, 1569).

[2] *Guerra d'Amore. Festa del serenissimo Gran Duca di Toscana Cosimo Secondo, fatta in Firenze il Carnevale del* 1615 (Florence, 1615); *Guerra di Bellezza. Festa a cavallo fatta in Firenze, per la venuta del serenissimo Principe D' Vrbino, l' Ottobre del* 1616 (Florence, 1616).

[3] Cf. *infra*, pp. 175–177.

[4] *Diar. Ferr.* in Muratori, *Rer. Ital. Script.* vol. XXIV, coll. 244, 245.

[5] *Loc. cit.*

PLATE V

1 THE CAR OF EUROPE AND AFRICA

2 THE CAR OF NIGHT

Triumphal chariots from *Feste nelle Nozze*, a Florentine tournament
held in 1579. See pp. 176, 177

It is surely implied in this passage that when the princes had arrived at houses where there were festivals 'with damsels and dances,' then they danced with these damsels. During the whole of this Carnival, from January 1st to March, the streets of Ferrara were full of people going about by night *in mascara*, Duke Ercole among them. On the last day of the Carnival there was a great banquet at which the Duke and all the House of Este appeared *in mascara*[1]. The custom soon spread to other Italian cities, and proved an enduring one.

When the Duke and Duchess of Mantua visited Ferrara in 1582, they thoroughly enjoyed the Carnival amusements, and they themselves would join in the masking. From a contemporary letter we learn how they would go about 'sempre in maschera e talvolta a piedi, mangiando per le strade, battendo a una a una tutte le porte d' una contrada, e cose simili giovanili e carnevalesche.'[2] When they went home they introduced these pastimes into their native city. A correspondent from Mantua wrote to Duke Alfonso d' Este in the same year:

'Non starò anco da avvisar Vostra Altezza Ser^ma che dopo il ritorno che hanno fatto questi Signori Serenissimi di costà in qua, le signore della corte, le gentildonne della città sempre sono andate in maschera vestite alla usanza ferrarese, con cappelletti alla ferrarese; con stanellette intorno e quando senza stanelle, con tabarretti intorno alzati suso delle bande, che io per prima non aveva veduto simil foggie in questa città.'[3]

Sir Thomas Hoby, the translator of Castiglione's *Courtier*, gives an account of a masquerie that came under his own observation:

On the Shrovetide Festival of 1549, the young Duke of Ferrandine visited Venice 'where he with his companions in Campo San Stefano shewed great sporte and meerye pastime to the Gentlemen and Gentlewomen of Venice, both on horsbacke in running at the ring with faire Turks and Cowrsars, being in a maskerie after the Turkishe maner, and on foote casting of eggs into the windowes among the Ladies, full of sweet waters and damask poulders.' At night he went to a banquet given in his honour and was killed in a quarrel arising out of the following

---

[1] *Diar. Ferr.* in Muratori, *Rer. Ital. Script.* vol. XXIV, coll. 245, 246.
[2] Angelo Solerti, *Ferrara e la Corte Estense* (Città di Castello, 1900), 'Carnevali ferraresi,' chap. XII, pp. cl ff.
[3] *Ibid.*

trivial incident: 'The Duke cumming in a brave maskerye with his companions went (as the maner is) to a gentlewoman whom he most fansied....There came in another companye of Gentlemen Venetiens in another maskerie: and one of them went in like maner to the same gentlewoman that the Duke was entreating to daunse with him, and somwhat shuldered the Duke, which was a great injurie.' In the brawl which followed the Duke lost his life[1].

English and French writers sometimes call this amusement a 'masquerie,' and the term may well be adopted as a convenient method of distinguishing the impromptu masking from the more formal masquerade. Both went back to traditional Carnival customs, but in Florence Lorenzo de' Medici had turned this custom into an aesthetic entertainment, while the princes of Ferrara had turned it into a kind of fashionable craze, the masquers going about the streets more or less continuously and indulging in any whim that came into their heads, going uninvited to supper-parties and balls, and using their incognito as an opportunity for dancing and flirting with the ladies of the company. Even if there is no absolutely certain example of this latter practice before the sixteenth century, yet it seems the inevitable result of the fact that the Ferrarese masquers were bent, not on giving an entertainment to others, but on amusing themselves[2].

The true character of the masquerie was evidently appreciated by Shakespeare, who in his early plays, where the scene is laid in Italy, makes the masque an impromptu social affair. Lyly also regarded it in the same light[3]. Sastrow witnessed this kind of pastime on the banks of the Rhine. He describes how, during the time of Carnival Kingdoms, male and female maskers go about in fancy dress, accompanied by musicians, and visit various gatherings, where 'they have the right of three dances with those who give the entertainments.'[4]

One result of the spread of the Italian Renaissance into France was that the masquerie, the masquerade, the intermedio, the balletto or figured dance, became French possessions, and were

[1] *Op. cit.* p. xxx.
[2] Cf. *Eliz. Stage*, vol. I, pp. 152, 153, 154 and note 1.
[3] Cf. *Euphues and his England*, in *The Complete Works of John Lyly*, ed. R. W. Bond (Oxford, 1902), vol. II, p. 103.
[4] *Social Germany in Luther's Time*, p. 274.

influenced by the French spirit. This phase of the history of the revels is important to us because the history of our English masque is as closely bound up with the history of the French *ballet de Cour* as it is with that of the Italian intermezzo and masquerade. It is, however, possible to deal very briefly with this part of our subject because it has already been admirably treated in M. Henri Prunières' *Le Ballet de Cour en France avant Benserade et Lully*.

It is not necessary to enumerate the various kinds of Italian revels which were brought to France, or to follow closely the process of absorption showing how they combined with or superseded older forms of entertainment such as the momerie and entremets. As M. Prunières points out, the French seem to have had no great liking for the masquerade by itself, but preferred to use it as an adornment of tournaments and other public functions. But it must be remembered that when the French came to Italy the original masquerade of Lorenzo de' Medici was being superseded by the later form, which consisted in a procession of elaborate triumphal chariots, and was in Italy very often the accompaniment of a tournament, or of a *bufolata*[1].

M. Prunières divides the masquerade performed in France from the time of Henry II into two main classes: (1) *mascarades à grand spectacle*, great open-air shows, and (2) *mascarades de palais*, shows performed on a smaller scale in a garden or room. Again this latter division he subdivides into (1) masquerades leading up to some complimentary speech, and (2) masquerades serving as a pretext for dancing and ballets[2]. The first kind seems to correspond roughly to the English entertainment, the second to the English masque.

The reign of Charles IX, or perhaps one should say, the reign of Catherine de' Medici, was a particularly important period in the history of French revels. The Italian influence was naturally at its height, the French Court swarmed with Italian musicians, artists, and dancing-masters; Catherine and her Italian maids of honour were continually performing masquerades. The conquest of Milan had led to a great vogue of figured dancing or

[1] Cf. *supra*, p. 100.   [2] *Op. cit.* p. 42.

ballets, and many of the Court entertainments were composed by Ronsard and other learned poets of the Pléiade group, who were busy spreading the ideals of the Italian humanists.

The two most cultivated nations of Europe were now in intimate contact with each other, and it was obviously the moment for fresh progress in the history of the revels.

The creative impulse arose almost simultaneously in France and Italy. Many years before Lorenzo de' Medici had felt the appeal of the old May games and Carnival processions, and had tried to turn them into real works of art expressive of the humanistic ideal. The same impulses were still at work in the latter half of the sixteenth century, but the innovators were setting before themselves a more ambitious project. They felt the attraction of masquerades and figured dances and divined in them possibilities of beauty as yet unrealised. They were also haunted by the dream of reviving not simply the antique figures and fables, but also the choric drama of the ancients, in which poetry and music and dancing were combined together.

About the year 1580[1] a little coterie of people interested in music and drama were accustomed to meet together in Florence at the house of Giovanni Bardi to talk over various aesthetic problems, and in particular to search out the secret that had given ancient music such an extraordinary effect on the mind. Before they could attain to this antique excellence, they felt it would be necessary to make many changes in the theory and art of music, as it was practised in their day, and especially they meant to wage war on counterpoint and on the habit of rendering the poetry unintelligible by trills, ornaments and a too frequent introduction of instrumental passages. Vincenzo Galilei and Giulio Caccini directed themselves to 'wedding their notes and words lovingly together,' determining, in Caccini's words,

'to place no value upon that music which makes it impossible to understand the words and thus to destroy the unity and meter, sometimes lengthening the syllables, sometimes shortening them in order to suit the counterpoint—a real mangling of the poetry—but to hold fast to that

[1] Cf. Angelo Solerti, *Musica, Ballo e Drammatica alla Corte Medicea dal 1600 al 1637* (Firenze, 1905); *Gli Albori del Melodramma* (Milan, 1904); *Le Origini del Melodramma* (Turin, 1903).

principle so greatly extolled by Plato and other philosophers: "Let music be first of all language and rhythm and secondly tone," but not vice versa, and moreover to strive to force music into the consciousness of the hearer and create there those impressions so admirable and so much praised by the ancients, and to produce which modern music through its counterpoint is impotent.'[1]

This latter aim was especially striven after by Ottavio Rinuccini and Giovanni Bardi, who were looking for a way of performing tragedy in music. The result of some years of tentative effort by the Camerata was, as is well known, the invention of Opera and Recitative.

The same ideals which inspired the members of the Camerata were at the same time animating the Pléiade poets and their friends, and indeed they found satisfactory expression earlier in France than in Italy. The Frenchmen, like the Florentines, were eager to effect a close union between music and poetry, but whereas the Italians, in making their musical reforms, had always the drama in their mind, and were searching for a more expressive and personal utterance, the French were chiefly con-cerned to exact from the composer a closer attention to the laws of prosody, to invent ballet in which the dance-rhythms should be based upon Greek metres, for, unhappily, they associated their plan of reformation with the abortive effort to revive classical metres in modern poetry[2].

In 1571 the poet Antoine de Baïf and the musician Thibault de Courville founded under royal patronage the *Académie de Musique et de Poésie*. The object of this institution was to afford opportunities for experiment and for putting into practice the new aesthetic theories of music and poetry and dancing, and also to create an intelligent and receptive public. It was the great hope of Baïf and his friends that they would ultimately be able to produce a drama composed in classical measured verse. This hope was not to be fulfilled. The work of the Academy was

[1] W. J. Henderson, *Some Forerunners of Italian Opera* (London, 1911), pp. 221–223. For the original passage see *Le Origini del Melodramma*, a collection of papers and discourses written by Caccini, Rinuccini, etc., expounding the new musical theories.
[2] Cf. Prunières, *op. cit.* pp. 63 ff.; Augé-Chiquet, *La vie, les idées et l'œuvre de Jean-Antoine de Baïf* (Paris, 1909).

interrupted by the Wars of Religion, but not before it had dis-
seminated the new ideas, and had influenced many of the Court
musicians, singers, and choreographers who were more practical
and worldly-wise than the learned Pléiade poets, and more
capable of translating their ideas into a form intelligible and
pleasing to the average men and women of society.

In 1581 the King of France determined to celebrate royally
the marriage that he had arranged between the Duc de Joyeuse
and Mdlle de Vaudemont, sister of the Queen. For this purpose
he summoned Ronsard, Baïf, the musician Claude Lejeune, and
others to prepare masquerades, combats, and ballets on foot and
on horseback performed in the ancient Greek manner. Seeing
all these preparations, it came into the mind of Catherine de'
Medici that she also should do something worthy of herself and of
the occasion; she therefore requested Balthazar de Beaujoyeulx, a
favourite valet de chambre, to prepare a great festival that should
surpass all others of the kind, and should advertise to the world
the power and wealth of the kingdom of France. Beaujoyeulx
was just the man for the purpose. He was an Italian by birth
(his real name being Baldassarino da Belgiojoso), a good violinist
and a man of some literary and great social abilities. In response
to the Queen's demand, Beaujoyeulx set himself to think out a
scheme which should be not only sumptuous and costly, but also
original. After a period of retirement, he returned to Court and
laid before the Queen his plan for the *Circe* or *Ballet comique de
la Reine*, and begged her to give him charge of all the arrangements. He could not look for the collaboration of artists and
musicians of the first rank, because they were all fully employed
by the King, but he was able to command the services of able
and distinguished men of whom some at least were connected
with the Academy of Music and Poetry.

Circe has been frequently described, but it holds such an important place in the history of the revels that a short account of
it must be given here[1]. The scenic arrangements were not

---

[1] Cf. *Balet comique de la Royne faict aux Nopces de Monsieur le Duc de
Joyeuse et de Mademoyselle de Vaudemont, sa sœur, par Baltasar de Beaujoyeulx,
Valet de chambre du Roy et de la Royne sa Mere.* Reprinted in P. Lacroix,
Ballets et Mascarades de Cour (Geneva, 1868), vol. I, pp. 16 ff.

original. The King and Queen sat beneath a dais at one end of
the hall, the spectators were arranged round the walls, some on
the level of the floor, and some in raised galleries. The main
body of the hall was used for the performance. To the right of
the sovereigns were set up an arbour or *bocage de Pan* and a
grotto surrounded by illuminated trees. To their left was *la voûte
dorée*, a recess for the musicians covered by clouds outside, and
brilliantly lit up within by artificial lights. At the far end of the
hall was the garden and palace of Circe, with passages left on
either side for the entry of dancers and chariots. It will be
noticed that Beaujoyeulx used the mediaeval system of dispersed
decorations and not the perspective scene dear to Italian architects.

The performance began at ten o'clock in the evening. After
a musical overture, a gentleman came running out of the palace
of Circe in evident terror, and delivered a long verse tirade to
the sovereigns, begging them to put an end to the enchantments
of the witch, Circe, who was holding him in captivity. Hardly
had he finished when Circe herself appeared, looked for him in
vain, and returned to her palace in anger.

Next there entered a procession of sirens and Tritons, singing
together. They were followed by a chariot made in the form of
a fountain bearing Thetis and Glaucus, surrounded by Nereids.
On golden steps at the foot of the fountain were grouped the
Naiads, who were the chief ballet-dancers of the evening, and
were all illustrious ladies of noble birth. Behind the chariot
came a choir of eight Tritons. The procession halted and after
some dialogue between Thetis and Peleus, the Naiads descended
and began to dance to the sound of violins. Suddenly Circe
appeared, and struck them motionless with a touch of her magic
wand, but Mercury at once descended in a cloud, and after song
and speech restored their powers by sprinkling them with moly,
and the interrupted dance began afresh. This infuriated Circe,
who renewed her spells, and having overcome even Mercury,
led them all captive into her palace.

Provoked by this monstrous wrong, all the powers of Heaven
and Earth gathered together for reprisals. Satyrs and Dryads

formed themselves into a rescue party, the nymph Opis summoned Pan (who was seated in his bower) to give them his help.
The four Cardinal Virtues hurried to the scene. Minerva
entered on a chariot drawn by a huge serpent and called upon
Jupiter, who immediately descended from Heaven on an eagle
to the sound of joyous chanting from la voûte dorée. Pan came
out of his bower, heading a troop of Satyrs armed with sticks.
All together, divinities and lesser spirits made a grand assault on
the palace. Circe defied them, but in vain. Jupiter struck the
enchantress with a thunderbolt and led her captive before the
King, to whom at the same time he presented his two children,
Minerva and Mercury. The Dryads danced for joy and brought
the disenchanted Naiads out of the palace, and then all the
nymphs together danced a *grand ballet*, or great figured dance.
After this the Naiads and Dryads made a reverence to the King,
and presented medals and emblems to the royal party and others
in the audience. The rest of the evening was passed in ordinary
ballroom dancing[1].

At first sight this entertainment may seem to differ but little
from many of the masquerades, intermezzi, and ballets which
preceded it. It differs from them, however, in two important
respects. Its component parts have been more carefully joined
together, and it has borrowed from the drama unity and consistent plot. 'La musique et la danse cessent d'interrompre
l'action pour y participer. Récits, airs, ballets, pantomimes ont
leur raison d'être au seul point de vue de l'expression dramatique.'[2]
As M. Prunières points out, it was not a profound work,

'mais une adroite adaptation au goût des courtisans français des théories
humanistes sur le drame antique. Disposant des seuls moyens de réalisa-
tion scénique dont se servent depuis vingt ans les chorégraphes royaux
pour leurs mascarades, Beaujoyeulx crée une œuvre originale en
mettant ces éléments usés au service de l'esthétique éclose en l'*Académie*
de Baïf.'[3]

Beaujoyeulx was well aware of the significance of his work,
and prefixed to the libretto of *Circe* an introductory notice

---

[1] Some early editions of the *Balet comique* are illustrated. The design for
the main scene is reproduced in Prunières, *op. cit.* p. 32.
[2] Prunières, *op. cit.* p. 93.   [3] *Ibid.* pp. 78, 79.

describing his aims and explaining his use of the term *ballet comique*. He fears that the reader may find the title strange, since never before has a ballet been printed or associated with comedy, but he feels the word is expressive because his work is really one well designed body, satisfying to the eye, the ear and the understanding[1].

The reception of *Circe* was all that its producers could desire. Laudatory sonnets were showered on Beaujoyeulx congratulating him on his great discovery, or rather, as it was thought, his revival of ancient drama and harmony of all the arts[2]. His work quickly gained a European renown, and provoked a quantity of imitations.

In France the ballet comique superseded the *mascarade à grand spectacle*, and for some years was looked upon as the normal form of Court entertainment for Shrovetide and great state occasions. It was, however, too expensive to admit of very frequent performance, and on less important occasions the courtiers contented themselves with the old masqueries, or *mascarades de palais*. These entertainments, however, were influenced by the ballet comique, and became more literary, musical, and dramatic. Finally they coalesced with the ballet in a hybrid form, to which M. Prunières gives the name of '*ballet-mascarade.*'

The ballet-mascarade consisted of a series of entries made by groups of performers. First came the musicians, masked and grotesquely disguised, then came the torch-bearers who ranged themselves in cadence round the dancing-place, then came various groups or quadrilles of ballet-dancers, who danced in turn and then joined together in the grand ballet or final figured dance. The ballet-mascarade was usually of a grotesque character and needed no long preparation nor elaborate mise-en-scène. It was possibly due to this that during the reign of Henry IV it seemed about to supersede the ballet comique.

During the first decade of the seventeenth century, every variety of entertainment was practised at Court, and only very

---

[1] Cf. *infra*, p. 248.
[2] Cf. Lacroix, *op. cit.* vol. I, pp. 9 ff.

scanty literary remains of the festivals have been preserved—
sometimes just a few songs or a programme of the proceedings.
During this period the dramatic side of the ballet was noticeably
weakening, but music was playing a more and more important
part, and this latter development was probably due to the presence
of Rinuccini and Caccini, who resided at the French Court
from 1601 to 1605.

With the production of the *Ballet d'Alcine* in 1610, the
dramatic conditions of the ballet comique re-asserted themselves, the only difference being that declamation had now given
way to recitative, and that the literary element was less important, and was practically superseded by song, pantomime and
expressive gesture. This type of ballet, which M. Prunières
calls the *ballet mélodramatique*, flourished from 1610 to 1621,
when it came to an end with the death of the Constable De
Luynes, who had supervised the Court ballets for some time,
and had a taste for grave and heroic themes. After the death of
this nobleman, the Duc de Nemours became responsible for the
planning of the ballets de Cour, and he preferred the grotesque
ballet-mascarade to the more pompous ballet comique, a pre-
ference which led to the vogue of the *ballet à entrées*.

The ballet à entrées was a combination of ballet-mascarade
and ballet mélodramatique. It consisted of various parts, each
of which had the structure of a ballet-mascarade (introductory
speech and entries) and then as a finale came a great chorus of
singers and musicians who announced the arrival of the dancers
of the grand ballet. This became the classical French ballet de
Cour, and flourished until the death of Louis XIII in 1643,
after which the ballet de Cour was superseded for a while by
Italian opera, then revived by Benserade and Lully, and finally
merged into French opera[1].

The French ballet was, as we have seen, deeply indebted to
Italian revelling. Its inventor was Italian by birth, and almost
all the materials of which it was composed came in the first

[1] This account of the development of the French ballet de Cour is based
upon Prunières (*op. cit.* chap. III, 'Évolution du Ballet de Cour'; cf. also
ibid., 'Conclusion,' pp. 244 ff.) and upon a study of the collection of
ballets published by Lacroix.

instance from Italy. Soon, however, France began to pay back
some of her debt. Rinuccini, for instance, studied the ballet
comique during his visit to France, and finding it greatly to his
taste determined to introduce it into his native country. This
happened in the early years of the seventeenth century.

In 1608 two great royal weddings took place in Italy, both
of which were very important in the history of European revels,
and one of which was particularly connected with our English
masque.

The first of these functions took place in Mantua[1] (the home
of Italian pastoral drama), and was a celebration of the marriage
between Francesco Gonzaga, Duke of Mantua, and the Infanta
Margherita of Savoy. Ottavio Rinuccini and many well-known
poets of the time were summoned to Mantua to prepare for this
festivity. Rinuccini composed a tragedy to be represented in
music in a theatre specially erected for the purpose. The music
for this opera was composed by Monteverde. A few days later
a comedy was performed, interspersed with marvellously complicated intermezzi, two of which have a special interest for us
on account of their connection with masque and ballet.

At the end of the third act, the main scene of the comedy
displayed a prospect of shadowy grottos full of dread nocturnal
creatures. Out of this gloomy place, Night, summoned by
Mercury, arose on starry chariot, while behind her there issued
out of the cave Dreams and Phantasms on little clouds resembling a dense smoke. On the cloud nearest to the chariot of
Night were Morfeo Forbetore and Fantaso who sang. Still
Night soared upwards, the sky darkening and the moon and
stars appearing as she arose, the Fates appeared riding on a
cloud, Jove entered on his chariot, and Aurora dawned gradually
and the air was lit up by a sudden comet.

The oncoming of night and the gradual approach of the
dawn was a favourite theme of Italian, French and English
revels and we shall meet with it again[2].

---

[1] *Compendio delle Sontuose Feste fatte l' anno M.DC.VIII. nella Città di
Mantova, per le Reali Nozze del Serenissimo Prencipe D. Francesco Gonzaga,
con la Serenissima Infante Margherita di Savoia* (Mantua, 1608).
[2] Cf. *infra*, pp. 198 ff., 227 ff., 236 ff.

The fifth intermezzo shows the influence of the French ballet de Cour.

The scenery consisted of the usual woods, hills, buildings and fountains, overhung by a cloud full of Dryads and Hamadryads. The sky opened, revealing a bower where Jove, Hebe and Hercules sat banqueting, and were waited on by many lesser divinities. Then there issued out of the various streets which divided the hills, men banded into troops of six, who came on, one after another, and danced in time to the singing of the nymphs in the clouds. The last two of these *quadriglie* danced moriscos, and finally all twenty-four of them (twelve on each side) danced a balletto which changed into a mock battle.

A few days later, Rinuccini produced the *Ballet of the Ungrateful Ladies*, modelled on the French ballet de Cour, but declaimed in recitative after the fashion of the new Italian opera. For this performance the arrangements of the theatre were very similar to those of our English masking-hall (England, of course, was the borrower). Opposite the scene was a series of semicircular steps, where the bulk of the noble audience were seated. Between these steps and the scene, a space was left empty for the ballet-dancers. Against the wall, to the right of the steps, was a stage for the accommodation of the ambassadors and other gentlemen, and opposite this was a similar stage for the musicians.

The scene consisted of the mouth of a great and deep cavern, at the far end of which was a fiery whirlwind. Approaching this terrible Hell-mouth came Venus, leading by the hand her son Cupid, while they spoke together in recitative to the accompaniment of musical instruments. Cupid then went into the mouth of Hell, and fetched up Pluto in order to terrify the obdurate Mantuan beauties who were invulnerable to his arms, by a sight of the punishment of the ungrateful ladies. At the summons of Pluto, a number of horrible and monstrous shades scattered flames on all sides, and then there appeared the condemned troop of ungrateful ladies, who were to perform the ballet. Two by two, to the sound of sad music, with many sorrowful gestures, they descended to the dancing-place and performed a melancholy ballet. Then, at a sign from Pluto, they separated into two companies, while Pluto walked through their midst, descended from the stage, and went up to the princess and addressed her in recitative. Again the ladies performed a ballet full of great desperation, after which Pluto drove them back to Hell, while one ungrateful lady who had remained behind on the stage uttered a piercing lamentation. Having received them, the

PLATE VI

1 A SEA-SCENE

2 A SCENE OF HELL

Designs by Parigi for *Le Nozze Degli Dei* (Florence, 1637), showing spectacular effects typical of the Italian Intermedii

mouth of Hell was closed, and the scene remained, showing a beautiful and delightful prospect.

In October, 1608, the wedding of the Grand Duke Cosimo de' Medici, Prince of Tuscany, with Maria Maddalena, Archduchess of Austria, was celebrated in Florence with extraordinary pomp and splendour. In the general history of the revels, this ceremony is perhaps less important than the Mantuan festival, but its influence on the English masque was very much greater[1].

On Sunday night, October 19th, there was a great nuptial banquet in the Palazzo Vecchio. When the meal was finished there appeared before the royal table the sea-shell of Venus bearing in its bosom her messenger the Breeze, who sang a song explaining her identity and her errand, and offering to the princely pair the whole Court of Venus who accompanied her, either seated in the shell or swimming in the sea. Then from the other side of the hall appeared Love enthroned on the chariot of Venus, drawn by black doves, and he offered up all his companions as a wedding gift. After this, a falling curtain revealed in the upper part of the hall a cloud full of celestial beings who sang a congratulatory madrigal. Finally, while the princes rested, two bands of youths performed a combat at barriers.

On Monday calcio was played in the Piazza of Santa Croce. Wednesday evening was spent in dancing, enlivened by *spettacoli di musica*, a kind of performance which came into fashion about this time and was sometimes known as a *veglia* or 'vigil.'[2] This particular veglia was called *Notte d'Amore*, and the words were composed by Francesco Cini. A scene was arranged at one end of the dancing-place, and at intervals the ordinary ballroom dancing was interrupted by the sudden fall of a curtain, and a masque-like performance began, the actors and dancers mingling with the spectators. The performance was divided into four acts or vigils. The subject was simply a glorification of the

[1] *Descrittione delle Feste fatte nelle Nozze de' Serenissimi Prencipi di Toscana, D. Cosimo de' Medici, e Maria Maddalena Arciduchessa d' Austria.*
[2] The *Ballo delle Grazie* which took place in 1615 is called a *veglia*. Cf. *Musica, Ballo e Drammatica*, pp. 87 ff.; *Gli Albor del Melodramma*, vol. I, pp. 26 ff.

passing moment. The burden of the songs was that Night had yielded her sceptre to Love. This piece had a deep influence on certain English masques, and we shall have to return to it later. At the end of the performance, ballroom dancing began again, and finally the night's festivity ended with a ballet danced by maidens and pages in pastoral disguise.

On Saturday evening, 25th of October, a comedy called the *Judgment of Paris*, written by Michelágnolo Buonarotti, was performed in a hall arranged in the form of a Roman circus. The scenery of the comedy and of the sumptuous intermezzi was designed by Giulio Parigi. To these intermezzi also we shall have to return later.

On Monday a new kind of entertainment took place on the Piazza of Santa Croce, which was 'un giuoco di cavalli a guisa di balletto.' The Piazza was surrounded by a platform for the accommodation of the spectators, and at one end of the Piazza was figured a mountain, rocky and wind-beaten, and down below was a cave with a forbidding-looking door barred and bolted. First of all there came out a great masquerade. There were Aeolus, king of the winds, Triton-trumpeters, sirens and other masked musicians. There were eight pages representing the effects of wind, cold, damp, dryness, etc. Then came a great triumphal car of Fame and another car of Ocean drawn by two whales, and inside it nymphs of seas, rivers and fountains all playing on musical instruments. In the most prominent position of the car sat Deiopeia, wife of Aeolus. After this procession had gone round the Piazza, Aeolus opened the grotto, and out rushed the winds, that is to say, a number of knights on horseback who proceeded to go through many ballet figures.

The rest of the entertainment consisted of mock fights and grand naval shows on the Arno. On the 7th of November, 1608, the festivities ended, having lasted almost three weeks.

With this entertainment we may close our survey of French and Italian revels. It has been necessary to trace the story down to this point because it was in the seventeenth century that English composers of masques were most deeply indebted to Italian artists, and this was unfortunate, for by this time the glory of the Italian Renaissance had faded, and the foreign influence was of very doubtful value. Italy's best work for the revels was done in the fifteenth and sixteenth centuries, when her people awoke to the possibilities of splendid living and a 'scenic public life,'[1] and her artists set to work to bring to perfection music, dancing, and the fine arts, and to discover or rediscover some method of expressing a world of ideal loveliness through the medium of all the arts working together in harmony.

The attempt failed, as it was bound to do, but not before it had produced some notable results, particularly after the Italian Renaissance had reached France. The end proposed was noble, though unattainable, and the constant striving after it gave rhythm and glow and colour to both life and art, and was the most important contribution made by Italy to the development of the revels.

[1] Cf. R. A. Taylor, *Aspects of the Italian Renaissance* (London, 1923).

CHAPTER V

The Early Tudor Masque

'Hys grace beyng yonge, and wyllyng not to be idell, rose in the mornynge very early to fetch May.' HALL.

W E left the history of the English revels in the middle of the fifteenth century, at a time when the poet Lydgate was introducing the allegory and symbolism of religious drama into the civic pageant, and the momerie or disguising. At that period the revels of England closely resembled those of France. During the second half of the century, while the Court of Burgundy was becoming the most important centre for late mediaeval chivalry, England was engaged in the Wars of the Roses, which were naturally not conducive to gaiety and expensive revels; although disguisings did take place from time to time both at Court and in the houses of the nobility[1].

With the accession of Henry VII, the history of the English revels took a fresh start. Henry, indeed, according to Bacon, did not find elaborate entertainments very congenial, 'in triumphs of justs and tourneys and balls and masks (which they then called disguises) he was rather a princely and gentle spectator than seemed much to be delighted'[2]; his wife, however, was a warm lover of such pleasures, and he himself evidently found it expedient to encourage plays and 'goodly disgysings' at Court; for a contemporary chronicler records the absence of these pastimes at Christmas as exceptional and due to illness: 'this cristmass i saw no disgysynges and but right few plays but ther was an abbot of misrule that made muche sport, and did right well his office.'[3] An Abbot or Lord of Misrule appeared at the Court almost every Christmas during the reign of Henry VII, and the custom was continued under Henry VIII until the year

[1] Cf. J. P. Collier, *Hist. of Eng. Dram. Poetry and Annals of the Stage* (London, 1879), vol. I, p. 38, note 1; *Household Books of John, Duke of Norfolk, and Thomas, Earl of Surrey*, ed. Collier for Roxburghe Club, pp. 339, 515, 517; *The Paston Letters*, ed. J. Gairdner (London, 1900), vol. III, p. 314.

[2] *King Henry VII*, in *The Works of Francis Bacon*, ed. James Spedding (London, 1858), vol. VI, p. 244.

[3] Reyher, *Les Masques Anglais*, p. 6, note 3. Cf. also Kingsford, *Chronicles of London*, p. 200; A. Feuillerat, *Le Bureau des Menus-Plaisirs* (Louvain, 1910), pp. 13, 14.

1520, and probably later still[1]. This mock monarch generally brought with him other traditional and popular pastimes, and there are references in the accounts of the time to tumblers, fools, 'players with Marvells,' companies of players belonging to various English towns or English noblemen, to disguising and May games[2].

With the accession of the first Tudor King, the Court began to develop into a lively centre of national drama and revelling, and one striking sign of this new development was the rise of new Court officials, whose business was in some way or another concerned with dramatic production. The task of providing amusement at Christmas and other festive seasons was now entrusted not only to the Lord of Misrule, but to the Master of the Revels, whose particular function was to organise the more practical part of the business, the provision of players' garments, masks, stage-properties, etc., and also to exercise powers of censorship. At first this work was done by someone who held other office at Court, but in 1545 Sir Thomas Cawarden was given '*officium Magistri jocorum revelorum et mascorum omnium et singulorum nostrorum vulgariter nuncupatorum revelles and maskes,*' as a permanent life appointment. From this time onwards, the office of the revels increased continually in size and importance, and gave employment to an increasing number of minor officials[3].

Companies of players had been gradually coming into existence during the latter half of the fifteenth century and were frequently welcomed at the Court of Henry VII; but the King had also his own dramatic company, which consisted of four men, '*lusores regis, alias, in lingua Anglicana, les pleyars of the Kyngs enterluds,*' a company which was increased to eight in the reign of Henry VIII, and may be traced almost to the end

[1] Cf. *Med. Stage*, vol. I, pp. 403, 404 and notes; Reyher, *op. cit.* pp. 58 ff. and notes. Both these authorities give further references.

[2] Collier, *op. cit.* vol. I, pp. 50–55; *Med. Stage*, vol. II, p. 257.

[3] The history of the office of the revels has been adequately treated in more than one authoritative work. Cf. Albert Feuillerat, *Documents relating to the Office of the Revels in the time of Queen Elizabeth*, in *Materialien*, vol. XXI; *Le Bureau des Menus-Plaisirs; Documents relating to the Revels at Court in the time of King Edward VI and Queen Mary*, in *Materialien*, vol. XLIV; E. K. Chambers, *Notes on the History of the Revels Office under the Tudors* (London, 1906), in *Eliz. Stage*, vol. I, chap. III, which gives further references.

of the Tudor period, although it does not seem to have played a very important part in the development of Court drama[1]. Richard Gibson, however, who was one of the King's four players, held an important position in the office of the revels, and the accounts which were kept by him form a valuable supplement to Hall's *Chronicle*, as a source of information about the disguisings and revels of the Tudor period. The gentlemen and children of the Chapel Royal played a much more important part than the King's players in the development of courtly drama and entertainment. The masters of the Chapel Royal were always distinguished musicians, and, from the time of Henry VII onwards, they were leading spirits in Court theatricals, composing the lyrics, and devising interludes, pageants and disguisings. The splendour and variety of the Court life of Henry VIII, for instance, owed much to the activities of William Cornish, Master of the Chapel, who had a considerable share in the work of elaborating the Tudor masque and disguising[2].

During his exile Henry VII must have become acquainted with the French dances and courtly fashions, and with the performances of the sociétés joyeuses, and some of these customs he probably introduced into his native country. French players appeared at Court on at least two occasions during his reign. The morisco, which, as we have seen, was then very popular on the Continent, at this time became a recognised part of the revels. The disguising (which sometimes included the morisco) was now performed with all the elaborate mise-en-scène of the French and Burgundian entremets, and as it is not likely that it had made much progress during the troubled period which preceded Henry's reign, it is permissible to regard this developed disguising as a product peculiar to the Tudor period.

---

[1] Cf. *Med. Stage*, vol. II, chap. XXIV, 'Players of Interludes,' especially pp. 187–193, which gives further references.
[2] Cf. C. W. Wallace, *The Evolution of the English Drama up to Shakespeare* (Berlin, 1912), chaps. I–VII, but his conclusions cannot be accepted unreservedly. For Gibson's accounts see *Revels* in J. S. Brewer, *Letters and Papers, Foreign and Domestic, of the reign of Henry VIII* (London, 1864), vol. II, pt II, pp. 1490 ff.

Collier quotes a long passage from *The Booke of all manner of Orders concerning an Earle's house*, in which detailed instructions are given for the proper performance of a disguising on Twelfth Night. The Fairfax MS, from which it was taken, has disappeared, but if it is genuine, it is a very important contribution to our knowledge of early Tudor revels. Some part of it, according to Collier, is dated 16 Henry VII, though the handwriting belongs to the latter half of the reign of Henry VIII[1].

It provides that the disguising shall not come into the hall until the interlude, comedy or tragedy is ended and that the procedure shall be as follows: First the disguisers are to come in preceded by three torch-bearers, who are to make their obeisance and either depart or stand aside while the minstrels also withdraw a little and play as the disguisers 'make their obeysaunce altogeder and daunce suche daunces as they be appointed' and then stand back, half of them on one side and half of them on the other side of the room 'if there be no women.' If, however, there are women they are to have 'the prehemynence of their standnge,' and it is only after they have danced and stood aside that the minstrels and torch-bearers are to fetch in the men who also dance and then place themselves on the opposite side of the hall. After this the 'Morris' is to 'come in incontinent...yf any be ordeynid.' Finally the men and women disguisers couple together and dance certain *basse* dances and rounds appointed by the Master of the Revels and return to their places.

It is worth noting that the morris-dancers are to 'com out oon after an outher' and then return in the same way into a 'towre, or thing devised for theim.' We find the same mode of arrival and departing in the Italian morisco, and it is also a feature both of the sophisticated and the country sword-dance[2]. There is no reason to suppose that it was always regular for the disguisers to arrive on foot and the morris-dancers in a machine.

---

[1] Collier, *op. cit.* vol. I, pp. 24, 25.

[2] Cf. *supra*, pp. 27, 86; *Med. Stage*, vol. I, p. 193, notes 1, 2, 3, 4, and vol. II, appendix J, 'Sword-dances'; and Thoinot Arbeau, *Orchésographie*, pp. 98 ff. In the morris-dance, surviving at the present day, the entrance and exit n single file are known as the 'morris-on,' and the 'morris-off.'

In this case the absence of elaborate pageantry is accounted for by the fact that the disguising is supposed to take place at the private house of a nobleman, and would naturally be planned on a smaller scale than the disguisings at Court.

Both disguisings and moriscos were sometimes combined with plays. On Epiphany, 1494, 'in Westminster halle was a greate bankett...where theyre was a playe, with a pageant of St george with a castle, and also xij lordes knights and Esquyers with xij dysguysed which dyd daunce.'[1]

In 1501, the marriage between Prince Arthur and the Princess Katherine of Aragon was celebrated with great splendour. There are several lengthy and detailed accounts of the ceremonies, and it is evident that the occasion was felt to be epoch-making; 'in my mynde it was the first such pleasant myrth and property that ever was heard in England of longe season.' Certainly, even Lille and Bruges under the Dukes of Burgundy could not boast of greater splendours than those which graced the English Court on this occasion[2].

The King caused Westminster Hall to be adorned with rich hangings and a huge cupboard of plate. On Friday evening when all the court was assembled there entered a 'most goodly and pleasant disguising convayed and shewed in pageantes proper and subtile.' A wonderfully devised castle was drawn into the hall by four great artificial animals. Eight disguised ladies were looking out of the windows of the castle, and on each of the four turrets sat a little boy, dressed like a maiden, who sang sweetly as the pageant advanced into the hall. The next event was the arrival of a lady, dressed like a Spanish Princess, who came in on a ship, that appeared to be sailing upon the sea, the ship's captain and crew speaking and behaving in nautical fashion. They cast anchor near the castle, and two 'goodly persons' called Hope and Desire descended by a ladder, approached the castle and informed the ladies that they were ambassadors from certain Knights of the Mount of Love, who wished to come and court them. The ladies, however, 'gaue their small aunsweare of vtterly refuse' and while the ambassadors were warning them of the grave consequences of their stubbornness in came the third pageant, which was shaped like a mountain, and contained eight goodly knights. As soon as the newcomers had been informed that

[1] Reyher, *op. cit.* p. 6, note 3.
[2] Kingsford, *op. cit.* pp. 234 ff.; *The Antiquarian Repertory*, ed. F. Grose, T. Astle (London, 1808), vol. II, pp. 249 ff.

negotiations had failed, they made a vigorous attack on the castle, reduced it to submission, and induced the ladies to descend into the hall and dance with them. During the dancing the three pageants were removed, and after a while the disguisers, half of whom were dressed in English costume and half in Spanish, themselves departed, and the Duke of York and a few other very distinguished members of the audience descended into the hall and danced basse dances.

On another evening in the same hall an interlude was performed, followed by a disguising 'shewed by two Pageantes,' the first of which was shaped like an arbor and contained twelve knights, who descended and danced many different dances and then stood aside. Then the trumpets blew, and in came a pageant 'made round after the fashion of a Lanthorne' with many windows and more than a hundred great lights, and all made so transparent that the 'xij goodly Ladyes disguised' could be clearly seen. These ladies came out and danced alone and then coupled with the knights.

On Thursday evening the Court again assembled in Westminster Hall, and as soon as silence had been secured two marvellous pageants were disclosed at the lower end of the chamber. These pageants, which were fastened together with a golden chain, represented two great mountains, one of them green, full of all kinds of trees and herbs and flowers, the other like a dark rock, scorched with the sun and full of metals and precious stones. On the sides of the first hill sat twelve disguised noblemen with musical instruments, and on the second hill sat ladies also with 'claricordes,' dulcimers, etc., among them a lady dressed like the Princess of Spain, seated upon the topmost peak. As the pageant moved up the hall towards the King, both companies of disguisers played 'so sweetly and with such noyse that in my mynde it was the first such pleasant myrth and property that ever was heard in England of longe season.' As soon as the pageants came to a standstill the lords danced 'deliberate, and pleasantly,' and then the ladies descended and coupled with the lords 'and daunced there a long season many and divers roundes and newe daunces full curiously and with most wonderfull Counteynance. In the meane season the two mountaines departed and evanished out of presence and sight.'

The description of the disguising at Richmond is somewhat difficult to follow.

The pageant was a glorious tower or tabernacle, made like a chapel and containing many lights, and a standing cupboard full of costly plate. The structure had two sto?es, eight disguised ladies were in the upper partition, eight disguised knights down below. The pageant was on wheels and was drawn into the King's presence by 'woddose' (wild men) and had apparently on either side of it wooden figures, representing a merman and a mermaid, and inside of it children of the Chapel singing very harmoniously. Before the lords descended to perform their dances they let loose conies which ran about the hall, and the ladies let fly doves and other birds before they too came down from the pageant to dance with the lords. 'Great laughter and disport they made.'[1]

The accounts of this wedding festivity make the nature of the Tudor disguising quite clear: it consisted of the entry of one or more groups of disguised persons (usually of two groups, one of men and the other of women) who danced first alone and then together. Very often the disguisers arrived in a pageant, descended into the hall to dance specially prepared dances, and then retired back into the pageant and were drawn out of the hall. They probably danced the fashionable society dances of the time. The basse dance was a slow, stately dance 'plein d'honneur et modestie,' which was fashionable in France and Italy during the fifteenth and the first half of the sixteenth century. The *ronde* was more lively than the basse dance. We have no information about 'the newe dances.'[2] As regards the mise-en-scène it is worth noticing that the disguising had now acquired the machinery and decoration and musical accompaniment of the civic pageant; and also that in form it corresponded very closely to the French entremets of 1377 and 1389[3]. Perhaps, however, the most important point about the show was that it had a certain dramatic quality; it was no longer a case of merely despatching a Presenter or Prologue to explain matters, 'the Masters of the Shippe and their Company in their counteynaunces *Speeches* and demeanour used and behaved themselves after the manner and guise of Mariners.' The ambassadors, Hope and Desire, make speeches to the ladies and the knights, the ladies give 'their small aunsweare of vtterly refuse.'

Henry VIII did not inherit his father's austere temperament, and his accession to the throne gave a great impetus to the development of the revels; indeed the first part of Hall's *Chronicle* of his reign is like the unrolling of a grand, highly coloured pageant. During the early years of Henry's life, the English

---

[1] *Harleian MS.* 69, printed in Reyher, *op. cit.* pp. 500 ff.

[2] Cf. Reyher, *op. cit.* chap. VIII, 'Les Danses,' and Thoinot Arbeau, *op. cit.*

[3] Cf. *supra*, pp. 44, 49.

Court with its quaint mummings and disguisings and gorgeously equipped joustings bears a very close resemblance to the Court of Philip and Charles of Burgundy. The solemn tournament was particularly cultivated by the youthful sovereign for, as his admiring chronicler remarks, 'The kyng beyng lusty, young, and couragious, greatly delited in feates of chyvalrie.'[1] These 'feates' of his are often worthy of some attention, because the barriers and the masque were closely connected with each other, even as late as the Stuart period, and in England, as in other countries, the solemn tournament greatly influenced the subject-matter of the masque.

The King's coronation in 1509 was celebrated by a magnificent tournament held at Westminster in which certain knights, scholars of Pallas, who were headed by a Goddess bearing a crystal shield, fought with other knights, called servants of Diana, headed by a gentleman bearing a golden spear. On the second day of the tournament Diana's servants had as their device 'A Pagente made like a Parke,' out of which issued real live deer who were killed by greyhounds and presented to the Queen[2].

The next year jousts were again held at Westminster, this time in honour of the Queen's churching.

The challengers were the King and three others, calling themselves '*Cure loial, Bon voloire, Bonespoir, Valiaunt desire*,' and collectively '*Les quater Chivalers de la forrest salvigne*.' The most noteworthy thing about the tournament was the elaborate pageant which brought the challengers into the hall. This pageant was made like a forest, with rocks and hills and dales, and a golden castle in the midst of it. It was drawn by a golden antelope ridden by two ladies and led in by 'certayne men appareiled like wilde men, or wood-houses, their bodies, heddes, faces, handes, and legges, covered with grene Silke flosshed....' When the pageant had come to a standstill in front of the Queen the six foresters who were seated on it blew their horns and 'then the devise or pageant opened on all sydes, and out issued the foresaied foure knyghtes....'[3]

On Candlemas Eve, 1520, a challenge for a tournament was

[1] *Henry VIII* by Edward Hall, with an introduction by Charles Whibley, in *The Lives of the Kings* (London, 1904), vol. I, p. 28 (the 2nd year). This text is reprinted from the 1550 folio edition printed by Richard Grafton.

[2] Cf. Hall, *op. cit.* vol. I, pp. 11–13 (1st year).

[3] Hall, *op. cit.* vol. I, pp. 22, 23 (2nd year); cf. also vol. I, pp. 53, 54 (4th year).

brought into the Queen's chamber by a lady richly attired and
borne in 'a tricke waggon' carried by 'foure Gentelmen appareled in long and large garmentes of blewe damaske bordered
with gold....'[1] This expression 'tricke waggon' is interesting
as showing the influence of the French revels. The French
word 'truc' was used to denote an elaborate device or ingenious
piece of mechanism used for pageantry, etc. It is noteworthy
that, in the accounts, the four gentlemen who accompanied the
waggon are said to be disguised as Italian maskers[2].

The Tudor tournament was becoming a kind of pageant or
disguising, and it was naturally very often closely connected
with the latter form of entertainment. On the 13th of February,
1511, there was a disguising which was practically a continuation
of the tournament of *Les quater Chivalers de la forrest salvigne.*
Hall's very full account gives a curious picture of the manners
of the time.

After supper the King and the Queen, the ambassadors and the
nobility, assembled in the white hall of the palace where an interlude
was performed, followed by 'divers fresh songes' and dancing. While
everyone was occupied with the dancing the King slipped quietly away,
and shortly afterwards a great pageant was wheeled in to the sound of
trumpets and out of it issued 'a gentelman rychely appareiled, that
shewed, how in a garden of pleasure there was an arber of golde,
wherein were lordes and ladies, muche desirous to shew pleasure and
pastime to the Quene and ladies....' A curtain which hung before the
pageant was removed revealing in the arbor six ladies, all dressed in
white satin and green, and in the garden the King and five others with
their names inscribed in letters of gold '*Cuer loyall, Bone voloyre,*' etc.
When the pageant had arrived before the prince 'then discended a
lorde and a lady by coples, and then the mynstrels, which were disguised,
also daunced, and the lorde and ladies daunced, that it was a pleasure
to beholde.' The pageant was put on one side where it might be kept
in readiness to convey the disguisers out of the hall, but the rude people
ran up and broke it to pieces and even made an assault upon the King
and his companions and stripped them of their garments until they were
forced back. 'So the kyng with the Quene and the ladyes returned into
his chamber, where they had a great banket, and all these hurtes were

[1] Hall, *op. cit.* vol. I, p. 182 (11th year).
[2] On the significance of this cf. *infra*, pp. 131 ff., and also Reyher, *op. cit.*
p. 29.

turned to laughyng and game, and thought that, all that was taken away was but for honoure, and larges: and so this triumphe ended with myrth and gladnes.'[1]

The tournament and disguising were still more closely linked together in an entertainment which took place on the 8th of October, 1518, when the marriage agreement between the Dauphin and the Lady Mary was celebrated with much magnificence:

In the Hall there was erected a rock, on top of which were a lady with a dolphin in her lap, and also five trees bearing the arms of Church, Empire, Spain, France, England, in token that these Powers were leagued together against the Turk. Ten knights came out of a cave, fought a tourney and returned, then the disguised ladies and gentlemen, who had been sitting on the lower part of the pageant, descended, danced, and suddenly the rock opened to receive the disguisers and instantly closed again. Then in came Report, riding upon Pegasus, and 'in Frenche declared the meaning of the rocke and the trees, and the Tournay.'[2]

The political symbolism of this disguising was to be often paralleled in later masques; it had, of course, long been a common feature of civic pageants, and it was often found in Italian performances. It is closely allied to that kind of political morality or interlude, which formed a link between the early religious moralities and the later chronicle play. One such piece Hall calls a disguising, and this play and others of the like kind were very often diversified by the insertion of masques, moriscos or disguisings[3].

Mock fights were very popular. Several of the Tudor disguisings took the form of an assault made by knights on a castle full of ladies[4].

In the year 1522 Wolsey invited the King and ambassadors of the Emperor to a supper-party. When the meal was finished he brought his guests into a great chamber, at the end of which was a large towered castle kept by eight ladies in Milanese costumes called 'Beautie, Honor,'

[1] Hall, *op. cit.* vol. I, pp. 25–27 (2nd year).
[2] *Ibid.* vol. I, pp. 171, 172 (10th year).
[3] Cf. Hall, vol. I, p. 256 (14th year); vol. II, pp. 79 (18th year), 109 (19th year). In the *Interlude of the Four Elements* there is a stage direction, 'also, if ye list, ye may bring in a Disguising.' Cf. Dodsley, *Collection of Old Plays*, ed. Hazlitt, vol. I, p. 5.
[4] Cf. Hall, *op. cit.* vol. I, pp. 40 (3rd year), 149 (7th year).

etc., and underneath the fortress sat more ladies dressed as Indians who were called 'Dangier, Disdain,' etc. The castle was attacked by eight lords, chief of whom was the King, called 'Amorus, Noblenes, Youth,' etc. These were led on by one dressed in crimson satin adorned with burning flames of gold, who urged the ladies to yield, but was defied by Scorne and Disdain. Then to a great peal of guns, and encouraged by Desire the knights hurled dates and oranges at the castle, which the ladies defended with rose-water and comfits. At last Lady Scorne and her followers were driven away and 'Then the lordes toke the ladies of honor as prysoners by the handes, and brought them doune, and daunced together verye pleasauntlye, which much pleased the straungers, and when thei had daunced their fyll, then all these dysvisered themselfes and were knowen....' In 1515, on Twelfth Night, a golden tent was brought into the hall at Greenwich. In front of it were four knights who fought against four others, until suddenly eight terrible wild men, dressed in green moss, 'came out of a place lyke a wood' and fought with the knights, who drove them out of the hall. Then six ladies and six gentlemen came out of the tent, danced, returned, and were conveyed out of the hall[1].

The plan of the latter disguising resembles that of the later Stuart masques, in which the appearance of the noble masquers was preceded by a grotesque dance or antimasque[2].

The disguising was sometimes combined with the momerie. In the fifteenth century, as we have seen, the two terms seem to have been synonymous, but in the Tudor period there was a clear distinction between them.

On the first Shrove Sunday of Henry's reign he gave a great banquet to all the foreign ambassadors in the Parliament Chamber at Westminster.

The Queen and the guests were seated, when the King suddenly disappeared to return shortly afterwards, with five others, all in fancy dress. They arrived in couples, the King and the Earl of Essex dressed as Turks, the next pair as Russians, and the last pair as Prussians. 'The torchebearers were appareyled in Crymosyn satyne and grene, lyke Moreskoes, their faces blacke: And the kyng brought in a mommerye. After that the Quene, the lordes, and ladyes, such as would had played, the sayd mommers departed....' After the banquet, when everyone was

<hr>

[1] Hall, *op. cit.* vol. I, pp. 239, 240 (13th year), and p. 143 (6th year). Cf. Brewer, *op. cit.* vol. II, pt II, p. 1502.

[2] For the morisco at Henry VIII's Court see Hall, *op. cit.* vol. I, p. 22 (2nd year); Brewer, *op. cit.* vol. II, pt II, p. 1494, and (2nd edit.) vol. I, pt II, p. 1123.

occupied with the dancing, the King once more disappeared and shortly afterwards in came first a drum and fife, then certain masked gentlemen as torch-bearers, and then another group of gentlemen of whom the King was one, all dressed alike and vizarded. After that six ladies came in in couples, 'Their faces, neckes, armes and handes, covered with fyne plesaunce blacke...so that the same ladies semed to be nigrost or blacke Mores....After that the kynges grace and the ladies had daunsed a certayne tyme they departed every one to his lodgyng.'[1]

The next year of his reign Henry entertained various ambassadors and foreign noblemen at Richmond.

When they had supped they went into the Queen's chamber and the King with fifteen others, all dressed alike, with white velvet bonnets, white plumes and masks 'came in with a momery,' played dice for a time with the Queen and the strangers, and then departed. This was followed by the sudden entry of six minstrels playing on their instruments, and after them fourteen gentlemen, all dressed alike and bearing torches, and finally, the King with five others disguised in 'whyte Satyne and grene.' Then some of the torch-bearers departed and returned with six ladies disguised as Spaniards, who danced with the King and his party and finally unmasked them[2].

In 1518 Wolsey entertained the French ambassadors who were in England for the purpose of concluding a treaty of marriage between the Princess Mary and the Dauphin of France. After the banquet six minstrels came in, followed by three gentlemen, each bearing a golden cup—the first cup being full of coins, the second of dice, the third of cards. 'These gentlemen offered to playe at monchaunce' and when they had done so, the minstrels played, and in came twelve disguised ladies each attended by a gentleman (the first couple being the English King and the French Queen) and the whole party accompanied by twelve disguised knights as torch-bearers. All thirty-six persons wore the same green satin costume 'and maskyng whoodes on their heddes.' They all danced at once and then disvisored[3].

The performance which followed the momerie seems to have been a disguising, although the disguisers wore the dress of masquers[4]. These examples make the difference between the

---

[1] Hall, *op. cit.* vol. I, pp. 15–17 (1st year).
[2] *Ibid.* vol. I, p. 21 (2nd year).
[3] *Ibid.* vol. I, pp. 170–171 (10th year).
[4] Cf. Reyher, *op. cit.* p. 29, note 1.

Tudor momerie and the Tudor disguising quite clear. The mumming has altered but little since 1377, it is still a cortège of masked and silent dice-players, a sophistication of a popular pastime. The disguising has not changed since the previous reign[1]. Sometimes (especially when it is combined with tourneys or moriscos) it takes the simple form described in the Fairfax MS cited by Collier[2].

We saw that a dramatic element was present in some of the famous disguisings of 1501. There is no reason to suppose that Henry VIII's disguisings were retrogressive in this respect. Hall, it is true, confines his attention chiefly to the decoration of the pageants, and the dresses of the performers, but even he occasionally indicates that there was speech; and we know from the account books that the children and gentlemen of the Chapel were often concerned in the entertainments, which certainly meant that there was both music and singing[3]. Hall, for instance, merely describes the appearance of the *Garden of Esperance*, but we know from an entry in the *Household Book* (Add. MS 21481) that William Cornish spoke a prologue. 'Of which garden Master Cornish showed by speech the effect and intent, inparelled like a stranger...and so declaring his purpose.'[4]

Brotanek[5] finds it a relief to leave for a while the 'tasteless' Mounts of Love and Wheeled Ships, etc., and to follow Henry VIII on his various Maying expeditions into the greenwood, but Brotanek's judgment of Court entertainments is surely unduly severe; for the disguisings, with their quaint pageants, their romantic chivalrous settings, have a certain naïve charm in spite of their stiffness and incongruity, and there is indeed a zest and a feeling of spring time and joie-de-vivre through all the earlier part of Hall's chronicle which is most attractive. The chronicler represents his hero as throwing himself with equal

---

[1] For further examples cf. Hall, *op. cit.* vol. I, pp. 57 (4th year), 153 (8th year).
[2] Cf. the disguising on New Year's night described by Hall, *op. cit.* vol. I, p. 143 (6th year).
[3] Cf. Brewer, *op. cit.* vol. II, pt II, pp. 1496, 1501.
[4] Brewer, *op. cit.* vol. II, pt II, pp. 1509; Hall, *op. cit.* vol. I, p. 153 (8th year). Cf. Reyher, *op. cit.* p. 119; Wallace, *op. cit.* p. 49, and chap. VII.
[5] *Op. cit.* p. 32.

gusto into folk-customs and courtly pleasures, if indeed there is any hard and fast distinction between them. We have seen that the momerie as played by Henry VIII was a sophistication of a popular game, and the same is probably true of the morisco, which in England was often combined with the May game and the Robin Hood play, both of them traditional rustic amusements[1], which were not always in favour with the authorities. In the first year of his reign, about the time of Twelfth Night, when the Christmas festivities were still going on, the king

'came to Westminster with the Quene, and all their train: And on a tyme beyng there, his grace, therles of Essex, Wilshire, and other noble menne, to the numbre of twelve, came sodainly in a mornyng, into the Quenes Chambre, all appareled in shorte cotes, of Kentishe Kendal, with hodes on their heddes, and hosen of the same, every one of theim, his bowe and arrowes, and a sworde and a bucklar, like out lawes, or Robyn Hodes men, wherof the Quene, the Ladies, and al other there, were abashed, as well for the straunge sight, as also for their sodain commyng, and after certayn daunces, and pastime made, thei departed.'[2]

The ordinary Court disguising did not take place in the morning, and it is obvious, I think, from the words of Hall, that this was an informal entertainment and that the astonishment of the Queen and her ladies was perfectly genuine. Next year Hall tells us how Henry kept the popular folk-custom of May Day by going out to the woods, with his knights and squires, and returning every man 'with a grene bough in his cappe.'[3]

Next year the first three days of May were celebrated by royal joustings at Greenwich and on their return from the woods the King and his company were met by a ship called *Fame*, which had for cargo Renown, and which sailed before them to the tilt-yard. In 1515 the royal party were entertained at a venison pic-nic by archers of the King's guard, disguised as Robin Hood men, and on their return were met by Lady May and Lady Flora driving in a chariot drawn by five horses, on each of which sat a lady called Pleasance, Sweet Odour, Vegetative, etc.[4]

---

[1] E.g. in 1502, 'about Mydsomer, was taken a felowe whych hadde renewed many of Robin Hodes pagentes, which named himselfe Greneleef.' Fabyan, *Chronicles*, ed. H. Ellis (London, 1811), p. 687.
[2] Hall, *op. cit.* vol. I, p. 15 (1st year).
[3] *Ibid.* vol. I, pp. 18, 19 (2nd year).
[4] *Ibid.* vol. I, pp. 28, 29 (2nd year); pp. 146, 147 (7th year).

The royal Mayings are very good instances of the sophistication of popular custom; we must, however, be wary of regarding them as peculiarly English, and using them as evidence that the Tudor sovereigns wished to encourage native custom and foster a purely national drama. The distinctions between various types of revelling at this period seem to have been social rather than national; Robin Hood and Maid Marion have their French prototypes, the May game was played in French and Italian villages, and was a favourite amusement of Lorenzo de' Medici. The strong, peace-loving government of the Tudors, and the dramatic and aesthetic activity at their Courts, did indeed produce conditions most favourable to the development of our national drama; but it does not seem that this was the conscious aim of either Henry VII or Henry VIII. What they did desire for England was a full share of Continental culture, which meant, of course, the introduction of Humanism and other ideals of the Italian Renaissance. Not only the ideals. The gay revels of Italy made an irresistible appeal to the high-spirited, sensual King of England, and in 1512 he introduced into a slightly scandalised Court the notorious Italian masquerie.

Hall's account[1] of the first English masque has been the subject of considerable controversy:

'On the daie of the Epiphanie at night, the kyng with xi. other wer disguised, after the maner of Italie, called a maske, a thyng not seen afore in Englande, thei were appareled in garmentes long and brode, wrought all with gold, with visers and cappes of gold, and after the banket doen, these Maskers came in, with sixe gentlemen disguised in silke bearyng staffe torches, and desired the ladies to daunce, some were content, and some that knewe the fashion of it refused, because it was not a thyng commonly seen. And after thei daunced and commoned together, as the fashion of the Maskes[2] is, thei toke their leave and departed, and so did the Quene, and all the ladies.'

This passage has caused students of the masque considerable, and I cannot help feeling rather unnecessary, difficulty. In what did the novelty of this entertainment consist, how did it differ from preceding mummings, disguisings, etc.? Before giving my

---

[1] Hall, *op. cit.* vol. I, p. 40 (3rd year).   [2] Cf. *infra*, p. 132, note 1.

own opinion it will be well to summarise the chief views and supporting arguments that have already been put forward.

Sir A. Ward's opinion that the novelty of the performance consisted in the wearing of masks is untenable in view of the undoubted fact that wearing a mask was common in morris-dances and mummings[1], and there is more to be said for the theory (upheld by Soergel and Evans) that the innovation consisted in the fact that the masquers danced with the audience[2], so that whereas the disguising was a kind of theatrical performance, the masque was little more than an improvised masked ball.

M. Brotanek argues that the novelty was merely a matter of costume[3], and compares Hall's words with the entry of the revels accounts:

'...and for the nyght of the Ephephany 12 nobyll personages, inparylled with blew damaske and yelow damaske long gowns and hoods with hats after the maner of meskelyng in Etaly.'[4]

'In dieser Notiz, wo es sich doch nur um eine summarische Beschreibung der zu bezahlenden Costüme handelt, wird also auch die Maskerade als italienisch bezeichnet. Das bringt uns auf den Gedanken, dass der Ausdruck, "after the maner of meskelyng in Etaly," und der correspondierende bei Hall, "disguised after the maner of Italie, called a maske" *einzig und allein auf das Costüm zu beziehen ist.*'

In support of this he calls attention to the fact that the expression

---

[1] Masks were not essential to disguisings. Cf. Reyher, *op. cit.* p. 29, note 2.

[2] According to Dr Chambers (*Eliz. Stage*, vol. I, pp. 150 ff.), this was really a 'new-old mode,' for maskers danced with spectators in the Kennington mumming of 1377. I have given reasons for doubting this (*supra*, pp. 39, 40), and for believing that dancing with the assembled guests was a practice of fashionable Italian maskers (*supra*, pp. 100 ff.). It occurred at the performance of Sannazaro's *Farsa* in 1492 (*Opere Volgari*, Venice, 1741, vol. II, pp. 123 ff.). Mahomet laments as he is driven out of a temple. Faith comes out of the temple, makes a long speech, retires, the temple is moved up the hall. Gladness enters, sings, scatters flowers, a trumpet blows, the Prince of Capua and others appear 'in mumia,' dressed alike, dancing with torches in their hands. Each takes a lady and dances with her. This suggests that the Italian masquerie developed dramatically through being sometimes combined with other entertainments. It looks like an early, simple form of the *veglia*, an entertainment in which ballroom dancing was interrupted at intervals by the arrival of masquers, who after some dramatic business descended from the stage to mingle with the ordinary guests.

[3] R. Brotanek, *op. cit.* pp. 67 ff.

[4] Brewer, *op. cit.* vol. II, pt II, p. 1497.

'after the maner of Italie' is grammatically dependent on the word 'disguised,' so that Hall's true meaning is that whereas in former masquerades the maskers or disguisers had been dressed in 'shorte garmentes' or as Russians, Turks, Prussians, etc., they were now dressed in Italian costumes, 'garmentes long and brode, wrought all with gold, with visers and cappes of gold,' and that this was 'the thyng not seen afore in England.' Brotanek then discusses the strange behaviour of the Court ladies. The masquers, it will be remembered, asked them to dance and 'some were content, and some that knewe the fashion of it refused, because it was not a thyng commonly seen.' It is sometimes thought that there is a slight contradiction here. Holinshed[1] evidently felt a difficulty, for while using this passage from Hall, he omits the words 'that knewe the fashion of it' and 'because it was not a thyng commonly seen.' According to Brotanek, all contradiction disappears if we admit that it was the masquing dress that was not seen before in England, and the entry of masquers that was the thing not commonly seen. The passage may then be interpreted as follows: some of the ladies refused to dance because they knew that it was good form (the fashion of it) to affect shocked surprise at the entry of maskers and mummers which, according to Brotanek, was looked upon as something a little out of the common. This astonishment was indeed, Brotanek maintains, a recognised part of the proceedings: witness for instance the abashment of the ladies when Henry VIII and his courtiers came into the Queen's chamber disguised as Robin Hood and his merry men; the general surprise caused by Henry's arrival in a pastoral masque at Cardinal Wolsey's banquet; the picture in the Bodleian MS, when one of the dancing ladies holds up a hand as if in astonishment and deprecation; the scene in *Timon of Athens* when Timon is taken by surprise by the masque of Amazons who interrupt his banquet. The behaviour of the ladies, therefore, in no way shows that the masque was a novelty in England in 1512.

Reyher, who has made a very careful study of the whole

Chronicles of England, Scotland, and Ireland (London, 1808), vol. III, p. 567. He has 'maske' for 'maskes,' as have some of Grafton's editions.

question, has dealt with Brotanek's argument point by point, and I think with complete success[1]. That the masquing costume was a novelty he admits and indeed emphasises. From Hall's description, from a French description of the meeting between the English King and the Emperor at Calais, and from the revels accounts, it is clear the masquing costume consisted of long and broad garments with hoods and hats and vizards. This, I may add, closely resembles the costume worn by those who took part in the masqueries at Modena and Ferrara and Mantua.

'Mais toute la nouveauté du spectacle n'est pas dans le costume: les explications circonstanciées et toutes spéciales que Hall croit devoir donner sur l'attitude des dames, les danses, et les conversations des cavaliers avec les spectatrices "comme il est d'usage dans les Maskes," semblent bien indiquer que le "Maske" n'est pas seulement un travestissement, mais un divertissement dont le costume italien n'est qu'un des éléments.'

As regards the attitude of the Court ladies, Reyher seems to me to show more insight into the situation, and into the niceties of language, than does Brotanek.

'Il nous semble que si le mot *fashion* était employé dans le sens de "mode," Hall aurait plutôt écrit *who knew the fashion*, ce qui voudrait plutôt dire "qui étaient au courant des usages." En tout cas, il est tout à fait contraire aux faits de dire que les personnages déguisés et masqués étaient "not commonly seen"; rien n'était moins rare. L'on y était habitué, à la cour, depuis des siècles....'

Reyher denies that the examples adduced by Brotanek prove that affected astonishment was the regular reception expected by the masquers. The Robin Hood pastime was an informal frolic and proves nothing either way.

As to the masque at Wolsey's banquet: 'Holinshed et Cavendish, avant lui, racontent en effet que le cardinal simula, pour conserver l'illusion de l'impromptu, de prendre les bergers pour des étrangers.' The scene from *Timon of Athens* proves nothing, the date of the play is too late, and the exact meaning of the speeches uncertain. No conclusion can be drawn from the picture of Jehan de Grise: the lady holds up her hand, it is true,

[1] Reyher, *op. cit.* pp. 18–28, 491–494 (appendix I).

but she evidently has not refused to dance, and the next lady does not even hold up her hand. Anyhow, the document dates from before 1344. Brotanek seems also to forget that to express astonishment is not the same thing as to refuse to dance; and the subsequent history of the masque proves conclusively that the refusal to dance was most emphatically *not* a recognised part of the proceedings.

These criticisms seem to me incontrovertible, and even more objections may be urged against Brotanek's theory. In the first place, he is putting a strained interpretation on words, that after all are not so very obscure. When Hall first uses the word 'maske' he may—though I think it unlikely—mean a masking garment and not a masker or a masking game, but when he says 'thei daunced and commoned together as the fashion of the Maskes is,' the word 'maskes' must surely mean maskers[1], and the whole phrase imply that a special kind of behaviour was expected of those who appeared in the new masquing dress. We may compare with these words Hoby's account of the Venetian masquerie. 'The Duke cumming in a brave maskerye with his companions went (*as the maner is*) to a gentelwoman whom he most fansied.'[2] The revels accounts are not altogether to the point here, for they are necessarily concerned with the clothes, rather than with the dances, evolutions and manners of the masquers; and nobody denies that the strange costume was a striking feature of the new masque. But there is one interesting entry in the revels accounts. On the 7th of March, 1519: 'and for a *Revylls callyed a maskalyn* after the gyse and maner of the contrey of Ettaly...viij meskelyn hatts...viij myskellyng hodys for lords...viij long meskelyn gownys.'[3] The expression 'a Revylls callyed a maskalyn' is to my mind conclusive that the word *mask* or *maskelyn* (it existed in many variant forms) meant primarily entertainment, not costume.

The question then arises, what was the precise nature of this

---

[1] This use of the word was foreign rather than English, but cf. *infra*, p. 156. Some editions read 'maske,' which here must mean masking game.
[2] Cf. *loc. cit. supra*, p. 102.
[3] Reyher, *op. cit.* p. 19, note 3; Brewer, *op. cit.* vol. III, pt I, p. 35, entry 113.

novel entertainment? The greatest weakness in Brotanek's argument is that he entirely fails to make good his point that there was no essential difference between the 1512 masque and previous Court entertainments. The momerie and disguising of 1510, which he cites to prove continuity, prove exactly the reverse, and show that the disguising was essentially a piece played before an audience, in which only disguisers danced together, whereas in the masque, the masquers chose out ladies in the audience for their dancing partners. Indeed, 'to mask with' came to be a recognised expression for this dancing of the masquers with members of the audience. The mumming of 1377, cited by Dr Chambers, does not really disprove this difference; for although performers and spectators danced at the same time, still the mummers probably 'kept themselves to themselves,' and did not choose partners from the aristocratic audience. But indeed, in treating of the distinction between masques and the earlier mummings and disguisings, it is necessary to remember that in the Tudor period there was a real distinction between the mummings and disguisings themselves, so that the masque need not differ from them both in precisely the same way. The distinction has already been made clear, more than once, and here it is enough to say that there is more affinity between the masque and the mumming, than there is between the masque and the disguising. The latter entertainment had become altogether artificial and sophisticated; the mumming and the masque were neither of them as yet very far removed from the popular street processions of Christmastide and Carnival. But there was a difference, and the nature of this difference is made quite clear by Reyher. The mummers might dance after their arrival in the hall, but their main object was to play a game of mumchance in complete silence; the object of the masquers was to choose each a lady out of the assembled company, to entertain her with dancing and *gallant conversation*. The gallantry and *risqué* talk of the masquers became proverbial, and was often contrasted with the silence of the mummers: 'I come to present you with a Mask...or rather more properly I may call it a Mumming, because the presenters have scarce a word to say for themselves,'[1] but on the other hand, the brother of the Duchess of Malfi desires her to 'give o'er these chargeable revels:

> A visor and a mask are *whispering rooms*
> That were never meant for virtue' (Act I, sc. 2, I).

Sometimes one and the same entertainment could be both a mumming and a masque, 'hauing daunced...they fel to dicing... being both Maskers and mummers...after they had masked and mummed, away they went.'[2] This passage makes it clear that even when the two 'ludi' were combined they still remained quite distinct from one another[3]. A more famous instance of the combination of the two pastimes is the masque brought by Henry VIII to the banquet of Cardinal Wolsey:

> 'The banquets were set forth, with masks and mummeries, in so gorgeous a sort, and costly manner, that it was a heaven to behold. There wanted no dames or damsels, meet or apt to dance with the maskers,...I have seen the King suddenly come in thither in a mask, with a dozen of other maskers, all in garments like shepherds.' On this occasion the guests were much startled by a salute of guns which greeted the arrival of the masquers, who after some preliminary parleying entered the room in couples. The Lord Chamberlain acted as interpreter between them and their host—for they were supposed to know no English. They announced that they had come to play at mumchance with the ladies, and when they had done so, there occurred the well-known incident of the disvisoring and of the Cardinal's failure to identify the King.

The two activities of these maskers are kept quite distinct from one another; they have come to play mumchance with the ladies 'and then after to dance with them, *and so to have of them acquaintance*,' the last expression being probably a euphemism for flirtation[4].

Reyher quotes in this connection some interesting passages from the *Arresta Amorum*, a collection of burlesque decrees made by the Court of Love[5].

---

[1] Heywood and Rowley, *Fortune by Land and Sea* (London, 1655), Act V, sc. I.

[2] *Choice, Chance and Change* (1606), in *Occasional Issues of Unique or very Rare Books*, ed. A. B. Grosart (Manchester, 1881), vol. XVII, pp. 45, 46.

[3] For other examples see Reyher, *op. cit.* pp. 14–20 and notes.

[4] Cavendish, *The Life of Cardinal Wolsey*, ed. S. W. Singer (London, 1825), vol. I, pp. 49 ff.

[5] *Op. cit.* pp. 21, 22. See also G. Bouchet, *Les Serées*, ed. C. E. Roybet (Paris, 1881), vol. I, pp. 131 ff.; vol. V, pp. 5, 6.

The fifty-second judgment deals with an imaginary dispute between husbands and the masquers. The former complain that when they are at pleasant social gatherings, with their wives and daughters, the gallantry arrive 'en masque,' choose demoiselles, take them away into a corner, make love, dance with them, and stay until midnight. The husbands suggest that the 'mignons' should be allowed an hour's masquering, half-an-hour for dancing, half-an-hour for conversation (for they consider there is no love-making that cannot be got through in half-an-hour), and that after that time the masquers must either unmask or retire.

In the early years of the sixteenth century Francis I found it an amusing pastime to disguise himself and his 'mygnons' in 'habitz dissimulez et bigarrez, ayans masques devant leurs visaiges, allans à cheval parmy la ville et alloient en aucunes maisons jouer et gaudir; ce que le populaire prenait mal à gré.'[1] It is interesting to learn from Hall that these amusements of the French King were shared by certain young Englishmen, who evidently wished to introduce them into the English Court; but were very promptly thwarted by the authorities:

'Duryng this tyme remayned in the Frenche court...diverse...young gentelmen of England and they with the Frenche kyng roade daily disguysed through Parys, throwyng Egges, stones and other foolishe trifles at the people, whiche light demeanoure of a kyng was muche discommended and gested at. And when these young gentelmen came again into England, they were all Frenche, in eatyng, drynkyng and apparell, yea, and in Frenche vices and bragges,...so that nothing by them was praised, but if it were after the Frenche turne.' So that when these 'young minions' were banished from Court their fall was little 'moned emong wise men.'[2]

It seems to me that there is abundant and indisputable evidence for Reyher's view that the real novelty lay in the introduction of a new element of gallantry and intrigue[3]. The masque, in

[1] *Journal d'un Bourgeois de Paris* (1515–1536), ed. L. Lalanne (Paris, 1854), p. 55. [2] Hall, *op. cit.* vol. I, pp. 175, 178 (10th year).
[3] This does not seem to have been appreciated, however, by later writers. It is the one point in Reyher's work to which M. Prunières takes exception. Cf. *infra*, p. 141, note 1. Robert Withington, *English Pageantry* (Cambridge, Harvard University Press, 1918), vol. I, p. 121, refers back to his article, 'After the Manner of Italy,' in *Journal of English and Germanic Philology*, July, 1916, pp. 423 ff. This article summarises the views of other scholars, but leaves the problem unsolved. The author, however, makes the sound suggestion that the solution will be found when a proper study is made of Italian festivals. He does not seem to realise, however, that Reyher had

fact, was the notorious masquerie, which became fashionable first in Modena and Ferrara, then spread to the whole of Italy and France, and finally reached England (probably by way of France) in 1512.

Once it is realised that it was the masquerie (not a new kind of dramatic entertainment, but a notorious social custom from Italy) that was introduced into England in 1512, all the supposed difficulties vanish. In cases of this kind, we shall get nearer the truth by the exercise of a little historical imagination than by the employment of a too precise and subtle analysis of descriptions which are probably quite simple and straightforward; for we are not dealing with written literature that can be classified with scientific exactness, but with fluid revels, fashions and social practices, recorded by sycophantic chroniclers, and described in diaries and letters of men of the world and gay young ladies; none of whom would care particularly about exact definition, though they would be quick enough to seize upon a new fashionable game or foreign mode. Moreover, the main difference between various 'ludi' and revels often lies in just those variations of setting, background, social atmosphere and mood, etc., that are almost impossible to convey by a bare description. Let us then try to get the masque of 1512 against its proper background of past history and contemporary social custom.

already supplied the clue by his description of the masquing customs of France and Italy (cf. particularly Reyher, *op. cit.* pp. 27, 28), and has misunderstood Reyher's attitude on an important point, i.e. the behaviour of the ladies in 1512, for he remarks, 'Reyher surmises that perhaps good manners or court etiquette demands an exhibition of surprise on the part of those before whom the masquers appear; but he does not understand why such surprise should prevent the ladies from accepting the cavaliers' advances' ('After the Manner of Italy,' *op. cit.* p. 428). But Reyher is not offering a surmise, he is criticising a suggestion of Brotanek (Reyher, *op. cit.* p. 493). The nature of the 1512 masque is discussed by Christoph Wilhelm Scherm in *Germanisch-romanische Monatsschrift*, Aug., Sept. 1912, pp. 469 ff. Scherm does not appear to be acquainted with Reyher's work, but he reaches a conclusion almost identical with his, i.e. that the novelty consisted in the attitude of the masquers to the spectators. He does not seem to realise the importance of the masquing customs of Modena and Ferrara. I think that Hall, throughout his work, distinguishes more closely between the disguising and masque than Scherm will allow. I do not think it is necessary to assume that when masques are mentioned as inserted in plays, etc. (in the early Tudor period) they were *necessarily* just the old disguisings under another name. There is no proof of this.

We saw in the first chapters how at the heart of most European festive games there lay a primeval revel: the arrival of a band of disguised and often masked persons, whom, for want of a better name, we called the mummers. In the early Tudor period, apart from aristocratic imitations of popular customs, the staple form of amusement was the solemn tournament and stereotyped disguising which is so fully illustrated in Hall's *Chronicle* and the Harleian manuscripts. It is easy enough to picture the scene— a man, gorgeously dressed, rides into the banqueting hall on a magnificent charger. It is William Cornish, Master of the Chapel Royal, who announces that certain ladies and gentlemen are very anxious to show sport and pastime to the Queen and ladies. The Queen makes courteous answer, and a pageant is drawn in, to the sound of minstrelsy. A trumpet blows, the curtain which veiled the pageant drops down, displaying an artificial garden or forest; conventional, brightly coloured, glittering with gold, made with a light-hearted disregard of the laws of verisimilitude or perspective. Round its side, beneath the trees of green silk, are ranged gentlemen and children of the Chapel, disguised as foresters, who sing and play, while a troop of noble ladies, wondrously disguised, step down from a central arbour of gold, and dance certain new dances specially prepared for the occasion. They are followed by a band of disguised knights who do likewise; and then they all—disguised lords and ladies—couple together and dance basse dances and rondes, or other stately dances imported from France. After this they retire back into their pageant and are drawn out of the hall. The performance is charming, even gay, but quite proper and in conformity with a strict Court etiquette. The show belongs to the later Middle Ages, the atmosphere is that of the *Morte d'Arthur* and the *Roman de la Rose*. But meanwhile people in society are beginning to talk about certain amusing, but rather doubtful, revels which have been practised in Italy for some years, and are now becoming fashionable in France, and are sure to appeal to a man of Henry VIII's temperament.

So now we leave the formal Tudor Court, and travel in

imagination to Italy, the home of the Kalends and the Saturnalia. At Maytide and Carnival and the eve of St John, the streets of the lively Italian cities swarm with maskers, mummers, buffoons, bands of disguised citizens, mock kings and queens surrounded by their turbulent courts of love, etc. Buffoonery and satire are in the air. At Florence the masquerade is particularly popular, and that seems to be not so much a traditional custom itself as the parody of traditional custom. It is crude and rather monotonous; but Lorenzo de' Medici and his friends realise that it has possibilities, and they proceed to alter its character. Now instead of a rabble of maskers dressed as women, marching or dancing to monotonous, popular songs, we watch gay bands of courtiers disguised as sellers of sweetmeats or other typical characters, and accompanied and explained by songs written to new and varied dance measures. Sometimes there is a still more elaborate masquerade, and all through the night a great triumphal chariot rolls through the streets of Florence, surrounded by torch-bearers, musicians and choristers, who celebrate in song the splendid masquers in the car, and explain the significance of the classic myth which they are meant to represent. In Ferrara, as in Florence, the autocratic princes gain popularity by taking a lively interest in the amusements of their subjects. At Carnival time a kind of madness seems to descend upon the house of Este. Storms of wind and snow do not check their wild, nocturnal progress through the streets. On one occasion the Carnival is protracted for many weeks, and masquing becomes a passion. Supper-parties and dances are invaded by bands of masked young men, and the whole Court goes about continually in masquing costume. The habit spreads, first to Mantua, then all over Italy and even further afield; and it is fashionable for masquers—even in foreign countries—to wear the Ferrarese masquing costume. Gossip follows in the wake of the masquerie. Funny stories, full of esprit gaulois, are told about the French 'masqueurs,' and it is perfectly understood that the masquerie is just an excuse for flirtation and amorous adventures. So, naturally, when Henry VIII introduces the custom into the English Court it has a rather mixed reception.

Some of the ladies, apparently, have heard nothing about it, and when the masquers come into the room in an unwonted manner and disguise, they probably attribute it to a sudden whim of the King's (like his impromptu Robin Hood pastime) and accept the invitation to dance in all innocence. Others are less ignorant and more wary; as soon as they see the ample garments, the masking hoods and hats, they realise that the notorious Italian masquerie is being introduced into England by the English King, and they know very well what it means, they know all about the unsavoury reputation of the 'masqueurs,' and they are not prepared to compromise themselves by taking part in any such performance, or at least not until it has been sanctioned by respectable English society. Judging by the historical situation, and the most natural and obvious meaning of the words used by Hall, I have no doubt that this is an essentially true account of what happened on the night of Epiphany, 1512.

The opposition, it seems, died out almost at once. But, as a matter of fact, even under the patronage of Henry VIII, the English Court masque was an expurgated version of the Continental masquerie. For just as the real mumming was a popular house-to-house visitation, and King and courtiers only pretended to be mummers, so in a sense, they only pretended to be masquers, coming from outside, uninvited, to take part in the Court festivities. When an attempt was made at the English Court to imitate the undignified behaviour of the French King and his minions (and the practice of the masquerie was what gave most offence to their subjects), it was, as we have seen, promptly and sternly suppressed. However, no doubt in England as in other countries, the masque (which was not only a Court amusement) often afforded opportunity for licentious behaviour. M. Prunières[1] considers that Reyher has attributed too much importance to the Italian masquerie. Such an essentially undramatic custom, he thinks, could never have led to the dramatic, or at least semi-dramatic ballet and masque. M. Prunières, however, seems to be taking it for granted that the English masque and the French ballet de Cour had the same historical development. But this is

[1] *Op. cit.* p. 27, note 1.

not the case. The French ballet was the result of deliberate experiments made by artists who were trying to build up a new genre out of the raw material supplied by the fusion of Italian masquerade, intermezzo and balletta or figured dance with the French spectacular tournament. The English masque came from a combination of the Italian masquerie and the Tudor disguising; and how far this was the result of conscious experiment we have no means of knowing; perhaps William Cornish and other artists connected with the Chapel Royal may have been pursuing some definite artistic ideal, but they have left no record of their intentions; and it does not seem very likely. The process may be traced in Hall, and it does not look deliberate.

For some time the distinction between the old and new pastimes was quite clear-cut. In the disguising, the performers never mingled with the spectators, and the mise-en-scène was often elaborate. The masque, on the other hand, was still obviously rather a social ceremony than a dramatic performance, and there was no mise-en-scène. For instance, hoods are frequently mentioned as part of the masquing costume, communing with the ladies and a final unmasking are regular parts of the performance[1].

Masking was a favourite diversion of both the courts that met on the Field of the Cloth of Gold. Many splendid masqueries, or companies of masquers, would go with the French King to visit the English Court at Guisnes, while at the same time Henry would set out as chief masquer to be entertained by the Queen of France at Arde. On one such occasion the French and English masquers met by the bank of Anderne 'and eche compaigny passed by other without any countenaunce makyng or disviseryng.'[2]

From Hall's description it is clear that some slight alterations were taking place in the character of the masquerie. The appearance of masquers disguised as Hector, Hercules, etc., suggests that the masquerie was approximating to the more dramatic masquerade, although the main features of the masquing dress—the

---

[1] Hall, *op. cit.* vol. I, pp. 171 (10th year), 247 (14th year).
[2] *Ibid.* vol. I, p. 217 (12th year).

hoods and ample garments—were still retained. Hall comments on the variety of the French masquing suits; in England the usual custom was for each band of masquers to be dressed alike, though there might be variations in the details of the costume. Originally the masquers were always men, but that particular rule was very quickly discarded, although the members of each masquerie, or band of masquers, were usually of the same sex. When there were two sets of masquers, one of men and one of women, the performance was known as a double masque.

In 1532 Henry visited France and entertained the French King at Calais, and Hall's description shows how few changes had been made in the masquerie during the twenty years that had elapsed since its first introduction into England[1]. But while the simpler form of the masquerie continued to be practised, a more complicated kind of masque was at the same time coming into existence.

In the nineteenth year of his reign Henry gave the French ambassadors a magnificent and varied entertainment at a banqueting house at Greenwich, specially erected for the purpose.

When the King and the Queen were seated, a person appeared, richly attired to represent Fame, and made a solemn oration, expressing satisfaction at the league between the French and English Kings, and the result of the cardinal's mediation. After this, members of the King's Chapel came in singing, the singers being divided into two groups of eight, each group accompanied by a person in rich apparel, who engaged in a dialogue or débat, 'theffect whereof was whether riches were better then love.' As they could not agree they each called in three knights, who fought a fair battle over a golden barrier, which suddenly fell down between them, finally an old man entered and concluded that both love and riches 'be necessarie for princes.'

'Then at the nether ende, by lettyng doune of a courtaine, apered a goodly mount, walled with towers...with all thinges necessarie for a fortresse...on this rocke sat eight Lordes...and then they sodenly descended from the mounte and toke ladyes, and daunced divers daunces.'

Then out of a cave issued out the ladie Mary doughter to the kyng and with her seven ladies...these eight Ladies daunced with the eight Lordes of the mount, and as thei daunced, sodenly entred six person-

---

[1] Hall, *op. cit.* vol. I, p. 220 (12th year); and also *ibid.* vol. II, pp. 24 (16th year), 220 (24th year).

ages, appareled in cloth of silver...and these persones had visers with sylver berdes...these Maskers tooke Ladies and daunced lustly about the place.

Then sodenly the kyng and the viscount of Torayne were conveighed out of the place into a chambre thereby, and there quicklie they ii. and six other in maskyng apparell...greate, long, and large, after the Venicians fashion and over them great robes, and there faces were visard with beardes of gold: then with minstrelsie thei viii. noble personages entred and daunced long with the ladies, and when they had daunced there fyll, then the quene plucked of the kynges visar, and so did the Ladies the visars of the other Lordes, and then all were knowen.'[1]

This entertainment is a disguising followed by two masques, but the disguising itself has been influenced by the masque, for the lords of the mount descended and danced with the ladies in the audience—before the other disguised ladies came and danced with the disguised lords according to the regular procedure of disguisings.

The combat preceding the disguising is an example of a pastime which retained its popularity as late as the seventeenth century, and by the reign of James I the barriers had become a variant of the masque.

A few pages further on there is a description of a similar mixed entertainment:

After supper the King led the ambassadors into the great chamber of disguisings where there stood a fountain, a hawthorn tree and a mulberry tree and eight ladies in 'straung attier' sitting on a bench. A political play was performed in Latin by children, then four companies of masquers danced and then the King and seven other masquers danced with the eight ladies sitting round the fountain and afterwards were unmasked and recognised[2].

Sometimes the special masquing costume was used in other kinds of entertainment; it was worn, for instance, by the gentlemen who brought in the 'tricke waggon,' with the challenge for the tourney of 1520[3] and by courtly disguisers of 1518 whom Hall refers to as the 'Maskers.'[4] This, however, was not the most important result of the mingling of the old and new

[1] Hall, *op. cit.* vol. II, pp. 87–88 (19th year).
[2] *Ibid.* vol. II, pp. 108, 109, 110 (19th year).
[3] *Ibid.* vol. I, p. 182 (11th year).
[4] *Ibid.* vol. I, p. 171 (10th year).

pastimes; for the special masquing dress was destined to disappear; whereas the masque was to acquire as permanent possessions the decorative setting, the rehearsed dance and the dramatic quality of the mumming and the disguising.

The introduction of the masquerie gradually changed the spirit as well as the form of the courtly revels. The old-fashioned Tudor disguising belonged, as we have seen, to the world of the *Roman de la Rose*; the disguisers were mariners in a Ship of Fame, inhabitants of a Mount of Love, haunters of a beautiful garden of roses and pomegranates. The masquers were figures typical of different countries, trades or social classes, deities or heroes of classical antiquity. The distinction must not be pressed too closely; there is no absolute break; but it is roughly true to say that the old disguisers were generally lovers in the mediaeval dream-setting; the new masquers drew their inspiration from real life or from the learning of Renaissance Italy. Symbolism and allegory, however, lasted as long as the revels themselves.

In Edward VI's reign the most notable event in the history of the revels was the appointment of George Ferrars as Lord of Misrule[1]. Ferrars, who contributed to the *Mirror for Magistrates*, was a poet of some distinction in his own day, and he brought to the performance of his function an ingenuity which gained him high favour at Court; but was less welcome apparently to Sir Thomas Cawarden, Master of the Revels, who had to find the wherewithal for the proper presentment of the mock king's fanciful devices. The correspondence on this subject is copious and amusing. Usually Ferrars emphasises his need of Cawarden's advice, and offers his own suggestions tentatively, leaving many details entirely in the Master's hands. Sometimes, however, there are unmistakably signs of friction:

'It seemeth vnto vs that as towching the Apparell of our Counseilloures you have mistaken ye persons that sholde were them as Sir Robert

---

[1] Cf. *supra*, chap. II, and Albert Feuillerat, *Documents relating to the Revels at Court in the time of King Edward VI and Queen Mary*, in *Materialien zur Kunde des älteren englischen Dramas*, ed. W. Bang, vol. XLIV (Louvain, Leipzig, London, 1914), pp. 56 ff.

Stafforde & Thom*a*s wyndeham with other gentlemen that stande also apon their reputacion and wolde not be seen in london so torcheberer-lyke disgysed for asmoche as they ar worthe or hope to be worthe.'[1]

One of the letters to Cawarden is signed ' fferryes the lorde Myserabell.'[2]

The most interesting part of the correspondence is that which relates to a performance arranged by Ferrars, which is called in the accounts 'The triumph of venus & mars with their paiauntes maskes & othe*r* furniture.'[3] Cawarden is given instructions:

'Ffirst yow have to furneshe Venus in a chaire trivmfall and with her iij laides and her chaire to be carried on iiij mens bakkes & eche of theme a torche in his hand as yow thinke mete in howse compaine I ame appointed for to come forneshed as I wrote vntoo yow be me man

Than comes in mars in a chaire ffurneshed with torche and men ffor the carrien of hime ffurneshed acordenge as yow shall thinke gode also mars muste be harmed wiche armor shall have here yf yow woll or else whether he shall have painted harnes or not and haveng ...a naket Sworde with hime commethe iij gentlemen havenge iij targetes of his harmes and swordes in ther handes

Cupide shalbe a letell boy howe mvst be tremmed with a bow and arrows blinfelde accordenge as yow thinke hit mete....'[4]

In another letter Ferrars gives a list of performers:

' M[y lo]rdes persone,
Chancellour, Treasorer, Comptrollour, Vizchamberlaine, my lordes Counsaillours arayed in apparel accustumed.
The Marshall and his bande
Those persones be alredy furnyshed so yt yt nedyth not to provyde but only for these vnderwrytten.
Ydelnes Dalyance two Ladies straungely attyred
Cupide a small boye to be cladd in a canvas hose and doblett sylverd over with a payre of winges of gold with bow and arowes his eyes bended
Venus to come in with a Maske of ladies and to reskue Cupide from the Marshall Mars the god of battale to come in very triumphantly Brett shalbe mars they must haue three fayre targettes the rest shalbe their owne armure The herault cuoeur ardant To haue a fayre short garment and a cote armour painted with burning hartes persed with dartes.'[5]

[1] Feuillerat, *op. cit.* p. 59.   [2] *Ibid.* p. 93.   [3] *Ibid.* p. 125.
[4] *Ibid.* p. 93.   [5] *Ibid.* p. 94.

The marshal may have been Ferrars himself or else perhaps one of his officers. The Christmas Lord of the Inns of Court was known sometimes as the Constable Marshal[1]. The indications as to the form of the entertainment are unfortunately very vague. Venus entered first in a triumphal chariot, accompanied by a masque of ladies and possibly by Cupid. Then, it seems, the marshal followed with his band, but whether this also was a triumphal entry is not certain. The relevant entries in the accounts do not clear up the matter:

'John Carowe for a dragon for the seate of the pageaunt of marce prepared for the lorde of misrule...cuppes of wood turned for the chaiers...An ymage of Cupide to stond ouer venus pageaunt...and for cutting of leves for the headpeces of her torcheberers...iiij Chaiers by him turned for ye pageauntes for ma(r)ce and venus in the Tryvmphe of Cupid and for the Seates of the lorde of misrule....'[2]

Again, we cannot tell from Ferrars' letters whether Mars made his triumphal entry after Venus had rescued Cupid from the marshal, or whether he and his men came to the assistance of the goddess. It would seem, at any rate, that the main action of the piece consisted in some form of mock combat. Two points are particularly noteworthy. In the first place, the word 'mask' still stands for the *band of maskers*, and is a part of the *furniture* of the show; and secondly, the show itself is called a *Triumph* and is an imitation of the Italian *Trionfi*, with their triumphal chariots full of Greek gods and goddesses.

It was, probably, due to the presence of the Lord of Misrule, and the desire felt by him and others to amuse the young King, that the masques of this reign are mostly of a burlesque character. There was a 'dronken Maske,' a masque of 'covetus men with longe noses,' a masque of cats, a masque of monstrous bagpipes, and strangest of all a macabre 'Maske of deathes being medyoxs half man half deathe....'[3]

The reign of Mary has no particular importance in the history of the masque. There were masques of 'Arcules,' of

---

[1] Cf. *supra*, p. 23.
[2] Feuillerat, *op. cit.* p. 107.
[3] Cf. *ibid.* pp. 59, 116, 130, 145.

Venetian senators, 'Venusses,' 'Goddesses huntresses,' etc. [1] An undated letter addressed to 'Mr Carden' (i.e. Cawarden, Master of the Revels) suggests, I think, that the English revels were still felt to be somewhat inferior to those of other countries.

'Mr Carden I haue declareyd to the quens hynes how that you haue no other mask*es* thene such as has byne shewyd all Redy before the kyng*es* hynes & for that he hathe syne meny fayer & Ryche be yend the seys you thynke yt not honorab that he shuld se the lyeke here[2].'

[1] Feuillerat, *op. cit.* pp. xiv, xv.
[2] *Ibid.* p. 245.

CHAPTER VI

The Elizabethan Masque

'Shows and nightly revels, signs of joy and peace
Fill royal Britain's court.' CAMPION.

WHEN Henry VIII came to the throne there was a
sudden and very large increase in the expenditure of the
office of the revels[1]. Elizabeth inherited her father's
tastes; but it would seem that during her reign occasional efforts
were made to check the ever-increasing expenditure of the revels
office, old masques were sometimes refurbished, and Sir Thomas
Benger added a significant postscript to the revels accounts for
the year 1559–1560:

'Memorandum that the Chargies for making of maskes cam never to
so little a somme as they do this yere (i.e. £227. 11. 2) for the same did
ever amount aswell in the Quenes highnes tyme that nowe is, as at all
other tymes heretofore, to the somme of cccc[li] alwaies when it was
Leaste.'[2]

The Queen may have appreciated the need for economy, for
apparently she made no attempt to foster any new and striking
development of the masque. In the first years of her reign there
were masques of swart rutters, fishermen and fishwives, market-
wives, astronomers, shipmen and maidens of the country,
barbarians, patriarchs, Italian women and so on[3]. This kind of
masque that represented trades or professions, or special classes
of the community, was popular both in Italy and France, and
was most unlike the old mediaeval disguisings. It will be
remembered that the first production of Lorenzo de' Medici
was a masquerade of sellers of sweetmeats.

There are indications in the revels accounts that the Elizabethan masque had acquired the mise-en-scène of the disguising.
In the year 1559–1560 there were:

'Toe Maskes of men & one maske of wemen with there torche
berers & A Rocke of founteyne and other furnyture thereto apertenente

[1] Cf. Collier, *op. cit.* vol. I, p. 65; Feuillerat, *Le Bureau des Menus-
Plaisirs* (Louvain, 1910), p. 16.
[2] Feuillerat, *Documents relating to the Office of the Revels in the time of
Queen Elizabeth*, in *Materialien zur Kunde des älteren englischen Dramas*,
ed. W. Bang (Louvain, Leipzig, London, 1908), vol. XXI, p. 111.
[3] *Ibid.* pp. xiii ff.

prepared to be sett forth & shewen in ye quenes presence at whyghte Hall duringe ye tyme of Shroftyde whereof the Hole Charges will amounte by estymacion to c^{li} at the leaste.'[1] And again: 'And allsoo in the same yeare (i.e. 6 Eliz.) the ixth of Iune Repayringe and new makinge of thre maskes with thare hole furniture and diuers devisses and a Castle ffor ladies and a harboure ffor Lords and thre harrolds and iiij Trompetours too bringe in the devise with the men of Armes and showen at the Courtte of Richmond before the Quenes Maiestie....'[2]

The whole question of mise-en-scène in the Court and University drama of the Tudor period is carefully considered by Miss Campbell in chapters VI, VII, VIII of her work on *Scenes and Machines on the English Stage.* I think she establishes a strong probability that, at least in Elizabeth's reign, the neo-classical methods of staging were adopted for plays presented at the Court and at the Universities. The dumb shows inserted into the early classical tragedies seem to be English equivalents of the Italian intermezzi; and their stage directions suggest knowledge of Italian stage mechanisms. For the moment, however, the new scenery (supposing Miss Campbell's theory to be correct) was only applied to the drama, and the masque still retained the pageant setting of the old disguisings. At the same time the masque was so often incorporated into, or associated with, the play, that it could hardly remain quite unaffected by innovations in the staging of the Court drama. For instance, in 1565, the revels accounts contain entries of payments made to

'officers and Tayllors paynttars workinge vppon diuers Cities and Townes and the Emperours pallace & other devisses...provicions for A play maid by Sir percivall hartt's Sones with a maske of huntars and diuers devisses and a Rocke, or hill ffor the ix musses to Singe vppone with a vayne of Sarsnett Dravven vpp and downe before them &c.'[3]

Naturally the revels accounts give but scanty information as to the form of the masque in the reign of Elizabeth. There are, however, a few indications as to the nature of the action:

'One of the forenamed Maskes (i.e. one of the masques performed at Shrovetide, 1571) had going before it A Childe gorgevsly decked for Mercury, who vttered A speeche: & presented iij fflowers (wroughte in

[1] Feuillerat, *op. cit.* p. 110.   [2] *Ibid.* p. 116.   [3] *Ibid.* p. 117.

silke & golde) to the Queenes Maiestie, signefieng victory, peace, & plenty, to ensue. he had also ij torchebearers in Long gownes of changeable Taffata with him....'[1]

In Shrovetide, 1577, there was:

'A longe Maske of murrey satten...prepared for Twelf night, with a device of 7: speeches framed correspondent to the daie. Their Torchebearers vj: had gownes of crymsen Damask, and headepeeces new furnished, showen on Shrovetuysdaie night, without anie speeche.'[2]

In 1579:

'*A Maske of Amasones* in all Armore compleate...one with A speach to the Quenes maiestie delivering A Table with writinges vnto her highnes comyng in with musitions playing on Cornettes apparrelled in longe white taffeta sarcenett garmentes torche bearers with the troocheman wearing longe gownes of white taffeta...and after the Amasons had dawnced with Lordes in her maiesties presence in came.

An other Maske of knightes all likewise in Armoure compleate... and commyng in with one before them. with A speach vnto her highnes and delivering A table written their torch bearers being Rutters apparrelled. in greene satten Ierkines...the Amasons and the Knightes after the Knightes had dawnced A while with Ladies before her maiestie did then in her maiesties presence fight at Barriars.'[3]

The presenter, or trucheman, who went before the maskers, and delivered an introductory speech, was a regular figure in the Elizabethan period[4], but it is not possible to say at what date he penetrated into the masque, because the descriptions of masques in earlier reigns are mostly given by writers whose main interest is in dress and decoration. Perhaps he was there from the first, for he was a common figure in the earliest momeries, mummings, disguisings and sword-dances, and he survives still in the mum-

[1] Feuillerat, *op. cit.* p. 146.
[2] *Ibid.* p. 270.
[3] *Ibid.* pp. 286–287.
[4] '...vj bandes of ffethers for the Men maskers & one for the Tronchewoman....' *Ibid.* p. 218.

'Maskes. showen ⎫ Warriers vij with one shippmaster that
at Hampton Coorte. ⎬ vttered speche....
(1573/4) ⎭ Ladyes vij with one that vttered a speeche....'
Ibid. p. 213.

In Sept. 1589, '...garmentes for the furnishing of a maske for six Maskers & six torchebearers and of suche persons as were to vtter speches at the sheweng of the same maske Sent into Scotland to the king of Scottes mariage by her Maiesties comaundement...' *Ibid.* p. 392.

mers' play. The masque composed by George Gascoigne for
Viscount Montacute, in celebration of the double marriage
between his son and daughter and the daughter and son of Sir
William Dormer, shows very well how the introduction of a
presenter could lead to the literary development of the masque.

Gascoigne tells us how eight gentlemen related to the Montacutes
had already made all preparations for a Masque of Venetians, when it
occurred to them that the performance might appear rather pointless,
and so to remedy this they sent for the author and asked him to write
some verses for recitation by an actor, which should furnish a motive
for the arrival of Venetians. The poet fell back upon their family tree,
and calling to mind that the Montacutes were related to a family called
Mounthermer, and assuming a connection between the English family,
and the noble house of Montacute in Italy, he decided to bring in a
boy of twelve years old, supposedly a Mounthermer by his father's side,
and a Montacute by his mother, who should explain to the audience
that his father, having been killed in battle against the Turks, and he
himself taken prisoner, he had only lately been released by certain
Venetians, who being on their way home were shipwrecked on the
coast of England, where they heard of the marriage of the Montacute
family and were hastening to pay their respects.

All this the boy expounds at great length in pages of verse until he
breaks off at the entry of the masquers:

'They will not tarry long: lo! nowe I heare their drumme;
Behold, lo! nowe I see them here, in order howe they come.
Receiue them well, my lord, so shall I praye all wayes,
That God vouchsafe to blesse this house with many happie days.'

'After the maske was done, the Actor (i.e. the boy) tooke Master Tho.
Bro. by the hand, and brought him to the Venetians,' explaining that
he also is a Montacute:

'Make much of him, I pray you then, for he is of your name.
For whom I dare aduante, he may your Truchman bee,
Your herald and ambassadour; let him play all for me.'

'Then the Venetians embraced and receiued the same master Tho.
Browne, and after they had a while whispered with him, he torned to
the Bridegroomes and Brides,' making a congratulatory speech in verse
on behalf of the Venetian masquers[1].

The dramatic part of the masque (and also of earlier disguisings)
came partly from an expansion of the prologue, partly from an

---

[1] *Complete Poems of George Gascoigne,* ed. by W. C. Hazlitt, printed for
Roxburghe Library, 1869, vol. I, pp. 77 ff.

absorption of qualities belonging to the plays, interludes, tourneys and debates, etc., with which it was so often associated. A show which was to have been performed at the meeting of Queen Elizabeth and Mary Queen of Scots at Nottingham in 1562 is a good example of the latter process. The meeting between the two queens did not take place, but luckily the scheme of the proposed entertainment was drawn up, and was preserved among the papers of Sir William Cecil. It was entitled: *Devices to be shewed before the Queenes Majestie by waye of masking at Nottingham Castell, after the meetinge of the Quene of Scots.*

On the first night a prison, called 'Extreme Oblivion,' was to be set up in the hall and guarded by Argus or Circumspection and 'then a maske of Ladyes to come in after this sorte': first comes Pallas, then two ladies, Prudence and Temperance, riding upon lions, then six or eight lady masquers leading Discord and False Report in chains. They all march round the hall, and then Pallas declares that Prudence and Temperance have obtained Jupiter's permission to imprison Discord and False Report and to give to their jailor Argus a lock labelled *In Eternum* and a key labelled *Nunquam.* When this has been done then are 'th' inglishe Ladies to take the nobilite of the straungers, and daunce.'

On the second night an additional pageant, the Court of Plenty, was to be erected, with Ardent Desire and Perpetuity as its Porters, and the order of the proceedings to be as follows: Enter Peace in a chariot drawn by an elephant with Friendship riding upon its back, followed by six or eight lady masquers. They march round, Friendship declares that the gods are pleased with the doings of Prudence and Temperance and have sent Peace to keep them company in the Court of Plenty. Then the conduits of that building run with wine, 'duringe whc. tyme th' inglishe Lords shall maske wth. the Scottishe Ladyes.'

On the third night, Disdain, riding a wild boar and Prepencyd Malyce, in the likeness of a serpent, were to draw in an orchard with six or eight lady masquers sitting in it. Disdain declares that his master Pluto, highly indignant at the proceedings of the last two nights, has sent Malice to require either the freeing of Discord and False Report or the yielding up of Peace. But at this point Discretion enters leading a horse on which rides Hercules or Valiant Courage, and he explains that they have been sent to confound Pluto's devices, but that Hercules needs words of encouragement from Prudence and Temperance if his efforts are to be crowned with success. Discretion then approaches the Court of Plenty and asks Prudence how long she wishes Peace to dwell with herself and Temperance, and she replies by lowering a 'grandgarde' inscribed with the word *Ever.* Then he asks Temperance when Peace shall depart from herself and Prudence, and she lets down a sword inscribed with the word *Never*. Discretion arms Hercules with the grandgarde and sword, and a fight takes place, in which Disdain escapes with his life but Prepencyd Malyce is killed. 'After this shall come out of the garden, the vj or viij Ladies maskers, wth a songe,...as full of armony as maye be devised.'[1]

At first glance this show appears to be an interlude or morality, diversified with masques, but on more careful examination, as Reyher points out, it is discovered to be nothing of the kind. All the speeches are made by allegorical or mythological figures acting as presenter to various troops of masquers; so that the show is just a collection of ordinary masques, each with its presenter or prologue. But there is a difference. The actions described by the various presenters are performed in dumb show by allegorical figures who are not included in the masque proper; and moreover the various speeches and dumb shows are related to each other, and each contributes to the main action or plot—if such it can be called. 'Il semble que l'auteur ait essayé d'adapter un sujet de moralité à une mascarade ou, mieux encore, de les combiner.'[2] The weakness of the scheme lies in the failure to make the appearance of the masquers a central or even an integral part of the performance. It was evidently considered meritorious, for years later it was performed—with some alterations—for the entertainment of the French ambassador. Its chief interest lies, I think, in the fact that it is an experiment, and suggests that in England, as elsewhere, on one occasion at least, a conscious attempt was made to develop the form of the masque. There are references to it in the accounts[3].

In August, 1578, Elizabeth made a progress into Norfolk and Suffolk, and was given a brilliant welcome by the city of Norwich. There were daily shows and entertainments.

On Thursday, 'there was an excellent princely maske brought before hir after supper, by Mayster Goldingham, in the Privie Chamber; it was of gods and goddesses, both strangely and richly apparelled. The first that entred was Mercurie. Then entred two torch-bearers,...sixe

---

[1] Collier, *op. cit.* vol. I, pp. 178–181; also in Malone Soc., *Collections* (Oxford, 1908), vol. I, pt II, pp. 144 ff.   [2] Reyher, *op. cit.* pp. 125 ff.
[3] Feuillerat, *op. cit.* pp. 153 ff. For the view that the performance to which these accounts refer, should *not* be identified with the *Devices* planned in 1562, see *Collections, op. cit.* p. 144.

musitians,...playing very cunningly. Then two torch-bearers more.
Then Jupiter and Juno, Torchbearers,
>   Mars, Venus,
>   Torchbearers,
>   Apollo, Pallas,
>   Torchbearers,
>   Neptune, Diana,
and last came Cupid and concluded the matter. They marched once
about the chamber, and then Mercury made an introductory speech.

Then they marched about again, and Jupiter spoke to the Queen and
presented her with a riding wand of whale's fin curiously wrought.
His speech promised her his protection, and assured her that as he had
first given her sovereignty so he would give her still 'peerlesse power'
to rule and love; the wand being a token that she would 'in quiet rule
the lande.' Juno spoke next, giving a purse curiously wrought. Her
speech begins: 'Is Juno rich? No, sure she is not so,' and states that the
love the Queen has won from her subjects far exceeds riches, that she,
Juno, can neither give her anything better, nor take away the good she
has already found. And so the performance continued. Each made an
offering, accompanying it with appropriate speech. Before each couple
of gods appeared, the marching round was performed again.

After this, 'The gods and goddesses, with the reste of the maske,
marched aboute the chamber againe, and then departed in like manner
as they came in.' The Queen thanked the Mayor heartily and had
some private talk with him, and so passed the night to the joy of all
who saw her Grace 'in so pleasaunt plight.'[1]

It will be noticed at once that the culminating dance is
lacking from this performance, which is more nearly allied to the
old momeries than to the new Court masque. This is perhaps
natural in a provincial show. The name and fame of the fashionable ludus spread all over the country; but outside the sphere of
Court influence, or among the more conservative country gentlemen, there was probably little change in the nature of the usual
social recreations. The well-known picture of the masque at Sir
Henry Unton's wedding[2] depicts a ludus strikingly similar to
the masque given by the Mayor of Norwich. The masquers
walk in couples, each couple separated by torch-bearers, they are
headed by a presenter, and a messenger hurries up bearing a letter
in his hand, reminding us of Lydgate's 'lettre made in wyse of

---

[1] John Nichols, *Prog. Eliz.* vol. II, pp. 159–164.
[2] Cf. frontispiece to *Eliz. Stage*, vol. I.

balade...brought by a poursuyvant in wyse of Mommers....'[1]
The continual marching round in the Mayor's masque is rather
interesting, in view of the mysterious letter *m* in the margin of
Lydgate's manuscript. It will be remembered that the letter *m*,
or the word 'Marche,' appears in the margin of manuscript
versions of Breton religious plays, and is apparently a stage
direction, indicating that at certain points in the Prologue's
speech the whole company of actors were to march round in
procession. I believe that that gives us the clue to the meaning
of Lydgate's *m*, and the action of the Norwich masquers tends
to confirm this belief; for since the practice is not derived from
the Italian masquerades or masqueries, nor from the Tudor
Court disguisings (of the entremets type), the presumption is
that it is a survival from the old momeries. Almost the only
serious difference between this masque and entertainments such
as Lydgate's mummings and disguisings and the Burgundian
momerie of *Grace-Dieu*, is that in this particular masque,
besides the short introductory speech of the presenter, each
masquer spoke for himself or herself, as he or she arrived before
the royal seat; whereas in the earlier momerie and in the processional part of the Breton plays, the mummers, as they came
up, were introduced, described and interpreted by the presenter,
but said nothing themselves[2].

It is interesting to compare this provincial show with a
masque in a private house given towards the end of Elizabeth's
reign[3]. On the 16th of May, 1600, Rowland Whyte writes to
Sir Robert Sidney:

'There is to be a memorable maske of eight ladies. They have a
straunge dawnce newly invented....Those eight dawnce to the musiq
Apollo bringes; and there is a fine speach that makes mention of a ninth,
much to her honor and praise.' After the wedding, he writes again:
'After supper the masks came in, as I writ in my last; and delicate it was
to see eight ladies so pretily and richly attired, Mrs Fetton leade; and
after they had donne all their own ceremonies, these eight ladies maskers
chose eight ladies more to dawnce the measures. Mrs Fetton went to

---

[1] *Loc. cit. supra*, p. 54.
[2] Cf. *supra*, pp. 58 ff.
[3] *Prog. Eliz.* vol. III, pp. 498–499.

the Queen, and woed her·to dawnce. Her Majesty asked what she was? *Affection,* she said. *Affection,* said the Queen, is false. Yet her Majestie rose and dawnced.'[1]

At this fashionable entertainment, though there was probably some more or less dramatic business—at any rate an introductory speech—all the emphasis is on dress and dance; it is a masquerie, not a mumming re-christened.

Every fresh development of the Court masque meant increased expenditure, and Elizabeth was not inclined to be a munificent patroness of the revels. It is true that

'The coming of the Duke of *Alenzon* into *England,* opened a way to a more free way of living, and relaxed very much the old severe form of Discipline: The Queen danced often then, and omitted no sort of Recreation....Dances, Masques, and variety of rich Attires, were all taken up, and used, to shew him how much he was honoured.'

However, as soon as he was dismissed 'she as heartily endeavoured to reduce her nobility to their old severe way of living,' but without much success[2]. Elizabeth did her best work for the masque, not through direct encouragement, but by her habit of making progresses through England[3], spending her summer visiting the country houses of the nobility; on these occasions the house and grounds of the noble host became a kind of enchanted country, abounding in deities, nymphs and wild-men who met the Queen on her walks, and delivered long complimentary harangues in prose or verse. The same kind of thing took place in the streets of the country towns. Some weeks before the date fixed for the royal visit the Mayor and other civic authorities, the expectant host and the chief gentlemen of the countryside would be busy making preparations, buying up silks and other necessary properties, getting poets, schoolmasters, carpenters to work at pageants and devices for the welcome of the royal guest. Well-known musicians and literary men were hired for these occasions. Ferrars, sometime Lord of Misrule,

---

[1] *Prog. Eliz.* vol. III, pp. 498, 499. Note that Whyte uses 'masks' for 'maskers.'

[2] E. Bohun, *The Character of Queen Elizabeth* (London, 1693), p. 345.

[3] Cf. *Eliz. Stage,* vol. I, pp. 106 ff.; *Prog. Eliz.* vol. I, pp. 393 ff., 426 ff.; vol. II, pp. 94 ff.; vol. III, pp. 101 ff.; R. W. Bond, *Works of John Lyly* (Oxford, 1902), vol. I, pp. 403 ff.

Hunnis, Master of the Queen's Chapel, Churchyard, Gold-ingham, Gascoigne, wrote verses and planned devices for the welcome of the Queen at Kenilworth Castle in 1575. Church-yard was one of the poets to be employed by the civic autho-rities at Norwich in 1578, by whom his pains were 'but slenderly considered,' and at Bristol in 1574, where some of his speeches 'could not be spoken, by means of a Scholemaister, who envied that any stranger should set forth these Shows.' In 1578 Leicester diverted his sovereign with a pastoral written by Sidney, 'the subject of which was a Contention between a Forrester and a Shepherd for the May-Lady.'[1] It has been sug-gested[2] that it was Lyly who transformed the rites of the Cots-wold peasants into the fashionable pastoral entertainments, which were prepared for the visit of the Queen at Bissam, Ricort and Sudley in 1592.

There is, however, no space here to pursue the Queen any further on her holidays or to watch the indefatigable Churchyard as he astounds the simple provincials with a Mercury's Coach rivalling the triumphal chariots of Italy, or recovers from his disappointment when his show of water-nymphs is ruined by a thunderstorm so that 'we were all so dashed and washed, that it was a greater pastime to see us looke like drowned rattes, than to have beheld the uttermost of the shewes rehearsed.'[3] It must suffice to emphasise the fact that the Queen's habit of travel encouraged the development of the entertainment, a genre akin to but not identical with the masque, for the main business of the performers is to offer gifts, make complimentary speeches, engage in a debate or slight dramatic action, not to pave the way for an entry of a troop of masquers.

The anonymous 'masques' preserved in the collection of Henry Ferrers, Esq., of Baddesley Clinton, Warwickshire, seem to be more in the nature of entertainments, than of true masques, but since they consist only in speeches and dialogue unaccom-panied by stage directions, it is impossible to decide for what kind of performance they were intended; except that it is clear

[1] *Prog. Eliz.* vol. II, p. 133; vol. I, p. 407; vol. II, p. 94.
[2] Cf. Bond, *Works of John Lyly*, vol. I, pp. 379 ff.
[3] *Prog. Eliz.* vol. II, pp. 179–212.

that the speeches in Part I are all introductory to joustings. The songs and speeches in Parts II and III probably formed part of entertainments given to the Queen during a visit to Sir Henry Leigh's house. The underlying idea of the performance (given apparently on the first day, after dinner) was that the Queen had set free 'Captiue Ladies, Captiue Knights,' delivered the ladies from inconstancy, and had freed a knight from an enchantment, inflicted on him as a punishment for a piece of unfaithfulness. For 'the second daies woorke,' the chaplain makes a long speech, describing how 'Loricus,' finding old age creeping on him, retired to a hermitage to spend his last days in praying for the Queen and preparing for his end. His death is now to be expected at any time. Suddenly, however, a page brings the news that his master has begun to recover, owing to the health-giving presence of Her Majesty, to whom he has bequeathed

'*The whole Mannor of Loue*, and the appurtenaunces thereunto belonging:
> (viz.) Woodes of hie attemptes,
>   Groues of humble seruice,
>   Meddowes of greene thoughtes,
>   Pastures of feeding fancies....'

The masques seem to be full of allusions to events in Sir Henry Leigh's private life, and especially to his resignation, on account of old age, of the position of Queen's Champion, in virtue of which he had been wont to fight in a tournament on each anniversary of her accession[1].

There is the same combination of tournament and entertainment in the *Device exhibited by the Earl of Essex before Queen Elizabeth, on the Anniversary of her Accession to the Throne, Nov.* 17, 1595, for which Francis Bacon wrote the speeches[2].

The solemn tournament still played an important part in Elizabethan revels. When the French ambassadors came to England in 1581, a great triumph was prepared in which Philip Sidney and three others, calling themselves 'the four Foster Children of Desire,' were to be the chief challengers in a solemn tournament, and were to arrive on a machine called the

[1] *Prog. Eliz.* vol. III, pp. 195–213.
[2] *Ibid.* vol. III, pp. 371 ff.

'rolling trench,' ready to besiege the Queen's seat, which was called, and not without cause, 'The Castle or Fortresse of Perfect Beautie.'[1]

The devisers of this show meant to make it as splendid as possible, but it is more childish and absurd than the grand tournaments of Henry VIII's reign. It has lost the mediaeval glamour, and not yet acquired the grace and polish of the Stuart 'barriers.' It must have seemed a very crude performance to the foreign ambassadors, for at that same time, the humanists across the Channel were striving to satisfy the eye, ear and understanding, by the creation of the ballet de Cour.

During the greater part of Elizabeth's reign the entertainment was more dramatic and literary than either the barriers or the masque; but in 1594 the gentlemen of the Inns of Court produced as part of their Christmas merrymaking a piece which had almost all the characteristics of the developed Stuart masque.

In 1594[2] the gentlemen of Gray's Inn resolved to revive their traditional king-game, which had been discontinued for some three or four years. 'Whereupon, they presently made choice of one Mr Henry Holmes, a Norfolk gentleman, who was thought to be accomplished with all good parts, fit for so great a dignity; and was also a very proper man of personage, and very active in dancing and revelling.'[3] We may pass over the elaborate mock ceremonial which accompanied the 'honourable Inthronization' of the 'Prince of Purpoole' and proceed to the unfortunate events of the second grand night[4]. On that occasion (it was Innocents' Day at night) a very notable performance was expected of the 'Grayans,' and the ambassador of the Inner Temple was present 'as sent from Frederick Templarius, their Emperor, who was then busied in his wars against the Turk.' Unfortunately the stage was so crowded with people whose rank or sex forbade violence, that no entertainment could be provided and the ambassador and his train departed 'discontented and displeased,' and nothing took place except dancing

---

[1] *Prog. Eliz.* vol. II, pp. 312 ff.
[2] *Gesta Grayorum*, published in *Prog. Eliz.* vol. III, pp. 262 ff.
[3] *Prog. Eliz.* vol. III, p. 262.   [4] *Ibid.* pp. 277 ff.

and 'a Comedy of Errors (like to Plautus his Menechmus) was played by the players.' The night was afterwards called 'The Night of Errors.' Next day was spent in mock trials and consultation 'for the recovery of our lost honour.' The result was a show which although not actually a masque is yet of very great interest.

When the Prince and the Ambassador of Templaria were seated, they were presented with this device: 'At the side of the Hall, behind a curtain, was erected an altar to the Goddess of Amity; her arch-flamen ready to attend the sacrifice...round about the same sate Nymphs and Fairies,...and made very pleasant melody with viols and voices, and sang hymns...to her deity.' Then there came from another room three pairs of the famous friends of antiquity. Lastly, were presented *Graius* and *Templarius*...but the Goddess did not accept their service until the arch-flamen had performed mystic rites, the nymphs had sung hymns and they had renewed their devotions. Then the arch-flamen pronounced Graius and Templarius perfect friends and cursed any who should attempt to separate them. When the show was ended the Prince made the Ambassador a Knight of the Helmet[1].

On Twelfth Night the Grayans presented 'a shew which concerned his Highness's State and Government.'[1]

First there came six Knights of the Helmet, with three prisoners, attired like monsters and miscreants. The Knights gave the Prince to understand, that as they were returning from their adventures out of Russia, they surprised these three persons, which were conspiring against his Highness and his dignity. Then entered in the two goddesses Virtue and Amity, who disclosed to the Prince that these suspected persons were Envy, Male-content, and Folly. 'Then willed they the Knights to depart, and to carry away the offenders; and that they themselves should come in more pleasing sort, and better befitting the present. So the Knights departed, and Virtue and Amity promised that they two would support his Excellency against all his foes whatsoever, and then departed with most pleasant musick. After their departure, entred the six Knights in a very stately mask, and danced a new devised measure; and after that, they took to them Ladies and Gentlewomen, and danced with them their galliards, and so departed with musick.'[2]

This show may be compared with the Nottingham 'devices.' The chief sign of advance is that the masque is not simply part of the furniture of the show, but the show is made to *lead up* to

---

[1] *Prog. Eliz.* vol. III, pp. 281, 282. [2] *Ibid.* pp. 297, 298.

the masque. It is, apparently, a happy combination of the masque in the show, and the masque with presenters and introductory speeches. The step from this to the developed masque was very slight, and was in fact taken shortly afterwards by the same young lawyers, during the reign of the same Henry of Purpoole.

The morning after Twelfth Night, the Prince of Purpoole took a journey to 'Russia,' where he remained until Candlemas, when he intended to make a most triumphant return to his 'Court,' but was much disappointed by 'the Readers and Ancients of the House,' who had taken down all the scaffolds, and so prevented the performance of the 'very good inventions' which had been prepared. However, the Queen was anxious to welcome him, as she had in vain expected some amusement from the mock king at Christmas time. The Prince despatched a letter to the Queen, saying he was for the moment much weakened by sea-sickness, but hoped to recover his strength about Shrovetide, 'at which time I intend to repair to her Majesty's Court (if it may stand with her gracious pleasure) to offer my service, and relate the success of my journey.' Her Majesty answered: '"That if the letter had not excused his passing by, he should have done homage before he had gone away, although he had been a greater Prince than he was: yet," she said, "she liked well his gallant shews, that were made at his triumphant return." And Her Highness added further, "that if he should come at Shrovetide, he and his followers should have entertainment according to his dignity."' Consequently at Shrovetide[1] the Prince went to Court where the sports 'consisted of a mask, and some speeches that were as introductions to it.'

First entered five musicians representing 'an Esquire of the Prince's Company, attended by a Tartarian Page. Proteus the Sea-god, attended by two Tritons. Thamesis and Amphitrite, who likewise were attended by their Sea-nymphs.' The nymphs and Tritons sang a song in praise of Neptune: 'Of Neptune's Empire let us sing....' Then from a conversation between the Esquire, Proteus, Amphitrite and Thamesis, we learn that the Prince of Purpoole had caught Proteus, and refused to let him go, until he promised to bring to an appointed place the 'Adamantine Rock,' the magnetic cliff that brought with it the empire of

[1] *Prog. Eliz.* vol. III, pp. 309 ff.

the sea. But Proteus would only agree to do this on condition 'That first the Prince should bring him to a Power, Which in attractive virtue should surpass The wondrous force of his Iron-drawing rocks.' The Prince of Purpoole and seven of his knights have allowed themselves to be shut into the rock as hostages, for the performance of this covenant, and now the moment of trial has come. Proteus descants on the magnetic virtue of the adamantine rock, but the squire points out that the rock may draw iron, but the Queen attracts to herself the hearts of men, and the human heart moves the arm that can wield iron. Proteus acknowledges himself defeated.

'When these Speeches were thus delivered, Proteus, with his bident striking of adamant, which was mentioned in the Speeches, made utterance for the Prince, and his seven Knights, who had given themselves as hostages for the performance of the Covenants between the Prince and Proteus, as is declared in the Speeches. Hereat Proteus, Amphitrite and Thamesis, with their attendants, the Nymphs and Tritons, went unto the rock, and then the Prince and the seven Knights issued forth of the rock, in a very stately mask, very richly attired, and gallantly provided of all things meet for the performance of so great an enterprize. They came forth of the rock in couples, and before every couple came two pigmies with torches. At their first coming on the Stage, they danced a new devised measure, etc. After which, they took unto them Ladies; and with them they danced their galliards, courants, etc. And they danced another new measure; after the end whereof, the pigmies brought eight escutcheons, with the maskers devices thereupon, and delivered them to the Esquire, who offered them to her Majesty; which being done, they took their order again, and with a new strain, went all into the rock; at which time there was sung another new Hymn within the rock....

'For the present her Majesty graced every one; particularly, she thanked his Highness...and wished that their sports had continued longer, for the pleasure she took therein; which may well appear from her answer to the Courtiers, who danced a measure immediately after the mask was ended, saying, "What! shall we have bread and cheese after a banquet?"...her Majesty gave them her hand to kiss, with most gracious words of commendations to them particularly, and in general of Gray's-Inn, as an House she was much beholden unto, for that it did always study for some sports to present unto her.'

The masque of *Proteus and the Adamantine Rock* brings us to a turning-point in the history of the masque. It is the first piece that we know of which gives the norm of the masque as composed by Ben Jonson and his fellow-poets. Later masques were more elaborate, but with the exception of the antimasque all the elements are here: the introductory song and dialogue, the entry of the masquers, the masque dances, the revels, the final song and dialogue recalling the masquers to the scene and concluding the performance, and finally the motiving of the whole by a slight story and dramatic action.

It seems natural, at this point, to ask ourselves whether the developed masque was a genre peculiar to England or whether Davison and Campion were using foreign models[1], and even deliberately emulating the work of men like Beaujoyeulx and the members of the Camerata.

The fact that from the first French writers freely applied the term 'ballet' to the English masque, and English writers used 'masque' as a term for foreign 'ballets' and 'mascarades,' seems to suggest that the English masque is only the French ballet under another name, and resemblances between the two pastimes are undoubtedly very close. We must remember, however, that the masquerade-entertainment, in which divinities, nymphs, sibyls, shepherds, etc. sang, danced, made speeches, filed past in chariots, performed mock fights, was common to all western Europe, and the question is not whether there were resemblances between English and foreign revels, but whether the English lawyers were consciously following Beaujoyeulx in his attempt to create out of this formless fluid material a *ballet-comique*, a lyrical and choreographical drama, comparable to that of the ancient Greeks.

Certainly in the *Proteus and the Adamantine Rock* we have the firstfruits of a genre which did to a large extent fulfil the ideal of Beaujoyeulx; in this work, and still more in the later Stuart masques, the dance is made to speak, the comedy to sing, the eye, the ear and the understanding are equally satisfied. It is

---

[1] Note that Italian players visited Elizabeth's Court. Cf. Feuillerat, *op. cit.* pp. 225, 227–228. Cf. 'To Patruchius Vbaldinas by the comaundment of the Lord chamberleyne for the translating of certen speaches into Italian to be vsed in the maske....' *Ibid.* p. 301. For Italian artists at the English Court, cf. Reyher, *op. cit.* pp. 73–80; and Campbell, *op. cit.* pp. 77, 78, which gives further references. Cf. the excellent chapter in Brotanek, *op. cit.* pt IV, 'Fremde Einflüsse,' pp. 283 ff.

worth remembering that Campion, who contributed the first lyric, was particularly interested in musical reform, in coupling his words and notes 'lovingly together,' in substituting classical metre for English rhyme and rhythm, and, in fact, shared all the most cherished ideas of the Camerata and the Académie de Musique et de Poésie. This humanistic bias of Campion's, however, makes it all the more probable that if he and his associates were introducing something new and learned into the English revels, they would have made the fact quite clear. It may be noted that when Rinuccini introduced the new French ballet into Italy, his intention was quite obvious and unambiguous. It would probably have been equally difficult to overlook any attempt to introduce the new genre into England. In the *Gesta Grayorum*, *Proteus and the Adamantine Rock* is described very modestly: 'the sports, therefore consisting of a Masque, and some speeches that were as introductions to it.' Again we are told that 'at the Stroke of Proteus, the Prince and the seven Knights issued forth of the Rock *in a very stately mask*, very richly attired,' so that the term 'mask' is still primarily applied to the procession of masquers. It does not as yet apply to the performance as a whole, including the introductory speeches and songs by professionals. In fact, on careful examination, *Proteus* will be seen to be still true to the type of those masques in Henry VIII's reign which had coalesced with the earlier disguisings and had been absorbing some of the characteristics of the interlude. In *Proteus* all the early features are there. The masquers appear from a machine, dance by themselves, with the spectators, and then retire again to their machine, and the chief change is the more developed dramatic character of the introductory speeches, which supply the semblance of a plot and give unity to the whole performance. This improvement is the natural outcome of a process which had been going on since the beginning of the Tudor period, and was due partly to the association of the disguising and masque with the interlude and entertainment and stage play; partly again to the steady influence of the French and Italian masquerades, which was experienced both directly and through the mediation of dramatic entertainments at noble houses. For instance, in 1565 Baïf composed a *Mascarade de Mons. le Duc de Longueville*[1].

First of all there was a dance between rocks and trees. Then a fairy arrived, and announced that in a valley of the Pyrenees six maidens had refused the suit of six knights, who had appealed in their despair to the gods. Their prayer was heard and the maidens were transformed permanently into trees, the knights were changed into rocks, but might recover their true shapes when peace was concluded between France and Spain. She asked the king if he wished to disenchant the knights, and on a favourable sign from him, she waved her wand, and the knights issued out of the rocks and offered their grateful service to the house of France.

Proteus resembles this masquerade much more closely than it does the later *Ballet comique de la Reine*.

There is, then, no indication at all that the gentlemen of Gray's Inn were taking for their model the ballet de Cour, as shaped by Beaujoyeulx, although they can hardly have escaped from the general influence of French and Italian revellings; and since both ballets and masques were made out of much the same materials, and existed under very similar social conditions, they naturally bear a strong family likeness to each other.

Both in the French ballet and the English masque, however varied the forms of entertainment might be, there was one constant factor: the *raison d'être* of the whole performance was the arrival of noble personages disguised and masqued to dance a specially prepared dance. They might dance other dances as well, either all together or in groups, but there was one special dance in which they all took part which was the centre of the whole thing, and that dance was known in France as *le grand ballet*, in England as the main or grand masque dance. The chief features of the costume of the noble masquers were also very similar in the two countries. An important difference must, however, be mentioned. In France *le grand ballet* was a grand finale. In England it almost always occupied a more or less central position, and was followed by *revels* (i.e. ordinary ballroom dancing between masquers and audience) and by the final

[1] Baïf, ed. Marty-Laveaux, vol. II, pp. 331 ff. The mascarade is described by Brotanek, *op. cit.* p. 293, Prunières, *op. cit.* pp. 69, 70.

dramatic business of speech or song or both, and perhaps a final dance of the masquers, known as the 'going off,' or 'the last dance.'

The important place occupied by the revels is no doubt due to the origin of the masque in the Italian social masquerie; and probably the dramatic instinct, which was strong in England, made the masque writers incorporate the revels in a performance which had some kind of artistic unity, instead of allowing the masque to trail off into ordinary ballroom dancing. In spite of the later developments of the antimasque, the form of the English Court masque was more fixed and unchanging than that of the French ballet de Cour.

To sum up. The English masque grew up in a somewhat haphazard manner through the gradual combination and fusion of various pastimes, most of which were ultimately of foreign origin. The catholic taste of the Tudors led them to make their Court an attractive centre for humanism, national drama, folk-custom and foreign fashion; so that all these various activities were kept in continuous and fruitful contact with one another. To this fact, and to the poetic genius of the English nation, was chiefly due the literary and dramatic quality of the English masque.

CHAPTER VII

The Jacobean Masque

'A few Italian herbs picked up and made into a sallad
may find sweeter acceptance than all the most nourishing
and sound meats of the world.' JONSON.

URING the greater part of the Tudor period the English
revels were in a fluid condition, and it is not always
possible to draw hard and fast distinctions between
momerie, masque, tourney, and entertainment; towards the end
of Elizabeth's reign, however, the masque, having acquired the
setting and poetic quality of other revels and of the drama, was
shaped into a definite genre by the young lawyers of the Inns of
Court, though apparently more by accident than by deliberate
design. During the Stuart period this new masque[1] was developed
and elaborated under the patronage of two successive queens,
Anne of Denmark and Henrietta Maria of France, and, since
the new royal family were ready to expend vast sums on pleasure
and diplomatic advertisement, the Court of England soon rivalled
Paris and Florence as a centre of splendid revelling. The munificent patronage of the Stuarts was not, however, to prove an
unmixed blessing, for it enabled the stage architects to produce
those grandiose scenic effects which in the end disintegrated the
masque just as the intermedii choked the Italian drama; and
moreover, owing perhaps to the predominantly French character
of Scottish culture, the Stuarts were inclined to foster that foreign
influence which had such a baneful effect on the revels towards
the middle of the seventeenth century. However, during James I's

---

[1] Most of the masques of this period are printed in J. Nichols, *The Progresses of King James I* (London, 1828), in four volumes. A selection of
sixteen masques is given in H. A. Evans, *English Masques* (London, 1897).
As a matter of convenience, I refer in the footnotes to the most accessible
editions of the masques. For Jonson's masques I use *The Works of Ben Jonson*,
ed. F. Cunningham (London, 1911), vol. III. Brotanek and Reyher give
useful bibliographies of masques, in which they make a chronological list
of the masques and of the relevant contemporary allusions, letters, accounts,
etc., and refer to the various editions. Much information of this kind,
together with copious quotations, is gathered under the heading of each
masque, listed under the name of its author in *Eliz. Stage*, vol. III, chap.
XXIII, but unfortunately no masque written after the death of Shakespeare
is included.

reign, these unfortunate tendencies were kept in check by the powerful genius of Ben Jonson, and under his sway poet, architect, musician, and dancing-master worked together in harmony, and gave to the masque a very real artistic value[1]. The decline of the masque began in the reign of Charles I, when Jonson lost his position as chief masque writer to the Court through the enmity of his colleague Inigo Jones. This process of development and disintegration is the subject of the next two chapters.

Ben Jonson began his career as poet of the revels in 1603, when he was employed by Sir Robert Spenser to prepare entertainment for his royal guests, Queen Anne and Prince Henry, who were on progress from Scotland to London. For this purpose Jonson composed the *Satyr*, a charming pastoral entertainment, which was performed in the garden of Althorp, and which marked a great advance on the naïve shows and masquerades presented to Elizabeth at Norwich, Kenilworth and elsewhere. On this occasion, Ben Jonson introduced Queen Mab and a bevy of fairies, and expounded through the mouth of the Satyr the same attractive fairy lore that Shakespeare put into the mouth of Puck and Mercutio[2].

The excellence of the *Satyr* is so great that one would expect to find Jonson becoming immediately prominent as a composer of courtly revels. The first masques of the new reign, however, were written by other poets. In the autumn of 1603 Anne welcomed Prince Henry with a masque of which no record has survived, but which obviously showed no advance on the masque of *Proteus*, for the French ambassador regarded it as more like the informal masquerade which still flourished in France than the elaborate and dramatic ballet de Cour.

'Elle fit jl y'a quelques jourz vn ballet ou pour mieux dire vne masquarade champêtre. Car il n'y avoit ni ordre ni depense. Mais Elle se propose d'en faire d'autres plus beaux cet hiver en recompense et

[1] There is an admirable detailed study of Ben Jonson's masques, barriers, and entertainments in C. H. Herford and Percy Simpson, *Ben Jonson*, vol. II, pp. 249 ff.

[2] *The Progresses of King James I*, ed. John Nichols (London, 1828), vol. I, pp. 176 ff.

semble que le Roy et ses Principaux Ministres, qui sont toujourz en Jalousie de son Esprit, soient bien aises de le voir occupé en cet exercice.'[1]

For our knowledge of two of these more excellent masques which Beaumont expected we are dependent on the pen of that lively correspondent Dudley Carleton:

'On New yeares night we had a play of Robin goode-fellow and a maske brought in by a magicien of China. There was a heaven built at the lower end of the hall, owt of which our magicien came downe and after he had made a long sleepy speech to the King of the nature of the cuntry from whence he came comparing it with owrs for strength and plenty, he sayde he had broughte in cloudes certain Indian and China Knights to see the magnificency of this court. And theruppon a trauers was drawne and the maskers seen sitting in a voulty place with theyr torchbearers and other lights which was no vnpleasing spectacle. The maskers were brought in by two boyes and two musitiens who began with a song and whilst that went forward they presented themselves to the King. The first gave the King an Impresa in a shield with a sonet in a paper to exprese his deuice and presented a jewell of 40,000£ valew which the King is to buy of Peter Van Lore, but that is more than euery man knew and it made a faire shew to the French Ambassadors eye whose master would have bin well pleased with such a maskers present but not at that prise. The rest in theyr order deliuered theyr scutchins with letters and there was no great stay at any of them saue only at one who was putt to the interpretacion of his deuise. It was a faire horse colt in a faire greene field which he meant to be a colt of Busephalus race and had this virtu of his sire that none could mount him but one as great at lest as Alexander. The King made himself merry with threatening to send this colt to the stable and he could not breake loose till he promised to dance as well as Bankes his horse. The first measure was full of changes and seemed confused but was well gone through with all, and for the ordinary measures they tooke out the Queen, the ladies of Derby, Harford, Suffolke, Bedford, Susan Vere, Suthwell th' elder and Rich. In the corantoes they ran over some other of the young ladies, and so ended as they began with a song; and that done, the magicien dissolved his enchantment, and made the maskers appear in theyr likenes to be th' Erle of Pembroke, the Duke, Mons[r] d'Aubigny, yong Somerset, Philip Harbert the young Bucephal, James Hayes, Richard Preston, and Sir Henry Godier. Theyr attire was rich but somewhat too heavy and cumbersome for dancers which

---

[1] Beaumont to Villeroy (27 Oct. 1603), printed in *Eliz. Stage*, vol. I, p. 171, note 2.

putt them besides ther galliardes....The twelfe-day the French Ambassador was feasted publikely; and at night there was a play in the Queens
presence with a masquerado of certaine Scotchmen who came in with
a sword dance not vnlike a matachin, and performed it clenly....The
Sunday following was the great day of the Queenes maske.'[1]

The masquerade of Scotsmen, performed on Twelfth Night,
is interesting because Ben Jonson and his friend Sir John Roe
were present in the audience, but were thrust forth by the Lord
Chamberlain[2]. Perhaps Ben's comments on the performance
were too loud and caustic; his temper was not likely to be
improved by the fact that Samuel Daniel, who was 'at jealousies
with him,'[3] had been chosen to compose the great masque of the
season at which Queen Anne herself was to appear as chief
dancer.

As a social and diplomatic event the *Vision of the Twelve
Goddesses*[4] was of the highest importance, but aesthetically it was
not very significant, although it had a good reception at Court.
The scenic arrangements were old-fashioned, the hall at Hampton
Court being arranged in accordance with the system of dispersed
decoration which Italian architects had rendered obsolete. At
the upper end of the hall was the Cave of Sleep with the Temple
of Peace to the left of it, and at the lower end of the hall a
mountain from which the masquers were to descend. The
musicians were scattered, some placed in the cupola of the temple,
some dressed like savages sitting in the 'concaves of the mountain.'
The proceedings opened with the approach of Night, coming to
arouse her 'sonne Somnus,' who in obedience to her command
used his white wand 'to infuse significant visions to entertaine
the Spectators, and so made them seeme to see there a Temple,
with a Sybilla therein attending upon the sacrifices.' At this
point, apparently, a curtain fell down revealing the Temple of
Peace. Then 'Iris, the Messenger of Juno, descends from the

---

[1] Carleton to Chamberlain (15 Jan. 1604), quoted in *Eliz. Stage*, vol. III,
pp. 279, 280.
[2] Cf. *Ben Jonson's Conversations with Drummond of Hawthornden*, ed.
R. F. Patterson (London, 1923), p. 15.
[3] *Ibid.* p. 14.
[4] Printed in *Prog. James*, vol. I, pp. 305 ff. and *The Complete Works of
Samuel Daniel*, ed. A. B. Grosart (Blackburn, 1885), vol. III, pp. 185 ff.

top of a mountaine...and, marching up to the Temple of Peace, gives notice to the Sybilla of the comming of the Goddesses; and withall delivers her a prospective, wherein she might behold the figures of their Deities.' The sibyl then looks through the perspective glass, and, pretending that she can see the goddesses, describes them in verse giving their names and their allegorical significance.

'Which as soon as she had ended, the three Graces...appeared on the top of the mountaine, descending hand in hand before the Goddesses; who likewise followed three and three, as in a number dedicated unto Sanctity and an Incorporeall Nature....And betweene every ranke of Goddesses marched three Torch-bearers in the like severall colours, their heads and robes all dect with starres;...the Goddesses one after an other with solemne pace ascended up unto the Temple, and, delivering their presents to the Sybilla (as it were but in passing by), returned downe into the midst of the Hall, preparing themselves to their dance....Which dance being performed with great majesty and arte, consisting of divers straines, fram'd unto motions circular, square, triangular, with other proportions exceeding rare and full variety, the Goddesses made a pause, casting themselves into a circle (whilst the Graces againe sang to the musicke of the Temple), and prepared to take out the Lords to dance....'

This masque seems to have pleased Carleton, usually a somewhat supercilious critic of these toys:

'Through the midst from the top came a winding stayre of breadth for three to march; and so descended the maskers by three and three; which being all seene on the stayres at once was the best presentacion I have at any time seene.'[1]

The materials for the dresses, he tells us, were taken from the wardrobe of Queen Elizabeth.

'Only Pallas (i.e. Queen Anne) had a trick by herself for her clothes were not so much below the knee, but that we might see a woman had both feete and legs which I never knew before.'[2]

It is, however, difficult to share Carleton's approval of the *Vision*; neither the device nor the poetry was good. In spite of its elaboration and costliness it was less advanced than the masque

---

[1] Carleton to Chamberlain, in *Eliz. Stage*, vol. III, p. 280.
[2] *Loc. cit.*

of *Proteus* and not very far removed from the masque given by the Mayor of Norwich[1] or the masque at Henry Unton's wedding[2], or even from the ancient momerie of *Grace-Dieu*[3]. The double set of presenters—Sleep introducing the vision of the sibyl, and then the sibyl describing the masquers—was a novelty, but hardly a happy one. Particularly clumsy and absurd was the device of giving the sibyl a telescope, so that she might describe the goddesses before their entrance. One is inclined to agree with Ben Jonson in his summing up of poor Daniel as 'a good honest man...bot no poet.'[4]

At the end of the year there was a masque at the wedding of Sir Philip Herbert and Lady Susan Vere, which is briefly described by Dudley Carleton:

'Theyre conceit was a representacion of Junoes temple at the lower end of the great hall, which was vawted and within it the maskers seated with staves of lights about them, and it was no ill shew. They were brought in by the fower seasons of the yeare and Hymeneus: which for songs and speaches was as goode as a play. Theyre apparel was rather costly than cumly; but theyr dancing full of life and variety; onely Sr Tho: Germain had lead in his heales and sometimes forgott what he was doing.'[5]

All these masques seem to us now merely preludes to the Twelfth Night masque of 1605, which marks an epoch in the history of the revels, because it is the beginning of the collaboration between Ben Jonson and the famous architect Inigo Jones. The history of the masque, to a certain extent even the history of contemporary drama and poetry, is bound up with the history of this famous partnership.

Inigo Jones was first known to his contemporaries as a great traveller. He spent some time in Italy at the expense of the Earl of Arundel, and from there went north and found employment at the Court of Denmark. He came back to England full of enthusiasm for the work done by Italians in reviving classic architecture and classic methods of staging, and determined to introduce this new art into his native country. His indebtedness

[1] Cf. *supra*, p. 154.   [2] Cf. frontispiece to *Eliz. Stage*, vol. I.
[3] Cf. *supra*, pp. 69, 70.   [4] *Conversations*, p. 3.
[5] *Eliz. Stage*, vol. III, p. 377.

to Palladio is well known. The nickname given him later by Ben Jonson shows that he was known to share the Italian reverence for the work of Vitruvius. He had evidently studied the work of Serlio, the pupil of Baldassare Peruzzi, for we find him using the devices of Serlio at Oxford, where he arranged three changes of scene during the course of a tragedy, and his designs for masque settings show the influence of the satirical, tragic, and comic scenes in Serlio's *Architettura*. Of Jones' architectural work I am not competent to speak, nor do I possess the technical knowledge which would qualify me to pronounce upon the value of his work for the Court stage. As far as I can judge, one of his ambitions was to emulate the marvellous spectacular effects devised by Italian artists, although his designs are usually more restrained and imaginative than those of his foreign contemporaries. To Jones the masque was a grand spectacle, and he seems to have been very insensitive to its poetic and dramatic aspect, although occasionally his descriptions of scenery show gleams of imagination and are written in vigorous prose[1].

Ben Jonson's attitude was very different. He was first and foremost a learned poet, and if he undertook to write masques, it meant that the masque would have to be taken seriously, that the scholarship would have to be exact, the nymphs, goddesses, satyrs, etc., dressed in accordance with the true tradition of

[1] See on Inigo Jones: *Dictionary of National Biography*, art. *Inigo Jones*; P. Cunningham, J. R. Planché, J. Payne Collier, *Inigo Jones, A Life*, etc. (Sh. Soc. London, 1848); Reyher, *op. cit.* pp. 75–77, 192–201, 332 ff.; R. Blomfield, *A History of Renaissance Architecture in England* (London, 1897), vol. I, pp. 97–122, and articles in *The Portfolio* (London, 1889), vol. xx, pp. 88 ff., 113 ff., 126 ff.; W. Keith, in *The Builder*, vol. cvII, p. 312, vol. cvIII, pp. 331–333; W. J. Lawrence, *The Mounting of the Carolan Masques*, in *The Elizabethan Playhouse* (Stratford-upon-Avon, 1912), first series, pp. 91 ff.; L. B. Campbell, *op. cit.* chap. xII, 'The work of Inigo Jones and his contemporaries in England'; E. Welsford, *Italian Influence on the English Court Masque*, in *M.L.R.* vol. xvIII, no. 4, Oct. 1923; P. Simpson and C. F. Bell, *Designs by Inigo Jones for Masques and Plays at Court* (Walpole and Malone Societies, Oxford, 1924), cited as *Designs*. This magnificent volume is indispensable to all serious students of the masque. It contains an introduction, giving an account of the development of the masque and of the history of the Chatsworth collection, a descriptive catalogue of the designs, fifty-one plates, reproductions in the text of those designs by Parigi that were imitated by Inigo Jones.

antiquity, and above all there would have to be literary unity. To Ben Jonson the masque was not a grand display of scenic splendour, it was a dramatic poem with spectacular and musical elements. Here lay the seeds of future strife. It was not going to be easy for these two conscientious but irascible artists to work together harmoniously. For the moment, however, there was no difficulty, for Ben Jonson was in an unquestionably superior position. He was recognised as the dominant figure in the literary world, whereas Jones was still comparatively unknown, and his effort a few months later to introduce Italian methods of scene-shifting on the Oxford stage did not prove an unqualified success[1].

For his first Court masque Inigo did not attempt anything very ambitious. He contrived no changes of scene for the *Masque of Blackness*, although he did emulate other Italian spectacular devices, such as the artificial sea and the scene in perspective, and he abolished once for all the system of dispersed decorations, and concentrated his scenery on a raised stage at the far end of the hall. In front of this stage there hung a curtain, painted to represent a woody landscape, which, falling, displayed the masquers enthroned upon a splendid pageant, surrounded by mermen and sea-monsters. This strange spectacle it was the business of the poet to explain, and since Queen Anne had expressed a desire that she and her fellow-masquers should appear as blacka-moors, Ben Jonson had to invent a poetical justification for the sudden appearance of a number of negresses at the English Court:

Niger, accompanied by his daughters and their attendants, has arrived together with Oceanus at the Court of England. He explains to Oceanus that his daughters have fallen into a profound despair on hearing of the superior beauty of nymphs living in other parts of the world, and have been wandering, in obedience to a vision, in quest of a land 'whose termination (of the Greek) sounds *tania*,' where they hope to get cured of their blackness. At this point in the action the Moon goddess reveals herself, and explains that she has now come to announce that her prophecy has been fulfilled, in that the daughters of Niger have arrived at *Britania*, a land governed by 'bright Sol' (i.e. King James)

'Whose beams shine day and night, and are of force
To blanch an Æthiop and revive a corse.'

[1] Cf. *Prog. James*, vol. I, p. 558.

For this libretto Ben Jonson evidently took some suggestions from the Florentine tournament of 1579, which celebrated the wedding of Francesco de' Medici with the enigmatic lady Bianca Cappello[1]. It will be remembered that after the time of Leo X, the Italian masquerade usually consisted of a procession of triumphal chariots, and was very often combined with the tournament. The entertainment of 1579 was of this character.

The performance took place in the courtyard of the Pitti palace, where a fine theatre had been erected showing a grotto adjoining a lovely garden. This grotto opened out to the sound of loud music and was transformed into a loggia overlooking the sea, which was most realistically painted: '...il mare era dipinto, & il dipintore haueua fatto l' on-deggiare al mare, si ch'ei pareua, che veramente si mouessi, e frangessi, e franto biancheggiasse d'intorno a gli scogli; e gli scogli pareuano veri, & a viua forza vscir dell' acque; ma piu vero pareua il farsi, e 'l disfarsi della schiuma, che nasceua dall' onde rotte....'

The occasion of the tournament was a challenge made by three Persian knights, who were prepared to assert by force of arms the superiority of Persian beauties to all others in the world. A great number of marvellous triumphal cars filled with masquers and accompanied by music entered into the theatre during the course of the tournament, and among others there came one bearing the two ladies Europe and Africa who had come thither accompanied by their knights, because they could not bear that the Persian boast of the excelling beauty of the Continent of Asia should be allowed to pass unchallenged: 'Allora venne in campo vna Madreperla molto grãde, e risplendente, e tale, che ben mostraua d'essere stata gloria del profondissimo Oceano; risplendeua ella del suo proprio, e dell' altrui splendore: percioche ella era d'argento, & haueua nel suo candido seno due Donzelle, e due Caualieri, nel cui volto, e nel cui mouimento, e 'n tutto l' apparato: comeche straniero; si vedeua vn regio costume, e senza sapere chi le Donzelle si fussero, solo perciò, regine; & i Caualieri di grande, & alto

---

[1] In commenting on some remarks on this subject made by me in an article on *Italian Influence on the English Court Masque* in *M.L.R.* Oct. 1923, Professor Herford (C. A. Herford and Percy Simpson, *Ben Jonson*, vol. ii, p. 265, note 5) points out that both Inigo and Ben were six years old when this Italian tournament took place. I should, perhaps, have expressed my meaning more carefully, but I thought that the whole tenour of my article made it plain that I was referring to a *literary* influence, and was suggesting that the composers of the masque had read the Italian descriptive pamphlets. I should like also to add that, so far from trying to exaggerate Jonson's indebtedness to Italy, I was deliberately contrasting his originality with the plagiarism of later poets, and pointing out that whereas they copied and borrowed, he merely took a hint, and allowed it to quicken his own imagination.

affare stimati si sarieno; come inuero era; perche le due Donzelle si fingeuano per l'Europa, e per l'Affrica, che nõ potendo soffrire, che la gloria della belleza, e del valore dalla nemica Asia loro fusse occupata i due guerrieri menauano p[er] fare i Persiani de'loro orgogliosi vanti rimanere; & l'vna delle due vn suo liuto molto dolcemente sonaua, & l' altra vi cantaua sopra: & i Caualieri alla sua armonia stauano attenti... tutte queste cose faceuano vn'apparenza amorosamente altiera, e sopra qualunque altra diletteuole.; perche la Madreperla simigliaua vna naue rotonda: intorno alle sponde della quale essendo appoggiate le Donne, e i Caualieri: pareua, che i suoi nauicanti fussero la gioia, la bellezza, il diletto, e 'l valore; ella soauemente sopra l'acque marine ondeggiando veniua, tirata da due huomini acquatici, e sospinta, e retta da molte Ninfe, e Dee, e Dij del Mare, e dilettaua molto il vedere quasi in vn corpo solo tutte le contrarietà; perche per l' altezza del trionfo i Caualieri, & le Regine si vedeuano poco meno, che in aria: ma di celesti raggi circondati, oue essendo in aria nauicauano sopra l'onde del mare, e 'l mare ondeggiaua sopra la terra; degno carro delle due principali parti del mondo.'[1]

Compare with this description the account of the staging of the *Masque of Blackness*:

'First, for the scene, was drawn a *landt-schap* (landscape) consisting of small woods, and here and there a void place filled with huntings; which falling, an artificial sea was seen to shoot forth, as if it flowed to the land, raised with waves which seemed to move, and in some places the billow to break, as imitating that orderly disorder which is common in nature. In front of this sea were placed six tritons, in moving and sprightly actions, their upper parts human, save that their hairs were blue, as partaking of the sea-colour: their disinent parts fish, mounted above their heads, and all varied in disposition....Behind these a pair of sea-maids, for song, were as conspicuously seated; between which two great sea-horses, as big as the life, put forth themselves...upon their backs Oceanus and Niger were advanced....These induced the masquers, which were twelve nymphs, negroes, and the daughters of Niger; attended by so many of the Oceaniae, which were their light-bearers.

The masquers were placed in a great concave shell, like mother of pearl, curiously made to move on those waters and rise with the billow; the top thereof was stuck with a cheveron of lights, which indented to the proportion of the shell, strook a glorious beam upon them as they

---

[1] *Feste nelle Nozze del Serenissimo Don Francesco Medici Gran Duca di Toscana; et della Sereniss. sua Consorte la Sig. Bianca Cappello*, Composte da M. Raffaello Gualterotti (Florence, 1579), pp. 13 ff. For the description of the 'Madreperla' see pp. 31, 32.

were seated one above another: so that they were all seen, but in an extravagant order. On sides of the shell did swim six huge sea-monsters, varied in their shapes and dispositions, bearing on their backs the twelve torch-bearers, who were planted there in several graces....

These thus presented, the scene behind seemed a vast sea, and united with this that flowed forth from the termination, or horizon of which (being the level of the state, which was placed at the upper end of the hall) was drawn by the lines of prospective, the whole work shooting downwards from the eye; which decorum made it more conspicuous, and caught the eye afar off with a wandering beauty.'

It is evident that Ben Jonson and Inigo Jones took some hints from this Italian tournament, but there is no real plagiarism, the treatment of the theme is their own. As regards form, no very great advance has been made on earlier masques, although the sudden intervention of Æthiopia, the Moon goddess, gives an unusually dramatic turn to the poetic introductory speeches. The masque apparently made no very favourable impression on Dudley Carleton:

'At night we had the Queen's maske in the Banquetting-House, or rather her pagent. There was a great engine at the lower end of the room, which had motion, and in it were the images of sea horses with other terrible fishes which were ridden by Moors: The indecorum was, that there was all fish and no water.'[1]

But what chiefly annoyed him was to see the lady masquers with blackened arms and faces, which he describes to Chamberlain as 'a very lothsome sight,' and, again, he remarks to Winwood, 'you cannot imagine a more ugly sight than a troop of lean-cheeked Moors.'[2]

The Twelfth Night masque of 1606[3] celebrated the unfortunate union of the Earl of Essex and the Lady Frances Howard. It was a characteristic Renaissance affair—all the resources of all the arts called out to celebrate a wedding that was destined to end in divorce, a shameful second marriage, murder, and a great public scandal which did not leave even the throne untainted.

---

[1] R. Winwood, *Memorials of Affairs of State in the reigns of Q. Elizabeth and King James I* (London, 1725), vol. II, p. 44; and *Eliz. Stage*, vol. III, p. 376.

[2] *Loc. cit.*   [3] Jonson, *Hymenaei*.

The masque is described by Sir John Pory in a letter to Sir Robert Cotton:

'I haue seen both the mask on Sunday and the barriers on Mundy night. The Bridegroom carried himself as grauely and gracefully as if he were of his fathers age. He had greater guiftes giuen him then my lord Montgomery had, his plate being valued at 3000£ and his jewels, mony and other guiftes at 1600£ more. But to returne to the maske; both Inigo, Ben, and the actors men and women did their partes with great commendation. The conceite or soule of the mask was Hymen bringing in a bride and Juno pronuba's priest a bridegroom, proclaiming those two should be sacrificed to nuptial vnion, and here the poet made an apostrophe to the vnion of the kingdoms. But before the sacrifice could be performed, Ben Jonson turned the globe of the earth standing behind the altar, and within the concaue sate the 8 men-maskers representing the 4 humours and the fower affections which leapt forth to disturb the sacrifice to vnion; but amidst their fury Reason that sate aboue them all, crowned with burning tapers, came down and silenced them. These eight together with Reason their moderatresse mounted aboue their heades, sate somewhat like the ladies in the scallop shell the last year. Aboue the globe of erth houered a middle region of cloudes in the center wherof stood a grand consort of musicians, and vpon the cantons or hornes sate the ladies 4 at one corner, and 4 at another, who descended vpon the stage, not after the stale downright perpendicular fashion, like a bucket into a well; but came gently sloping down. These eight, after the sacrifice was ended, represented the 8 nuptial powers of Juno pronuba who came downe to confirme the vnion. The men were clad in crimzon and the weomen in white. They had euery one a white plume of the richest herons fethers, and were so rich in jewels vpon their heades as was most glorious. I think they hired and borrowed all the principal jewels and ropes of perle both in court and citty. The Spanish ambassador seemed but poore to the meanest of them. They danced all variety of dances, both seuerally and promiscue; and then the women took in men as namely the Prince (who danced with as great perfection and as setled a maiesty as could be deuised), the Spanish ambassador, the Archdukes Ambassador, the Duke, etc., and the men gleaned out the Queen, the bride, and the greatest of the ladies. The second night the barriers were as well performed by fifteen against fifteen; the Duke of Lennox being chieftain on the one side, and my Lord of Sussex on the other.'[1]

As far as its 'soul' is concerned, this masque is an improvement

[1] *The Court and Times of James I* (London, 1848), vol. I, pp. 42 ff.; and *Eliz. Stage*, vol. III, p. 379.

on the *Masque of Blackness*. Hymen, Reason, and Order are no mere presenters who furnish through set speeches an elaborate and unconvincing explanation of the appearance of the masquers, but they themselves take part in the rudimentary dramatic action, and by their words and actions turn the masque into a symbolical setting forth of the meaning of marriage. It should, however, be remarked that Ben Jonson in describing this masque uses the plural and not the singular form: 'On the night of the Masques which were two, one of men and the other of women,' for this shows that the word masque was still felt to apply primarily to the procession of masquers and not to the performance as a whole.

In 1608 Ben Jonson, in composing the Queen's *Masque of Beauty*, reverted to the form of the *Masque of Blackness*, probably because he was obliged to meet the views of the Queen, who desired that her masque should be a sequel to that which she had danced a few years before. The masque seems to have been a success. The Venetian ambassador wrote to his government that 'The apparatus and the cunning of the stage machinery was a miracle, the abundance and beauty of the lights immense, the music and the dance most sumptuous.'[1] The actual execution of the scenery does not, however, seem to have satisfied the exacting Ben Jonson. The chief device was that of the Throne of Beauty, which moved on the waters with a circular motion, while steps placed upon the throne moved in a different direction.

'And with these three varied motions at once, the whole scene shot itself to the land....The order of this scene was carefully and ingeniously disposed; and as happily put in act (for the motions) by the king's master carpenter. The painters, I must needs say (not to belie them), lent small colour to any to attribute much of the spirit of these things to their pencils. But that must not be imputed a crime either to the invention or design.'[2]

In February Ben Jonson and Inigo Jones worked together again, and produced one of the most beautiful of these early masques, *The Hue and Cry after Cupid*. In the first part of the masque Jonson dramatised the search of Venus for her son Cupid, an

---

[1] *Calendar of State Papers, Venetian*, vol. XI, p. 86, no. 154.
[2] Opinions differ as to whether or no Inigo Jones designed the scenery for this masque. There is no evidence to enable us to settle the question.

episode which Spenser had already worked out in *The Faerie Queene*. In this episode of Venus and Cupid, which is treated as a kind of antimasque, the God of Love is accompanied by

'twelve boys, most antickly attired, that represented the Sports, and pretty Lightnesses that accompany Love, under the titles of Joci and Risus....Wherewith they fell into a subtle capricious dance, to as odd a music, each of them bearing two torches, and nodding with their antic faces, with other variety of ridiculous gesture, which gave much occasion of mirth and delight to the spectators.'

Chamberlain calls this dance of the Jocund Sports a 'matachina,' that is to say a sword- or morris-dance[1].

In this masque Inigo Jones began experimenting with the scena ductilis, and produced that very popular device of the rock opening to a burst of loud music and disclosing a splendid interior scene[2].

In 1607 the Twelfth Night masque at Whitehall was composed by Thomas Campion:

The subject of the masque—which was in honour of the marriage of Lord Hayes—was a dispute between Flora, Goddess of Flowers, and Night, the representative of Cynthia or Diana, Goddess of Chastity. Night complains that Flora, together with Zephyr and the Sylvans, are wantonly insulting the Moon Goddess by celebrating the theft of one of her nymphs. That this is a dangerous thing to do is shown by the fact that already certain Knights of Apollo have been turned into trees:

'By Cynthia's vengement for their injuries
In seeking to seduce her nymphs with love.'

At this juncture Hesperus arrives with the news that Cynthia has been appeased by Phoebus and desires Night to retransform the trees into human shape. Night obeys, and the trees sinking three at a time beneath the stage are cleft into three parts out of which jump the Knights clothed in leafy garments. The Knights, after they have danced some masque dances, leave the dancing place and march back one by one to the upper stage, in order to make a solemn offering of their leafy disguise at Diana's tree. They then return to dance once more in their own resplendent masquing garments[3].

The idea of this masque may have been taken from the French

[1] *Prog. James*, vol. II, p. 189; *Eliz. Stage*, vol. III, p. 382.
[2] Cf. Campbell, *op. cit.* pp. 170, 171.
[3] *Prog. James*, vol. II, pp. 105 ff.; *Works of Thomas Campion*, ed. A. H. Bullen (London, 1903), pp. 148 ff.

masquerade composed by Baïf in the year 1565 [1]. The forty-two years' interval between the two works is paralleled by many other instances of English borrowings from Continental revels. Campion may have been attracted by this work of Baïf because he was interested in the musical and metrical experiments of Baïf and his colleagues of the Académie de Musique et de Poésie. Campion's masque is noteworthy for its numerous songs, choruses and chanted dialogue, and for the careful description of the very elaborate musical arrangements. The scenic devices are also interesting. The stage was built on two levels, the upper part reserved for the acting, the lower part for the masque dancing. The scene was not changed, but variety was gained by drawing back first that half of the front curtain which concealed the Bower of Flora, and then the other part of the curtain which concealed the rest of the scene, the House of Night and the Tree of Diana, planted on a hill-top in the middle of the back of the stage, overhanging the central grove where stood the nine golden trees concealing the Knights of Apollo. The trees were lowered by an engine placed beneath the stage, but 'either by the simplicity, negligence, or conspiracy of the painter, the passing away of the trees was somewhat hazarded.' [2] Round the House of Night 'were placed on wire artificial bats and owls, continually moving.' [3]

In August of the same year John Marston composed a masque for Lord and Lady Huntingdon's entertainment of their right noble mother, Alice Countess Dowager of Derby, the first night of Her Honour's arrival at the house of Ashby [4]. The masque was presented by gentlemen representing eight stars, the sons of Mercury. The staging was fairly complicated. The effect of variety was obtained by drawing back curtains at different times.

As soon as the guests had been ushered into their places, 'a travers slyded away; presently a cloud was seen move up and downe almost to the topp of the greate chamber, upon which Cynthia was discovered ryding.' The Moon Goddess was then joined by Ariadne, who floated up towards her on a cloud from the lower end of the hall. After some poetic speeches 'the travers that was drawn before the Masquers sanke

---

[1] Cf. *supra*, p. 165.   [2] *Works*, p. 164.
[3] *Ibid.* p. 150.   [4] *Prog. James*, vol. II, pp. 145 ff.

downe,' revealing eight knights with 'wisards like starres' enthroned beneath a great oak with a golden eagle perched upon it. After the dancing of the revels the performance was closed by some attractive lines spoken by Cynthia, heralding the coming of the day.

Ben Jonson chose as a subject for the Twelfth Night masque of 1609, in which the Queen herself was to take a part, 'A celebration of honourable and true Fame, bred out of Virtue.'[1]

The first scene which presented itself was an ugly hell full of smoke and fire. Into this hell come eleven witches summoned by Hecate and representing the Vices, Falsehood, Slander, and so on. The witches perform a wild dance, until suddenly there is a blast of loud music and the hags with their cauldron and their hell vanish away, while in place of them appears a glorious and magnificent building figuring the House of Fame, on top of which are discovered the twelve masquers sitting upon a throne triumphal 'erected in form of a pyramid and circled with all store of light.' From this palace a person dressed as Perseus and figuring Heroic Virtue descends and describes the masquers, who are supposed to be twelve great queens of antiquity. Fame now appears at the top of the building, while the masquers descend to the sound of music, come out through the doors of the House of Fame mounted upon four magnificent chariots drawn by griffins and eagles, and so are brought in triumph into the dancing place where they perform their measures.

This performance is a turning-point in the history of the masque, for it marks the acceptance of the antimasque as an integral part of the performance, and also it is the first work to show unmistakable traces of the influence of those Florentine revels of 1608[2], which were to have such a very great effect on the history of the English Court masque. Ben Jonson in his Preface lays upon the Queen part of the responsibility for the introduction of the antimasque.

'And because Her Majesty (best knowing that a principal part of life in these spectacles lay in their variety) had commanded me to think on some dance, or shew, that might precede hers, and have the place of a foil, or false masque: I was careful to decline, not only from others, but mine own steps in that kind, since the last year, I had an antimasque of boys; and therefore now devised that twelve women, in the habit of hags or witches, sustaining the persons of Ignorance, Suspicion,

1 *The Masque of Queenes Celebrated from the House of Fame.*
2 Cf. *supra*, pp. 113 ff.

Credulity, &c., the opposites to good Fame, should fill that part, not as a masque, but a spectacle of strangeness, producing multiplicity of gesture, and not unaptly sorting with the current and whole fall of the device.'

The origin of the antimasque is uncertain, but obviously Ben Jonson did not regard it as wholly an innovation. The principle of contrast and variety was latent from the first in mummings and disguisings, and many of the Tudor and a few of the Stuart masques were wholly grotesque in character. Both the performers of these grotesque dances and also the dances themselves were sometimes known as 'antics,'[1] and it is therefore possible that the proper form should be 'anticmasque,' a word which occurs in *The Masque of Flowers,* and is used sarcastically by Jonson in *The Masque of Augurs*[2]. Daniel and others use the form 'antemasque,'[3] but this would seem to be due to a misunderstanding caused by the fact that the grotesque dance usually preceded the main performance. Ben Jonson employed the word 'antimasque' because he appreciated the dramatic possibilities of the grotesque dance. In his description of *The Hue and Cry after Cupid,* Chamberlain emphasises the contrast between the 'wags' who danced the matachina 'and acted it very antiquely,' and the 'Twelve Signs' who 'descended from the Zodiac, and played their parts more gravely,' by calling the latter 'Master-Maskers.'[4] This description and the passage quoted above suggest, I think, that Jonson was using a familiar device in a new and striking way, and that this improvement in technique was begun in 1608, and perfected in 1609 in *The Masque of Queens.*

It is, however, impossible to understand the history of the antimasque without considering what was happening on the Continent. It will be remembered that in France at the beginning of the seventeenth century there flourished side by side

---

[1] Cf. 'Then enters Gamboles, dancing a single Anticke wth. a forme. After him, Autumne brings in his Anticke of drunkards.' *Mask of the Four Seasons,* in *Inigo Jones, A Life,* etc., p. 148.

[2] Cf. *infra,* p. 204.

[3] E.g. Chapman, White, and the author of *The Masque of the Twelve Months.* Cf. *infra,* pp. 191, 197, 211.

[4] *Prog. James,* vol. II, p. 189.

PLATE VII

1 ENTRY OF RUSTIC MUSICIANS
In *Les Fées des forêts de Saint-Germain* (Paris, 1625)

2 ENTRY OF THE 'GRAND CAN' AND HIS SERVANTS
In *La Douairière de Billebahaut* (Paris, 1626)

Grotesque scenes typical of the French ballet à entrées

C.L. Archives Photographiques, Paris   *Louvre dessins nos.* 32604, 32640

with the ballet de Cour the simpler and more informal ballet-masquerade which was usually of a grotesque character. *Le Ballet de la Foire Saint-Germain*, which was performed about 1606, is typical of this kind of entertainment, and undoubtedly had no small influence on the English masque[1].

The ballet began with the entrance of a small boy heralding the advent of the Miracle of the Fair of St Germain:

'C'est une homasse
Qui surpasse
Les effects du genre humain.'

Then a midwife entered and danced a ballet round the hall, after which there came in a huge wooden figure representing a fat woman decorated with combs, drums, mirrors, and other fairings of the kind. The midwife then proceeded to draw various sets of dancers out of the wooden figure: four astrologers, who danced a ballet, presented an almanack to the ladies in the audience, and retired; then four painters who pretended to paint in rhythm; then four operateurs[2] (i.e. pedlars) who, as they danced, distributed to the ladies phials of scent and some very coarsely worded recipes. Finally came four pickpockets who pretended to draw the teeth of the pedlars 'et au mesme instant leur couppoient la bourse.' After all these had left the stage Mercury entered with his lute and announced the subject of the main masquerade, which was to be the triumph of constant over inconstant love. First inconstant love entered with eight Knights and performed a lively ballet, then constant love followed with another eight Knights, who danced a more stately entry, and then both troupes combined to dance the grand ballet, which consisted of a series of figures imitating mock combats, until at last 'l'Amour constant triompha de l'Amour volage.'

The arrangement of *Le Ballet de la Foire Saint-Germain* is strikingly like the arrangement of the English Court masque, with its antimasque followed by divers masque-dances, only—and the difference is very important—in the French ballet there is no connection between the two parts of the performance. Later on, as we shall see, the English masque approximated more and more to the inconsequent ballet-masquerade, but for the time the French influence was counteracted by the stubborn genius of Ben Jonson.

[1] Lacroix, *Ballets et Mascarades de Cour de Henri III à Louis XIV*, vol. I, pp. 204 ff. The performance is described by Prunières, *op. cit.* pp. 103, 104.
[2] Cf. the drawing of an 'operator' among the masque designs.

It seems likely then that what happened was this: many English people knew something of what was happening in France, they were aware of the vogue of the ballet-masquerade, and desirous to see something of the kind introduced into the English entertainments, and it was easy to meet their requirements because the principle of contrast was latent in the masque from the beginning; grotesque masques had never been unknown in England, and were always popular. Ben Jonson would feel the pressure of the popular demand, and he also had to obey the express order of the Queen. It seems to me extremely likely that he deliberately invented the term antimasque and used it instead of the form anticmasque in the hope that he would be able to emphasise the fact that the antimasque was meant as a foil, and not as a mere variety entertainment. Perhaps already Ben Jonson felt that danger lay in the antimasque, and that if it were not used with the greatest care it would turn the masque into a farcical pantomime[1].

For the subject of *The Masque of Queens* Ben Jonson was indebted to certain Italian intermedii which were inserted into the *Giudizio di Paridi*, a pastoral comedy composed by Michel Agnolo Buonarotti and staged by Giulio Parigi in October 1608.

The first intermedio represented a wonderful translucent palace, on the top of which stood the Goddess of Fame displaying to the princely pair (i.e. the Grand Duke of Tuscany and his bride) a great company of their illustrious forebears, who sang a madrigal promising a like succession to the royal spouses. Then the door of the palace opened and the heroes entered in order to soar from thence to the heavenly glory that they had deserved. The palace then disappeared, and Fame remaining in the air began to rise up and was hidden in the clouds, and, as she soared, she sang how those who had shone on earth by exalted deeds should go with her to heaven, where she would transform them into eternal stars[2].

The Italian pastoral was acted only a few months before *The*

[1] W. Y. Durand makes a not very successful attempt to prove the antimasque a pre-Jonsonian phenomenon in *A Comedy on Marriage and some early Antimasques* (*Journal of English and Germanic Philology*, vol. VI, pp. 412 ff.).

[2] *Descrittione delle Feste fatte nelle Nozze de' Serenissimi Prencipi di Toscana, D. Cosimo de' Medici, e Maria Maddalena Arciduchessa d' Austria,* pp. 36, 37.

Masque of Queens, and the strong resemblance between the two can hardly be accidental. For his ugly hell Jonson may have taken some hints from the sixth intermedio which represented the Flaming Forge of Vulcan, or perhaps from the hell mouth represented in the *Ballet of the Ungrateful Ladies* which had been acted at the earlier Mantuan festival[1]. The device of drawing the masquers into the dancing place on triumphal chariots may well have been suggested by the elaborate sea cars which appeared on the Arno during the same Florentine marriage. Drawings of these cars appear in the same pamphlet that gives the designs for the intermedii of Parigi. Inigo Jones must, as we shall see, have possessed a pamphlet or pamphlets containing designs and a full description of the proceedings. For the moment he and Ben contented themselves with taking suggestions from the Italian work, and there was no plagiarism. Ben Jonson gives a detailed description of the House of Fame, and clearly it is not a replica of the 'Palazzo della Fama' of Giulio Parigi[2]. Later on, as we shall see, Inigo did not scruple to appropriate the designs of Parigi, but that was after he had gained complete control over the arrangements for the Court masque. Was Ben Jonson exercising a restraining influence upon him? The poet himself was quite ready 'to invade authors like a monarch,' but he was emphatically unwilling to sacrifice poetry and dramatic unity for the sake of reproducing Italian designs upon the stage at Whitehall. I think it will become clear, as we trace the later history of the masque, that this was at least one of the causes of the smouldering hostility between the two men, and of the quarrel that finally broke up their partnership. The difficulty may have been there from the very first, for already in his Preface to *Hymenaei* Jonson remarks scornfully upon the taste of the courtiers who preferred a few Italian herbs to the sound meats provided by himself. It is possible that Jonson's statement that

[1] Cf. *supra*, pp. 112, 113.

[2] In *Designs* there is a reproduction of Parigi's 'Palazzo della Fama,' and also a reproduction of Jones's House of Fame. It is worth noticing that the rough sketches for the *machina versatilis* in the corner of the page are inscribed in Italian: 'la Tribuna mnta [montata?] In vna nugola pieno dell lume con la fame dirutto.' Cf. plate IV and pp. 37, 83.

Fama Bona was represented according to the descriptions of Virgil and Cesare Ripa, his unusually emphatic insistence on Inigo's originality in devising the House of Fame—'the structure and ornament of which (as is profest before) was entirely Master Jones's invention and design....In which he profest to follow that noble description made by Chaucer of the place'—is really the reverberation of an argument in which the poet gained the day and could afford to be generous. But however that may be, the comparison of the *Masque of Queens* with the Italian intermedii and with a typical French ballet such as *La Foire Saint-Germain* increases our respect for Jonson's poetic tact and constructive ability.

The *Masque of Queens* fixed the norm of the masque for some years. From 1609 to 1617 Ben Jonson wrote masque after masque, all showing the same careful structure and unity of design, the antimasque being strictly kept in its place and serving as a real foil to the main action. The chief mark of Jonson's work at this period is the steady development of the literary and dramatic quality of the revels. Sometimes instead of composing an antimasque he will begin with a little comedy of manners, as in the *Irish Masque*, or in *Love Restored*, where he gives a vivid picture of the difficulty that the bourgeoisie experienced in gaining admission to the great Court functions, and where he takes the opportunity of mocking at the Puritans. Besides masques, Jonson wrote several poetic libretti for barriers, which present a striking contrast to the clumsy tasteless devices composed for Elizabethan tournaments.

While Ben Jonson was developing the dramatic side of the masque and barriers, Inigo Jones was perfecting the stage mechanism. In the *Masque of Oberon*, for instance, there were three changes of scene, obviously worked by means of the scena ductilis, and it is interesting that whereas the House of Fame in the *Masque of Queens* was wrought 'as in massy gold,' the palace of Oberon was translucent like Parigi's 'Palazzo della Fama.'

In 1610 the Queen's masque was prepared, not by Ben Jonson but by his rival Daniel. Why this happened is not quite certain.

Daniel's Preface to *Tethys' Festival*[1] is a veiled attack upon his rival, and suggests that Ben Jonson and Inigo Jones had been having difficulties, and that Daniel had taken sides with the architect. Both by his practice and his theory Daniel minimised the importance of the poetry, and emphasised the importance of the spectacular effect. His description of the scenery was given in Inigo's own words, possibly to annoy Ben. Daniel also discredited the practice of using exact scholarship in order to design the classical dresses with accuracy, and repudiated with contempt the idea of justifying himself against criticisms of the courtly spectators by an appeal to antiquity[2]. This was another hit at his rival. Daniel gave Inigo Jones plenty of scope for working out his grandiose designs and scene-changes, and consequently the masque had a very good reception. It was described with approval by John Finet:

'The *Prince's Creation* was upon *Monday* last (i.e. June 1610)....The next Day was graced with a most glorious *Maske*, which was double. In the first, came first in the little Duke of *Yorke* (N.B. representing Zephyrus) between *two great Sea Slaves*, the cheefest of *Neptune's* Servants (i.e. Tritons), attended upon by *twelve little Ladies* (N.B. Daniel says that there were eight and that they represented Naiades or Nymphs of Fountains), all of them the Daughters of Earls or Barons. By one of these Men a Speech was made unto the *King* and *Prince*, expressing the Conceipt of the Maske; by the other, *a Sword* worth 20000 Crowns at the least was put into the Duke of *York's* Hands, who presented the same unto *the Prince* his Brother from the first of those Ladies (i.e. the Queen) which were to follow in the next Maske.' In his speech Triton announced himself as the messenger of Tethys, who was shortly to appear in person attended by certain river nymphs, whom he proceeded to name and describe. 'This done, the *Duke* returned into his former Place in midst of the Stage, and *the little Ladies* performed their Dance to the Amazement of all the Beholders, considering the Tenderness of their Years and the many intricate Changes of the Dance; which was so disposed, that which way soever the Changes went the *little Duke* was still found to be in the midst of these little Dancers. These light Skirmishers having done their *devoir*, in came *the*

---

[1] *Prog. James*, vol. II, pp. 346 ff.; and *Works*, ed. Grosart, vol. III, pp 309 ff.
[2] Cf. *infra*, p. 254.

Princesses; first the *Queen*,'[1] etc., etc.,...The withdrawal of Zephyrus and his Naiads and the appearance of Tethys and her river nymphs coincided with a change of scene, the working of which Inigo Jones concealed by a new device: 'First, at the opening of the Heavens, appeared three circles of lights and glasses, one within another, and came downe in a straight motion of five foote, and then began to move circularly; which lights and motion so occupied the eyes of the spectators, that the manner of altering the scene was scarcely discerned; for in a moment the whole face of it was changed, the port vanished, and Tethys with her Nymphes appeared in their severall cavernes gloriously adorned.' Daniel ended up his masque in an unusual manner. The masque dances and revels were over, the masquers had retired to their caverns and vanished. 'When to avoid the confusion which usually attendeth the desolve of these shewes, and when all was thought to be finisht, followed another entertainement, and was a third shew no lesse delightfull than the rest.' Zephyrus marched in once more, accompanied by his Tritons, and was brought to a sudden halt by a flash of lightning followed by a speech from a Triton, who announced that Mercury had been sent to recall Tethys and her company; then 'Mercury most artificially, and in an exquisite posture, descends, and summons the Duke of Yorke, and six young Noblemen to attend him, and bring back the Queen and her Ladies in their owne forme....Hereupon the Duke of Yorke, with his attendants, departing to performe this service, the lowde musique soundes, and sodainely appeares the Queene's Majesty, in a most pleasant and artificiall grove, which was the third scene; and from thence they march up to the King, conducted by the Duke of Yorke, and the Noblemen, in a very stately manner.'[2]

Daniel concludes his description of *Tethys' Festival* by remarking on the unusual circumstance that all the performers of this masque were of good birth, and that torch-bearers had been omitted on account of the hot weather and the lack of space. The construction of *Tethys' Festival* is undramatic and clumsy, and it looks as if Daniel must have been deliberately adhering to the older type of masque in order to defy Ben Jonson and minimise the value of his innovations. This may have been the motive which led to his use of the term 'antemasque' or 'first show' instead of antimasque, the term which Ben Jonson employed, probably to emphasise the fact that the grotesque dance

---

[1] Winwood, *Memorials*, vol. III, p. 179; *Eliz. Stage*, vol. III, pp. 282, 283.
[2] *Prog. James*, vol. II, pp. 353 ff.; *Works*, ed. Grosart, vol. III, pp. 315 ff. The description of the scene-change is given by Daniel in the words of Inigo Jones.

was organically connected with the main performance. It is, however, possible that the word antemasque had to be employed here because only gentlefolk acted in *Tethys' Festival* and it was therefore necessary that it should be a double masque rather than a masque preceded by a grotesque and intentionally inferior antimasque.

Whatever we may think of the literary defects of Daniel's work (which is redeemed by one beautiful lyric)[1], by contemporary spectators these defects were forgiven, or probably not even noticed, owing to the splendour of the scenery devised by Inigo Jones. What did it matter that the masquers were all described before their appearance and no adequate motive given for their entry, when there were three changes of scene and each scene more magnificent than the last? Jones' prestige was now very high, and in future Ben Jonson was not to have things all his own way, and he might expect to find Inigo becoming a rival rather than a partner. However, in spite of the success of *Tethys' Festival*, the other masque poets followed the lead not of Daniel but of Ben Jonson.

In 1613 the marriage of the Elector Palatine with the Princess Elizabeth was the cause of protracted rejoicings in England. There were numerous grand water-shows on the Thames, splendid fireworks, and a number of masques preceded by a triumphal procession. It was an advertising campaign on a grand scale intended to impress other nations with the sense of England's power and importance[2].

The first of these masques was the *Lords' Masque* composed by Thomas Campion in collaboration with Inigo Jones. Campion represented his masque as a vision of Entheus or Poetic Inspiration, and the great moment of the piece came when certain stars danced to the singing of the beautiful lyric:

> 'Advance your choral motions now,
> You music-loving lights.'

[1] Quoted *infra*, p. 274.

[2] Cf. the description by Taylor, the Thames waterman, who gained some reputation as a poet, in *Prog. James*, vol. II, pp. 527 ff. Considerations of space have made it impossible to consider the diplomatic and political aspect of the Court masque. The masque as a form of diplomatic advertisement is the main theme of M. Sullivan, *Court Masques of James I* (New York, 1913).

According to the humour of this song, the stars moved in an exceeding strange and delightful manner, and I suppose few have ever seen more neat artifice than Master Inigo Jones shewed in contriving their motions, …about the end of this song, the stars suddenly vanished, as if they had been drowned amongst the clouds, and the eight masquers appeared in their habits, which were infinitely rich[1].

The fiery house of Prometheus and the transformation of the stars recall the 'Paradiso' which Leonardo da Vinci had constructed many years before to grace a royal wedding in Milan. It resembles still more closely a Florentine festivity of 1612 in which four noblemen appeared as four Medicean stars.

'Comparse Giove sopra una altissima nube et appresso di lui sedeva l'Inganno amoroso, et più a basso tra le nuvole apparivano le quattro stelle erranti intorno a Giove ritrovate dal sig^r. Galileo Galilei fiorentino, matematico di S. A.....Quando Giove finì il suo canto, si sentì alcuni tuoni per l'aria; scopertosi la nugola apparsero le quattro stelle che presto si trasmutorono in quattro cavalieri che si levorno in piede.'[2]

The construction of this masque is confused and poor, but there is much lyric beauty, and Inigo staged it magnificently. However, it does not seem to have pleased everyone, for Chamberlain writes to Carleton 'that night was the Lords' mask, whereof I hear no great commendation, save only for riches, their devices being long and tedious, and more like a play than a mask.'[3]

The two other masques celebrating the marriage of the Princess Elizabeth were presented by the Inns of Court and were written by Chapman and Beaumont respectively. They were great spectacular triumphs, and the masquers rode in solemn procession to Whitehall, so that as many people as possible might witness their splendour. For Chapman's masque[4] the performers and their assistants met at the house of Sir Edward Phillips, Master of the Rolls, and then set forth.

First there rode fifty gentlemen, with vassals attending. 'Next (a fit distance observed betweene them) marcht a mock-maske of baboons,

---

[1] Op. cit. p. 203.   [2] Solerti, Musica, Ballo, etc., p. 72.
[3] Chamberlain to Carleton, Court and Times of James I, vol. I, p. 226; and Eliz. Stage, vol. III, p. 243.
[4] Printed in Prog. James, vol. II, pp. 566 ff.; Works of George Chapman, ed. R. H. Shepherd (London, 1889), vol. I, pp. 341 ff.; The Plays and Poems of George Chapman, ed. T. M. Parrott (London, 1914), vol. II, pp. 435 ff.

attired like fantasticall travailers, in Neapolitane sutes and great ruffes, all horst with asses and dwarf palfries, with yellow foot-cloathes, and casting cockle-demois about, in courtesie, by way of lardges; torches boarn on either hand of them, lighting their state as ridiculously as the rest nobly.' Then went the two great triumphal cars, 'adorn'd with great maske-heads, festones, scroules, and antick leaves, every part inricht with silver and golde.'[1] In these chariots went the musicians six in each dressed like Virginian sun-worshipping priests; then the chief masquers who were dressed as Virginian princes, and in front of the masquers torchbearers who were also dressed as Indians.

The masque itself must have been well worth seeing. The opening up of the great rock which revealed the masquers in a shining mine of gold, the singing and worshipping of the Virginian priests while the sun set in a golden evening sky, must have been really beautiful. The performance seems to have been appreciated by contemporaries[2] although some people found the speeches too long[3].

Beaumont's masque is interesting on account of Sir Francis Bacon's share in its production:

On Tuesday it came to Gray's Inn and the Inner Temple's turn to come with their Mask, whereof Sir Francis Bacon was the chief contriver; and because the former came on horseback and open chariots, they made choice to come by water from Winchester-place in Southwark, which suited well with their device, which was the Marriage of the River of Thames to Rhine; and their shew by water was very gallant by reason of infinite store of lights very curiously set and placed; and many boats and barges with devices of light of lamps with three peals of ordnance, one at their taking water, another in the Temple-garden, and the last at their landing; which passage by water cost them better than £.300. They were received at the Privy Stairs; a great expectation there was that they should every way excel their competitors that went before them, both in devise, daintiness of apparel, and, above all, in dancing, wherein they are held excellent, and esteemed the properer men. But by what ill planet it fell out, I know not; they came home as they went without doing anything; the reason whereof I cannot yet learn thoroughly, but only that the Hall was so full that it was not possible to avoid it, or make room for them; besides that most of the Ladies were in the Galleries to see them land, and could not get in. But

[1] *Prog. James*, vol. II, p. 567.
[2] *Court and Times of James I*, vol. I, pp. 226, 227.
[3] Cf. *infra*, p. 257.

the worst of all was, that the King was so wearied and sleepy with setting
up almost two whole nights before, that he had no edge to it. Whereupon,
Sir Francis Bacon ventured to entreat his Majesty, that by this disgrace
he would not as it were bury them quick; and I hear the King should
answer, that then they must bury him quick, for he could last no longer;
but withall gave them very good words, and appointed them to come
again on Saturday. But the grace of the Mask is quite gone, when their
apparel hath been already showed, and their devices vented, so that
how it will fall out God knows; for they are much discouraged and out
of countenance, and the world says it comes to pass after the old proverb,
'the properer men the worse luck.'[1]

However, when it was performed it won great applause and
approbation from the King and all the company. It was well
written in good blank verse, as was to be expected since Francis
Beaumont was the author. The device was as follows:

'Jupiter and Juno, willing to do honour to the Marriage of...
Thamesis and Rhine, employ...Mercury and Iris for that purpose....
Mercury...springs forth an anti-masque all of spirits or divine natures;
but yet not of one kind or livery (because that had been so much in
use heretofore); but, as it were, in consort, like to broken music....He
raiseth four of the Naiades out of the fountains, and bringeth down
fire (four?) of the Hyades out of the clouds to dance. Hereupon Iris
scoffs at Mercury, for that he had devised a Dance but of one sex, which
could have no life; but Mercury...calleth forth out of the groves four
Cupids, and brings down from Jupiter's altar four statues of gold and
silver to dance with the Nymphs and Stars. In which Dance, the Cupids
being blind and the statues having but half-life put into them, and
retaining still somewhat of their old nature, giveth fit occasion to new
and strange varieties both in the music and paces. This was the First
Anti-masque.
    Then Iris,...in token that the Match should likewise be blessed with
the love of the common people, calls to Flora...to bring in a May dance,
or rural dance, consisting likewise not of any suited persons, but of a
confusion or commixture of all such persons as are natural and proper
for country sports. This is the Second Anti-masque.
    Then Mercury and Iris...seem to leave their contention; and Mer-
cury...brings down the Olympian Knights, intimating that Jupiter
having...revived the Olympian Games...had enjoined them, before
they fell to their Games, to do honour to these Nuptials. The Olympian

    [1] Chamberlain to Carleton, in *Prog. James*, vol. ii, pp. 589 ff.; *Court and
Times of James I*, vol. i, pp. 227, 228 (cf. also p. 229); *Eliz. Stage*, vol. iii
p. 234.

Games portend to the Match celebrity, victory and felicity. This was the main Masque.

The fabric was a mountain with two descents, and severed with two traverses. At the entrance of the King, the first traverse was drawn and the lower descent of the mountain discovered, which was the pendant of a hill to life, with diverse boscages and grovets upon the steep or hanging ground thereof; and at the foot of the hill...fountains running with water, and bordered with sedges and water flowers....

The Statues enter....At their coming, the musick changed from violins to hautboys, cornets, &c. and the air of the musick was utterly turned into a soft time, with drawing notes, excellently expressing their natures; and the measure likewise was fitted into the same, and the Statues placed in such several postures, sometimes all together in the centre of the Dance, and sometimes in the four utmost angles, as was very graceful, besides the novelty. And so concluded the First Anti-Masque....

The Second Anti-masque rusheth in, they dance their measure, and as rudely depart; consisting of a Pedant; May Lord, May Lady; Serving man, Chamber-maid; a Country Clown or Shepherd, Country Wench; an Host, Hostess; a He-baboon, She-baboon; a He-fool, She-fool, ushering them in; all these persons appareled to the life, the men issuing out of one side of the boscage, and the women from the other. The musick was extremely well-fitted, having such a spirit of country jollity as can hardly be imagined; but the perpetual laughter and applause was above the musick. The Dance likewise was of the same strain; and the dancers, or rather actors, expressed every one their part so naturally and aptly, as when a man's eye was caught with the one, and then past on to the other, he could not satisfy himself which did best. It pleased his Majesty to call for it again at the end, as he did likewise for the First Anti-Masque, but one of the Statues by that time was undressed.'[1]

Francis Bacon may possibly have been concerned in the production of the *Masque of Flowers*[2], by which the gentlemen of Gray's Inn celebrated the disgraceful marriage between the Earl of Somerset and the Countess of Essex.

'The Sunne, willing to doe honour to a Marriage betweene two noble persons of the greatest island of his universal empire, writeth his Letter of Commission to the two seasons of the year, the Winter and the Spring,...directing the Winter to present them with sports, such as are commonly called by the name of Christmasse sportes, or Carnavall sportes; and the Spring with other sportes of more magnificence.

And more especially, that Winter...take knowledge of a certaine

[1] *Prog. James*, vol. II, pp. 593 ff.   [2] *Ibid.* pp. 735 ff.

Challenge...betweene Silenus and Kawasha upon this point, that Wine was more worthy then Tobacco....This to be tried at two weapons, at Song and at Dance...in the dayes of the solemnitie of the same Marriage.

The same Letter containeth a second speciall direction to the Spring, that whereas of ancient time certaine beautifull youths had bin transformed from Men to Flowers, and had so continued till this time, that now they should be returned againe into men, and present themselves in Maske at the same Marriage.

All this is accordingly performed, and first the two Seasons Invierno and Primavera come in, and receive their dispatch from the Sunne, by Gallus, the Sunne's Messenger; thereupon Winter brings in the Challenge, consisting of two Anticke-ma[s]kes, the Anticke-maske of the Song, and the Anticke-maske of the Dance.

Then the Spring brings in the Maske itself, and there is first seene in the fabrique a faire garden upon a descending ground, and at the height thereof there is a stately long arbour or bower arched upon pillars, wherein the Maskers are placed, but are not discovered at the first, but there appeare onely certaine great tufts of flowers betwixt the collumnes. Those flowers upon the charm doe vanish, and so the Maskers appeare every one in the space inter-column of his arch.'[1]

It is worth noting that among the antimasquers appears Pantaloon, a well-known character of the Italian improvised comedy, and also characters representing various trades or professions in the realistic French manner. It is also interesting that 'morascoes' were danced on this occasion during the revels when ordinary ballroom dancing took place[2].

The same infamous marriage was celebrated by Campion in his *Squires' Masque*[3]. The construction of this is worse than usual, and even the lyrics are not particularly attractive. Inigo Jones did not plan the scenery.

'The workmanship whereof was undertaken by M. Constantine, an Italian, architect to our late Prince Henry: but he being too much of himself, and no way to be drawn to impart his intentions, failed so far in the assurance he gave that the main invention, even at the last cast, was of force drawn into far narrower compass than was from the beginning intended.'

---

[1] *Prog. James*, vol. II, pp. 736 ff.   [2] *Ibid*. p. 744.
[3] *The description of a Maske: presented in the Banqueting roome at Whitehall, on Saint Stephens night last, At the Mariage of the Right Honourable the Earle of Somerset: And the right noble the Lady Frances Howard,* reprinted in *Works of Thomas Campion,* ed. A. H. Bullen, p. 217.

Apart from the employment of an Italian as architect, this masque is interesting because it shows the tendency of the anti-masque to turn into mere pantomime. One of the antimasques is reminiscent of the *Ballet of the Winds* performed in the Floren-tine festivities of 1608[1], but this resemblance may be merely accidental. After the revels at the end of the performance, 'Straight in the Thames appeared four barges with skippers in them and withal this song was sung:

> Come ashore, come, merry mates,
> With your nimble heels and pates:' etc.

At the conclusion of this song the twelve skippers in red caps danced 'a brave and lively dance, shouting and triumphing after their manner.'[2]

In 1617, *Cupid's Banishment*, a very curious masque written by Robert White, was presented to Queen Anne by 'younge gentlewomen of the Ladies' Hall, in Deptford at Greennwich,' apparently a kind of finishing school for aristocratic girls num-bering among its pupils two godchildren of the Queen. The plot of the masque was grounded upon the 'choosinge of a Kinge and Queene by Fortune's doome; which is a sporte our litle Ladies use on Candlemasse night,' and it expressed the idea that Hymen can bring about a chaste union of hearts among Diana's nymphs, even in an 'academy Where Modesty doth onely sway as Governesse,' and where Cupid is naturally kept at arm's length. The plan of *Cupid's Banishment* differed from that of an ordinary masque, for the masquers, two of whom sang songs, were revealed at the beginning of the proceedings, and remained in full view of the audience until the end of the masque, when they descended to dance in letters Anna Regina, Jacobus Rex, and Carolus P., and other figures devised by 'Mr. Ounslo, Tutor to the Ladies Hall.' It is odd that this modest academy should have chosen an 'Ante-maske, all of Bacchus' children,' who showed 'the severall humers of drunkards, and many pretty figures befitting that vayne.'[3]

---

[1] Cf. *supra*, p. 114; *Descrittione*, pp. 52 ff.
[2] *Op. cit.* p. 226.
[3] *Prog. James*, vol. III, pp. 283 ff.

All these masques written at this time by writers other than Ben Jonson show the increasing popularity of the antimasque and the tendency to multiply the grotesque dances and to emulate the bizarre inconsequence of the French ballet-masquerade; they help us to realise how strenuously Ben Jonson was resisting popular pressure in his attempt to keep the antimasque in a subordinate position. Gradually, however, even Ben was forced to give way, and the masques prepared by him in the year 1617 mark a fresh stage in his submission to foreign influence. It is significant that this year the Queen's French musicians performed a ballet at the English Court[1].

Although Chamberlain 'heard no great speach nor commendations of the maske neither before nor since,'[2] there are few of Ben Jonson's masques more charming than the *Vision of Delight* which was presented at Court in 1617.

For the first scene there was 'A street in perspective of fair building discovered.' Into this 'Delight is seen to come as afar off, accompanied with Grace, Love, Harmony, Revel, Sport, Laughter: and followed by Wonder.' Delight in 'stylo recitativo' then summons the antimasques:

'Let your shows be new as strange,
Let them oft and sweetly vary;
Let them haste so to their change
As the seers may not tarry.
Too long t'expect the pleasing'st sight,
Doth take away from the delight.'

After this comes the antimasque, 'A She-monster delivered of six Burratines, that dance with six Pantalones,' and then Delight chants once more:

'All sour and sullen looks away,
That are the servants of the day;
Our sports are of the humorous Night,
Who feeds the stars that give her light,
And useth than her wont more bright,
To help the *Vision of Delight*.'

The chanting continues while Night rises with her chariot and the Moon also, and then Night 'hovering over the place' sings:

'Break, Phant'sie, from thy cave of cloud,
And spread thy purple wings;
Now all thy figures are allowed,
And various shapes of things;

[1] Cf. Brotanek, *op. cit.* p. 286.   [2] Sullivan, *op. cit.* p. 105.

> Create of airy forms a stream,
> It must have blood, and nought of phlegm;
> And though it be a waking dream,
> CHORUS. Yet let it like an odour rise
> To all the Senses here,
> And fall like sleep upon their eyes,
> Or music in their ear.'

Then the scene changes to cloud, from which Phantasy breaks forth and summons the next antimasque of Phantasms in a long speech of nonsensical doggerel. After the dance of the Phantasms an Hour descends and the scene changes to the Bower of Zephyrus, while Peace sings:

> 'Why look you so, and all turn dumb,
> To see the opener of the New Year come?
> My presence rather should invite,
> And aid and urge, and call to your delight;
> The many pleasures that I bring
> Are all of youth, of heat and life and spring,...
> CHO. We see, we hear, we feel, we taste,
> We smell the change in every flow'r,
> We only wish that all could last,
> And be as new still as the hour.'

But even as Wonder expresses boundless astonishment, Phantasy promises fresh surprises, and, 'to a loud music, the Bower opens, and the Masquers are discovered as the Glories of the Spring.' Wonder exclaiming, 'Whose power is this? What god?' Phantasy explains that it is all due to the presence of the Monarch. The Masquers then descend, dance their entry and revel with the ladies, after which Aurora appears (the Night and Moon being descended) and this epilogue follows:

> 'AUR. I was not wearier where I lay
> By frozen Tithon's side to-night;
> Than I am willing now to stay,
> And be a part of your delight.
> But I am urged by the Day,
> Against my will, to bid you come away.
> CHO. They yield to time, and so must all.
> As night to sport, day doth to action call;
> Which they the rather do obey,
> Because the Morn with roses strews the way.'

For the idea of this masque Jonson was almost certainly indebted to the description of Florentine revels to which we have already referred. Among the many triumphal chariots which added to the splendour of the wedding tournament of 1579 was the Car of Night, which was drawn into the Pitti Palace by two black animals.

In the car was the figure of Night asleep, and overhead hovered her son Aether, while 'Nel mezo erano molte ombre, e fantasmi fatte di velo negro, in guisa, che traspareuano, e con diuerse attitudini mostra-uano hauer paura, & *delle loro bocche vsciua vn negro fumo, ma di soaue odore.*' When the chariot of Night had arrived in front of the royal box it passed, and Night awaking from her sleep sang a madrigal to the accompaniment of a viol:

> '*Fvor dell' humido nido*
> *Vscita con le mie presaghe schiere*
> *Di Fantasmi, di Sogni, e di Chimere*
> *La Notte io son....*'[1]

This description I feel sure struck Jonson's imagination and suggested to him the invocation to Phantasy made by Night and the Chorus. But he was still more deeply influenced by the *Notte d' Amore*, a series of musical spectacles or 'vigils' which were performed during the Florentine festivities of 1608 at a ball held in the Palazzo Vecchio.

The guests were dancing, when suddenly a curtain fell from the front of the stage and displayed a view of the western quarter of Florence with its neighbouring mountains, but more woody than in reality. Across this scene came Hesperus on a floating cloud, who called upon the Night to give rest to weary mortals, for the sun was hidden and had yielded to her his power. Night thereupon appeared, bringing with her Oblivion, Silence, Repose, Sweet Sleep. But then Love also arrived, bringing with him Play, Laughter, Dancing, Song, Contentment and a band of Cupids, and he prayed Night to grant him dominion over these few hours; because all the beauties assembled together had made, in spite of her, a new day. Night yielded and departed with her troop, whereupon Love and his followers, having descended among the spectators, sang a chorus and danced in time to their singing. This brought the first vigil to an end, and the ballroom dancing began again, for every vigil was ended by the dancing together of lords and ladies.

The scene of the second vigil was *a lovely garden 'pieno d' alberi fioriti, e verdi compartiti da prati, e quadri, e fonti, e logge, e cerchiate, e simili vaghezze ingannatrici degli occhi.' Stars appeared in the sky, 'e non riuedendo in quel sito l' oscurità solita della Notte, vna d' esse*

[1] *Feste nelle Nozze*, etc., pp. 24-26.

domandò oue ell' era, ò se pure il Sol retrogradaua.' The Moon then appeared and, marvelling at the splendour she beheld, bade the Stars descend to admire these new wonders. Then Endymion entered the garden and, seeing his beloved Moon, adjured her by their ancient love, to descend on to that spot where Love had gathered together the flower of lovers and of beauties, and to spend the calm nocturnal hours in joy and gladness. Then Endymion, the Moon and the Stars danced and sang together, Love added his summons to mirth and dancing and the second vigil ended.

More hours passed by, the guests danced and made merry in company with the new masquers, until at last they grew weary, and to revive their flagging interest the scene changed, and displayed '*Castelli in aria, monti, rupi, mari, edifici ardenti, e rouinanti, con huomini, altri, che nauicauano, altri cadeuano, con altre varietà d' apparenze di quelle, che si soglion' esser rappresentate da' sogni, tutto sostentato dall' arco Celeste.' The nocturnal Hours flew across the scene and one of them called loudly upon Dreams and upon Morpheus 'rapprēsētator delle figure humane, e Itatone delle mostruose, e Panto¹ delle materiali.'* Upon this the Dreams appeared—monstrous, stunted, unfinished forms—who danced together until one of them asked the flying Hours whither they were being driven, for this was no place for them, here where the Lovers—like so many Arguses—were keeping a delightful vigil. But Love told the Dreams that although the Lovers present were happy and must not be troubled by vain visions, nevertheless the Dreams might amuse them by dancing among themselves. Thereupon they began an extravagant dance, imitating various actions, but always starting another movement before they had finished the first. Then in chorus, Love and his followers dismissed the monstrous Dreams and bade them go away and disturb those who are asleep:

'E noi tornando, à gl' amorosi inuiti,
Guidiam balli d' Amor, balli graditi.'

The dancing now began again until the approach of daybreak, when the scene changed back again to the garden, and the Morning Breeze was seen in the air. Summoned by the Morning Breeze Aurora arrived, leaving Tithonus alone in the sky to bewail the loss of his bride and to shower curses upon the Morning Breeze. Aurora was induced by Love to descend among the spectators and so delay for a while the coming of the Sun. Then the Lovers, the Stars, Endymion, Aurora and the Morning Breeze, all danced and sang together and invoked blessings upon the princely assembly. But at last Aurora heralded the coming of the Sun, and one by one all the deities departed, bewailing the

¹ For a discussion of the forms *Itatone* and *Panto* cf. Welsford, *Italian Influence on the English Court Masque*, in *M.L.R.* vol. XVIII, No. 4, Oct. 1923, p. 404, note 1.

transitory nature of all earthly happiness. Then finally appeared Apollo bringing in the Day, and ready to drive off the company to perform actions worthy of the light. After a brief argument with Apollo, Love and his followers went out singing

'Oh' chiaro, oh' lieto giorno...,' etc.[1]

There is, I believe, no doubt about Jonson's indebtedness to this performance. The general idea of his *Vision* is similar to that of the *Notte d' Amore*. In both pieces Night is invoked, Phantasms are summoned to perform grotesque dances, an Hour appears, great wonder is expressed at all the glories of the time, which are felt to be due, in the case of the Florentine spectacle, to the presence of an assembly of such noble lovers, in the case of the English masque, to the presence of King James, and finally in both pieces Aurora appears, the audience is dispersed and dismissed cheerfully to the day's work. In both pieces the chorus is sung by personifications of the more cheerful emotions. The nonsense talked by Ben Jonson's Phantasy may have a slightly sarcastic reference to the queer unfinished dances of the monstrous Phantasms in the *Notte d' Amore*, and his poetical epilogue was probably suggested by the dramatic business of the last vigil[2]. In all this there is nothing that can be called plagiarism; Jonson has taken suggestions from the *Notte d' Amore*, but he has not made any actual borrowings, nor has he imitated it at all closely, nor is it the only source of his inspiration.

The *Vision of Delight* shows the influence of France as well as of Italy. The first antimasque is obviously an imitation of the first part of the *Ballet de la Foire St-Germain*[3], in which the

---

[1] *Descrittione delle Feste*, etc., pp. 28–32 (from which all the following descriptions and quotations are taken). For the poetical libretto cf. *Notte Damore* del S. Francesco Cini. Rappresentata tra Danze, nelle Nozze del Sereniss. D. Cosimo de' Medici, Principe di Toscana e della Serenissima Arciduchessa Maria Maddalena d' Austria, In Firenze l' Anno MDCVIII, reprinted in Solerti, *Musica Ballo*, etc., pp. 263 ff. I have italicised those passages which have been imitated by the author of *Luminalia*. Cf. *infra*, pp. 236 ff.

[2] Of course, I am aware that there is a strong family likeness between all masques, ballets, intermedii, etc., which are usually based on a few stock themes. Nevertheless my impression of Jonson's indebtedness to specific Italian works has been strengthened, not weakened, by a fairly wide reading of Italian, French and English descriptions of Court entertainments.

[3] Cf. *supra*, p. 185.

midwife brought various groups of dancers out of the huge
wooden female figure representing the Fair. Jonson's Burratines
and Pantaloons are stock figures of the Italian *commedia dell' arte*,
but they may have reached England by way of France, for the
Italian actors were popular both at Parisian fairs and at the
Parisian Court. It was not long after this time that the *Mountebanks' Masque*[1] was performed at Gray's Inn, and although only
a fragment of it remains it is sufficient to show that it was deeply
influenced by the French ballet, and particularly by this ballet
which influenced Jonson's *Vision*. The sayings of Paradox, and
the recipes of the Mountebanks, recall the recipes and almanacks
that were distributed among the audience at the French entertainment. Many years later some of these French recipes were
translated by Davenant for his masque *Salmacida Spolia*.

The introduction of two antimasques in the *Vision* shows that
Jonson was having to accommodate himself to the prevailing
fashion, and compose his masques *à la mode de France*. He
resented the necessity. Phantasy's speech has a satirical ring,
and in *Neptune's Triumph*, a masque performed some years later,
Jonson introduces a cook who considers himself equal if not
superior to the poet, and makes himself responsible for the antimasques.

'Cook. But where's your Antimasque now all this while?
　　　I hearken after them.
Poet. Faith, we have none.
Cook. None!
Poet. None, I assure you, neither do I think them
　　　A worthy part of presentation,
　　　Being things so heterogene to all device,
　　　Mere by-works, and at best outlandish nothings.
Cook. O, you are all the heaven awry, sir!
　　　For blood of poetry running in your veins,
　　　Make not yourself so ignorantly simple.
　　　Because, sir, you shall see I am a poet,
　　　No less than cook, and that I find you want
　　　A special service here, an antimasque,
　　　I'll fit you with a dish out of the kitchen,
　　　Such as I think will take the present palates,

[1] *Prog. Eliz.* vol. III, pp. 332 ff.

> A metaphorical dish! and do but mark
> How a good wit may jump with you. Are you ready, child?
> (Had there been masque, or no masque, I had made it.)
> Child of the boiling-house!
>
> . . . . . .
>
> And, brother poet, though the serious part
> Be yours, yet envy not the cook his art.'

Again in the *Masque of Augurs* after John Urson has danced with his bears, the Groom asked: 'But what has all this to do with our mask?' and Vangoose answered:

'O sir, all de better vor an antickmask, de more absurd it be, and vrom de purpose, it be ever all de better. If it go from de nature of de ting, it is de more art: for dere is art, and dere is nature, yow sall see. *Hocos Pocos! paucos palabros!*'

And again in *Time Vindicated*, when Fame protests against the kind of entertainment desired by those curious people Ears, Eyes, and Nose, as

> '...fit freedoms
> For lawless prentices on a Shrove-Tuesday,
> When they compel the Time to serve their riot;
> For drunken wakes and strutting bear-baitings,
> That savour only of their own abuses,'

the answer comes

> 'EYES. Why, if not those, then something to make sport.
> EARS. We only hunt for novelty, not truth,'

and Fame concedes with reluctance:

> 'I'll fit you, though the Time faintly permit it.'

The foreign influence was shown, not only in the development of the antimasque, but also in the tendency to make the masque operatic. In the *Vision* Delight declaims her first speech in recitative, a style which as we have seen originated in Italy, and since the year 1610 had ousted all spoken monologue and dialogue from the French ballet de Cour. A few months after the performance of the *Vision of Delight*, Ben Jonson's *Masque of Lethe* was presented to the Baron de la Tour, Ambassador Extraordinary of the French King; and we are told that 'the whole Masque was sung after the Italian manner, *stylo recitativo*, by Master Nicholas Lanier (i.e. a Frenchman frequently employed in the preparation of masques); who ordered and made both the scene and the music.'¹ Jonson's poetry is particularly charming, and so far is he from allowing the grotesque element to predominate that he makes the masquers dance the antimasque as well as the main masque²; the former being performed while they are still supposed to be ghosts 'in several gestures as they lived in love, the latter after they have drunk a draught of Lethe, and have in consequence been born again as men.'

In 1618 Ben Jonson and Inigo Jones composed *Pleasure reconciled to Virtue,* the performance of which was a very important social event, since it marked the first appearance of Charles, Prince of Wales, as chief masquer. The masque, however, seems to have given little satisfaction: '...it came far short of the expectacōn & Mr Inigo Jones hath lost in his reputacōn in regard some extraordinary deuise was looked for (it being the Prince his first Mask) and a poorer was never sene.'³ Nor did Ben Jonson fare better. Sir Edward Harwood mentions the antimasque 'beinge of little boyes dressed like bottells and a man in a tonne wᶜʰ the bottells drew out and tost too and fro, not ill liked the conceite good the poetry not so....'⁴ And according to Nathaniel Brent 'diuers thinke fit he (i.e. Ben Jonson) should returne to his ould trade of bricke laying againe.'⁵ The masque was described in detail by the Venetian Busino, and his account of it is particularly interesting, because it enables us to compare the description left by the poet with the impression made by the performance on an eye-witness. It must, however, be remembered that much of the meaning of the masque would be obscure to a foreigner who could not easily follow the speeches and

---

¹ Jonson, *op. cit.* vol. III, p. 112.
² It is possible that in this too we have a trace of the French influence. Sometimes in the French ballets courtiers would take part in one or more of the *Entrées,* and then retire and change their clothes, ready to re-appear suitably dressed for the *Grand Ballet.* Cf. Prunières, *op. cit.* pp. 165, 166.
³ W. Sherburne, in *State Papers, Domestic, James I,* vol. xcv, No. 10. Quoted in Sullivan, *Court Masques of James I,* p. 118.
⁴ Sir Edward Harwood to Sir Dudley Carleton, in *S.P.D. James I,* vo . xcv, No. 8. Quoted in Sullivan, *op. cit.* p. 118.
⁵ Nathaniel Brent to Dudley Carleton, in *S.P.D. James I,* vol. xcv, No. 12. Quoted in Sullivan, *op. cit.* p. 118.

songs. A slightly summarised version of Busino's letter is given in the *Calendar of State Papers*:

'In the middle of the theatre there appeared a fine and spacious area carpeted all over with green cloth. In an instant a large curtain dropped, painted to represent a tent of gold cloth with a broad fringe; the background was of canvas painted blue, powdered all over with golden stars. This became the front arch of the stage, forming a drop scene, and on its being removed there appeared first of all Mount Atlas, whose enormous head was alone visible up aloft under the very roof of the theatre; it rolled up its eyes and moved itself very cleverly. As a foil to the principal ballet and masque they had some mummeries performed in the first act; for instance, a very chubby Bacchus appeared on a car drawn by four gownsmen, who sang in an undertone before his Majesty. There was another stout individual on foot, dressed in red in short clothes, who made a speech, reeling about like a drunkard, tankard in hand, so that he resembled Bacchus's cupbearer. This first scene was very gay and burlesque. Next followed twelve extravagant masquers, one of whom was in a barrel, all but his extremities, his companions being similarly cased in huge wicker flasks, very well made. They danced awhile to the sound of the cornets and trumpets, performing various and most extravagant antics. These were followed by a gigantic man representing Hercules with his club, who strove with Antaeus and performed other feats. Then came twelve masked boys in the guise of frogs. They danced together, assuming sundry grotesque attitudes. After they had all fallen down, they were driven off by Hercules. Mount Atlas then opened, by means of two doors, which were made to turn, and from behind the hills of a distant landscape the day was seen to dawn, some gilt columns being placed along either side of the scene, so as to aid the perspective and make the distance seem greater. Mercury next appeared before the king and made a speech. After him came a guitar player in a gown, who sang some trills, accompanying himself with his instrument. He announced himself as some deity, and then a number of singers, dressed in long red gowns to represent high priests, came on the stage, wearing gilt mitres. In the midst of them was a goddess in a long white robe and they sang some jigs which we did not understand. It is true that, spoiled as we are by the graceful and harmonious music of Italy, the composition did not strike us as very fine. Finally twelve cavaliers, masked, made their appearance, dressed uniformly....These twelve descended together from above the scene in the figure of a pyramid, of which the prince formed the apex. When they reached the ground the violins, to the number of twenty-five or thirty began to play their airs. After they had made an obeisance to his Majesty, they began to dance in very good time, preserving for a while the same pyramidical figure, and with a variety of steps. Afterwards they changed places with each other in various ways, but ever ending the jump together. When this was over, each took his lady, the prince pairing with the principal one among those who were ranged in a row ready to dance, and the others doing the like in succession, all making obeisance to his Majesty first and then to each other. They performed every sort of ballet and dance of every country whatsoever.... Last of all they danced the Spanish dance, one at a time, each with his lady, and being well nigh tired they began to lag, whereupon the king, who is naturally choleric, got impatient and shouted aloud Why don't they dance? What did they make me come here for? Devil take you all, dance. Upon this, the Marquis of Buckingham, his Majesty's favourite, immediately sprang forward, cutting a score of lofty and very minute capers, with so much grace and agility that he not only appeased the ire of his angry lord, but rendered himself the admiration and delight of every body....The prince, however, excelled them all in bowing, being very formal in making his obeisance both to the king and to the lady with whom he danced, nor was he once seen to do a step out of time when dancing, whereas one cannot perhaps say so much for the others. Owing to his youth he has not yet much breath, nevertheless he cut a few capers very gracefully....The king now rose from his chair, took the ambassadors along with him, and after passing through a number of chambers and galleries he reached a hall where the usual collation was spread for the performers, a light being carried before him. After he had glanced all round the table he departed, and forthwith the parties concerned pounced upon the prey like so many harpies. The table was covered almost entirely with seasoned pasties and very few sugar confections. There were some large figures, but they were of painted pasteboard for ornament. The repast was served upon glass plates or dishes and at the first assault they upset the table and the crash of glass platters reminded me precisely of a severe hail storm at Midsummer smashing the window glass. The story ended at half past two in the morning and half disgusted and weary we returned home.

Should your lordships writhe on reading or listening to this tediousness you may imagine the weariness I feel in relating it.'[1]

Pleasure reconciled to Virtue was performed a second time, so that the Queen, who had been absent from the Court at Twelfth Night, might see it. Ben and Inigo succeeded on this occasion in vindicating their reputation by composing new and lively antimasques.

[1] *Calendar of State Papers, Venetian,* vol. XV, 1617–1619, pp. 110 ff. For a fuller version see Sullivan, *op. cit.* pp. 114 ff., quoting *Venetian Transcripts,* vol. CXLII, p. 68.

We now turn to a group of masques, some of them widely separated in time, but linked together by similarities of style or subject-matter, and most of them standing more or less outside the main stream of courtly tradition.

In 1619 Thomas Middleton composed the *Masque of Heroes*[1], which was presented by gentlemen of the Inner Temple 'as an Entertainement for many worthy Ladies.'

The masque opens with the entrance of Doctor Almanack, coming from the funeral of December or the Old Year, who engages in an amusing conversation with Fasting Day and Plum Porridge, and is then joined first by New Year, and then by Time, who is thus greeted:

> 'NEW YEAR. ...O, I honour that
> Reverent figure! may I ever think
> How precious thou'rt in youth, how rarely
> Redeem'd in age!'

Then follow two antimasques (spelt ante-masques in the list of *dramatis personae*), the first of Candlemas Day, Shrove Tuesday, Lent, Ill May-Day, Midsummer-Eve, and First Dog-Day, the second of three Good Days, three Bad Days, and two Indifferent Days. These 'pleasures of low births and natures,' not being grateful to the New Year, he is comforted by Doctor Almanack by disclosing to him the secret that:

> 'By the sweet industry of Harmony,
> Your white and glorious friend;
> Even very deities have conspir'd to grace
> Your fair inauguration. ...

At which loud music heard, the first cloud vanishing, Harmony is discovered, with her sacred choir...' and sings:

> 'New Year, New Year, hark, hearken to me!
> I am sent down
> To crown
> Thy wishes with me:
> Thy fair desires in virtue's court are fil'd;
> The goodness of thy thought
> This blessed work hath wrought,
> Time shall be reconcil'd.
> Thy spring shall in all sweets abound,
> Thy summer shall be clear and sound,
> Thy autumn swell the barn and loft
> With corn and fruits, ripe, sweet, and soft;
> And in thy winter, when all go,
> Thou shalt depart as white as snow.'

---

[1] *Works of Tho. Middleton*, ed. A. Dyce (London, 1840), vol. v, pp. 133 ff.

'Then a second cloud vanishing, the Masquers themselves are discovered sitting in arches of clouds, being nine in number, heroes deified for their virtues,' and the song is continued.

The masquers then descend and dance, encouraged by Harmony:

> 'Move on, move on, be still the same,
> You beauteous sons of brightness;
> You add to honour spirit and flame,
> To virtue grace and whiteness;
> You whose every little motion
> May learn strictness more devotion...' etc.

The revels follow, and then 'Time re-entering, thus closes all.

> TIME. The morning gray
> Bids come away;
> Every lady should begin
> To take her chamber, for the stars are in.

(Then making his honour to the ladies)

> Live long the miracles of times and years,
> Till with those heroes you sit fix'd in spheres!'

The author himself comments on the simplicity of his plot:

> 'This nothing owes to any tale or story
> With which some writer pieces up a glory;
> I only made the time, they sat to see,
> Serve for the mirth itself, which was found free;
> And herein fortunate, that's counted good,
> Being made for ladies, ladies understood.'

This piece of Middleton's is by no means the only masque in which the plot is nothing but a symbolical setting forth either of the particular holiday which was being celebrated, or else more generally of the flight of time, the succession of day and night, the round of seasons, months, and festivals. For instance the *Masque of the Twelve Months*[1], which was probably performed in honour of Prince Henry about seven years earlier,

---

[1] Printed in *Inigo Jones, A Life*, etc., pp. 131 ff. For a discussion of the date of this masque cf. *Eliz. Stage*, vol. IV, p. 58. For a discussion of the possible connection between the masque and a design by Inigo Jones cf. W. J. Lawrence, *Inigo Jones—An Identification*, in *Times Lit. Supp.*, 24 Oct. 1924, and a letter in reply from W. W. Greg, *The Masque of the Twelve Months, Times Lit. Supp.*, 30 Oct. 1924. The design is described in *Designs*, p. 85, and is tentatively assigned to Carew's masque *Coelum Britannicum*. I do not think the design corresponds to the description of the scene of the *Masque of the Twelve Months*, which consisted of a heart-shaped fortress, stuck with banners and plumes, situated in a bower.

shows 'the full pompe of the yeare, Contracted, yett much amplified here.'

The first scene represents a bower into which Madge Howlet enters 'hooting, going vp towards ye King,' but is hailed by Pigwiggen 'You, myne hostesse of the Ivie bushe! What make ye hooting in theis walkes?' Pigwiggen has been sent by the fairy Queen to attend upon 'Bewty, who in her charmed fort sittes close hereby, enthron'd, and raignes this night great President of all those princely revells that in ye honor of our fairy king are here to be presented.' They retire, while in answer to a summons sung by the 'Twelve Spheres,' Beauty's Fort, made in likeness of a heart, opens up and allows Beauty and Aglaia to issue out of it, 'the two Pulses beating before them up towardes ye King.' Beauty then gives Aglaia the following absurd explanation of the meaning of the scene and the action:

'BEAUTY. …This heart, therefore, is neither man's nor woman's, but the heart of the yeare; signifying that the whole yeares cheife virtues and bewties are now to be contracted in one night, as the whole worldes are in one year.

AGLAIA. A contraction greate and princely.

BEAUTY. To performe w^{ch}, we are to induce, in their effectes the foure Elementes and the foure Complexions; of whose apt composition, all the Bewtie of the world is informed. [This refers to the antimasques, which were to be performed by eight pages who were lying asleep round the Fort, and were supposed to represent Spark, Atom, Drop, Ant, a little Cupid, a little Fury, a little Fool, a little Witch, the sons of the Elements and Complexions.]

AGLAIA. Of all wch y^r excellence [i.e. Beauty, to whom she is speaking] is presented as abstract.

BEAUTY. Being amplified wth other personages infinitely more bewtifull.' [This refers to the masquers, who were to appear as the twelve months, attended by torchbearers representing Moons dressed as huntresses.

Beauty goes on to act as a guide to the scenery:]

'AGLAIA. Of whate use are those banners and bandrolls stucke upon the forte?

BEAUTY. They are the Yeares ensignes, whose Hearte this is suppos'd, expressing in amorous mottos, inscrib'd in them, the triumphant love and loyaltie included. To this our glorie of the yeare, and his most peaceful employer.

AGLAIA. What are those plumes stucke in ye middst and toppe, as that heartes pride, and his affections scope?

BEAUTY. The ensignes of the darling of the yeare, delicious Aprill [i.e. Prince Henry?].

AGLAIA. What's the motto there?

BEAUTY. *His virtus nititur Alis.* They are the winges of virtue, twixt wch. (spight of fate) shee ballances herselfe, and staies her state; and thus much for our necessarie relation.'

After this at an alarm from the Pulses, the 'eight Pages starte up, and fall into their Antemasque,' and then at the sound of loud music a second 'antemasque' is performed by Moons, dressed as huntresses who serve as torchbearers to 'The Moneths, our Masquers, and newe rising sunnes.' At last at the close of masque dances and revels, Somnus hovers in the air, the masquers are summoned to rest, dance their going off, and the entertainment comes to an end.

More attractive than this tasteless production is the so-called *Masque of the Four Seasons*[1], which was probably performed about the same time, and was not really a masque but an entertainment at a banquet. It is by no means a masterpiece, but it does show that mingling of courtliness and classic grace with sympathy for the real country life and country pastimes, which is characteristic of English pastoralism at its best.

The same kind of spirit pervades the *Sun's Darling*[2], 'a moral Masque' by Dekker and Ford, which describes the progress of Raybright, child of the Sun, who is offered all possible delights and benefits by the four seasons in turn, but rejects them all at the bidding of his attendant Folly, and his false sweetheart Humour. The masque is full of lyrics, many of them most charming. In the third act, for instance, we are in the House of Summer.

'Enter Raybright, Humour, Plenty, Folly, Country-fellows, and Wenches.

Song.

Haymakers, rakers, reapers, and mowers,
Wait on your Summer-queen;
Dress up with musk-rose her eglantine bowers,
Daffodils strew the green;
Sing, dance, and play,
'Tis holiday;
The Sun does bravely shine
On our ears of corn.

---

[1] *Inigo Jones, A Life*, etc., pp. 143 ff.
[2] *The Dramatic Works of John Ford*, ed. W. Gifford (London, 1827), vol. II, pp. 359 ff.

Rich as a pearl
Comes every girl,
This is mine, this is mine, this is mine;
Let us die, ere away they be borne.'

In 1638, a time when the fashionable taste was all in favour of over-elaboration and conventional gallantry, Thomas Nabbes composed two masques[1] in the old style, *The Spring's Glory* and *A Presentation Intended for the Prince His Highnesse on His Birthday the 29th of May*. In the latter masque, Time who is the chief presenter disputes with 'certaine ignorant, and yet Great undertaking Almanack-makers,' then brings in May, attended by Flora and Vertumnus, and when they have sung he commands May to introduce a morris-dance; and finally 'whilst the Scoene is varied into a glorious expression of *Elizium*,' he summons certain 'brave Heroick shadowes' who are the eight masquers representing eight Princes of Wales. In *The Spring's Glory* the plot turns on a rivalry between Venus and Cupid on the one side and Ceres and Bacchus on the other. Christmas, Shrovetide, and Lent appear to help settle the dispute, and finally the Spring acts as a moderator between the parties. Both these masques would appear to have been composed under the influence of Middleton's *Masque of Heroes*.

Middleton had a hand in preparing a good many pageants, civic shows, and other public revels of his day, and he composed— assisted by William Rowley—*The World Tost at Tennis*[2], which seems to have been the first masque composed for the theatre.

---

[1] *The Works of Thomas Nabbes*, ed. A. H. Bullen (London, 1887), vol. II, pp. 224 ff., 256 ff.

[2] *The Works of Thomas Middleton*, ed. A. Dyce (London, 1840), vol. V, pp. 157 ff. Mr W. J. Lawrence thinks that this masque was written for performance by the Prince's Men at Denmark House, and was intended as an entertainment for the King; Prince Charles hoping by this means to appease the King's wrath against the particular company who had recently acted a distasteful play. But the King refused to see the masque, so it was acted at an inn called the Princes' Arms. See art. in *Times Lit. Supp.*, 8 Dec. 1921, *Early Substantive Theatre Masques*. In this article Mr Lawrence also discusses the masques of Nabbes and Dekker. His main thesis is that the Jacobean public theatres had no scenic resources unknown to the Elizabethan stage, that when masques were reproduced on the public stage there was no attempt to reproduce the Court method of staging, and that passages in the plays which suggest some scenic elaboration are really Court versions.

Although the piece is entitled 'A Courtly Masque,' and is said to have been intended for a royal night, it is not an orthodox Court masque in form, for although there are various songs and dances, the performance is not arranged so as to lead up to and provide a motive for the appearance of a group of masquers— the *sine qua non* of an orthodox masque.

In *The World Tost at Tennis* Jupiter and Pallas appear to a discontented scholar and soldier, and show them by various object lessons that they have need to complain rather of themselves than of their environment. First of all as an example to them of

> '...What the young world,
> In her unstable youth, did then produce,'

the nine Muses and the nine Worthies descend from the upper stage, are described by Pallas, dance and make their exit. Then Time enters, complains of Deceit and Pride, and as an example of the effects of these vices, 'Music striking up a light fantastic air, the Five Starches, White, Blue, Yellow, Green, and Red, all properly habited to express their affected colours, come dancing in....' When the starches have departed, Jupiter comments on them:

> 'These are the youngest daughters of Deceit,
> With which the precious time of life's beguil'd,
> Fool'd, and abus'd; I'll shew you straight their father,
> His shapes, his labours, that has vex'd the world
> From age to age,
> And tost it from his first and simple state
> To the foul centre where it now abides:
> Look back but into times, here shall be shewn
> How many strange removes the world has known.

Loud music sounding, Jupiter leaves his state; and to shew the strange removes of the world, places the orb whose figure it bears in the midst of the stage; to which Simplicity, by order of time having first access, enters....' Various characters hand on the orb from one to another until at last 'as an ease to memory, all the former removes come close together; the Devil entering, aims with Deceit at the world; but the world remaining now in the Lawyer's possession, he, expressing his reverend and noble acknowledgment to the absolute power of majesty, resigns it loyally to its royal government; Majesty to Valour, Valour to Law again, Law to Religion, Religion to Sovereignty, where it firmly and fairly settles, the Law confounding Deceit, and the Church the Devil.'

Middleton himself, if we may judge from his prologue, did

not feel quite clear as to the category to which this curious piece should belong.

> 'This our device we do not call a play,
> Because we break the stage's laws to-day
> Of acts and scenes...
> There's one hour's words, the rest in songs and dances.'

The plan prefixed to the libretto shows that if the piece differs from an ordinary play it differs still more from an ordinary masque.

THE FIGURES AND PERSONS

Properly raised for employment through the whole Masque.

First, three ancient and princely Receptacles, Richmond, St James's, and Denmark House.

A Scholar.	Pallas.
A Soldier.	Jupiter.
The Nine Worthies [*The Nine Muses*].	

The first Song and first Dance.

Time, *a plaintiff, but his grievances delivered courteously.*
The five Starches, White, Blue, Yellow, Green, and Red.

The second Dance.

Simplicity.	*The Intermeddler.*
Deceit.	*The Disguiser.*

The second Song.

A King.	*A Sea-Captain.*
A Land-Captain.	*Mariners.*

The third Song and third Dance.

The Flamen.	*The Lawyer.*

The fourth and last Dance, the Devil an intermixer.

Nabbes' *Microcosmus*[1], 'a morall maske, presented with general liking, at the private house in Salisbury Court,' has much in common with *The World Tost at Tennis*, and still more with

[1] Nabbes, *op. cit.* vol. II, pp. 159 ff.

The Sun's Darling and his own *Presentation on His Highness'
Birthday*.

The piece opens with a horrified appeal made by *Nature* to her
husband *Janus* 'the figure of eternall providence' against the chaos
which she sees around her. 'The 4 *Elements* and their creatures dance
a confused dance to their owne antique musicke: in which they seeme
to fight with one another: and so goe forth confusedly.' They are,
however, calmed by *Love*, and 'the first Scene appeares; being a sphaere
in which the 4. *Elements* are figur'd, and about it they sit imbracing
one another.' In the second act we are introduced to *Physander*, a
'master-peece of Natures workemanship,' a 'little world.' *Physander*
is betrothed to *Bellanima*, but enticed away by *Malus Genius* and
encouraged by the four *Complexions* and the five *Senses*, he leaves her
for *Sensuality*, who forsakes him as soon as he has ruined his health
in her service. The erring *Physander* then returns to *Bellanima*, is
healed by *Temperance* and *Bonus Genius*, tried at the court of *Conscience*,
and acquitted, and then finally 'the last Scene is discover'd, being a
glorious throne: at the top whereof *Love* sits betwixt *Justice*, *Temperance*,
Prudence and *Fortitude*, holding two crownes of starres: at the foote
upon certain degrees sit divers gloriously habited and alike as *Elysij
incolae* (i.e. dwellers in Paradise); who whil'st *Love* and the *Vertues*
lead *Physander* and *Bellanima* to the throne, place themselves in a figure
for the dance.'

This piece is not remarkable for lyric beauty, but it does show
ingenuity and considerable constructive ability, and is a better
piece of work than *The World Tost at Tennis*. It is divided into
acts and scenes, but otherwise is more like a masque than the
former work, since it requires elaborate decorations and several
scene changes, and leads up to the disclosure of masquers. The
dramatic element, however, predominates, and it is not certain
how far the masque-like parts of the entertainment—particularly
the scene changes—were actually displayed at Salisbury Court,
for we are told on the title-page that it is set down according
to the intention of the author, which seems to imply that his
intention was not wholly carried out.

The attempt to adapt the masque to the requirements of the
theatre had two chief results. In the first place it led to the
production of a type of play with something of the didactic
abstract character of the earlier moralities, and secondly it led

to a loosening of the form of the masque, and consequently to the occasional use of the term as a designation for any masque-like play or entertainment, particularly such as were acted by 'gentlemen of quality' at private houses instead of by players on the public stage. The most notable instance of this vague use of the term masque is Milton's *Comus*, which he calls a masque, but which Sir Henry Wotton describes more appropriately as a 'dainty piece of entertainment.' The surpassing excellence of *Comus* has led to its being treated as a thing apart, but as a matter of fact it is only an unusually admirable example of a class of entertainment or play which was fairly common at the time, and of which several examples are found among Shirley's dramatic works, for instance, *Honoria and Mammon, The Triumph of Beauty, Ajax and Ulysses.* These entertainments and masque-like plays or morals, and a few old-fashioned masques like those of Nabbes, remain true for the most part to the style of the earlier English Renaissance, at a time when the Court masque was being developed in a very different direction and was absorbing the worst characteristics of foreign revels.

PLATE VIII

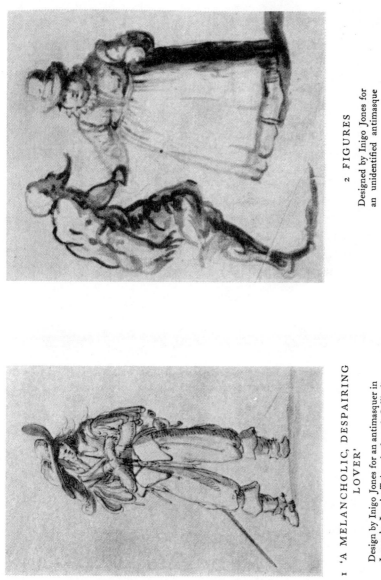

2 FIGURES

Designed by Inigo Jones for
an unidentified antimasque

1 'A MELANCHOLIC, DESPAIRING
LOVER'

Design by Inigo Jones for an antimasquer in
Jonson's *Love's Triumph through Callipolis*

Copyright of His Grace the Duke of Devonshire

CHAPTER VIII

The Caroline Masque

'At masks and plays, is not the bays
Thrust out, to let the plush in?' SHIRLEY.

WITH the accession of Charles I a new impulse was given to the masque. His Queen Henrietta Maria had quite as keen a taste for these pleasures as had her predecessor Anne of Denmark, and she did not content herself with appearing among the silent masquers, but sometimes took a speaking part in courtly pastorals, a circumstance which led to the libellous outburst of Prynne with all its disastrous consequences. King Charles did not hold aloof from his wife's pleasures, as James I had done, but frequently appeared in person as chief masquer. Sometimes both he and the Queen took part in a double masque, sometimes there would be two great royal masques in one year, the King presenting a masque to the Queen on Twelfth Night, and the Queen returning the compliment on Shrove Tuesday. It was only natural that French influence should be strong on these Caroline revels, but the unfortunate result was that the process of decay was much accelerated, and even Ben Jonson, who in 1631 collaborated with Inigo Jones in the preparation of two Court masques, was unable to resist the tendency of the time.

The argument of *Love's Triumph through Callipolis* turned on the difference between false and true love, and celebrated the chaste affection uniting the King and Queen of England. This kind of subject was to prove popular at the Caroline Court, where spiritual or platonic love was a constant theme for discussion among the ladies of Henrietta Maria, and the masque naturally reflected the topic of the hour.

This particular masque opened with the appearance of Euphemus sent from heaven to Callipolis, the city of beauty or goodness, to declare to her Majesty a message from the God of Love, saying that 'in the suburbs or skirts of Callipolis were crept in certain sectaries or depraved lovers, who neither knew the name or nature of love rightly, yet boasted themselves his followers, when they were fitter to be called his furies: their whole life being a continued vertigo, or rather a torture on the wheel of love than any motion either of order or measure. When suddenly they leap forth below, a mistress leading them, and with antic gesticulation and action, after the manner of the old pantomimi, they dance over a distracted comedy of love, expressing their confused affections in the scenical persons and habits of the four prime European nations.

> A glorious boasting lover.
> A whining ballading lover.
> An adventurous romance lover.
>
> A phantastic umbrageous lover.
> A bribing corrupt lover.
> A froward jealous lover.
>
> A sordid illiberal lover.
> A proud scornful lover.
> An angry quarrelling lover.
>
> A melancholic despairing lover.
> An envious unquiet lover.
> A sensual brute lover.

All which, in varied intricate turns, and involved mazes, exprest, make the ANTIMASQUE: and conclude the exit, in a circle.'

The rest of the masque, which was the occasion for a number of fine scenic effects, was occupied in showing the nature of true love, of which Charles himself was the great exemplar.

Designs for the various lovers in the antimasque are preserved at Chatsworth, and show that Inigo Jones copied some of them from the designs of the famous French engraver Jacques Callot[1]. Ben Jonson still held out against the division of the antimasque into entries, but this was to be his last stand.

At Shrovetide of this same year Ben Jonson and Inigo Jones composed the Queen's masque *Chloridia* as a counterpart to the King's masque *Love's Triumph through Callipolis*. The foreign influence was now predominant; the antimasque was divided up into a number of entries, the revels occurred at the end of the performance after the manner of the ballet de Cour[2], and for the grand finale Inigo Jones reproduced a device that had been employed years before by Parigi in the intermedio of *The Palace of Fame*:

'...sparue subito il Palazzo, e la fama, restata in aria, cominciò à salire all' insù, e si nascose trà le nuuole, cantando....'[3]

---

[1] *Balli di Sfessania*, nos. 641–664. Cf. E. Meaume, *Recherches sur la vie et les ouvrages de Jacques Callot* (Paris, 1860), vol. II, pp. 312 ff.; *Designs*, pp. 53–55; Reyher, *op. cit.* pp. 407, 408.   [2] Cf. Prunières, *op. cit.* p. 93.

[3] Cf. *supra*, p. 186; *Descrittione delle Feste*, p. 37.

We may compare with this the wording of the description in *Chloridia*:

'Here, out of the earth ariseth a Hill, and on the top of it a globe, on which FAME is seen standing with her trumpet in her hand; and on the hill are seated four persons, representing POESY, HISTORY, ARCHITECTURE, and SCULPTURE; who together with the Nymphs, Floods, and Fountains, make a full quire; at which FAME begins to mount, and moving her wings flieth, singing, up to heaven....

FAME being hidden in the clouds, the hill sinks, and the heaven closeth.'

Apparently this particular device was not successful, for Ben Jonson makes sarcastic allusion to:

'The ascent of Lady Fame, which none could spy,
Not they that sided her, Dame Poetry,
Dame History, Dame Architecture too,
And Goody Sculpture, brought with much ado
To hold her up....'[1]

Ben Jonson's word, however, is not altogether to be trusted, for by this time he was engaged in a violent quarrel with Inigo Jones. Some time before he had told Drummond of Hawthornden that: 'He said to Prince Charles of Inigo Jones, that when he wanted words to express the greatest villaine in the world he would call him ane Inigo. Jones having accused him for naming him, behind his back, A fool: he denied it; but, sayes he, I said He was ane arrant knave, and I avouch it.'[2] But now Ben Jonson was not going to find it safe to speak his mind freely about his rival. When he satirised him in a Court play, Inigo Jones was able to get the most offensive passages expunged, and even so the play was not liked. A friend wrote to him:

'I heard you censured lately at court, that you have lighted too foul upon Sir Inigo, and that you write with a porcupine's quill, dipt in too much gall';[3]

and again the same correspondent, alluding to his satire on the royal architect, says:

'If your spirit will not let you retract, yet you shall do well to repress any more copies of the satire; for to deal plainly with you, you have

[1] *An Expostulation with Inigo Jones.*
[2] *Conversations*, p. 41.   [3] Cf. Jonson, *Works*, vol. III, p. 210.

lost some ground at court by it; and as I hear from a good hand, the King, who has so great a judgment in poetry (as in all other things else), is not well pleased therewith.'[1]

At the beginning of the Stuart period Ben Jonson was powerful, Inigo Jones almost unknown. Now the position was reversed, and since the breach was not to be healed, it was Ben Jonson who had to go under. For the following Court masques Inigo Jones appointed a different poet, and though Ben Jonson composed a few royal entertainments he was never again asked to prepare a great Court masque. From this time onwards the masques were really created entirely by Inigo Jones with the help of various tame poets acting under his orders.

The ostensible cause of the dispute was trivial enough, for Sir John Pory, in a letter to Sir John Puckering, says that Ben Jonson was discarded

'by reason of the predominant power of his antagonist, Inigo Jones, who this time twelvemonth was angry with him for putting his own name before his in the title-page, which Ben Jonson made the subject of a bitter satire or two against Inigo.'[2]

Both the antagonists, like other men of genius before and since, were ludicrously childishly sensitive to slights, but it is only just to add that the real cause of their dispute lay deeper than hurt vanity. Unfortunately their artistic ideals were incompatible, and it was their very devotion to their respective arts that made peace between them impossible. It will be easier to judge between them after we have seen Inigo at work unhampered by Ben's clamorous assertion of the rights of poetry.

In 1632 Inigo Jones chose as his poet Aurelian Townshend[3]. Townshend had a certain lyric gift, but he was a third-rate poet and a far more submissive colleague for Inigo than the masterful Ben Jonson. He concludes his first masque on a note of humility:

'Those that will prayse the structure and changes of the Scene. The sweetenesse and variety of the Musicke. Or the Beauty of the Figures, and Paces, I thinke may doe it with cause enough.

---

[1] Loc. cit.

[2] Court and Times of Charles I, vol. II, pp. 158, 159.

[3] Aurelian Townshend's Poems and Masks, ed. E. K. Chambers (Oxford, 1912).

But for the Invention and writing of the Maske, I was as loath to be brought vpon the Stage as an vnhansom Man is to see himselfe in a great Glasse. But my Excuse, and Glory is, The King commanded, and I obeyed.'[1]

In this first masque of Townshend and Jones the subject was apparently planned by both of them[2].

'The King and Queenes Majesty having signified their pleasure to haue a new Maske this New yeare, Master *Inigo Jones* and I were employed in the Invention. And we agreed the subie[ct] of it should be a Triumphe in *Albipolis* the chiefe City of *Albion*. The Triumpher, *Albanactvs*, and *Alba* this Ilands Goddesse.' The first scene displayed a 'Romane Atrium,' underneath a serene sky, out of which came a cloud bearing Mercury, the messenger of Jove, who had descended to earth and was joined by the chorus: '*Orpheus, Amphion, Arion,* and three old Poets and Musicians more.' In *voce recitativa* Mercury announces to the Queen that Jove is about to show her The Triumph of Albanactus.

'A Triumph: Mighty, as the Man design'd
To weare those Bayes, Heroicke, as his mind.'

After some choruses and songs 'Mercury is Re-assumed into Heaven in Pompe. Here the Scene is changed into the Forum of the City of *Albipolis*, and *Albanactus* triumphing, attended like a Roman Emperor is seene a farre off to passe in pomp.' The scene then changes to an amphitheatre with various people sitting in it, and Platonicus and Publius discuss in prose dialogue the Triumph which has just taken place, Publius, the plebeian, being most interested in the external show, Platonicus the patrician in the inner meaning. Both together remain to witness 'such kind of pastimes as Victorious Emperors were wont to present as spectacles to the People,' which are here 'produced for Anti-Maskes vpon the stage.' This 'enterlude' being passed, 'the Scene is changed into a pleasant Grove of straight Trees, which rising by degrees to a high place, openeth itself to discover the aspect of a stately Temple.... In this groue, satt the Emperour *Albanactvs*, attended by fourteene Consuls....' These are the masquers. Cupid then appears in a cloud, and Diana in a chariot, and both descend to the scene shooting at the masquers, and particularly at Albanactus, who, yielding to the gods, moves down the steps while the chorus of sacrificers sing:

'Subdu'd by Albas eyes
Come downe, Loves Sacrifice!'

All this means, as we are told in the preface, that the conqueror has been conquered and subdued to love and chastity. After the main masque

[1] *Ibid.* p. 78.   [2] *Ibid.* pp. 57 ff.

dance has been performed, the King takes his seat by the Queen to watch the rest of the performance.

The scene was then varied to 'a prospect of the King's Pallace of *Whitehall,* and part of the Citie of *London,* seene a farre off, and presently the whole heauen opened, and in a bright cloud were seene sitting fiue persons, representing *Innocency, Justice, Religion, Affection* to the Countrey, & *Concord,* being all Companions of *Peace....*These moving towards the earth sing together as followeth....Then from the vpper part of the heauen, was seene to follow this: Another more beautifull cloud, in which alone triumphant sat *Peace,...Proclaiming her large Benefits, and the Worlds Ingratitude....*The Five in the lower Clowde confessing her great *Bounty,* Answere....When the fiue persons which first descended were come to the earth, the cloud that bare them, was in an instant turned into a richly adorned Throne. And out of the foure corners of the Scene proceede 4 Gods, *Neptune, Plutus, Bellona, and Cebele, complaining of ease and Plenty....*

> Peace.
> *Earths Rulers, stay!*
>
> The foure Gods.
> *Doth soft Peace call?*
>
> Peace.
> *Yes: and will streight employ yee All.*
>
> The foure Gods.
> *How, and wherein?*
>
> The 5. in the lower Clowde.
> *Give eare, your Charge doth now begin.'*

Peace gives them their charge, telling them that they are all to serve England and the King of England in the way appropriate to them.

> 'The Foure Gods reply:
> *When* Peace *commands such pleasing things,*
> *From* Love *and* Time *wee'l steale their wings.*

For a Conclusion, the Gods, Poets, and Priests ioyne, and sing a Valediction to *Hymens Twin* the *MARY-CHARLES.'*

This masque is clumsily arranged and it is not wholly original. If we may take a hint from an allusion in Ben Jonson's *Expostulation,* it would seem that some at least of the friction which arose over the performance of *Chloridia* was due to Inigo's attempt to reproduce an old stage device of Giulio Parigi's. When the restraining hand of his colleague was removed, Jones made use of Parigi's designs for almost every masque which he composed[1]. The design for the 'Romane Atrium' is adapted from Parigi's design for the *Tempio della Pace*, in *Il Giudizio di Paridi*[2]. The last scene of *Albion's Triumph* may have been suggested to Inigo by Parigi's design for the second intermedio of the same play. This design shows the usual landscape scene with a view of the city of Florence in the distance, and in the middle of the stage Father Arno reclining on the ground with his six nymphs on either side of him. In a cloud at the left-hand top corner of the scene sits the goddess Flora, and lower down and more to the centre of the stage in another cloud and encircling glory, sits Astraea upon an eagle with six maidens in a semi-circle round her. This design is composite, and does not represent any one moment of the actual performance, for the libretto informs us that Flora descended to earth before the appearance of Astraea out of the cloud[3]; but it is this composite picture which seems to have suggested that part of *Albion's Triumph*, where a 'Landscipt' with 'part of the citie of London seene afarre off' is the scene of a dialogue between Peace sitting on a throne in the upper part of the heaven and five deities in a lower cloud.

Far more obvious and undeniable, however, is Inigo's indebtedness to the sixth intermedio of Parigi.

The scene of this intermedio was a superb temple in which there appeared simultaneously the goddess of Peace descending in a cloud and her throne rising up from beneath the earth. The goddess was accompanied by a large following of abstractions, among whom were Innocence, Justice, Adoration, Affection to the Country, Concord, who were, however, dressed differently from the corresponding companions of Peace in *Albion's Triumph*. As soon as Peace was enthroned in her Temple, there appeared four clouds from the four quarters of the scene, and on each cloud was a chariot bearing a deity, Bellona drawn by elephants, Sibele drawn by lions, Pluto by black horses, Neptune by white horses. Peace having interrogated them charges them to serve the noble couple each according to his proper office. At this sentence the gods rejoice because no one is excluded, and they prepare to perform

---

[1] All these designs are reproduced by W. J. Lawrence, in his interesting article, *A Primitive Italian Opera*, in *The Connoisseur*, vol. xv (1906), pp. 235 ff., and also in *Designs*. [2] Cf. *Designs*, p. 62.
[3] *Descrittione delle Feste*, pp. 37, 38.

with joy and promptitude the commands laid upon them. The intermedio ends with the opening up of the heavens and a glorious celestial vision of deities followed by a marvellous aerial dance[1].

The resemblance between the arrangement of the last scene of *Albion's Triumph* and the design for the second intermedio may be accidental, but the likeness between grouping, action, and literary structure of this scene and the sixth intermedio is so close that it must be due to deliberate imitation. Probably Inigo borrowed from himself as well as from other people, for it would seem that his design for the temple of Albanactus was a modification of his earlier design for the palace of Oberon[2].

The King's Twelfth Night masque was followed on Shrove Tuesday by the performance of *Tempe Restored*, 'a Masque Presented by the Queene, and fourteene Ladies, to the King's Majestie.' The only share taken by Aurelian Townshend was the writing of the verses. 'The subject and Allegory of the

---

[1] *Descrittione delle Feste*, pp. 46 ff. Parigi's design is reproduced in *Designs*, p. 62.

[2] In the Chatsworth collection there is a group of designs (nos. 42–45) which has puzzled the editors of *Designs*. Design 42 shows the rocks opening to reveal Oberon's palace. Design 44 closely resembles this drawing in general arrangement, but the palace is altered, and has as its most conspicuous feature an imposing central figure of a stag, who is bayed at by hounds, and shot at by cupids. As the editors justly remark: 'the cupids, stag, and dogs do not seem appropriate attributes of the Fairy King,' and as they point out the difficulty is increased by the fact that design 45 is 'an elaborated sketch for the details of the palace' in design 44, and yet shows a 'technical mastery not elsewhere discernible in Inigo Jones's early work,' and they suggest that 'we have here evidence of a remodelling of the transformation scene in *Oberon*, for some later and unidentified masque.' This is no doubt the correct solution, but the masque can I believe be identified, for it is none other than *Albion's Triumph*, and I am convinced that designs 44, 45, were intended for that moment in the masque when 'the Scene is changed into a pleasant Grove of straight Trees, which rising by degrees to a high place, openeth itself to discover the aspect of a stately Temple....In this groue, satt the Emperour *Albanactus*, attended by fourteen Consuls.' This revelation of the masquers is followed by a dialogue in which Cupid and Diana encourage one another to shoot at the masquers, and the Chorus below also adds its voice: 'Bow-bearing Gods, shoote, shoote, and hit, And make our Caesar greater yet.' Thereupon Cupid and Diana shoot at the masquers and Albanactus descends with a stately dignity befitting 'Love's Sacrifice.' The cupids, hounds and stag are inappropriate attributes of the Fairy King, but most appropriate attributes of the Imperial victim of chaste love, the noble prey of the boy Cupid and the huntress Diana. Cf. *Designs*, pp. 44, 45, 46, and plates VII, VIII. The design of Oberon's palace is also reproduced n Herford and Simpson, *Ben Jonson*, vol. II.

Masque, with the descriptions, and Apparatus of the Sceanes were invented by *Inigo Jones*, Surveyor of His Majestie's worke.' It does him no credit. The construction of the masque is weak and insignificant, the elaborate allegory set out at the end is clumsy, unattractive, and almost totally unrelated to the actual performance. The plot such as it is was borrowed from the *Ballet comique* of Beaujoyeulx[1], and it is really remarkable that Inigo remained so completely uninfluenced by the dramatic character of his original. The French ballet was not, however, the only source of this masque. There is in the Chatsworth collection a design for side wings, which exactly corresponds to part of the description of Circe's bower in the Vale of Tempe, and these side wings are copied from Parigi's design for the garden of the nymph Calypso in the island of Ogygia[2]. Inigo betrays the source of his inspiration when he writes: '*Palas* and *Circe* returnes into the Scene with the *Nymphes*, and *Chorus*; and so concluded the last *Intermedium*.'

The next two Court masques were presented by the Inns of Court, and it was perhaps owing to this that Inigo Jones does not seem to have been able to domineer over the poets as he had become accustomed to do; for Shirley's preface 'To the Four Equal and Honourable Societies of the Inns of Court' leaves us in no doubt that he regarded the *Triumph of Peace* as his own work.

'This entertainment, which took life from your command, and wanted no motion or growth it could derive from my weak fancy, I sacrifice again to you, and under your smile to the world....I dare not rack my preface to a length. Proceed to be yourselves (the ornament of our nation), and when you have leisure to converse with imaginations of this kind, it shall be an addition to your many favours, to read these papers, and oblige beside the seals of your other encouragement, the humblest of your honourers, James Shirley.'[3]

The great Inigo Jones had to be content with mention in a footnote at the end of the piece, together with William Lawes and Simon Ives, who composed the music.

---

[1] Cf. *supra*, pp. 107 ff.
[2] Cf. *Designs*, pp. 69, 70.
[3] *The Dramatic Works and Poems of James Shirley*, ed. A. Dyce (London, 1833), vol. VI; *James Shirley*, ed. E. Gosse (Mermaid Series), p. 439.

Shirley, however, did not turn his independence (if indeed he had it) to any very good account. There is no principle of unity in *The Triumph of Peace*; the antimasques are many and have practically no connection either with one another or with the main masque. They are, however, presented in a more dramatic and literary way than were the French entries or the antimasques of Aurelian Townshend. Shirley follows Jonson in introducing a certain amount of realistic comedy into his masque. One antimasque, for instance, is danced by various characters representing a carpenter, painter, tailor, and other work people employed in the preparation of the revels, who break in and insist on being admitted to the entertainment. The conversation between Fancy, Opinion, and Laughter suggests that Shirley like Jonson may have been obliged by public opinion to follow a fashion of which he did not altogether approve.

<blockquote>

'FAN.   How many antimasques have they? of what nature?
              For these are fancies that take most; your dull
              And phlegmatic inventions are exploded.
              Give me a nimble antimasque.
OPIN.   They have none, sir.
LAUGH. No antimasque! I'd laugh at that, i'faith.
JOL.   What make we here? No jollity!
FAN.   No antimasque!
              Bid 'em down with the scene, and sell the timber,
              Send Jupiter to grass, and bid Apollo
              Keep cows again; take all their gods and goddesses,
              For these must farce up this night's entertainment,
              And pray the court may have some mercy on 'em,
              They will be jeered to death else for their ignorance.
              The soul of wit moves here; yet there be some,
              If my intelligence fail not, mean to show
              Themselves jeer majors; some tall critics have
              Planted artillery and wit murderers.
              No antimasque! let 'em look to 't.'

</blockquote>

It is the easier to believe that Shirley did not approve of the exaggeration of the antimasque, because his later masque *Cupid and Death*[1] shows that he could rival Jonson in the composition of a poetical and well-planned masque; and in the famous quarrel

---

[1] Cf. *infra*, pp. 261 ff.

between Inigo and Ben, Shirley's sympathies were obviously with the poet.

> 'Among all sorts of people
> The matter if we look well to,
> The fool is the best, he from the rest
> Will carry away the bell too.
> All places he is free of,
> And fools it without blushing,
> At masks and plays, is not the bays
> Thrust out, to let the plush in?'[1]

And again in *The Royal Master* Shirley adopts Jonson's tone in speaking of masque writing:

> 'I do not say I'll write one, for I have not
> My writing tongue, though I could once have read:
> But I can give, if need be, the design,
> Make work among the deal boards, and perhaps
> Can teach them as good language as another
> Of competent ignorance. Things go not now
> By learning; I have read, 'tis but to bring
> Some pretty impossibilities, for anti-masques,
> A little sense and wit disposed with thrift,
> With here and there monsters to make them laugh:
> For the grand business, to have Mercury,
> Or Venus' dandiprat, to usher in
> Some of the gods, that are good fellows, dancing,
> Or goddesses; and now and then a song,
> To fill a gap:—a thousand crowns, perhaps,
> For him that made it, and there's all the wit!'[2]

Shirley followed Jonson in adhering to the custom of putting the revels in the middle of the masque, and he closes *The Triumph of Peace* with the appearance of Amphiluche, the morning twilight, an episode which is particularly charming both for its lyrics and its prose description of the scenery.

Nevertheless, *The Triumph of Peace* owed its great success not to its literary value but to the grandeur of the triumphal chariots in which masquers and antimasquers rode through London, to the magnificence of the dresses, the beauty of the

---

[1] Shirley, *The Bird in a Cage*, act V, sc. 1.
[2] *The Royal Master*, act II, sc. 1.

music, and above all to the many marvellous scene-changes contrived by Inigo Jones. The first scene, which represented 'the
forum or piazza of peace,' emulated but was not a copy of the
Tempio della Pace, the most gorgeous and ingenious of all
Parigi's intermedii. There is a design in the Chatsworth collection which 'shows a translation into the terms of the Ionic
Order' of the design by Parigi. From the pencilled sketch of
the border we can tell that this design must have been intended
for Shirley's masque. According to the editors of *Designs*, 'It
looks as if Webb, to whom this drawing may safely be assigned,
had begun to adapt Parigi's Temple into Shirley's Forum of
Peace, but that Inigo Jones, reflecting that he had made use of
this composition shortly before from another masque, decided
to replace it by a fresh design.'[1] Perhaps, however, Shirley may
have had something to do with Inigo's second thoughts.

Thomas Carew's masque *Coelum Britannicum*[2] was performed
very shortly after *The Triumph of Peace*, and is even more
rambling and chaotic than its predecessor. It displays almost all
the worst vices of the masque at this period, but although it gives
opportunity for many antimasques and spectacular scenes, it
shows an increase rather than a reduction of the literary element,
for there are a number of long and very dull tirades put into the
mouths of Mercury and Momus. Again the masque is full of
borrowings. For part of the first scene Inigo Jones made use
of the side wings of Parigi's first intermedio of *The Palace of
Fame*[3]: and another scene was I believe suggested by the last
part of the fourth intermedio, in which a cloud appeared in the
middle of the sky, and opening up revealed Immortality seated
on a globe clad in an azure starry robe, and attended on one side
by Apollo and the Nine Muses and on the other side by a chorus
of ten poets of various ages and of various nations[4]. In Carew's
masque two clouds come down, the first bearing Religion, Truth,
and Wisdom, the second Concord, Government, and Reputation.

[1] *Designs*, p. 80.
[2] Reprinted in *The Poems of Thomas Carew*, ed. A. Vincent (London,
1899), pp. 191 ff.
[3] Cf. *Designs*, p. 83.
[4] *Descrittione delle Feste*, p. 42.

These being come down in an equal distance to the middle part of the air, the great cloud began to break open, out of which struck beams of light; in the midst, suspended in the air, sat Eternity on a globe; his garment was long, of a light blue, wrought all over with stars of gold, and bearing in his hand a serpent bent into a circle, with his tail in his mouth. In the firmament about him was a troop of fifteen stars, expressing the stellifying of our British heroes; but one more great and eminent than the rest, which was over his head, figured his Majesty[1].

Carew and Inigo Jones may have taken some hints from the French *Ballet d'Harmonie,* danced on the 14th of December, 1632, where Apollo first appeared, and then Atlas and Hercules were seen bearing up the celestial globe, and later Momus entered followed by seven or eight 'bouffons.'[2] Inigo's design for Atlas bearing up the globe resembles a drawing of the same figure which adorned one of the chariots appearing in the Florentine Tournament of 1616, and was designed by Parigi and engraved by Jacques Callot[3].

On Shrove Tuesday, 1635, the Queen's masque was prepared by William Davenant, who succeeded Ben Jonson as poet laureate. Davenant seems to have had easy relations with Inigo Jones; he was apparently less self-effacing than Townsend, more so than James Shirley. He seems to have filled just the rôle against which Jonson rebelled. He was acknowledged as joint author of the masque, but in the libretto his name followed that of Inigo Jones. They collaborated in the invention of the plot and the writing of the argument, but Inigo wrote all the descriptions of scenes, dances, dresses, etc., leaving to Davenant the composition of dialogue and lyric[4].

The first scene of *The Temple of Love* disclosed a grove 'and afar off on a mount,' a shady bower, and various cypress walks 'representing the place where the souls of the ancient poets are fained to reside.' Into this pleasant spot comes a chorus of ancient Greek poets, and Divine Poesy, descending from heaven in a cloud, announces the coming of Indamora. In time past, she says, poets have sung of false love, now it

[1] *Op. cit.* p. 232.
[2] Lacroix, *op. cit.* vol. IV, pp. 211, 217.
[3] No. 638, *Carro del Sole*; cf. Meaume, *op. cit.* p. 311; *supra*, p. 100.
[4] There is an explicit statement to this effect at the end of *Salmacida Spolia* (cf. *infra*, p. 242), and there is no reason to doubt that the division of labour was the same in the case of the other masques.

behoves them to hymn that which is true. Divine Poesy and her poets retire, while 'the whole scene changeth into mist and clouds, through which some glimpse of a Temple is here and there scarcely discern'd,' and three magicians enter from hollow graves underground, conversing together about the danger that is threatening from Indamora, through whose influence they fear the Temple of Chaste Love will be disclosed, unless they can produce strong counteracting spells. As a result of their incantations various antimasques are called up, first an entry of the earthy, the fiery, the airy, and the watery spirits, then other entries of quarrelling men, alchemists, drunken skippers, etc., brought in by each set of spirits in turn. In the seventh entry there is an obvious allusion to the Puritans, and probably to Prynne in particular, for this antimasque 'Was of a modern devil, a sworn enemy of poesy, music, and all ingenious arts, but a great friend to murmuring, libelling, and all seeds of discord, attended by his factious followers, all which was exprest by their habits and dance.

After these was an entry of three Indians of quality, of Indamora's train in several strange habits, and their dance as strange.' Then a 'Persian page comes leaping in,' and having made a speech about certain knights who had become platonic lovers, retires, and is followed immediately by certain noble Persian youths, who make their entry and dance. 'Their dance ended, the mist and clouds at an instant disappear, and the scene is all changed into a sea somewhat calm, where the billows moving sometimes whole, and sometimes breaking, beat gently on the land, which represented a new and strange prospect; the nearest part was broken grounds and rocks, with a mountainous country, but of a pleasant aspect, in which were trees of strange form and colour, and here and there were placed in the bottom several arbours like cottages, and strange beasts and birds...expressing an Indian landscape. In the sea were several Islands, and afar off a Continent terminating with the horizon.' A barque comes out of a creek. In this barque sits Orpheus with other sailors, pilots, etc., and 'he, playing one strain, was answered with the voices and instruments of the Brachmani joined with the priests of the Temple of Love, in extravagant habits sorting to their titles.' The barque heaved on the sea, and then returned to port whence it came. 'The barque having taken port, the Masquers appear in a maritime chariot, made of a spungy rockstuff mixt with shells, sea-weeds, coral, and pearl, borne upon an axle tree with golden wheels without a rim, with flat spokes like the blade of an oar coming out of the waves.' On the highest part of this chariot, which was drawn by sea monsters, sat Indamora, Queen of Narsinga, 'in a rich seat, the back of which was a great skallop shell.' The chariot moved upon the sea to the accompaniment of music and the voices of the chorus. 'The song ended, all the forepart of the sea was in an instant turn'd to dry land, and

1 APPEARANCE OF LOUIS XIII AND HIS COURTIERS AS DEMONS IN A MOUNTAIN GROTTO

2 PANTOMIMIC DANCE OF THE DELIVERANCE OF RENAUD FROM ENCHANTMENT

Scenes designed by Francini for *La délivrance de Renaud* (Paris, 1617), a typical French ballet mélodramatique

(For music, résumé of plot, description of method of scene-changing by means of rotatory disks, reproduction of upper half of Scene 2, see Prunières, *Le Ballet de Cour en France avant Benserade et Lully*, pp. 251 ff., 153, and frontispiece)

Indamora with her contributary ladies descended into the room, and made their entry. Then, for intermedium the music began again....' A song was sung and then the masquers, having reposed, danced their second dance, after which, 'the Queen being seated under the State by the King, the scene was changed into the true Temple of Chaste Love,' a magnificent building which had satyrs instead of columns and seemed to be of burnished gold. Into this Temple entered Sunesis and Thelema, who, assisted by the chorus, sang a dialogue on the joining together of Will and Reason in Love. During the singing of this song a cloud comes down from heaven, opens, and out of it comes Chaste Love, crowned with laurel and holding two laurel garlands in his hand. As he descends, the cloud closes and ascends heavenwards. Then Chaste Love, Sunesis, Thelema, Divine Poesy, Orpheus and the rest of the poets, go up towards the State, while the great chorus follows behind them accompanying their progress with a song. This done, they retire again to the scene, Indamora and the ladies begin the revels with the King and lords, which continue for most of the night[1].

Although Davenant's poetry is very mediocre, there is certainly more unity and design in *The Temple of Love* than there is in Shirley's *Triumph of Peace*, or in the masques of Carew and Townshend. All Davenant's masques approximate more or less closely in form to the French *ballet mélodramatique*, which flourished in Paris from about 1610 to 1621, and is described by M. Prunières as

'un genre dramatique bien défini. Intermédiaire entre l'opéra et le *ballet-mascarade*, il répond à l'amour des français pour la danse expressive et pour le théâtre. Il est rationnel, voluptueux et magnifique; il séduit les yeux, les oreilles et les esprits.'[2]

And again of one of them M. Prunières speaks in words very applicable to *The Temple of Love*:

'L'action en est claire, exposée par un grand nombre de récits, de dialogues, de chœurs et de scènes de pantomime.'[3]

Nothing is wanting in fact except imagination. Divine Poesy plays a part in Davenant's masque, but she has no real influence over it, nor over the French *ballet mélodramatique*. Davenant

---

[1] Sir Wm Davenant, *Dramatic Works*, ed. by James Maidment and W. H. Logan (Edinburgh, London, 1872), vol. I, pp. 281 ff.
[2] *Op. cit.* p. 121.
[3] *Loc. cit.*

seems to have been influenced by the French ballet in his choice of subject-matter as well as in his method of construction. The appearance of magicians and enchanters, of various realistic figures in the antimasque, are all typical of the French ballet; and by his employment of exotic and oriental settings Davenant already shows signs of that taste for 'heroic' literature which was to be the predominant influence for a while in the drama and opera of the Restoration. In his treatment of platonic love Davenant indulges in some good-natured satire directed against modes of thought prevalent among the Court ladies, and in this as in other of Davenant's masques there are many references to the political difficulties of the time springing from the conflicting ideals of Cavalier and Puritan.

Davenant was undoubtedly influenced by the French ballet, but both he and Inigo Jones were far more deeply indebted to Italy than to France. In 1616 Giulio Parigi designed chariots and costumes for a grand triumphal tournament which was held in the Piazza Santa Croce, Florence. At this tournament Indamoro, King of Narsinga, fought Gradametus for love of the Indian Queen Lucinda, who arrived in the theatre enthroned on a triumphal chariot surrounded by maidens, Indian soldiers, and 'Sacerdoti Brammanni.'[1] Davenant evidently took the names *Indamora, Narsinga*, and the idea of introducing 'Brachmani' from this performance. The main scene of Indamora's appearance was taken from Parigi's fourth intermedio of *Il Giudizio di Paridi*, and in this case the debt was by no means trivial. A comparison of the English and Italian descriptions will show how closely Davenant has followed his source. In the intermedio:

'...la Scena si fece mare placido, e quieto, e le sue riue apparuero vestite d' alberi incogniti à noi, e frà essi vedeuansi quà, e là sparse case fatte di palme, e di canne...l' aria piena di pappagalli, e simil varietà d' vccelli, e per terra huomini nudi, come costuman nell' Indie Occidentali.' Into this sea there came a ship bearing Amerigo Vespucci with Hope, Boldness, Strength, and other soldiers and sailors at the prow. (Here the description differs from that of the masque scene.) As the ship neared land a madrigal was sung, and 'al pari della barca,

<hr/>

[1] Cf. *supra*, p. 100, note 2. Callot's illustrations of this entertainment are vigorous and vivid. Cf. nos. 633–635, and Meaume, *op. cit.* pp. 307 ff.

era cominciata à sorger dell' acqua vno scoglio, che poi si conobbe esser il carro della Tranquillità, tirato da due foche marine. Era questo scoglio pieno di nicchi, e coralli, con musco, e altre marauiglie del mare. In cima d' esso staua la Tranquillità....'[1]

Parigi's design for this intermedio bears a very interesting resemblance to two designs of Inigo Jones which were evidently intended for the *Temple of Love*. The first of these designs represents an Indian shore and sea, but it only shows the side wings, and is nothing but a rough sketch imitating Parigi's design[2]. The other design is labelled 'Calm Sea, rocky landscape, an antique barge coming out of creek.'[3] It is a first rough draft for the main scene of *The Temple of Love*, but its connection with design 229 becomes much clearer when we compare it with Parigi's design for the second intermedio; for strangely enough it is the Italian not the English drawing which gives the best idea of the main scene of the English masque; since the car of Tranquillity corresponds closely to the verbal description of the car of Orpheus[4].

On Twelfth Night, 1638, the King's masque *Britannia Triumphans*[5] was presented at Whitehall, the authors being Inigo Jones and William Davenant. In the light of later events the subject of the masque appears very pathetic.

'Britanocles, the glory of the western world hath by his wisdom, valour, and piety, not only vindicated his own, but far distant seas... and reduc'd the land, by his example, to a real knowledge of all good acts and sciences. These eminent acts, Bellerophon, in a wise pity, willingly would preserve from devouring time...and gives a command to Fame, who hath already spread them abroad that she should now at home, if there can be any maliciously insensible awake them from their pretended sleep, that even they with the large yet still increasing

---

[1] *Descrittione delle Feste*, pp. 41, 42. Parigi's design is reproduced in *Designs*, p. 95.

[2] No. 229. It is reproduced in *Designs*, plate XXV B.

[3] No. 230. The editors of *Designs* connect this design with the *Temple of Love*; but point out that it lacks 'details, intended to give it an Indian character,' that the border of the scene does not correspond either with the drawing or the description, and that the 'cloud with personages in it does not appear in this scene in the masque.'

[4] Cf. *Designs*, pp. 94–97 and plates XXV, XXVI, XXVII.

[5] Davenant, *Dramatic Works*, vol. II, pp. 245 ff.

number of the good and loyal may mutually admire and rejoice in our happiness.'

The first scene showed English houses 'intermixt with trees' and a distant view of London. Into this scene came Action and Imposture, and after some dialogue, in which Action complains of

> '...such as impute
> A tyrannous intent to heavenly powers,
> And that their tyranny alone did point
> At men, as if the fawn and kid were made
> To frisk and caper out their time, and it
> Were sin in us to dance...'

they are followed by Merlin who invokes ancient imposters, and then 'The whole Scene was transformed into a horrid hell, the further part terminating in a flaming precipice, and the nearer parts expressing the suburbs, from whence enter the several Antimasques.' There were six entries of these antimasques, one of which was an entry of 'mock music of 5 persons,' which is reminiscent of the entries of grotesque musicians in the French ballet. After the antimasques are ended Bellerophon arrives, and again Merlin makes an invocation at which the hell vanishes, and there appears in its stead a forest and a castle, the scene of a 'mock Romanza.' After this little burlesque had been enacted, Imposture departed, and 'in the further part of the Scene, the earth open'd and there rose up a richly adorn'd palace, seeming all of Goldsmiths' work, with porticoes vaulted on pillasters running far in: the pillasters were silver of rustic work, their bases and capitols of gold. In the midst was the principal entrance, and a gate; the doors' leaves of bass-relief, with jambs and frontispiece all of gold. Above these ran an architrave, freize, and cornice of the same; the freize enricht with jewels; this bore up a ballestrata, in the midst of which, upon a high tower with many windows, stood Fame...in one hand a golden trumpet, in the other an olive garland....When this palace was arrived to the height, the whole scene was changed into a Peristilium of two orders, Doric and Ionic, with their several ornaments seeming of white marble, the bases and capitals of gold; this, joining with the former, having so many returns, openings, and windows, might well be known for the glorious Palace of Fame.' The chorus of poets entered, Fame sang, and 'the Masquers came forth of the Peristilium, and stood on each side, and at that instant the gate of the Palace open'd, and Britanocles appeared....The Palace sinks, and Fame, remaining hovering in the air, rose on her wings singing, and was hidden in the clouds.' The masquers then descend into the room, and the scene changes to Britain; Merlin invokes a new chorus of modern poets, who make their address to the Queen. Again the scene changes and shows a sea and a haven with a citadel on the rocks, 'from whence the sea-nymph Galatea came waving forth, riding on the back of a dolphin....Being arrived to the midst of the sea, the dolphin stayed, and she sung, with a Chorus of music....Which done, she gently past away, floating on the waves as she came in. After this, some ships were discern'd sailing afar off several ways, and in the end a great fleet was discovered, which passing by with a side wind, tackt about, and with a prosperous gale entered into the haven, this continuing to entertain the sight whilst the dancing lasted.'

The wording of the preface to *Britannia Triumphans*, which speaks of 'Masques with shewes and intermedii,' makes it clear that the approximation to the foreign type of entertainment was by now an accepted fact; and again in this masque we find striking borrowings from Parigi.

Long before when they prepared the *Masque of Queens*, Ben Jonson and Inigo Jones had sought inspiration from the first intermedio of the *Giudizio di Paridi*; and now Inigo returns to his precious pamphlet, and copies the same intermedio with a fidelity which perhaps he might have displayed already in 1608, had he not been restrained by Ben Jonson. In Chatsworth there are two designs for the main scene of this masque, one showing only the main building of the Temple of Fame at the back and centre of the stage, and the other showing the side wings or peristilium of two Orders. The design for the temple is simply a copy of Parigi's palace of Fame (although it is clear that Inigo did not make his palace translucent), but the side wings in the English and Italian drawings are different. It will be noticed also that the English libretto resembles the Italian description, particularly in the words describing the upward flight of Fame, a striking effect which Inigo had already tried to emulate in *Chloridia*. The action of the central scene of *Britannia Triumphans* follows the action of the intermedio more closely than does the action of the *Masque of Queens*[1].

The King's Twelfth Night masque was followed on Shrove Tuesday by the Queen's masque *Luminalia or The Festival of Light*[2]. According to Professor Brotanek and Mr Simpson,

---

[1] Cf. *supra*, pp. 183, 186.
[2] Reprinted in *Miscellanies of the Fuller Worthies' Library*, ed. A. B. Grosart, vol. IV.

Davenant collaborated with Inigo Jones in the composition of this masque[1], but if so, it seems likely that Davenant was responsible for the songs, and possibly for the prose description, but not for the action and the argument, which is more chaotic than any other of his masques, and recalls the formlessness of *Tempe Restored*. Like *Tempe Restored*, too, is the lengthy and complicated argument or interpretation of the plot, which has but the very slightest connection with the masque as it actually appears. This looks like the hand of Inigo Jones, and the preface suggests that he must bear the blame[2].

'The King's Majesties Masque being performed, the Queene commanded *Inigo Jones* Surveyor of her Majesties works, to make a new subject of a Masque for herselfe, that with high and hearty invention, might give occasion for variety of Scenes, strange aparitions, Songs, Musick and dancing of severall kinds: from whence doth result the true pleasure peculiar to our English Masques, which by strangers and travellers of judgement, are held to be as noble and ingenious, as those of any other nations.'

It is odd that by the wording of this preface Inigo or his colleague should make such a definite claim to originality, for in no other masque is the plagiarism so blatant and so extensive. *Luminalia* is in fact nothing else but a clumsy adaptation of Francesco Cini's *Notte d'Amore*, altered to suit the form of the English masque, and combined with an imitation of the aerial dance in Parigi's *Triumph of Peace*.

The masque opens with the fall of a curtain discovering 'a Scene all of darknesse, the neerer part woody, and farther off more open with a calme River, that tooke the shadowes of the Trees by the light of the Moone, that appear'd shining in the River; there being no more light to lighten the whole Scene than served to distinguish the severall grounds, that seemed to run farre in from the eye: with this Scene of darknesse was heard the voyces of Birds of Night...there arose out of the hollow caverns of the earth a duskie cloud, and on it a Chariot enricht and drawne by two great owles....' In it was Night...'She tels she came to give repose to the labours of mortals: but seing all things here tending

[1] Cf. *Beiblatt zur Anglia*, XI, 177–181; *Designs*, p. 13, note 1.
[2] But cf. *Designs*, Introduction, p. 13. I am sorry to differ from Mr Simpson in my estimate of this masque. I share his admiration of the designs, but the masque as a whole seems to me chaotic, and inferior in unity and poetic imagination to its Italian original.

to feasts and revels, she with her attendants will give her assistance, though it serves but as a foile to set off more nobler representation.' Night sings, and from the sides of the scene appear her attendants—Oblivion, Silence and the four nocturnal hours or vigils[1]. (We may compare the appearance of these with that of the corresponding Italian characters, for the descriptions of their dresses are practically identical.) The chariot of Night stays in the middle of the air, and 'after some dialogue with her attendants, shee ascends singing, and is hidden in the clouds.' (This is the third occasion on which Inigo Jones imitated the ascent of Lady Fame in Parigi's intermedio.)

The attendants of Night call forth certain antimasques. These antimasques are divided up into entries and are so like the entries of a typical French ballet de Cour that it would not be surprising to learn that they were borrowed from one of them[2]. 'Most of these Antimasques,' we are told, 'were presented by Gentlemen of Qualitie.'

'These Antimasques being past, the scene of night vanished; and *a new and strange Prospect of Chimeras appea'rd* [sic], *with some trees of an unusuall forme, Mountaines of gold, Towers falling, Windmils, and other extravagant edifices, and in the further part a great City sustained by a Rain-bow, all which represented the City of Sleepe*[3]. *One of the Vigils in song called forth Sleepe, who appeared comming out of a darke cave, with three of his principall sonnes. Morpheus the presenter of humane shapes. Iceles, of fearfull visions. And Phantaste, of anything that may be imagined. Sleepe, a fat man in a black robe, and over it a white*

---

[1] Each of the four divisions of *Notte d' Amore* is called a *vigilia*, a word having the same origin and meaning as *veglia*, 'a vigil, an evening party,' which came to be used as the name for a particular kind of entertainment, that was fashionable at the beginning of the seventeenth century (cf. *supra*, p. 113 and note 2). The *veglia* bears a close resemblance to the ballet de Cour and the Court masque, for it consists of the introduction of bands of masquers who proceed to dance with the spectators, and has a more or less consistent plot. (For a possible early form of it cf. *supra*, p. 131, note 2.) The chief difference between the masque and the *veglia* was that in the former the introduction of the masquers was the central event and the ostensible *raison d'être* of the evening's entertainment, in the latter the masquers were introduced in a series of intermedii inserted into a ball instead of into a play. This difference was hardly noticeable in the Caroline period owing to the increasing incoherence and over-elaboration of the Court masque, but it still existed as a comparison of *Luminalia* and *Notte d' Amore* proves. Callot's etchings of a *veglia* performed in 1616 show that the arrangement of hall and stage was identical with that made for a Court masque. Cf. nos. 630–632. The design entitled 'Primo Intermedio della veglia della Liberatione di Tirreno fatta nella Sala delle Comedie del Ser.mo Gran Duca di Toscana il Carnovale del 1616,' is reproduced in Prunières, *op. cit.* plate IV.

[2] In the *Ballet du grand Demogorgon*, performed in 1633 (?), there was an entry of nocturnal characters and creatures, and also a 'Grand Ballet dansé par les incubes et succubes.' Cf. Lacroix, *op. cit.* vol. IV, pp. 265 ff., 271 ff.

[3] *Designs*, plate XL.

mantle, on his head a girland of Grapes, with a Dormouse sitting before, in his hand a golden wand.' (In *Notte d' Amore* 'il sonno' is dressed in exactly the same way.)

Then 'the sonnes of Sleepe bring in these Antimasques of dreames. For the fourth entry appear 'five feathered men, inhabitants of the City of *Sleepe*....Here an Antique ship was seen farre within the Scene, sailing in the aire.' Of the fifth entry we are told: 'From the Temple of the Cocke, seated by the haven of the City of Sleepe, the principall Mariners or Master Mates in rich habits...make their entry.

...These Antimasques being past, the Heaven began to be enlightned as before the Sunne rising, and the Sceane was changed into *a delicious prospect; wherein were rowes of Trees, Fountains, Statues, Arbors, Grota's, walkes, and all such things of delight, as might expresse the beautifull garden of the Britanides.* The morning Starre appeares in the Aire, sitting on a bright Cloud, in forme of a beautifull youth.' From the other side of Heaven comes Aurora 'in a Chariot touch'd with gold, borne up by a rosie coloured Cloud....*Hesperus askes Aurora, why the Sunne is so long in comming, and whether being weary of his last journey, he is gone to take his rest.*' Aurora replies that the sun has yielded his office to 'a terrestriall Beautie' and bids him descend and summon the Flamens and Arch-Flamens to celebrate with divine hymns 'this God-desse of brightnesse with those faire Nymphs dependants on her splendor.' The Morning Star then descends singing, while Aurora passes through the air, and as he descends 'the Chorus of Arch-Flamines and Flamines of the Britanides come forth...habited in rich habits of severall colours, as they are described by the Ancients.' Hesperus leads them down into the room towards the State; they sing in chorus, and there is a 'Saraband as they move back....Here the further part of the Garden opened, and the Masquers are seene, the Queenes Majestie being seated high, and the Ladies somewhat lower on two degrees....The Masquers dance... and her Majestie seated under the state by the King, in the further part of the Scene appeared a heaven full of Deit[i]es or second causes, with instruments and voices, together with the Muses of Great Britaine and Chorus of Arch-Flamines and Flamines sing this last song.' After which 'the upper part of the heaven opened, and a bright and transparent cloud came forth farre into the Scene, upon which were many Zephyri and gentle breasts (breezes?), with rich but light garments tuck'd about their wasts, and falling downe about their knees, and on their heads girlands of flowers: These to the Violins began a sprightly dance, first with single passages, and then joyning hands in rounds severall wayes. Which Apparition for the newnesse of the Invention, greatnesse of the Machine, and difficulty of Engining, was much admir'd, being a thing not before attempted in the Aire.' The masquers then danced the revels with the lords.

We may compare with this the final dance in the intermedio of Peace:

'...S' aperse il Cielo in tre luoghi, e vi si vide vn gran numero di Celesti, che applaudendo à tal sentenza, cominciarono à cantare... mentre, dalle due aperture delle bande, vscirono in fuor due nugole piene d' aurette, e zeffiri, che vagamente vestiti, e presi per mano, mossero vn ballo tondo, con gran merauiglia degli spettatori, come di cosa non più tentata in aria.'[1]

A comparison of *Luminalia* with *Notte d' Amore* will show at once how deeply indebted was Inigo Jones (or his poet-collaborator) to Francesco Cini. The most salient instances of borrowing I have emphasised by printing in italics the corresponding passages in the English and Italian descriptions. It is impossible to say whether or no there was a similar correspondence between the Italian and English staging, because, unfortunately, I have been unable to find any designs for the *Notte d' Amore* although there are many illustrations of the rest of the festivities.

Among the designs in the Chatsworth collection there are a few that stand apart from the rest, and seem to show an even finer quality of imagination. Of these the 'Cloudy Night piece,'[2] and the 'City of Sleep over a Rainbow,'[3] are certainly designs for *Luminalia*, and it has occurred to me that the fourth might be intended for that masque and possibly represent the 'Temple of the Cock seated by the haven of the City of Sleep.'[4] The design, which is unfinished, shows a temple rising up either out of the sea or out of the sea of cloud, the water or clouds welling up in little waves and breakers between the columns. Over the temple porch is a winged head crowned with sickles, and obviously

[1] *Descrittione delle Feste*, p. 49.
[2] *Designs*, plates XXXVIII, XXXIX.   [3] *Ibid.* plate XL A.
[4] This is the design that Messrs Bell and Simpson (cf. *Designs*, p. 85) assign tentatively to *Coelum Britannicum* on account of the signs of the Zodiac and Mr W. J. Lawrence to the *Masque of the Twelve Months* on account of the heart. Cf. *supra*, pp. 210, 211. I am extremely dubious about my own suggestion, but I let it stand because it does not seem much more uncertain than any of the others. I base it upon the predominance of the idea of 'Time' and the symbolism of the two figures who correspond to the clear contrast between light and darkness, which is the idea on which *Luminalia* is founded.

representing Time. The sculpture around the porch evidently represents the signs of the Zodiac. Lower down on each side of the temple in the midst of the waves are two figures leaning on their hands brooding, one with face turned upwards, one looking down to the water, probably representing either Light and Darkness, or Morning and Evening. The water or cloud floats round a heart in such a way as to make it look almost like a dim reflection of the winged head of Time up above[1]. The design is beautiful and has a certain quality of mystery which is absent from most of the others. It would be interesting to know whether these designs were of Inigo's own invention or whether he took them from Italian originals.

The last masque before the outbreak of the Rebellion was *Salmacida Spolia*[2], which was danced by the King and the Queen in 1640. It is fully illustrated by the designs of Inigo Jones preserved at Chatsworth. There were many changes of scene, and some of Inigo Jones' grandest feats were produced on this occasion. The sovereigns, we are told, were as full of enthusiasm for masques as ever they had been in the past, but it is quite clear that a storm was brewing. Lady Carnarvon refused to take part in the masque if it were performed on Sunday. Protests against the ever-increasing extravagance of the Court—for the cost of these masques was stupendous—had been made for some years, and Shirley's *Triumph of Peace* had been written partly as a disclaimer of the views of the Puritan law clerk Prynne, who lost his ears because of a foul-mouthed attack on women actors, which was supposed to reflect upon the Queen. Echoes of the coming storm are heard in the argument of *Salmacida Spolia*.

'A curtain flying up, a horrid scene appeared of storm and tempest; no glimpse of the sun was seen, as if darkness, confusion, and deformity, had possesst the world, and driven light to heaven, the trees bending, as forced by a gust of wind, their branches rent from their trunks, and some torn up by the roots: afar off was a dark wrought sea, with rolling billows, breaking against the rocks, with rain, lightning and thunder: in the midst was a globe of the earth, which at an instant falling on fire, was

---

[1] It appears so to me, but no one else has noticed it, and I may well be mistaken.

[2] Davenant, *Works*, vol. II, pp. 301 ff.

turned into a Fury, her hair upright, mixt with snakes, her body lean, wrinkled, and of a swarthy colour...in her hand she brandisht a sable torch, and looking askance with hollow envious eyes, came down into the room.' This Fury then invoked evil spirits to bring discord throughout England, and at her summons three others entered, and together they danced a wild antimasque. This being past, the scene changed into a landscape, showing all such things as might express a country at peace, rich and fruitful, and out of the heavens came a silver chariot, in which were two people, Concord, a woman, and a young man in a carnation costume signifying the Good Genius of Great Britain. 'Being arrived at the earth, and descended from the chariot, they sing this short dialogue, and then departed several ways to incite the beloved people to honest pleasures and recreations, which have ever been peculiar to this nation.

> BOTH. Oh who but he could thus endure
> To live, and govern in a sullen age,
> When it is harder far to cure,
> The People's folly than resist their rage?'

(All this alludes to the controversy that arose over the *Book of Sports*.) After that followed nineteen entries of antimasques, in the first of which appeared an 'operator,' who distributed recipes and 'many other rare secrets' some of which were literally translated from the recipes in the *Ballet de la Foire Saint-Germain*.

'The Antimasques being past, all the Scene was changed into craggy rocks and inaccessible mountains, in the upper parts where any earth could fasten, were some trees, but of strange forms, such as only grow in remote parts of the Alps, and in desolate places; the farthest of these was hollow in the midst, and seemed to be cut through by art, as the Pausilipo near Naples, and so high as the top pierced the clouds, all which represented the difficult way which heroes are to pass ere they come to the throne of Honour.' The Chorus of the beloved people came out led by Concord and the Good Genius; they advanced up to the State, greeting the Queen Mother in song, and presenting another poem inviting the appearance of the King on the throne of Honour. (In the libretto this poem is headed 'To be printed not sung,' another sign of French influence, for many of the literary remains of the French ballet were programmes intended for distribution among the audience, not songs to be recited or sung.) When the chorus had done this, they returned to the stage and divided, six on each side, while the further part of the scene disappeared, and the central rock opened and revealed Charles and the other masquers seated upon the throne of honour. While the chorus greeted with an outburst of song the appearance of the King, a great cloud of various colours came down from the sky, obliterating in its descent the throne of honour, and in this cloud were seated Queen Henrietta Maria and her ladies, dressed as Amazons. 'When this heavenly seat touched the earth, the King's Majesty took out the Queen, and the lords the ladies, and came down into the room, and danc't their entry.'

The dramatic business of the masque was over, not so the spectacular effects devised by Inigo Jones; for when the King and Queen were seated in the throne of State, the scene changed, and there was displayed a prospect of London with bridges going over the Thames and people passing to and fro over the bridges. The proceedings ended with a great galaxy of deities descending in various clouds. 'The invention, ornament, scenes and apparitions, with their descriptions, were made by Inigo Jones, Surveyor General of His Majesty's works. What was spoken or sung, by William D'avenant, Her Majesty's servant. The subject was set down by them both.'

This, then, was the last masque performed at the English Court for many years. With the fall of the Stuart monarchy the social conditions which made the masque possible came to an end, and the few masques which were performed after this date are merely belated examples of a form of art that had long lost its *raison d'être*. Before leaving the subject it would be well perhaps to consider what effect Inigo Jones had on the masque in the period when his sway was undisputed. During this time unity of action and to a large extent lyrical beauty were lost, and indeed the whole literary value of the masque was sacrificed to give the fullest possible scope for magical transformation scenes.

The further question arises what was the artistic value of the scenes and designs of Inigo. We can judge in part from the designs for dresses and scenery which are still preserved at Chatsworth. On studying these drawings the first feeling is one of astonishment at the great resources of the Court stage at this time, and one is inclined to think that Ben Jonson was unreasonable in his desire to keep Inigo Jones in a subordinate position. But there is another side to the picture. We have seen that all the Caroline masques are full of hints, imitations, and actual borrowings taken from French ballets and Italian intermedii, and most of them from a particular pamphlet or pamphlets describing the Florentine festival which took place in 1608. So it looks as if Inigo Jones in his high-handed dealings with the poets was actuated not so much by zeal for his own ideal of art, as by a passionate determination to introduce the artistic ideals of other nations into England. In mastery of stage mechanism he was probably second to none. His originality is more dubious. Was he, perhaps, as Ben Jonson hints more than once, merely an ingenious stage carpenter anxious to produce a certain spectacular effect but indifferent to the beauty of the masque as a whole? If this were so, the case for Ben Jonson would become very much stronger, for it is easy to understand his chagrin at having to modify his poetry in order to fit in not with the equally original views of the architect, but with ideas that he had borrowed wholesale from Italy and France.

On the other hand, it must be admitted that Ben Jonson never charges Inigo with his Italian borrowings (unless his reference to 'Italian herbs' and to 'twice conceived thrice paid for imagery' alludes to them), and he would hardly have failed to use any and every weapon against his antagonist. Perhaps, however, he realised that his own record was not blameless, and of course at that time plagiarism was not regarded with the modern severity which is mainly due to competitive industrialism and our exaggerated respect for property. Moreover the borrowings of Inigo Jones are piecemeal, and he combines what he has taken from Parigi with other inventions that are probably his own. His favourite words 'feasible,' 'conduce,'[1] and various gibes of Jonson's, suggest that it was not lack of originality, but love of harmonious design combined with insensibility to poetry, that caused the friction.

Is it possible that this failure of originality in the Caroline masque was due not so much to Inigo's habit of plagiarism, as to a general failure of inspiration in the nation as a whole? The history of the masque ends abruptly with the outbreak of civil war, but it could hardly have lasted much longer even if there had been no revolution. The last masques of Ben Jonson show that even he was powerless to hinder the process of disintegration, and by the time *Luminalia* and *Salmacida Spolia* were written the masque had come to be little more than an operatic panto-

[1] Cf. Jonson, *A Tale of a Tub*, act V, sc. 2.

mime. During the reign of James I the masque in spite of all its faults was an expression of a living ideal. The classical deities were not mere conventional abstractions, but inhabitants of a golden world. The lyrics were full of the rhythm and lilt of the dance. The whole performance was a radiant idealised present-ment of courtly revels. During the Caroline period all this was changed. There was an unpleasing mingling of pompous deities and realistic contemporary types; the setting became tasteless and extravagant; the lyrics were no longer dancing songs, but gallant neatly-turned compliments expressed in regular metre. Gradually the spirit of the dance faded out of the English masque, and when this happened the day of the masque was over, for in spite of all the efforts of the dramatists it was never really turned into art; it was always a form of amusement and revelling, closely bound up with the social system, and therefore unable to survive the social revolution of the Puritans. The masque even at its best was an attempt rather than an achievement, but although it never quite gained an intrinsic and permanent value, it had a deep, fruitful, and lasting influence on English poetry.

PART TWO

The Influence of the Masque

✿✿✿✿✿✿✿✿✿✿✿✿✿✿✿✿✿✿✿✿✿✿✿✿✿✿✿✿✿✿✿✿✿

CHAPTER IX

The Influence of Poetry on the Masque

'For thy excelling rapture, ev'n through things
That seems most light, is borne with sacred wings:
Nor are these musics, shows, or revels vain,
When thou adorn'st them with thy Phoebean brain.'
                                                    CAMPION.

IT is said that Michael Angelo once made a statue of snow,
and by that action he unconsciously symbolised no small part
of the artistic activity of several centuries. Many of the
artists, who have left their mark on the churches, the palace
walls, the very streets of Italian cities, spent much time and
trouble in creating a loveliness that melted almost as quickly as
Michael Angelo's snow statue. A few weeks' festival—then
the gorgeous pageants and miraculous stage decorations were
broken up; a night's merrymaking—then the ideas of a Leonardo
da Vinci or a Raphael had come to fruition, caused a momentary
pleasure, and passed away into an almost complete oblivion.

Was it sheer waste? Or were the artists able to enshrine in
their more permanent works something of the colour and gaiety
of Renaissance social life, just because they did not disdain to
give aesthetic dignity even to the frivolous amusements of their
fellow-citizens? This is the question to which the next few
chapters will be devoted, and although our immediate concern
is with the interaction between English masques and English
poetry, Ben Jonson and Inigo Jones cannot be fully understood
if Callot and Beaujoyeulx, Parigi and Rinuccini, are ignored.

A conscientious artist responsible for the planning of Court
functions was confronted by two problems: he had to give unity
to a production in which music, poetry, painting, and dancing
all played a part: he had to give beauty to a performance which
was chiefly appreciated as an advertisement of wealth and an
opportunity for flattery and political propaganda. These two
problems, which were not really separable from one another,
found different solutions in different countries. In France and
Italy, as we have seen, attention was directed chiefly to the first
difficulty, and members of the Pléiade and the Camerata tried

to revive the old Greek lyric drama, which they regarded as a harmony of all the arts. Their attempt to adjust the arts to one another resulted, however, not in an equilibrium, but in an organic unity in which one or other of the arts predominated.

In Italy music was the vital principle of opera, the most important result of the aesthetic development of the Italian Court festival. As to the merits of this Italian opera there have always been grave differences of opinion. To some it appears the very consummation of art; but others hold that the attempt to combine music and drama, or rather to make drama subservient to music, is bound to be unsatisfactory, because it is impossible to appreciate at one and the same moment a pictorial effect which is stationary, a musical effect which is progressive, and a dramatic effect which depends on suspense and crisis.

In France the arts were adjusted to one another in a different way, and at first it was dancing, rather than music, which held the most important place in Court entertainments. The motives that led to the invention of the French ballet de Cour are stated explicitly by Beaujoyeulx in his preface to the *Balet comique de la Royne*.

'Pour autant, amy Lecteur, que le tiltre et inscription de ce livre est sans exemple, et que l'on n'a point veu par cy-devant aucun Balet avoir esté imprimé, ny ce mot de Comique y estre adapté, je vous prieray ne trouver ny l'un ny l'autre estrange; car quant au Balet, encores que ce soit une invention moderne, ou pour le moins repetée si loing de l'antiquité, que l'on la puisse nommer telle, n'estant, à la verité, que des meslanges geometriques de plusieurs personnes dans un (dansans?) ensemble, sous une diverse harmonie de plusieurs instrumens; je vous confesse que, simplement representé par l'impression, cela eust eu beaucoup de nouveauté et peu de beauté, de reciter une simple comedie; aussi cela n'eust pas esté ny bien excellent, ny digne d'une si grande Royne qui vouloit faire quelque chose de bien magnifique et triomphant. Sur ce, je me suis advisé qu'il ne seroit point indecent de mesler l'un et l'autre ensemblement et diversifier la musique de poesie, et entrelacer la poesie de musique, et le plus souvent les confondre toutes deux ensemble: ainsi que l'antiquité ne recitoit point ses vers sans musique, et Orphée ne sonnoit jamais sans vers. J'ay toutesfois donné le premier tiltre et honneur à la dance, et le second à la substance, que j'ay inscrite Comique, plus pour la belle, tranquille et heureuse conclusion où elle se termine, que pour les personnages qui sont presque tous Dieux et

Deesses, ou autres personnes heroïques. Ainsy, j'ay animé et fait parler le Balet, et chanter et raisonner la Comedie, et y adjoustant plusieurs rares et riches representations et ornemens, je puis dire avoir contenté en un corps bien proportionné l'œil, l'oreille et l'entendement. Vous priant que la nouveauté ou intitulation ne vous en fasse mal juger; car estant l'invention principalement composée de ces deux parties, je ne pouvois tout attribuer au Balet, sans faire tort à la Comedie, distinctement representée par ses scenes et actes; ny à la Comedie sans prejudicier au Balet, qui honore, esgaye et remplit d'harmonieux recits le beau sens de la Comedie.'[1]

It is clear from this that Beaujoyeulx intended to harmonise the intellectual and the sensuous elements in the ballet, but to do so by giving 'the first title and honour to the dance, the second to the substance.' Now here surely Beaujoyeulx is on the right lines. In the case of drama proper, spectacle and music are apt to spoil the play by overwhelming it or by destroying all veri-similitude, but this need not happen when the action is not a drama or enacted story, but a dance or enacted emotion, a symbolic representation of a condition rather than an imitation of an event; because, in the latter case the movements of the actors are progressive in the same way as the music is progressive, and the lyric feeling, which inspires the dancing and the poetry, is more or less static as the scenery is static. The one valid ob-jection to putting the dance in the central position is that dancing is of all arts the most ephemeral, and also that where dancing predominates, poetry is apt to vanish. The intellectual element in the revels disappeared even more swiftly in Paris than in London.

The English method of developing the Court revels was strikingly different from that of either France or Italy. In the first place, since the genius of the English nation was literary, the masque in so far as it approximated to permanent art, approximated not to spectacular opera or ballet, but to poetic drama; and its permanent effect on English art is to be studied, not in picture galleries or on the walls of great houses, but in the pages of the old dramatists, song writers, and pastoral poets.

[1] Lacroix, *op. cit.* vol. I, pp. 14, 15.

The consequence of this literary bias was that, when English-men attempted to turn the masque into a work of art, it was the second not the first of our problems which engaged most of their attention. In England the poets tried to turn masques into literary masterpieces which would stand the test of time, but for the accomplishment of their purpose they had to achieve some kind of harmony between the arts, they had to find some way of making the music and scenery and dancing expressive of the poetic idea of the performance. Perhaps however it is misleading to say that English poets *tried* to turn the masques into literary masterpieces, for few of them took the masque seriously enough to evolve a theory. In England the masque grew up in a characteristically haphazard way, and if at last it did turn into something capable of fulfilling the ideals of a Beaujoyeulx or a Rinuccini, this was due not to the labours of any English academy but to the fact that for a fairly lengthy period Ben Jonson and Inigo Jones had to work together, and that Ben Jonson was stubbornly resolved to stand out for the supreme dignity of the poet. If Ben Jonson was prepared to write masques, no man was justified in dismissing the masque as a trifle. Most of the other poets followed his lead in practice, but it was left to Ben to formulate the theory of the masque in his preface to *Hymenaei*:

'It is a noble and just advantage that the things subjected to under-standing have of those which are objected to sense; that the one sort are but momentary, and merely taking; the other impressing and lasting: else the glory of all these solemnies had perished like a blaze, and gone out, in the beholders' eyes. So short lived are the bodies of all things, in comparison of their souls. And though bodies ofttimes have the ill-luck to be sensually preferred, they find afterwards the good fortune (when souls live) to be utterly forgotten. This it is hath made the most royal princes, and greatest persons (who are commonly the personaters of these actions) not only studious of riches, and magnificence in the outward celebration or shew, which rightly becomes them; but curious after the most high and hearty inventions, to furnish the inward parts, and those grounded upon antiquity and solid learnings: which though their voice be taught to sound to present occasions, their sense or doth or should always lay hold on more removed mysteries. And howsoever some may squeamishly cry out, that all endeavour of learning and sharpness in these transitory devices, especially where it steps beyond their little, or (let me not wrong 'em), no brain at all, is superfluous; I am contented these fastidious stomachs should leave my full tables, and enjoy at home their clean empty trenchers, fittest for such airy tastes; where perhaps a few Italian herbs, picked up and made into a sallad, may find sweeter acceptance than all the most nourishing and sound meats of the world.

For these men's palates, let not me answer, O Muses. It is not my fault if I fill them out nectar and they run to metheglin.'

This preface shows clearly how Jonson's aims differed from those of the inventor of the ballet de Cour. Beaujoyeulx aimed at a combination of sensuous attraction and intellectual appeal, but substance was to be in second place; Ben Jonson, finding in poetry the only principle of permanence, aimed at giving to the masque an esoteric as well as an exoteric character. His composition was to be at one and the same time a poetic libretto suitable to the occasion and a dramatic poem independent of its accompaniments of dancing and scenery, and capable of surviving the Court performance for which it was primarily intended. The other arts in fact were the mortal body of the masque, but poetry was its immortal soul.

It is obvious that a theory of this kind could not be put into practice without arousing opposition on the part of those concerned with the other arts, and the famous *Expostulation with Inigo Jones*, in which Ben Jonson pours out his sense of injury, is of great interest, because at bottom the quarrel was an aesthetic not a personal one, and in the more reasonable passages of his satire Jonson elucidates his own positive ideal of the masque by showing us how this ideal of his conflicted with that of his antagonist.

> 'Master Surveyor, you that first began
> From thirty pounds in pipkins, to the man
> You are: from them leaped forth an architect,
> Able to talk of Euclid, and correct
> Both him and Archimede; damn Archytas,
> The noblest inginer that ever was:
> Control Ctesibius, overbearing us
> With mistook names out of Vitruvius;
> Drawn Aristotle on us, and thence shewn
> How much Architectonice is your own:

Whether the building of the stage or scene,
Or making of the properties it mean,
Vizors or antics; or it comprehend
Something your sur-ship doth not yet intend...
What is the cause you pomp it so, I ask?
And all men echo, you have made a masque.
I chime that too, and I have met with those
That do cry up the machine and the shows;
The majesty of Juno in the clouds,
And peering forth of Iris in the shrouds;
The ascent of Lady Fame, which none could spy,
Not they that sided her, Dame Poetry,
Dame History, Dame Architecture too,
And Goody Sculpture, brought with much ado
To hold her up: O shows, shows, mighty shows!
The eloquence of masques! what need of prose,
Or verse or prose, t'express immortal you?
You are the spectacles of state, 'tis true,
Court-hieroglyphics and all arts afford,
In the mere perspective of an inch-board;
You ask no more than certain politic eyes,
Eyes that can pierce into the mysteries
Of many colours, read them and reveal
Mythology, there painted on slit deal.
Or to make boards to speak! there is a task!
Painting and carpentry are the soul of masque.
Pack with your pedling poetry to the stage,
This is the money-got, mechanic age.
To plant the music where no ear can reach,
Attire the persons as no thought can teach
Sense what they are; which by a specious, fine
Term of [you] architects, is called Design;
But in the practised truth, destruction is
Of any art beside what he calls his.
Whither, O whither will this tireman grow?
His name is Σκηνοποιος, we all know,
The maker of the properties; in sum,
The scene, the engine; but he now is come
To be the music-master; tabler too;
He is, or would be, the main *Dominus Do-*
All of the work, and so shall still for Ben...
O wise surveyor, wiser architect,
But wisest Inigo; who can reflect
On the new priming of thy old sign-posts,
Reviving with fresh colours the pale ghosts

> Of thy dead standards; or with marvel see
> Thy twice conceived, thrice paid for imagery;
> And not fall down before it, and confess
> Almighty Architecture, who no less
> A goddess is than painted cloth, deal board,
> Vermilion, lake, or crimson can afford
> Expression for; with that unbounded line
> Aimed at in thy omnipotent design!'[1]

This dispute was not merely a result of the recurrent difficulty of adjusting the spectacular and literary elements in the art of the theatre, for in the case of the masque the crux was not whether spectacle should or should not be allowed to overweight the poetry, but rather who was to be responsible for the planning of the whole performance, of which both poetry and scenery were essential parts. Jonson was perfectly willing to give Jones scope for the designing of splendid scenery, as long as he was content to illustrate the poetry, but that would mean that the poet had a share in the designing of the scene, and in fact at the beginning of the Stuart period Jonson does seem to have usurped some of the functions of the stage architect[2]. Then again, there was the same difficulty over the attiring of the classical and allegorical personages; according to Jonson their dresses should be designed with strict regard to symbolical archaeological accuracy, but Jones, whose favourite words were 'feasible' and 'conduce,'[3] was chiefly concerned with effectiveness of colour and outline, and in the end, as we know, he was left free to 'attire the persons as no thought can teach sense what they are.'

Ben Jonson had to maintain the rights of poetry not only against Inigo Jones, but against the taste of the courtiers. He was determined to supply 'high and hearty inventions...grounded upon antiquity and solid learning,' but they cried out that 'all endeavour of learning and sharpness in these transitory devices...

---

[1] Jonson, *op. cit.* vol. III, pp. 211, 212.

[2] Cf. Jonson's description of the *Masque of Beauty*: But, before, in midst of the hall...I had placed January in a throne of silver'; again, 'Here a curtain was drawn...and the scene discovered which...I devised should be an island floating on a calm water.'

[3] Cf. Jonson's satirical treatment of In-and-In Medlay, the architect who prepares the masque in the *Tale of a Tub*, V, 2, and is always repeating these two words.

is superfluous,' and their views were supported by Inigo Jones and the poet Daniel.

'And shall we who are the poore Inginers for shadowes, & frame onely images of no result, thinke to oppresse the rough censures of those, who notwithstanding all our labour will like according to their taste, or seeke to auoid them by flying to an Army of Authors, as idle as our selues?...

And for these figures of mine, if they come not drawn in all proportions to the life of antiquity (from whose tyrannie, I see no reason why we may not emancipate our inuentions, and be as free as they, to vse our owne images) yet I know them such as were proper to the busines, and discharged those parts for which they serued, with as good correspondencie, as our appointed limitations would permit.'[1]

Now here I think it must be admitted that the objectors had some justice on their side. The masque, even at its best, was too light a structure to support a great weight of antiquarianism, and if it failed of immediate appeal, the failure could not be excused by classical footnotes. This however does not invalidate Jonson's main contention that the masque should be grounded upon some poetic idea, and that the scenes and actions should be expressive as well as spectacular. Again, however, we must allow for the probability that Jonson sometimes composed his masques with a view to their permanent place in the library, rather than to their effective production in the masquing hall. The *Vision of Delight*, for instance, is particularly charming as a poem, but it does not seem to have had a very favourable reception[2], and perhaps public opinion was not so entirely in the wrong as we are inclined to suppose. The first antimasque is certainly rather unattractive and pointless, and although there is only a bare reference to it in the libretto, it must have filled up quite a considerable part of the performance, and may perhaps have altered and marred the balance of the whole piece.

The fact is that, in their eagerness to exalt their respective arts, both Inigo and Ben forgot that the soul of the masque was neither poetry nor carpentry but dancing. If, keeping that

[1] *Tethys Festivall.*
[2] 'I haue heard no great speach nor commendations of the maske neither before nor since.'—Chamberlain to Carleton, 18 January, 1617, quoted in Sullivan, *op. cit.* p. 105.

in mind, they had curbed their egoisms and together had sought to solve the problem of creating a harmony of the arts, perhaps the English masque might have reached greater heights and have lasted longer than it did. As it was, however, Ben Jonson's conception of the masque, though one-sided, was more fruitful than that of Inigo Jones and the ordinary courtier, for although it did not lead to the creation of a new genre such as opera or ballet, it did lead to the production of a few lyrical masterpieces, and it did draw the masque and literature closer together. If Court opinion was against Ben Jonson, he had discerning admirers who lamented his defeat, and realised that it was a disaster to art.

> 'Then for your songsters, masquers, what a deal
> We have? enough to make a commonweal
> Of dancing courtiers, as if poetry
> Were made to set out their activity.'[1]

> 'Those shallow sirs, who want sharp sight to look
> On the majestic splendour of thy book,
> That rather choose to hear an Archy's prate,
> Than the full sense of a learned laureat,
> May, when they see thy name thus plainly writ,
> Admire the solemn measures of thy wit,
> And like thy works beyond a gaudy show
> Of boards and canvas, wrought by Inigo.'[2]

Ben Jonson failed in the end, but his power at Court lasted long enough to enable him to put his ideas into practice without any serious hindrance. So that leaving his external difficulties, we may now turn to his work and judge from that how far he was able to carry out his plan of giving permanent literary value to the courtly revels.

The first difficulty which confronted Jonson was the choice of a subject which should be both suitable to the occasion and also of general interest. This difficulty was increased by the fact that often the poet could not invent freely, but had to comply with suggestions made by the masquers themselves.

[1] Jo. Rutter, *An Elegy upon Ben Jonson*, in Jonson, *op. cit.* vol. III, p. 513.
[2] Richard West, *On Master Ben Jonson*, in Jonson, *op. cit.* vol. III, pp. 517, 518.

Jonson in his preface to *Chloridia* throws some light on the method of plot-making.

'The King and Queen's Majesty having given their command for the invention of a new argument, with the whole change of the scene...
it was agreed it should be the celebration of some rites done to the goddess Chloris....
Upon this hinge the whole invention moved.'[1]

That expresses very neatly a characteristic of the masque which differentiates it from drama. The drama is a story with crisis and dénouement; the masque is an invention moving upon a hinge, or, to put it another way, it is the logical working out of an idea which has to be taken for granted. The hinge of a masque was as a rule some riddling compliment of the sovereign, or an actual event, which was represented as taking place in Olympus or Arcadia or as being so magnificent an affair that divinities were brought down to celebrate it.

In these cases the subject of the masque was strictly occasional; and it was very difficult for the poet to give to it more than a temporary interest, and most of the masque writers did not try to do so: to them the masque was but a toy[2].

There were, however, exceptions. Campion introduced the *Lords' Masque* as the creation of Entheus or Poetic Fury, who had been released by Orpheus and separated from the Frantics by whom he had been held captive:

'ORPHEUS. Too, too long,
      Alas good Entheus, hast thou brooked this wrong.
      What! number thee with madmen! O mad age,
      Senseless of thee, and thy celestial rage!
      For thy excelling rapture, ev'n through things
      That seems most light, is borne with sacred wings:
      Nor are these musics, shows, or revels vain,
      When thou adorn'st them with thy Phoebean brain.
      Th' are palate-sick of much more vanity,
      That cannot taste them in their dignity.
      Jove therefore lets thy prisoned sprite obtain
      Her liberty and fiery scope again;

---

[1] Italics mine.
[2] Cf. Daniel, *op. cit.* p. 306, and the concluding words of *Albion's Triumph*.

PLATE X

APPEARANCE OF THE QUEEN AND HER LADIES AS 'ELEVEN
DAUGHTERS OF THE MORN' RELEASED FROM THE
PRISON OF NIGHT (?)

Design by Inigo Jones possibly for Jonson's *Love Freed from Ignorance and Folly*

Copyright of His Grace the Duke of Devonshire

> And here by me commands thee to create
> Inventions rare, this night to celebrate,
> Such as become a nuptial by his will
> Begun and ended.'

Again, Chapman, a kindred spirit to Ben Jonson, pours scorn on 'certain insolent objections made against the length of my speeches and narrations' for the *Masque of the Middle Temple and Lincoln's Inn*, and affects to despise his critics on the ground that 'Every vulgarly-esteemed upstart dares break the dreadful dignity of ancient and authentical poesie.' Chapman was too indignant to write clearly, but the accusation against him seems to have been that his lengthy speeches and dialogues were not inserted for their interest or beauty, but from sheer necessity, because without them the meaning of the device and its 'application to the persons and places, for whom and by whom it was presented,' could not have been understood. In reply Chapman affirmed

'that as there is no poem nor oration so general but hath his one particular proposition; nor no river so extravagantly ample, but hath his never-so-narrow fountain, worthy to be named; so all these courtly and honouring inventions, having poesy and oration in them, and a fountain to be expressed, from whence their rivers flow—should expressively arise out of the places and persons for and by whom, they are presented; without which limits they are luxurious and vain.'[1]

That was all very well, but it did not really meet the criticism. It was quite understandable that many should wish the device and purport of a masque to be sufficiently plain without long explanatory speeches. And if a masque was to be a piece of literature, it was necessary that it should be freed from the limitations caused by too close a connection with the persons who presented it or whom it was intended to honour.

Ben Jonson, a greater artist than Chapman, seems to have seen this. His best masques can be enjoyed apart from any knowledge of the occasioning circumstance. Sometimes he introduces the masques by means of a little comedy of manners[2]. Sometimes he confines the complimentary 'hinge' of his inven-

---

[1] *Masque of the Middle Temple and Lincoln's Inn.*
[2] Cf. *Love Restored, News of the New World Discoverie in the Moon*, etc.

tion to the rather vague notion of the beneficent influence proceeding from King James, and transforming the present circumstances, and so gives fancy free play, and produces a charming little piece such as *The Golden Age Restored*, in which the Iron Age with its antimasque of evils is expelled by Astraea and the Golden Age, who have come down from Heaven bringing with them 'far-famed spirits of this happy isle,' Chaucer, Gower, Lydgate, Spenser, and the masquers, demi-gods, who once were souls, from the Elysian bowers.

'*The scene of light discovered.*

The first DANCE

PAL. Already do not all things smile?

AST. But when they have enjoyed a while
The Age's quickening power:

AGE. That every thought a seed doth bring,
And every look a plant doth spring,
And every breath a flower.'

Occasionally Jonson achieves a masque which is independent of its moment. *The Masque of Lethe*, for instance, is a graceful fantasy which could easily be adapted for performance on an ordinary stage:

'The SCENE discovered is, on the one side, the head of a boat, and in it CHARON putting off from the shore, having landed certain imagined ghosts, whom MERCURY there receives, and encourageth to come on towards the river LETHE, who appears lying in the person of an old man. The FATES sitting by him on his bank; a grove of myrtles behind them, presented in perspective, and growing thicker to the outer side of the scene. MERCURY, perceiving them to faint, calls them on, and shows them his golden rod....

LETHE. Stay; who or what fantastic shades are these
That Hermes leads?

MER.   They are the gentle forms
Of lovers, tost upon those frantic seas
Whence Venus sprung.

LETHE.   And have rid out her storms?

MER. No.

LETHE. Did they perish?

MER. Yes.

LETHE. How?

MER. Drowned by love.'

But Mercury and the Fates wonder whether the death of the lovers has really taken place:

'MER.   I 'gin to doubt, that Love with charms hath put
This phant'sy in them; and they only think
That they are ghosts.

1 FATE. If so, then let them drink
Of Lethe's stream.

2 FATE. 'Twill make them to forget
Love's name.

3 FATE. And so, they may recover yet....

Here they all stoop to the water, and dance forth their Antimasque in several gestures, as they lived in love: and retiring into the grove, before the last person be off the stage, the first Couple appear in their posture between the trees, ready to come forth changed.'

Then follows the masque dance and the revels with the ladies, during which Cupid and Mercury dispute together, and each tries to influence the lovers:

'CUP. Why, now you take me! these are rites
That grace Love's days, and crown his nights!
These are the motions I would see,
And praise in them that follow me!...

MER. Look, look unto this snaky rod,
And stop your ears against the charming god;
His every word falls from him is a snare:
Who have so lately known him, should beware.

    Here they dance their Main DANCE.

CUP. Come, do not call it Cupid's crime,
You were thought dead before your time;
If thus you move to Hermes' will
Alone, you will be thought so still.
Go, take the ladies forth, and talk,
And touch, and taste too: ghosts can walk.
'Twixt eyes, tongues, hands, the mutual strife
Is bred that tries the truth of life.
They do, indeed, like dead men move,
That think they live, and not in love!...

MER. Good Fly, good night.

Cup. But will you go?
　　Can you leave Love, and he entreat you so?
　　　Here, take my quiver and my bow,
　　　My torches too; that you by all may know
　　　　I mean no danger to your stay:
　　　This night I will create my holiday,
　　　　And be yours naked and entire.
Mer. As if that Love disarmed were less a fire
　　Away, away.

　　　　They dance their going out.'

Ben Jonson was not the only poet to produce masques of literary value, for indeed he wrote nothing that surpassed, or even equalled, William Browne's *Masque of the Inner Temple*[1], which is remarkable both for the beauty of its style and the excellence of its subject-matter.

In the first scene, Sirens, seated on a cliff overhanging the sea, sing an exquisite lyric, which is intended to entice Ulysses and his men to disembark, and so fall into the hands of 'mighty Circe, daughter to the Sun ':

'...she that by charms can make
The scaled fish to leave the briny lake,
And on the seas walk as on land she were;
She that can pull the pale moon from her sphere....'

In the second scene Circe and the Sirens entering into a wood find Ulysses asleep and waken him with a charm:

'THE CHARM

'Son of Erebus and Night,
Hie away; and aim thy flight
Where consort none other fowl
Than the bat and sullen owl;
Where upon the limber grass
Poppy and mandragoras
With like simples not a few
Hang for ever drops of dew.
Where flows Lethe without coil
Softly like a stream of oil.
Hie thee thither, gentle Sleep:
With this Greek no longer keep.

---

[1] Reprinted in *The Poems of William Browne*, ed. G. Goodwin (London, 1894), vol. II, pp. 169 ff.

> Thrice I charge thee by my wand;
> Thrice with moly from my hand
> Do I touch Ulysses' eyes,
> And with the jaspis: Then arise,
> Sagest Greek....'

Having awakened Ulysses Circe entertains him, first with an antimasque danced by those whom she had transformed into monsters, and then by a second more graceful dance performed by her attendant nymphs. Ulysses then intercedes with Circe for his companions:

> 'Give leave that (freed from sleep) the small remain
> Of my companions on the under plain
> May in a dance strive how to pleasure thee
> Either with skill or with variety.'

His desire is granted, and in the third scene Ulysses wanders through a fair woodland glade, awakens his sleeping comrades by touching them with Circe's wand, and incites them to the masque dances and the revels.

Browne, in dedicating his masque to the honourable society of the Inner Temple, says that it was 'done to please ourselves in private,' and perhaps it was the quiet unostentatious character of its production which enabled the poet to free his work from the tasteless flattery which was customary at Court.

In 1653, several years after the performance of the last great royal masque, Shirley composed *Cupid and Death*, 'to make good a private entertainment,' and was pleasantly surprised when it was presented before the Portuguese ambassador[1]. In writing this masque Shirley grappled with a problem even harder than that which confronted Ben Jonson; for he endeavoured, not without success, to give poetic value and organic unity to that later type of masque which consisted of a series of almost unrelated musical interludes and entries of grotesque dancers. In *Cupid and Death*, although Shirley provides for a number of scene changes, many songs and dances, and a great variety of incidents, everything is organically connected, everything illustrates the central idea of the masque.

The first scene represents 'A Forest; on the side of a hill, a fair House, representing an Inn or Tavern; out of which cometh an HOST, being a jolly, sprightly old man,...after him, a CHAMBERLAIN.' To this

[1] *The Dramatic Works and Poems of James Shirley*, ed. Gifford and Dyce (London, 1833), vol. VI, pp. 347 ff.

tavern come several strange visitors: first Cupid attended by Folly and Madness, and then Death who is led in by the Chamberlain and passes into the hostel, not without causing some consternation.

> 'CHAM. ...A curse upon his physnomy!
> How was I surpris'd! t'was high time to comfort me;
> I felt my life was melting downward.'

At this point Despair comes in with a halter, and offers to leave a legacy to the Chamberlain if he will bring him into the presence of Death. The Chamberlain however gives him some wine, which cheers him so greatly that he no longer desires Death, and the only legacy that he leaves the Chamberlain is the halter. After this incident the Chamberlain who had departed with Despair, re-enters with the Host, and describes his dreadful experience during the past night:

> 'CHAM. Death and his train are gone;
> I thank heaven he's departed. I slept not
> One wink to-night, nor durst I pray aloud,
> For fear of waking Death; but he at midnight
> Calls for a cup to quench his thirst, a bowl
> Of blood I gave him for a morning's draught,
> And had an ague all the while he drunk it.
> At parting, in my own defence, and hope
> To please him, I desir'd to kiss his hand,
> Which was so cold, o' th' sudden, sir, my mouth
> Was frozen up, which as the case stood
> Then with my teeth did me a benefit,
> And kept the dancing bones from leaping out:
> At length, fearing for ever to be speechless,
> I us'd the strength of both my hands to open
> My lips, and now feel every word I speak,
> Drop from it like an icicle.
>
> HOST. This cold
> Fit will be over. What said Cupid?
>
> CHAM. He
> Was fast asleep.
>
> HOST. The boy went drunk to bed:
> Death did not wake him?
>
> CHAM. It was not necessary in point of reckoning;
> Death was as free as any emperor,
> And pays all where he comes; Death quits all scores.
> I have the *summa totalis* in my pocket,
> But he without more ceremony left
> The house at morning twilight.

Host. Ha! they knock.
Get thee a cup of wine to warm thy entrails.'[1]

Again the Chamberlain goes out to see Love off the premises, and on his return he describes the mischievous trick that he has played on the parting guests, for he has exchanged the arrows of Cupid and Death. In the next scene we watch the dire results of the Chamberlain's practical joke.

'The scene is changed into a pleasant Garden, a fountain in the midst of it; walks and arbours delightfully expressed; in divers places, Ladies lamenting over their Lovers slain by Cupid, who is discovered flying in the air.

Enter a LOVER, playing upon a lute, courting his MISTRESS; they dance.

Enter NATURE, in a white robe, a chaplet of flowers, a green mantle fringed with gold, her hair loose. They start, and seem troubled at her entrance.' Nature tells them to fly, but before they can do so: 'Enter CUPID, who strikes the Lover, and exit.' Nature deplores it. After this Death arrives followed by old men and women with crutches, whom he promptly shoots at; but his shot, so far from being deadly, seems to have a rejuvenating effect, for they drop their crutches and embrace. 'They dance with antic postures, expressing rural courtship.' Then six gentlemen come in 'armed, as in the field, to fight against three: to them DEATH; he strikes them with his arrow and exit; and they, preparing to charge, meet one another and embrace. They dance.'

After this our old friend the Chamberlain returns leading two apes, for he now gains his livelihood by showing these animals at fairs. Death comes in and strikes the Chamberlain who at once falls in love with his apes. 'Enter a SATYR, who strikes him on the shoulder, and takes away his Apes.' This disaster so overwhelms the mischievous Chamberlain that he takes out the halter, that had been left him by Despair, and goes away to hang himself, while the satyr and apes indulge in a heartless bout of dancing.

'Upon the sudden, a solemn music is heard, and Mercury seen descending upon a cloud, at whose approach the others creep in amazed. In a part of the scene, within a bower, Nature discovered sleeping.' Mercury summons Cupid and Death before him, wakens Nature and pronounces solemn judgment. He commands Cupid and Death to change darts, limits Cupid's power to cottages, and decrees that Death's power is not to extend over men of art and honour. Finally, in order to comfort Nature who is mourning for her lost children, Mercury promises to reveal the blest condition of the slain lovers.

'The scene is changed into Elysium, where the grand Masquers,

[1] *Loc. cit.* p. 356.

the slain Lovers, appear in glorious seats and habits.' A song and the grand masque dance follows, and finally Mercury reappears and closes the performance.

> 'Return, return, you happy men,
> To your own blessed shades again,
> Lest staying long, some new desire,
> In your calm bosoms raise a fire:
> Here are some eyes, whose every beam
> May your wandering hearts inflame,
> And make you forfeit your cool groves,
> By being false to your first loves.
> Like a perfuming gale o'r flowers,
> Now glide again to your own bowers.'[1]

This achievement is particularly astonishing on account of the formlessness of Shirley's earlier and more famous masque *The Triumph of Peace*.

If the poets were to transform the masque into a poetic or dramatic genre they had somehow to make it independent of music, dancing, and scenery. There were two ways of doing this. The poet could try to describe or to transpose into poetry something of the charm of the masque setting; or he could write a poetic libretto which at the time of performance was adorned and enhanced by the sister arts, but was no more dependent upon them than an ordinary book is dependent upon its illustrations. It was the latter method that Jonson advocated in theory[2], and occasionally followed in practice.

In some of his masques, Ben Jonson almost entirely ignores the 'bodily part.' 'The scene changes,' 'the scene of light discovered' are the only references to the setting of *The Golden Age Restored*. In *Love Restored* there are no references to scenery at all, though the words of Robin Goodfellow seem to indicate that a palace or dwelling-place of Cupid was shown upon the stage. In two lines of verse there is the only reference to the college of augurs, the design for which is preserved at Chatsworth[3].

In most of his masques, however, Ben Jonson describes the

---

[1] *Loc. cit.* p. 367.
[2] Cf. *supra*, pp. 250, 251.
[3] 'APOL. Yond, yond afar,
   They closed in their temple are....' *The Masque of Augurs.*

scenery, and there is no doubt that they gain in beauty thereby; for, after all, the setting was more than a mere accessory, it was part of the idea of the masque as originally conceived. The primary purpose of the masque libretto was not to preserve the poet's work from oblivion, but to give some account of the Court functions for the sake of those who had not gained admission, or who wished to preserve some memorial of a remarkable performance, and it therefore presented the public not only with the poet's original invention but also with his impression of the work of his collaborators. A poet who ignored music and dancing and background might have written an attractive lyrical drama, but he had not given permanent aesthetic value to the masque.

The masque, then, was partly the poet's creation, partly the source of his inspiration. Shirley's *Triumph of Peace* is not very attractively written, but there is a certain charm in his description of the final scene, and of the appearance of Amphiluche who represents 'that glimpse of light, which is seen when the night is past, and the day not yet appearing.'

In Browne's *Circe* [1], as in Milton's *Comus*, the loveliness of the background is conveyed by poetic imagery rather than by description of the staging, but the account of Ulysses wandering through the forest glade is very vivid, and the description of the second scene (both verse and prose) is inspired by the actual or anticipated work of the scene painter:

'Yond stands a hill crown'd with high waving trees,
Whose gallant tops each neighb'ring country sees,
Under whose shade an hundred silvans play,
With gaudy nymphs far fairer than the day;
Where everlasting spring with silver showers
Sweet roses doth increase to grace our bowers;
Where lavish Flora, prodigal in pride,
Spends what might well enrich all earth beside,...
Midway the wood and from the levell'd lands
A spacious yet a curious arbour stands,
Wherein should Phoebus once to pry begin,
I would benight him ere he get his inn,
Or turn his steeds awry, so draw him on
To burn all lands but this like Phaeton....

[1] *Masque of the Inner Temple.*

While CIRCE was speaking her first speech, and at these words, "Yond stands a hill, &c." a traverse was drawn at the lower end of the hall, and gave way for the discovery of an artificial wood so near imitating nature that I think, had there been a grove like it in the open plain, birds would have been faster drawn to that than to Zeuxis' grapes. The trees stood at the climbing of an hill, and left at their feet a little plain, which they circled like a crescent. In this space upon hillocks were seen eight musicians in crimson taffety robes, with chaplets of laurel on their heads, their lutes by them, which being by them touched as a warning to the nymphs of the wood, from among the trees was heard this Song...

THE SONG IN THE WOOD

What sing the sweet birds in each grove?
Nought but love.
What sound our echoes day and night?
All delight.
What doth each wind breathe as it fleets?
Endless sweets.'

Of all the masque writers, Ben Jonson seems to have caught most of the glamour of the masque settings, and his descriptions are no mere catalogues, for he does not supply us with detailed information as to the devices and mechanism of Inigo's art, but he does give a vivid impression of its charm by suggesting the effect it had on himself and others. His prose prefaces and descriptions, besides conveying the attractiveness of the scenery, have an intrinsic literary value; for indeed their theme (the theme of most poetry) is the vain longing to seize and hold the glory of the moment and to make it last for ever.

'The honour and splendour of these Spectacles was such in the performance as, could those hours have lasted, this of mine now had been a most unprofitable work. But when it is the fate even of the greatest and most absolute births to need and borrow a life of posterity, little had been done to the study of magnificence in these, if presently with the rage of the people, who (as a part of greatness) are privileged by custom to deface their carcases, the spirits had also perished.'[1]

Description he realises is altogether inadequate: 'Yet that I may not utterly defraud the reader of his hope, I am drawn to give it those brief touches which may leave behind some shadow of what it was: and first of the attires....'[2]

---

[1] *The Masque of Blackness.*　　　　　　[2] *Hymenaei.*

Jonson's 'brief touches' kindle the imagination, and rouse the desire to see a masque:

'The first face of the scene appeared all obscure, and nothing perceived but a dark rock, with trees beyond it, and all wildness that could be presented: till, at one corner of the cliff, above the horizon, the moon began to shew, and rising, a SATYR was seen by her light to put forth his head and call[1].

...With a strange and sudden music, they (i.e. the witches in their "horrid hell") fell into a magical dance, full of preposterous change and gesticulation. In the heat of their dance, on the sudden was heard a sound of loud music, as if many instruments had made one blast; with which not only the HAGS themselves, but the hell into which they ran, quite vanished, and the whole face of the Scene altered, scarce suffering the memory of such a thing; but in the place of it appeared a glorious and magnificent building, figuring the HOUSE OF FAME, in the top of which were discovered the twelve Masquers, sitting upon a throne triumphal, erected in form of a pyramid, and circled with all store of light.'[2]

Jonson's prose is not only vivid, every now and then it has 'a dying fall,' a regretful cadence, that suggests a mysterious unseizable beauty. 'From their backs were borne out certain light pieces of taffata, as if carried by the wind, and their music made out of wreathed shells.'[3] The vast sea, which by the art of perspective Inigo made to flow forth from the horizon, 'caught the eye afar off with a wandering beauty.'[4] There is a glamour even in the dressing of the masquers: 'The ladies' attire was wholly new, for the invention, and full of glory; as having in it the most true impression of a celestial figure.'

'Their descent was made in two great clouds, that put forth themselves severally, and, with one measure of time, were seen to stoop; and fall gently down upon the earth. The manner of their habits came after some statues of Juno, no less airy than glorious. The dressings of their heads rare; so likewise of their feet: and all full of splendor, sovereignty, and riches.'[5]

Was the glory really present in the masque scene, or was it

---

[1] *The Masque of Oberon.*　　　　[2] *The Masque of Queens.*
[3] *The Masque of Blackness.*　　　　[4] *Ibid.*
[5] *Hymenaei.* Cf. Pory's more prosaic description of the masquers '...who descended vpon the stage, not after the stale downright perpendicular fashion, like a bucket into a well; but came gently sloping down.' Cf. *supra*, p. 179.

mostly in the imagination of the poet? Sir Dudley Carleton describes the *Masque of Blackness* to his friend, and where Jonson saw a vast sea flowing forth and bearing onwards a strange and wonderful pageant of sea-beings, he saw 'a great engine at the lower end of the room, which had motion, and in it were the images of sea-horses with other terrible fishes, which were ridden by the Moors: The indecorum was, that there was all fish and no water.'[1] Ben Jonson was probably more nearly right than Dudley Carleton. Contemporary opinion went beyond Jonson in appreciation of Inigo's work, the beauty and even grandeur of Inigo's ideas can be judged from the drawings at Chatsworth, and he was too great and conscientious to have been contented with a very inferior execution of his designs. There were, however, flaws, and the mechanism did not always work smoothly[2]. To be over-critical is not necessarily a sign of intelligence. For the poet, at any rate, the merest hint of beauty is enough, his imagination is far too busy following out the hint, developing it, recreating it, for him to pay much attention to minor or even important imperfections. So that Bowles may inspire Coleridge, and vulgar tavern music may send Sir Thomas Browne into a fit of deep divinity, and the glitter and glow of the masque may suggest to Fuller the thought of Heaven 'where there are joyes for ever more.'[3]

If Jonson was to rescue the masque from oblivion he had somehow to capture and enshrine in his poetry the charm and grace of the dancing, the gaiety of the revels, which far more than painting and carpentry were the true soul of the masque. The movements of the dancers are described in many of the masque lyrics which were sung while the masquers were resting,

'Breathe again, while we with music
Fill the empty space';[4]

---

[1] *Prog. James*, vol. I, p. 473; *Eliz. Stage*, vol. III, p. 376.
[2] Cf. Campion, *Masque at the Marriage of the Lord Hayes*, op. cit. p. 164: '*Either by the simplicity, negligence, or conspiracy of the painter, the passing away of the trees was somewhat hazarded.*' Note that the masque was not staged by Inigo Jones.
[3] Cf. *infra*, p. 406.
[4] Campion, *The Lords Masque*, op. cit. p 209.

or when the chorus greeted the appearance of the masquers:

> 'Shake off your heavy trance,
>   And leap into a Dance
> Such as no mortals use to tread:
>   Fit only for Apollo
> To play to, for the Moon to lead,
>   And all the Stars to follow.'[1]

Sometimes these masque lyrics were true dancing songs, the feet of the masquers keeping time to the singing. Such was the song to which the trees danced at the marriage of the Lord Hayes, such was the magnificent lyric which greeted the dancing stars at the Lord's Masque, composed by Campion.

But even Campion cannot surpass the best of Ben Jonson's masque songs:

> 'Have men beheld the Graces dance,
>   Or seen the upper orbs to move?
> So these did turn, return, advance,
>   Drawn back by Doubt, put on by Love.'[2]

> 'In curious knots and mazes so,
>   The Spring at first was taught to go;
> And Zephyr, when he came to woo
>   His Flora, had their motions too:
> And then did Venus lean to lead
>   The Idalian brawls, and so to tread
> As if the wind, not she, did walk;
>   Nor prest a flower, nor bowed a stalk.'[3]

Sometimes Jonson makes of his songs a mystical interpretation of the dances. For instance, in the *Masque of Beauty* the first dance ended in the form of a diamond, while a loud tenor voice celebrated the event in song:

> 'So Beauty on the waters stood,
>   When Love had severed earth from flood!
> So when he parted air from fire,
>   He did with concord all inspire!
> And then a *motion* he them taught,
>   That elder than himself was thought.
> Which thought was yet the child of earth,
>   For Love is elder than his birth.'

---

[1] Francis Beaumont, *Masque of the Inner Temple and Gray's Inn*, printed in Nicholl's *Progresses of King James I, op. cit.* vol. II, p. 599.
[2] *Love Restored.*   [3] *The Vision of Delight.*

Again in *Pleasure Reconciled to Virtue* Daedalus the wise comments on the movements of the masquers:

> 'DAED. Come on, come on! and where you go,
> So interweave the curious knot,
> As ev'n the observer scarce may know
> Which lines are Pleasure's, and which not.
>
> First figure out the doubtful way,
> At which awhile all youth should stay....
>
> Then as all actions of mankind
> Are but a labyrinth or maze:
> So let your dances be entwined,
> Yet not perplex men unto gaze....
>
> For dancing is an exercise,
> Not only shows the mover's wit,
> But maketh the beholder wise,
> As he hath power to rise to it....'

> 'DAED. O more and more! this was so well,
> As praise wants half his voice to tell,
> Again yourselves compose:
> And now put all the aptness on,
> Of figure, that proportion
> Or colour can disclose:
>
> That if those silent arts were lost,
> Design and picture, they might boast
> From you a newer ground....
>
> Begin, begin; for look, the fair
> Do longing listen to what air
> You form your second touch:
> That they may vent their murmuring hymns
> Just to the [time] you move your limbs,
> And wish their own were such.'

Ben Jonson accompanies the revels as well as the masque dances with songs, and no other poet has caught so much of the spirit of the courtly revels into his masque poetry

> 'The male and female used to join,
> And unto all delight did coin
> That pure simplicity.
> Then Feature did to Form advance,
> And Youth called Beauty forth to dance,
> And every Grace was by.'[1]

[1] *The Golden Age Restored.*

'Here all the day they feast, they sport and spring,
Now dance the Graces' hay, now Venus ring:
To which the old musicians play and sing.

SAR. There is Arion, tuning his bold harp,
From flat to sharp.

POR. And light Anacreon,
He still is one....

POR. Nor is Apollo dainty to appear
In such a quire; although the trees be thick,

PRO. He will look in, and see the airs be quick,
And that the times be true....

CHO. See! all the flowers,

PRO. That spring the banks along,
Do move their heads unto that under song....

This sung, the island goes back, whilst the Upper Chorus takes it from them, and the MASQUERS prepare for their figure.

CHO. Spring all the graces of the age,
And all the loves of time;
Bring all the pleasures of the stage,
And relishes of rhyme.
Add all the softnesses of courts,
The looks, the laughters, and the sports;
And mingle all their sweets and salts,
That none may say the triumph halts.'[1]

Sometimes Jonson conveys to us the charm and grace of the revels by his prose as well as by his poetry:

'This speech being ended, they dissolved: and all took forth other persons (men and women) to dance other measures, galliards, and corantos: the whilst this SONG importuned them to a fit remembrance of the time....Their dances yet lasting, they were the second time importuned by speech....At this, the whole scene being drawn again, and all covered with clouds, as a night, they left off their intermixed dances, and returned to their first places; where, as they were but beginning to move, this SONG, the third time, urged them....Here they danced their last dances, full of excellent delight and change, and in their latter strain, fell into a fair orb or circle; REASON standing in the midst, and speaking....With this, to a soft strain of music, they paced once about, in their ring, every pair making their honours, as they came before the state: and then dissolving, went down in couples, led on by HYMEN, the bride, and auspices following, as to the nuptial bower.'[2]

---

[1] *The Fortunate Isles.*   [2] *Hymenaei.*

There is nothing sad in these words, and yet, somehow, through some subtlety of rhythm perhaps, beneath them runs that undercurrent of pathos and regret which is in all dance music. In this case perhaps also there is the regret of the poet, whose words have not quite captured all the beauty of his vision. For Ben Jonson did not quite succeed, his masques have not the permanence and detachment of immortal poetry. The student knows and loves them, but they have not become part of the nation's soul. Interpreted by historic imagination, by knowledge of contemporary history, they live again, but they do not shine by their own light—and Jonson knew it.

'Hitherto extended the first night's solemnity, whose grace in the execution left not where to add unto it with wishing....Such was the exquisite performance as, beside the pomp, splendour, or what we may call apparelling of such presentments, that alone (had all else been absent) was of power to surprise with delight, and steal away the spectators from themselves. Nor was there wanting whatsoever might give to the furniture or complement; either in riches or strangeness of the habits, delicacy of dances, magnificence of the scene, or divine rapture of music. Only the envy was, that it lasted not still, or, now it is past, cannot by imagination, much less description, be recovered to a part of that spirit it had in the gliding by.'[1]

So Ben Jonson failed as he was bound to do, and we are left wondering whether his failure was deserved as well as inevitable. Might it not be argued that his aims were less lofty than those of his fellow-workers on the Continent, who sought for a harmony of the arts? That harmony may be unattainable but at least it is a generous ideal[2], and beside it how thin and meagre appears Ben Jonson's idea of the masque, how ungenerous his attempt to minimise the work of others and to free just his own share in the performance from that curse of mortality which lay upon 'the bodily part which was of Master Inigo Jones his design and act.'[3]

---

[1] *Hymenaei.*
[2] Cf. Baron von Hügel, *The Mystical Element of Religion* (London, 1923), vol. II, p. 165. He regards Wagnerian opera as 'a great Music-Drama and multiform yet intensely unified image of life itself,' and uses it to illustrate the comprehensive character of true religion.
[3] *The Masque of Blackness.*

But in truth Ben Jonson at his best did not really try to turn the masque into a lyrical drama independent of its environment. He strove (in fact if not in theory) to make the masque into something which combined the solidity and permanence of poetry with the grace and vitality of the revels. In *Comus* and to a certain extent in Browne's *Circe* the imagination is carried straight into the world of poetic magic, and the banqueting hall is forgotten. In the best of Jonson's masques the imagination reaches the world of poetic magic, but reaches it by way of the banqueting hall. Never for a moment are we unconscious of the brilliant assembly, the glittering stage, the conventional symmetrical scenery, the wistful Elizabethan music. In reading the work of other masque writers we are conscious of these things and indeed of little else. It is an easy matter to reconstruct the scene of a great Court masque from one of Davenant's or Townshend's libretti. It is an easy matter to picture those great social functions of the past in all their grandeur and brilliance, in all their stiff artificiality and false taste. But Jonson gives us both the actual and the ideal truth of the old Court function. He does not simply create for us a golden world, he does not simply recreate for us the courtly festivals, but by occasional brief touches he re-awakens in us those strange mixed feelings which must have stirred in the more imaginative among contemporary spectators, the feeling that not just the masque but the proud gay brilliant society that gave rise to it was a work of art too wonderful to end, mingled with the regretful sense of unreality and evanescence.

> 'We see, we hear, we feel, we taste,
> We smell the change in every flow'r,
> We only wish that all could last,
> And be as new still as the hour.'[1]

> 'O, you wake then! come away,
> Times be short, are made for play;
> The humorous moon too will not stay....

After this they danced their last dance into the work. And with a full SONG the star vanished, and the whole machine closed.

---

[1] *The Vision of Delight.*

> O yet how early, and before her time,
> The envious morning up doth climb,
>   Though she not love her bed!
> What haste the jealous Sun doth make,
> His fiery horses up to take,
>   And once more shew his head!
> Lest, taken with the brightness of this night,
> The world should wish it last, and never miss his light.'[1]

Milton, who has made his Lady and her brothers turn away from revelry and overcome the love of earthly pleasure, ends his masque on a note of exultation. His masquers earn 'a crown of deathless praise,' they 'triumph in victorious dance,' the Attendant Spirit soars up to a paradise of 'everlasting summer.' But many masques end with the thought not of eternity but of the swift flight of time and of the inevitable end of beauty and delight. Even the solid Daniel felt something of the pathos which lay behind the gay brilliance of the masquing hall.

> 'Are they shadowes that we see?
> And can shadowes pleasure giue?...
> But these pleasures vanish fast,
> Which by shadowes are exprest:
> Pleasures are not, if they last,
> In their passing, is their best.
> Glory is most bright and gay
> In a flash, and so away.
> Feed apace then greedy eyes
> On the wonder you behold.
> Take it sodaine as it flies
> Though you take it not to hold:
> Then when eyes haue done their part
> Thought must length it in the hart.'[2]

Ben Jonson tried to catch the short-lived beauty of the masque and 'length it in the heart.' But if it is difficult to achieve a harmony of all the arts, it is far more difficult to achieve harmony between the spirit of enduring poetry and the spirit of fleeting sensuous revelry, and this was what Jonson all but succeeded in doing. As the result of his attempt he created no perfect poem such as *Comus*, but he did make many lovely lyrics

---

[1] *The Masque of Oberon.*　　　　　　[2] *Tethys Festival.*

and he did, by bringing the spirit of poetry into the masque, help to keep alive the spirit of the dance in English literature; he did rescue from oblivion and hand down to posterity something of the charm of the old Court festivals, something of the glamour which surrounded the masquers, as they trod their measures at Whitehall or Hampton Court, or went in triumphant procession down the Thames or through the streets of London.

> 'How near to good is what is fair!
> Which we no sooner see,
> But with the lines and outward air
> Our senses taken be.
> We wish to see it still, and prove
> What ways we may deserve;
> We court, we praise, we more than love:
> We are not grieved to serve.'

Then comes

'the last Masque-Dance...and after it, this full SONG.

> What just excuse had aged Time,
>   His weary limbs now to have eased,
> And sate him down without his crime,
>   While every thought was so much pleased!
> But he so greedy to devour
>   His own, and all that he brings forth,
> Is eating every piece of hour
>   Some object of the rarest worth.
> Yet this is rescued from his rage,
> As not to die by time or age:
>   For beauty hath a living name,
>   And will to heaven, from whence it came.'[1]

---

[1] *Love freed from Ignorance and Folly.*

CHAPTER X

The Influence of the Masque on the Drama

'Canst thou bind the sweet influences of the Pleiades?'

T H E value of the Court masque lies in its dynamic quality rather than in any intrinsic excellence. Ben Jonson's attempt to transform it into a work of art, though unsuccessful, was not fruitless, for much of the literature of the time was permeated by the influence of the poetic masque and entertainment, and we shall misinterpret the work of the Elizabethan poet and playwright unless we remember that he had to cater for a public accustomed to a spectacular social life.

The drama was particularly susceptible to the masque influence, because the two genres were of kindred origin, and often associated in practice. This is true of the European theatre as a whole. The religious play began life as a ritual, it grew and flourished in an atmosphere of civic pageantry, it was reborn as a secular amusement, in the gay, glittering Courts of Italy.

In England as in Italy, the secular drama was cradled at Court: the masters, gentlemen and children of the Chapel Royal, were often employed in the production of plays, and the much discussed interlude, which is often taken as a starting-point of English dramatic history, is apparently just the old religious play, adapted to the needs of the banqueting hall by a little group of humanists, associated with Sir Thomas More. The English drama, therefore, arose in a musical and spectacular environment.

In the Tudor Court there was constant interaction between play and entertainment. From the pages of Hall's *Chronicle* we gather that moralities were freely embellished with masques and morris-dances; that plays and disguisings were often performed in close conjunction; that symbolical pageants, celebrating diplomatic events, might be almost indistinguishable from political interludes; and, finally, the chronicler, by his vague use of the term 'disguising,' suggests that there was no very hard and fast distinction between a dramatic performance and a revel[1]. This

---

[1] Hall, for instance, calls the morality play which offended Wolsey a 'disguising.' Cf. Hall, vol. II, p. 79 (18th year), and Brotanek, *op. cit.* p. 119.

state of affairs continued into the reign of Elizabeth: for it is hard to categorise the various shows prepared for the amusement of the Queen on progress, and moreover the lyrical and spectacular tradition of the entertainment was to a certain extent preserved by the children's companies and the actors in the private theatres, who formed connecting links between the Court and the public stage[1]. The children were not the only actors who kept the masque and drama in touch with one another, for the common players also were frequently at Court, where they performed both ordinary stage plays, and also those parts of the Court masque which were beyond the powers of the noble amateurs[2]. It was natural enough that the players should insert masques and masque-like episodes into ordinary stage plays, and that these spectacular interludes should prove very popular. For the ordinary theatre-goer was glad to be given some idea of famous Court functions, and then, as always, he had a keen relish for music, dancing, and spectacular display; for however much critics may despise these things, the average play-goer regards them as the most attractive part of a theatrical performance.

The influence of the masque not only caused interruptions in the action of certain plays, but it affected as we shall see the structure and spirit of the popular drama as a whole, and was a potent factor in the building up of certain dramatic forms, romantic comedy, dramatic romance, and the lyrical tragedy of Shakespeare, Webster, and others.

The dramatic experiments of the University wits owe much to the influence of the revels, and the continued interaction of the play and entertainment.

In 1584 George Peele's drama *The Arraignment of Paris*[3] was presented before Queen Elizabeth by the children of the Chapel Royal.

---

[1] Cf. W. J. Lawrence, *The Elizabethan Playhouse*, Series I, Papers I, XI; Chambers, *Eliz. Stage*, vol. I, chap. VII; vol. II, chaps. XII, XVII; vol. III, chap. XIX; F. E. Schelling, *Elizabethan Drama* (London, 1908), vol. I, chap. III.

[2] *Eliz. Stage*, vol. I, pp. 200, 201.

[3] *Dramatic Works of Greene and Peele*, ed. Dyce (London, 1874), pp. 347 ff.

The play opens with a ghost prologue, then, amid much irrelevant pastoral business, the competing goddesses appear, and each of them tries to influence the judgment of Paris by presenting a show. When he has made the fateful decision Paris is arrested by Mercury and the Cyclops on a charge of stirring up celestial strife, and his trial in the neighbourhood of Diana's bower affords opportunity for the introduction of several songs, dances, and spectacular effects. Finally Paris is despatched to Troy, and the golden ball is delivered to Diana, who decides that nobody but the nymph Zabeta (i.e. Queen Elizabeth) is worthy to receive it.

'The Music sounds, and the Nymphs within sing or solfa with voices and instruments awhile. Then enter Clotho, Lachesis and Atropos....' These three Fates sing a Latin chant and 'lay down their properties at the Queen's feet,' and then each in turn makes a complimentary speech, Diana delivers the ball of gold into the Queen's own hands, and the divinities altogether speak or sing the epilogue.

This pastoral play of Peele's is closely related to the masque. It is entirely lyrical in spirit, it is interspersed with songs, dances, spectacular devices and masque-like shows, it is devised as an elaborate compliment to the Queen, and is lacking in the proper dramatic detachment from the occasion and audience. *The Arraignment of Paris* is indeed more like a masque than is Milton's *Comus*, for its final compliment is not a mere epilogue, but a dénouement. This is a defect, for although Peele leads up to his flattery most ingeniously, he does not succeed in fusing compliment, lyric, and story into an artistic whole: the appearance of Ate 'from lowest hell' should surely prelude 'the tragedy of Troy,' instead of leading to a piece of extravagant flattery written in pastoral style.

Something of the same irrelevance and incoherence is occasionally shown in the use made of the induction, a dramatic convention which was possibly borrowed from the Court entertainment. Greene, for instance, pretends that his *Comical History of Alphonsus, King of Arragon* (a blood and thunder play with a happy ending) has been composed by the goddess Venus, who appears at the opening of the drama. 'After you have sounded thrice, let Venus be let down from the top of the stage.' Venus, it seems, dissatisfied with the negligence of the poets, has determined to turn authoress herself, and helped by the Muses she will

'...describe Alphonsus' warlike fame,
And, in the manner of a comedy,
Set down his noble valour presently.'[1]

Venus, like many inexperienced writers, cannot resist commenting on the progress of the story; she reappears at the beginning of each act, and finally hints at her intention of composing a sequel:

'Now, worthy Muses, with unwilling mind
Venus is forc'd to trudge to heaven again...
Meantime, dear Muses, wander you not far
Forth of the path of high Parnassus' hill
That, when I come to finish up his life,
You may be ready for to succour me....

Exit Venus; or, if you can conveniently, let a chair come down from the top of the stage, and draw her up....Exeunt omnes, playing on their instruments.'[2]

This absurd induction has no bearing at all upon the plot, and must surely have been composed for the sake of those who, through their experience of masques and entertainments, had come to regard the entry or descent of divinities as indispensable to a dramatic performance.

Greene's *The Scottish Historie of James IV* has an interesting induction:

'Music playing within. Enter after OBERON, King of Fairies, an ANTIC, who dance about a tomb placed conveniently on the stage; out of which suddenly starts up, as they dance, BOHAN, a Scot, attired like a ridstall man, from whom the ANTICS fly.' Oberon however remains, and soon strikes up a friendship with Bohan, who expresses his hatred for the world and offers to produce sound reasons for his misanthropy:

'BOH. Now, king, if thou be a king, I will show thee whay [why] I hate the world by demonstration. In the year fifteen hundred and twenty, was in Scotland a king, over-ruled with parasites, misled by lust, and many circumstances too long to trattle on now, much like our court of Scotland this day. That story have I set down. Gang with me to the gallery, and I'll show thee the same in action by guid fellows of our country-men; and then, when thou see'st that, judge if any wise man would not leave the world if he could.'[3]

Oberon and Bohan then watch the enacting of Bohan's jig, which is

[1] Act I, Prologue.   [2] Act V, Epilogue.   [3] Induction.

the romantic tale of the King of Scots, Queen Dorothea, and the Countess Ida. Between the acts Bohan and Oberon discuss what they have
seen, Oberon presents various dumb shows by way of comment on the
action, and both refresh themselves with lighter entertainment: 'To them
a round of Fairies, or some pretty dance[1]....Enter Slipper with a companion, boy or wench, dancing a hornpipe, and dance out again[2]....
Enter a round, or some dance, at pleasure.'[3] In Act IV, sc. 3, there is a
'dance of Anticks'; Act V, sc. 2, is preluded by the stage direction: 'After
a solemn service, enter from the COUNTESS OF ARRAN's house a service,
with musical songs of marriages, or a mask, or pretty triumph.'

This induction is more pointed than the induction to *Alphonsus*,
but it is not wholly successful. The distinction between induction and play is not maintained, for Slipper and Nano, Bohan's
sons, and occasionally Oberon, run in and out of the action in a
confusing manner; some of the dumb shows are quite irrelevant;
and the lyrical and dance episodes are too obviously inserted,
simply to relieve tension—as indeed Greene himself points out:

> 'Now after this beguiling of our thoughts,
> And changing them from sad to better glee,
> Let's to our cell, and sit and see the rest,
> For, I believe, this jig will prove no jest.'[4]

Again:

> 'The rest is ruthful; yet to beguile the time,
> 'Tis interlac'd with merriment and rhyme.'[5]

Greene's naïve avowal of his motive is enlightening. The
dramatists were expected to divert their audiences with interludes
of music and dancing, and their use of the induction was a clumsy
attempt to prevent these interludes from confusing the dramatic
action, while giving them at the same time some more or less
rational connection with the plot. The induction, however, was
not really a satisfactory solution of the problem, because the
induction was simply an elaboration of the rôle of the presenter
and so obviously more suitable to the masque than to the drama.
A silent procession or symbolical pageant may need introduction
and interpretation; but a well-written drama should be self-
explanatory, and in it the presenter's rôle is likely to be otiose,
and an elaborate induction confusing.

[1] Act I, sc. 3. [2] Act II, sc. 2. [3] Act IV, sc. 5.
[4] Act II, sc. 2. [5] Act III, sc. 3.

However, in spite of their defects, these hybrid, masque-like plays had a fascinating atmosphere of unreality and enchantment, and they never quite lost their popularity. Dekker's *Pleasant Comedy of Old Fortunatus* published in 1600 illustrates the unbroken continuity of English dramatic history, and shows how the influence of the masque helped to preserve the mediaeval tradition.

At the very beginning of our period John Lyly composed a number of plays, which prepared the way for the romantic comedies of Shakespeare. Lyly aspired to the Mastership of the revels, his plays were performed by the Children of Blackfriars before a cultivated audience, and naturally his work, like the work of Greene and Peele, bears a family likeness to the masque. Lyly, however, had a sense of form that was lacking in the other University wits, and was able to make a more satisfactory use of the influence of the revels. The difference of method is very interesting. For instance, Peele keeps us among Olympians and Arcadians until the final act, when we are suddenly jolted into the presence of Queen Elizabeth; but Lyly, on the other hand, conveys his tribute to the maiden Queen by telling a consistent story of Endymion's love for the Moon goddess, a story which from beginning to end is both a moral allegory, and a veiled description of Court intrigue. Instead of ending an ordinary play with a complimentary masque-like dénouement, Lyly sheds his compliment over the whole plot. Instead of framing a realistic story in a masque-like induction, Lyly makes his whole action approximate to the symbolical movement of the masque, and his very slight intrigue is carried out by characters, cold and colourless as masque presenters, who engage in cultivated wit contests, and move about in a gentle pastoral setting, which is perfectly congruent with fairy dances. Instead of producing a patchwork of masque and drama, Lyly consciously or unconsciously invented a new kind of society comedy which was dramatic in form, but in spirit akin to the courtly revels; and his plays may be regarded as imaginative renderings of the ordinary Court life, just a little idealised; or as dramatic versions of Court festivals, just a little faded. Shakespeare had only to add his own magic touch to

Lyly's structure, and the result was the creation of Romantic Comedy.

Shakespeare preserved intact the form of Lyly's comedy, but he gave it a much richer and more substantial content by dropping the mythological disguise and severing the connection with courtly flattery and intrigue. Rosalind, Viola, and the rest are genuine human beings, engaged in love affairs and farcical adventures, which have no symbolical meaning or ulterior motive. Yet although Shakespeare enriches and enlivens and humanises Court comedy, he does not change its spirit. Shakespeare's comedy is neither critical nor realistic, there is plenty of room in it for song and dance, background is almost as important as adventure, gesture is almost as interesting as personality, his comic characters are certainly made of flesh and blood, but 'they fleet the time carelessly as they did in the golden world.'

As You Like It, for instance, is a series of tableaux and groupings. The intrigue is tangled up at the beginning, and hurriedly unravelled at the close, but all the really attractive part of the play is a mere interlude, a picturesque idyll of the Forest of Arden. Music is only less important than pictorial effect. There are three scenes which simply serve to introduce song. Finally, the play is definitely connected with the masque by the introduction of Hymen, who appears as *deus ex machina*, and solves all discords to the accompaniment of still music.

Twelfth Night by its very name suggests thoughts of masque and revelry and carnival, which suit well with the 'uncivil rule' of Sir Toby and his companions. The opening line gives us the key in which it is written:

'If music be the food of love, play on.'

The musical Fool gives unity to the play. He forms a connecting link between the 'sotie' of Sir Toby and his fellow-roisterers and the half-playful romance of the main theme, and he brings the play to a close by singing a nonsense song, which seems to draw over the whole comedy the veil of unreality and illusion.

In *The Merchant of Venice* the spirit of the revels infects the Belmont scenes, where the casket is chosen to music, where Lorenzo and Jessica, seated together on a moonlit bank, watch the stars and summon the musicians to 'wake Diana with a hymn.' Here as in the *Midsummer Night's Dream* Shakespeare has extracted the quintessence of Lyly's work and realised its latent, unused beauty.

Lyly's influence, however, was not wholly romantic, for Ben Jonson as well as Shakespeare owed much to it. In *Cynthia's Revels or The Fountain of Self Love* Jonson copies Lyly in drawing a picture of Court life by means of a slight fantastic intrigue, carried out by characters representing both abstract qualities and real living people. Jonson, however, caricatures instead of idealising contemporary society, and the performance culminates in the production of a masque composed by the virtuous scholar Crites, i.e. Ben Jonson himself, in which Cupid enters disguised as Anteros, and makes a long prose speech introducing the masquers, who are disguised as virtues. The second masque is introduced by Mercury, who makes a similar prose speech. Then follows '*Music. A Dance by the two Masques joined, during which* Cupid *and* Mercury *retire to the side of the stage.*' There are three other masque dances, after which Cynthia insists on the dancers unmasking, and revealing themselves in their true characters as vices.

It is noteworthy that Ben Jonson composed *Cynthia's Revels* before he had written any independent Court masque, and that the masques inserted into this play are of the simpler processional type. In England the masque seems to have found its earliest fulfilment in the drama; Lyly was inventing Court comedy just about the time when in France Beaujoyeulx was inventing the ballet comique, and several years before the elaboration of the masque by Gentlemen of the Inns of Court. There was indeed constant interaction between the two kinds, and this is well illustrated by the *Masque of Oberon*. Jonson obviously borrowed the idea of this masque from the *Midsummer Night's Dream*, which was itself indebted to *Endymion* and to earlier masques and entertainments, and then Shakespeare in his turn borrowed an antimasque of satyrs from Jonson's *Masque of Oberon*, and inserted it into *The Winter's Tale*[1].

In James I's reign, when the masque became more elaborate

[1] Cf. *infra*, p. 284.

and dramatic, its influence upon the drama naturally increased. The public craved for a taste of courtly splendour, the dramatists inserted elaborate masques into their plays, and sometimes actors would reproduce on the public stage antimasques which they themselves had already performed at great Court functions. This happened in the case of the antimasque, borrowed by Shakespeare from Ben Jonson:

'Pol. ...Pray, let's see these four threes of herdsmen.

Serv. One three of them, by their own report, sir, hath danced before the king; and not the worst of the three but jumps twelve foot and a half by the squier....

Re-enter Servant, with twelve Rustics habited like Satyrs. They dance, and then exeunt.'[1]

Another instance is the morris-dance in *The Two Noble Kinsmen,* which appears to be a reproduction of one of the antimasques in Beaumont's *Masque of the Inner Temple*[2].

The insertion of an increasing number of lyrical interludes and episodes was not the only manifestation of the influence of the masque on seventeenth-century drama. Just as in Elizabeth's reign romantic comedy was shaped under the influence of the Court revels, so again in the Jacobean period a new wave of masque influence coincided with the change of dramatic style and a tendency to turn tragedy and comedy into dramatic romance.

The romance differed from earlier types of drama chiefly by the complication and ingenuity of its plot. About 1609 or 1610 the public seem to have tired of plays written in one dominant mood, and to have craved for more excitement and emotional variety. Whether the tale ended sadly or happily mattered little, as long as the dénouement was reached by a long and winding path, and the journey enlivened by astonishing events, sudden turns of fortune, and frequent changes of mood. Whatever the ultimate reason for this change of taste may have been, it is obvious that the masque helped to satisfy, even if it did not help to excite, this new craving for the marvellous and sensational. The last plays of Shakespeare and many of the works of Beaumont

---

[1] *The Winter's Tale,* act IV, sc. 3, ll. 341 ff.
[2] Cf. *The Two Noble Kinsmen,* act III, sc. 5, ll. 1–108, and *supra,* p. 195.

and Fletcher would seem to have been written in response to this new demand. Later still, at the beginning of the Caroline period, dramatists such as Ford and Shirley, who were particularly influenced by the masque, show a distinct tendency to revert to the older methods of religious drama, and to compose plays which were not only spectacular but abstract and allegorical.

This tendency to fuse masque and drama is illustrated in Beaumont and Fletcher's *Four Plays or Moral Representations in One*, which occupies the same midway position between the two kinds as does Peele's *Arraignment of Paris* or Jonson's *Cynthia's Revels*.

The action of the play takes place at the Court of Lisbon, where the nuptials of the King and Queen of Portugal and Castile are being celebrated by dramatic performances. In the opening scene we see the huisher Frigoso ushering the courtiers and city wives into their places, the royal couple enter and are addressed by 'a Poet...with a Garland':

> 'Four several Triumphs to your princelie eyes,
> Of Honour, Love, Death, and Time, do rise
> From our approaching subject....
> ...Then how dare we
> Present, like apes, and zanies, things that be
> Exemplified in you....'

After this the first representation, a typical romantic drama, begins, and we see Dorigen, wife of Sophocles, preserving her virtue against the solicitations of Martius. When all has ended happily Diana descends to announce the show of *Honour's Triumph*, which consists of a procession of the chief characters of the play, certain allegorical figures and a triumphal chariot.

The audience discuss what they have seen until Cupid descends to announce the next representation, the play of *Love*, which deals with the illegal but constant love of Violante and Gerrard. There are several dumb shows in the course of this play which are neither interludes nor symbolical interpretations of the story, but essential portions of the plot performed in pantomime. The play ends with a Triumph, after which there is a flourish, and a Prologue enters to announce an important change of subject:

> 'Now turn we round the scene; and, great sir, lend
> A sad and serious eye to this of Death;
> This black and dismal triumph....'

A very sombre procession conducting a 'chariot with Death, drawn by the Destinies,' closes the tale of how the lustful Lavall brought ruin upon himself, and how the innocent as well as the guilty were involved in his punishment.

Again the Prologue enters:

> 'From this sad sight ascend your noble eye,
> And see old Time helping triumphantly,
> Helping his master, Man....'

This last representation is a morality with masque-like characteristics, and corresponds closely in form to plays and masques such as the *World Tost at Tennis* and *The Sun's Darling*[1]. It is interspersed with dances and spectacular devices:

'Jupiter and Mercury descend severally to soft music....Enter Plutus, with a troop of Indians singing and dancing wildly about him, and bowing to him....Industry and the Arts discovered....Plutus stamps, and Labour rises....They carry Anthropos to a rock, and fall adigging. Plutus strikes the rock, and flames fly out....Enter Vain-Delight, Pleasure, Craft, Lucre, Vanity, &c. dancing, and masked, towards the rock, offering service to Anthropos. Mercury from above. Music heard. One half of a Cloud drawn, Singers are discovered; then the other half drawn, Jupiter seen in glory.

> MERC. Take heed, weak man! those are the sins that sunk thee;
> Trust 'em no more; kneel, and gives thanks to Jupiter.
>
> ANTH. Oh, mighty power!
>
> JUP. Unmask, ye gilded poisons!—
> Now look upon 'em, son of Earth, and shame 'em;
> Now see the faces of thy evil angels:
> Lead 'em to Time, and let 'em fill his triumph;
> Their memories be here forgot for ever!'

This episode is in itself a kind of compressed masque, in which an antimasque is followed by a revelation of a divine being.

After a song has been sung by Mercury, the Triumph enters, and then the King of Portugal brings all to a conclusion by giving his interpretation of the performance:

> 'By this we note, sweetheart, in kings and princes
> A weakness, even in spite of all their wisdoms....'

As a piece of craftsmanship this work is most interesting. The authors have set before themselves the same problem which was attacked by Greene and Peele in *King James IV* and in *The Arraignment of Paris*, but they bring to its solution a mastery

---

[1] Cf. *supra*, pp. 277 ff.

of technique unknown to the University wits. The scheme is carefully planned and exactly worked out. The courtly revels are transplanted on to the public stage, but without that sudden and unprepared lapse from dramatic detachment which spoils *The Arraignment of Paris*. The induction makes an admirable framework for the four representations and has some intrinsic interest; there is never any confusion between the characters of the induction and the characters of the play they are witnessing; each play is carefully plotted to illustrate some idea that can in each case lead up to an imposing final triumph, and is not without relevance to the situation of the newly wedded pair for whom it is represented. So far the play is a triumph of constructive skill, yet it is not a masterpiece. The joints are too obvious and the unity is the unity which joins together the parts of a machine, not the unity which animates a living organism. Moreover it lacks point. It does not give (except in the short opening scene) a vivid picture of Court life, it somehow fails to convey to us the charm of the revels, it does not tell any one story, it does not work out any one idea. There is no just cause why these four plays should be joined together. Apparently the authors are experimenting, they are seeking a form which will enable them to supply their audience with a maximum amount of variety by joining together (without blending) realistic comedy, romance, tragedy, pageant, masque, and morality. This kind of motive is admirable enough in an energetic manager of a music hall, but it is not likely to prove the mainspring of a dramatic masterpiece, and the *Four Plays in One* for all its careful construction has less vital unity than Shakespeare's loose-jointed rambling romances *Cymbeline* and *The Winter's Tale*.

Whatever may have been the ultimate motive for Shakespeare's sudden change of dramatic method, there is no doubt that his latest plays satisfied the public demand for emotional variety and spectacular effect, and were full of those masque-like episodes that the public loved.

In the romances, even more than in the early comedies, Shakespeare lingers over scenes of lyrical or pictorial beauty, and hurries unduly over matters of greater dramatic importance.

How lovingly, for instance, he lengthens out the sheep-shearing scene in *The Winter's Tale*, how he lingers on the picture of Imogen in her bed-chamber, reading herself to sleep with the tale of Tereus, until even her foe turns poet.

Once again gesture and background become almost as important as character and plot. In *The Winter's Tale*, for instance, in the middle of the tragic business of Hermione we overhear the messengers describing the wonders of Delphi and the 'ceremonious, solemn, and unearthly' pageantry of sacrifice, although dramatically their conversation is unnecessary.

Even poor Antigonus meets his absurd ending in romantic surroundings, and later in the same scene Shakespeare interrupts the comic business with the picture of the old weather-beaten shepherd, bending over the 'pretty barne': 'Now bless thyself: thou mettest with things dying, I with things new born....This is fairy gold, boy, and 'twill prove so.'[1]

The shepherd's words sum up the meaning of Shakespeare's latest work, and help us to understand why *The Winter's Tale* in spite of its grave dramatic flaws has more true dramatic unity than *Four Plays in One*. Of course joining together two plays by means of a chorus is no more and no less excusable than joining together four plays by means of an induction. But *The Winter's Tale* has more unity than the *Four Plays* because it has more significance, because it passes one at least of those tests of dramatic excellence, which have been well defined by Mr William Archer: 'Does the play *say* something and *mean* something?... In seeing or reading it, have we not merely enjoyed a pastime, but undergone an experience?'

Certainly *The Winter's Tale* says something and means something. It is not just an attempt to unite two plays by means of a chorus, it is an attempt to turn tragedy into comedy by means of Father Time. People demanded variety entertainments, Shakespeare supplied them with plays in which all things worked together for good, people demanded plays which combined the attraction of masque and drama, Shakespeare supplied them with romances, in which even the darker aspects of life were

[1] *The Old Drama and the New* (London, 1923), p. 136.

invested with an enigmatic beauty. In these last plays of his there are gross improbabilities, inconsistencies of character, clumsy dramatic devices; pseudo-historical events, tragic situations, comic and masque-like episodes are jumbled together in them with a wantonness worthy of Greene or Peele; yet underneath the incongruous medley there runs a kind of enchanted tune, now loud, now almost inaudible, an accompaniment which in some strange way atones for all the surface discords and inconsistencies:

'PERICLES. But, hark, what music?... HEL. My lord, I hear none.
PER.   None!
      The music of the spheres! List, my Marina.'[1]

Undoubtedly Shakespeare has something to say in his latest plays, he has to speak of a mysterious reconciliation with existence.

The attempt to trace the connection between the revels and the public stage is well worth making, because it calls our attention to the fact that there was a spiritual as well as a formal kinship between the two kinds, and that the romantic tendencies in the drama seem always to have been strengthened when the influence of the masque was particularly potent. At first, this appears odd, for the Court masques were composed by those who believed in classical rather than in romantic theories of art.

Romance is notoriously difficult to define, but most people would agree that it is in some way connected with a sense of distance and the appetite for the unfamiliar. The love of Othello and Desdemona, for instance, was perilously romantic because each approached the other from afar, each saw the other as the inhabitant of an alien but more beautiful world.

'She swore, in faith, 'twas strange, 'twas passing strange;
'Twas pitiful, 'twas wondrous pitiful.'

Though exploited by diplomatists and conventionalised by the courtiers, the masques always satisfied this craving for romance. The masque was 'a spectacle of strangeness'; the masquers often wore an exotic disguise; originally they really did arrive unexpectedly, and always, in theory, their appearance came as a sudden revelation—they had travelled from far-away lands, they had dropped from the clouds, or even from another world.

[1] *Pericles*, act v, sc. 1, ll. 225–230.

It is of course a commonplace that the beings of Shakespeare's romance and romantic comedy move in a world that is just removed from the world of reality. We see them from afar, yet the inhabitants of Shakespeare's fairyland are people of like passions with ourselves. Most comedy, even if it is not realistic, has some critical reference to reality ; it upholds the best social usage and laughs at eccentrics and idealists; it isolates and exaggerates certain traits of men and manners in order to point out their absurdity. But Shakespeare, though he often exaggerates, does not make exaggeration the principle of his art, and his business with men and manners is delight rather than criticism. He does not people Bartholomew Fair with walking 'humours,' he peoples a fairy world with ordinary men and women. He does not advise us to come close and use the pruning knife, he persuades us to stand a little way off and enjoy the rose tree. For Shakespeare's comedy is not a judgment but an embrace, it expresses faith in life, as the masque expresses faith in the social order.

In all romance there is an element of joy, or at least of acceptance, which is not unconnected with the sense of distance. By escaping from the immediacy of his own sensations the romantic is enabled to value experience and emotion for their own sake, and to find matter for enjoyment even in his grief. There are few scenes in Shakespeare more romantic than the scene in which Lorenzo and Jessica linger in the moonlight 'on such a night as this....' Each tale that they recall is a tale of sorrow, but the pain has gone. Dido is simply a lovely figure by a far-off sea, and her love stirs neither pity nor terror, but only the sense of beauty. In human destiny, as in the stars overhead, the lovers can only hear the music of the spheres.

In the romantic mood feelings of pleasure and pain lose their insistency, and are submerged in an overwhelming sense of remote beauty. This is perhaps the reason why tragedy and comedy are so often mingled in romantic drama, and why all distinction between them is lost when the spirit of romance is quite predominant.

In romantic comedy and romance human life is regarded as something to be expressed rather than analysed, experienced rather than understood, enjoyed rather than reformed. In his earlier comedy Shakespeare concentrates quite simply on happiness; in his later work he speaks with a more uncertain voice of a harder reconciliation. In both cases he excites the distrust of those who believe that all artists should be artist philosophers, that all literature should be social propaganda, and that romance should be renounced as a deceitful glamour, which blinds men into accepting ugly facts that it is their duty to destroy. The criticism is understandable, but it has far more justification when it is directed against the masque, rather than against romantic comedy.

The battle of romance and rationalism has always raged with a special heat around the fact of sex and the fact of nationality, and both of these facts are always treated romantically in the masque, that is to say they are treated not as subjects for criticism, but as subjects for panegyric and paean and idealisation. The physical side of love is indeed frankly recognised by the masque writers, but it is treated as a symbol of a spiritual union, which is, in its turn, symbolic of a wider social harmony. The masque writers were bound to represent both marriage and monarchy, not as faulty human institutions, but as joyful mysteries, they were forced by the conditions under which they worked to adopt an attitude of acceptance towards the social life with which they were dealing. This enforced orthodoxy led, as it was bound to do, to a stiff insincerity, very alien from the true spirit of romance. Behind the masque there did indeed lie a national enthusiasm, which was genuine enough; but this enthusiasm could not be adequately or truthfully embodied in flattery of King James, and by the time the masque had reached its highest development this enthusiasm was already on the wane.

The masque found not only its earliest, but also its best fulfilment in the drama. It was romantic in its influence, rather than in its nature. Poetic acceptance of Court weddings and government officials is not very edifying, but Shakespeare takes this dull orthodoxy and transforms it into an inspired interpretation of life. The masque writers are patently insincere; but Shakespeare is either wholly truthful or an arch-deceiver, for he mingles facts and fancy so cunningly, he imitates nature so convincingly, that almost he persuades us that romance is inherent in the human situation.

A great deal of what has already been said about the interaction between play and entertainment applies not merely to comedy, but to the drama as a whole; for the hybrid plays of the University wits and others were as near akin to tragedy as to comedy; and tragedy no less than comedy was subject to the continuous influence of the courtly revels. The influence of the masque played a part, though a small one, in the building up of Shakespearian tragedy, and it is by its effect on tragedy that the value of the masque influence must finally be judged.

Masques and pageants were frequently inserted into Elizabethan tragedies. A sudden change from masquing to murder, from revelry to revenge, was a favourite tragic motif, and even when the masque did not actually bring about the catastrophe, it deepened the horror, and brought with it a stifling atmosphere of intrigue and corruption. All this is too well known to need any further emphasis.

Elaborate dumb shows were regularly inserted between the acts of the early Senecan revenge plays. These dumb shows were equivalent to the Italian intermedii, and were probably in the first case borrowed from Italy[1]. Their kinship with the masque is apparent, and they owe their popularity to the music and spectacle with which they were usually accompanied. English dumb shows can be roughly divided into three main groups. (1) pantomimic summaries of the action which is to follow; (2) pantomimic summaries of action which is essential to the plot but not to be enacted in the play; (3) symbolical interpretations of the action.

It was an easy transition from the regular or sporadic dumb show to the spectacular or lyrical episode arising out of the action introduced fairly naturally as part of the ceremonial of the Court life which was being portrayed. The dramatists were particularly fond of elaborating the pomp of death. A good example of

---

[1] Cf. Cunliffe, *Italian Prototypes of the Masque and Dumb Show*. Publications of the Modern Language Association, vol. XXII, 1907, pp. 140–156.

these lyrical episodes occurs in Webster's *The White Devil*, where Cornelia sings her dirge 'of the earth earthy.' Webster seems to call attention to the fact that this episode is an extra-dramatic picture by his method of introducing it:

'Fran. de Med. I found them winding of Marcello's corse;
And there is such a solemn melody,
'Tween doleful songs, tears, and sad elegies,—
Such as old grandams watching by the dead
Were wont to outwear the nights with....

Flam. I will see them;
They are behind the traverse; I'll discover
Their superstitious howling. [Draws the curtain.

Cornelia, Zanche, and three other Ladies discovered winding Marcello's corse. A Song.'

The dangerously romantic quality of the dirge episode is particularly apparent in the death of Penthea in *The Broken Heart*, who (like the heroine, Calantha) dies to slow music:

'Soft sad music.

Orgilus. List, what sad sounds are these,—extremely sad ones?
Ith. Sure, from Penthea's lodgings.
Org.   Hark! a voice too.
Song within.
O, no more, no more, too late....
Ith. O, my misgiving heart!
Org.   A horrid stillness
Succeeds this deathful air; let's know the reason:
Tread softly; there is mystery in mourning.'

Then the scene changes to Penthea's apartment: 'Penthea discovered in a chair, veiled; Christalla and Philema at her feet mourning.' Ithocles and Orgilus enter and learn the manner of her death:

'Phil.   She called for music,
And begged some gentle voice to tune a farewell
To life and griefs: Christalla touched the lute;
I wept the funeral song.
Chris.   Which scarce was ended
But her last breath sealed-up these hollow sounds,
"O, cruel Ithocles and injured Orgilus!"
So down she drew her veil, so died.'

The masque-like episodes in Ford's plays arise professedly out of the plot and have a certain charm, yet they weaken the fibre of the drama, and their main purpose seems to be to play upon the gentler emotions. We may contrast with them the magnificent episode of the banquet aboard Pompey's galley, which arises quite naturally out of the action, and is by no means unrelated to the main theme of *Antony and Cleopatra*.

Professor Schücking's comment on this episode is very instructive:

'The poet seems to have taken a great delight in depicting this feast. At the end almost the whole company are drunk; they join hands, dance, and, as was the custom at Egyptian revels, unite their hoarse voices in an attempt to sing the burden of a song. This may be productive of a certain stage effect, but it completely *isolates the scene*, detaching it from the context of the whole in a manner which is unequalled even in Shakespeare. There are other cases of the procedure employed in the second part of that act, in which the whole action is made to follow the example of the dancers and keep turning round on the same spot.'[1]

Whether the adverse criticism is sound or not, Schücking is undoubtedly right in calling attention to the isolation of this scene, which certainly is related to the symbolical masque-like episode. For a space the action pauses, while attention is concentrated upon the significance rather than upon the happenings of the drama. In this grotesque yet terrible picture Shakespeare expresses the meaning of his play, and sums up a whole chapter of world history.

The masque influence made itself felt, not only by causing interruptions in the action, but by permeating the form and spirit of tragedy in a way that is easier to feel than to define. In the Elizabethan age masquerading was so much in the air that insensibly, inevitably, it coloured the imagination of playwright and play-goer, and infected the epical imitative play with something of the symbolic dance movement of the masque. To us the masque has become meaningless, so that to an important shade in the many-coloured picture of Elizabethan drama we are colour-blind, and it is hard for us to realise that sometimes it is not

[1] Levin L. Schücking, *Character Problems in Shakespeare's Plays*, p. 135.

merely isolated episodes but the whole action of the play which is best appreciated, if it is regarded, not only as a sequence of events, but also as a kind of expressive movement. The most striking examples are *The Duchess of Malfi* and *King Lear*.

The value of *The Duchess of Malfi* is usually supposed (unjustly I believe) to rest almost entirely on the fourth act. This act is quite the most unrealistic part of the whole play. Regarded as actual events the tortures Flamineo devises for his sister are wildly improbable and also disgusting. But it is not as actual happenings that they affect our imagination: 'As they are not like inflictions *of this life* so her language seems *not of this world*...her tongue has a snatch of Tartarus and the souls in bale.'[1] On both occasions when I have seen this play acted, I have found to my astonishment that this spiritual torment was brought out and deepened by performance, and this not through any superlatively fine rendering of the part of the Duchess, but through the structure and composition of the act. The idea of *The Duchess of Malfi* is the idea of the unconquerable sufferer, attacked by corruption, horror, and misery, in their foulest forms, yet remaining untouched and undefeated. This idea becomes particularly apparent in the dance of madmen. The Duchess, sitting white and motionless among the howling, lumbering madmen, is a figure not easily forgotten, and it is noteworthy that Webster made his meaning clearest through a kind of masque. Dancing like music (though not to the same extent) is an art that can 'express abstract, unlocalised, unpersonified feelings more completely than painting or poetry.'[2] The action of drama must lead to a suspension of disbelief, the dance movement has only to express emotion. For instance, the orgy of violent deaths which so often closes an Elizabethan tragedy is apt to arouse uncomfortable amusement in a modern spectator, but the effect of the same idea expressed in a dance, rather than a drama, might be very different. We can imagine the horror of a danse macabre performed by the Russian Ballet.

Of course, I do not mean to say that Webster's play is

[1] C. Lamb, *Specimens from English Dramatic Poets.*
[2] J. Harrison, *Ancient Art and Ritual*, p. 233.

symbolical. No doubt the fourth act of *The Duchess of Malfi* is primarily intended as a representation of events, but these events have surely been deliberately fashioned into a kind of grim ritual and, when Bosola enters to chant his dreadful dirge for the living, all verisimilitude is for a while abandoned. Webster's play is not symbolical, but it is infected with the spirit of the masque.

In *King Lear*, besides the ordinary movement of the story, there is another and profounder movement by which the two great sufferers press forward into an ever-deepening darkness, an ever-increasing isolation. This movement into darkness is also a movement into reality, a ruthless tearing away of everything, power, comfort, habit, reserve, until there is nothing left but naked humanity, the absolute bare bone of fact, and it culminates in that moment when Lear greets poor Tom:

'Is man no more than this? Consider him well. Thou owest the worm no silk, the beast no hide, the sheep no wool, the cat no perfume. Ha! here's three on 's are sophisticated; thou art the thing itself; unaccommodated man is no more but such a poor, bare, forked animal as thou art. Off, off, you lendings! Come; unbutton here.'[1]

Here, then, at the very heart of the play occurs the strangest of all great tragic scenes. It is not a dramatic situation, there is nothing to be done, no decision to be made. Movement ceases and time stands still, and the world becomes but a background to three wild figures, Poor Tom, the Fool, King Lear, all in various degrees of mental torture and disease, standing on the storm-swept heath, in utter helplessness and desolation, the only people at all capable of succouring them an old banished courtier and a grief-crazed nobleman. At this crisis of the play action yields to passivity, and yet the effect is not statuesque, for the world around is neither still nor silent. The whole heavens are convulsed by those forces of evil which have penetrated into the very centre of human personality and attacked reason itself. Through the outbursts of Lear and the sudden broken ejaculations of his companions we are made to feel the horror of the scene in nature, we are given the impression of loneliness and emptiness combined with a ghastly uproar. There is the same kind of horror in the

[1] Act III, sc. 4.

situation of the human sufferers. For these three outcasts life has come to a complete standstill, all the ordinary occupations of every day are ceased. The sufferers on the heath have nothing left to them but their own bodies, and there is nothing whatever that they can do. But theirs is no numbed passivity. It would seem that all ordinary life movements have stopped, that there may be entire concentration on the most awful and exhausting movement of all, the passion of mental agony at white heat.

In *King Lear* there are no intrusive lyrical interludes, no momentary changes from the tragic to the romantic or symbolical key, but the central scene of the play is lyrical, and the whole drama has something of that ambivalence which gives such a peculiar quality to the fourth act of *The Duchess of Malfi*.

It is not my intention to suggest that Shakespeare wrote *Lear* under the direct influence of the masque—that would be absurd. My point is that Shakespeare could hardly have produced it had he been catering for an audience less accustomed to hybrid forms, and to the frequent insertion of masques, less responsive to lyricism and symbolism, more eager for consistency and veri-similitude, and that the chief justification of the masque influence and the special lyrical moment is that they made possible the diffused lyricism of Shakespearian tragedy.

Many modern realists, however, would deny that this lyricism is desirable, and since the demand for verisimilitude is not ex-clusively modern, but has been made by dramatic critics in all ages, their objections can hardly be disregarded, but must be met by an appeal to the first principles of dramatic art, if the influence of the masque is to be justified. What is a drama, and why should it be more realistic than any other kind of poem?

A drama is a story which is told through the medium of living bodies moving about an allotted space for a limited period of time. Such a story must obviously be of smaller scope than the story handled by the epic poet, it must obviously conform in some way to the unities of Time, Place and Action, however broad may be the interpretation of these rules or principles. A good dramatist, however, will not content himself with the choice of a theme which is sufficiently limited to be easily handled upon the stage, but he will try to find a story whose significance is dependent upon those very limitations which are practically inseparable from theatrical performance. This means that the dramatist is bound not only to say less than the epic poet, but to say something quite different, and it is just possible that in this difference between the proper subject-matter of epic and drama we shall find a clue to the real nature of dramatic excellence.

The word epic conjures up the thought of size and of space. 'Epic poetry must be an affair of evident largeness.'[1] It describes human achievement on a grand scale, it represents humanity dealing triumphantly with circumstance, it embodies the ideals of a whole people. The interest of an epic may centre in a single individual but he is regarded as a representative of his tribe, a leader, a king of men, an upholder of the tradition. Again, the interest of an epic may be concentrated upon a single event, but the hero moves towards the deed with a certain kingly dignity and leisure. Time is ample, space is vast. The issue is a great one, but the chief emphasis is not upon the issue but upon the glory of the adventure. In the *Chanson de Roland*, for instance, the emphasis is not so much upon the question as to whether Roland will or will not blow his horn, as upon the unrolling of the disastrous events that followed his magnificent abstention. The *Battle of Maldon* deals in the same spirit with a very similar subject. Again, the epic poet dwells lovingly on the details of appearance and actions and surroundings, and this is natural, because epic is primarily concerned with the innate worth of human life. Now tragedy is the very converse of epic. The tragic hero is not the ideal representative of the tribe, he is rather a man at odds with his environment. He does not move with a gracious ease towards his doom, but he stands at the cross roads faced with the choice that shall have irrecoverable consequences, and bound to take a decisive step in a limited period of time. Odysseus, for instance, need not hurry over his preparation for the killing of the suitors, but Hamlet is engaged in a dreadful race against the clock, and much of the dramatic interest of the play lies in the uncertainty as to whether he will succeed in mastering

[1] Lascelles Abercrombie, *The Epic*, p. 50.

his mood before the King has succeeded in effecting his downfall. The epic suggests expansion of space, but drama, and especially tragedy, suggests limitation of time.

Stories which turn upon momentous choices to be made in a limited time are obviously well suited to the 'three hours traffic of the stage,' but their dramatic value lies in their poignancy, not in their possible verisimilitude. Few men can experience heroic adventure, but most men have to make important decisions, and all men share the knowledge that they have but a short time in which to achieve their purposes. Tragedy comes home to the bosoms and businesses of men, it penetrates into the very heart of human experience, and ennobles not our achievements but our struggles.

But there is another side. A great drama is more than an exciting story, and a great tragedy must, like the epic, be 'an affair of evident largeness,' it must have a universal application, it must say something worth saying about the life of men. Tragedy is both smaller and larger than epic. Pious Aeneas is the ideal representative of imperial Rome; Hamlet is a unique personality, he is also Everyman. The tragic moment is that moment when for a short while things hang in the balance, it is also a moment in eternity. Without the feeling of limited time there can be no dramatic intensity; without the feeling of unlimited significance there can be no tragic greatness.

The problem before the dramatist is to do justice to both sides of his art, and he is frequently helped to do this by some lyrical convention which he inherits from the past. The most un-mistakable instance of this is the Greek chorus, which relieves the dramatic tension by setting present happenings against a background of 'old unhappy far-off things' and of universal human destiny. In Elizabethan drama, the chorus, when it survived at all, was put to the improper use of filling up gaps in the action and turning the play into a kind of dramatic epic, but the true function of the Greek chorus was fulfilled by that under-current of lyricism, which every now and then would rise to the surface, and which was partly due, not to the survival of an ancient ritual, but to the influence of a living social custom. In the hands of an inferior dramatist these lyrical moments were only too apt to be either mere ornamental excrescences or else temporary lapses from high tragedy into romance. But in the hands of a Shakespeare, or even of a Webster, these lyrical pauses are not really separable from the essential movement of the play. When Lear and Cordelia enter as prisoners, Lear does not cease to be Lear[1], rather he has arrived at one of those supreme moments which occur in real life as well as on the stage, when the whole being of a man, all his latent greatness, suddenly rushes up into full consciousness and attains supreme expression. At such a moment, in life as well as in drama, time is pierced and eternity breaks through the gap. At such a moment a man may speak broken prose, but he thinks poetry.

It has always been possible to divide up great artists into two groups. There are those who eschew, as far as is possible, all excellences proper to other kinds of art, who keep easily within the technical limits of their own medium, and if anything tend to contract, rather than to expand, those limits. And then there are those who are always tending to stretch their art to breaking point, to pour in new wine with such a lavish hand that it seems almost impossible that the old wine skins should remain intact. Yet remain intact they do. There seems to be no particular reason for regarding either of these types as superior to the other; artists of the first group leave on one's mind an impression of easy mastery and fine ascetic intelligence, artists of the second group rouse admiration by the display of power, held in check by an unrelenting judgment and self-discipline. For this kind of artist (when he is great) gathers up into his work many of the excellences proper to other kinds, but he never allows these excellences to obscure the fundamental quality of his own form of art. Shakespeare and Michael Angelo may infuse into their creations something of the moving quality of a great symphony,

---

[1] In an article in *The Times Literary Supplement*, 26 May, 1921, this episode is used as an illustration of the theory that in 'the greatest plays there are moments when the play ceases and something else happens:...Lear ceases to be Lear,...circumstance falls away like scenery, and a universal voice is heard speaking the language of the absolute.' This passage is discussed in Archer, *op. cit.* pp. 385, 386, 387.

but they never allow their own forms, their own reasoned utterances, to melt away into vague emotional sound. The story of Lear swells in volume until it fills the world, yet it never ceases to be the story of Lear, and therein lies the whole justification for the influence of the masque; for Shakespeare's blending of lyricism and drama, of realism and romance.

Shakespeare unites these things because at heart they are one. Life is lyrical, ordinary men and women do as a matter of fact think, speak, and enact poetry. Aeschylus, Shakespeare, and Racine are realists, for they reveal reality. 'See deep enough and you see musically the heart of nature being everywhere music if you can only reach it.'[1]

[1] Carlyle, *Heroes and Hero-worship.*

CHAPTER XI

The Influence of the Masque on Poetry

'...revealing
    A tone
Of some world far from our's
Where music, and moonlight, and feeling
    Are one.'   SHELLEY.

THE influence of the masque on English literature is a
theme for a book rather than a chapter, and here I cannot
do more than suggest certain ways in which the masque
touched the imagination of Spenser and Milton, and helped to
supply those two great non-dramatic poets with a mode of expression which could be readily understood and appreciated by their
readers. I pass over the lyric with reluctance; but lack of space
forbids the consideration of how the masque kept song-writers and
musicians in touch with one another, and by causing them to write
dancing poems helped to impart that dance-like quality to English
song which shows itself so attractively in the long lingering
rhythms, the quick turns, and varying cadences of Campion's
poetry.

The pictorial quality of Spenser's imagination is manifested
obviously and crudely in the complaints and visions which he
wrote in imitation of Petrarch and the Pléiade poets. In *The
Ruins of Time*, where he adopts the same form, the connection
between this emblematic art and pageantry is made quite explicit.
The poet describes how he was sitting one day by the banks of the
Thames, when the ruined city of Verulam appeared to him in
the form of a woman, who bewailed her fate and the mutability
of all human things, and then vanished away leaving him to his
own reflections, which took visual and significant shapes as 'an
image all of massie gold...a stately tower...a bridge,' and so on:

'So inlie greeuing in my groning brest,
And deepelie muzing at her doubtfull speach,
Whose meaning much I labored foorth to wreste,
Being aboue my slender reasons reach;
At length by demonstration me to teach,
Before mine eies strange sights presented were,
Like tragicke Pageants seeming to appeare.'[1]

[1] *The Ruins of Time*, ll. 484 ff.

In the same way Spenser makes it clear that the adventures of the knights in *The Faerie Queene* may rightly be regarded as pageants. In Book II, canto I, Sir Guyon meets with the Red-cross Knight whose adventure was the subject of Book I, and the Palmer who accompanies Sir Guyon congratulates the Red-cross Knight on his past achievements, and laments the fact that toils still lie in front of him and his companions:

> 'For all I did, I did but as I ought.
> But you, faire Sir, whose pageant next ensewes,
> Well mote yee thee, as well can wish your thought.'[1]

The masque influenced Spenser even more deeply than did the pageant; but it was the provincial masque, which was near allied to the old momeries, rather than the gay masqueries of fashionable society, that most stirred his imagination. In Book III Britomart or Chastity enters into the House of Love and waits there until the evening, always expecting the onslaught of some hidden foe:

> 'All suddenly a stormy whirlwind blew
> Throughout the house, that clapped euery dore,
> With which that yron wicket open flew,
> As it with mightie leuers had bene tore:
> And forth issewd, as on the ready flore
> Of some Theatre, a graue personage,
> That in his hand a branch of laurell bore,
> With comely haueour and count'nance sage,
> Yclad in costly garments, fit for tragicke Stage.
>
> Proceeding to the midst, he still did stand,
> As if in mind he somewhat had to say,
> And to the vulgar beckning with his hand,
> In signe of silence, as to heare a play,
> By liuely actions he gan bewray
> Some argument of matter passioned;
> Which doen, he backe retyred soft away,
> And passing by, his name discouered,
> *Ease*, on his robe in golden letters cyphered.
>
> The noble Mayd, still standing all this vewd,
> And merueild at his strange intendiment;
> With that a ioyous fellowship issewd
> Of Minstrals, making goodly meriment,

---

[1] *The Faerie Queene*, bk II, cant. I, st. 33.

With wanton Bardes, and Rymers impudent,
All which together sung full chearefully
A lay of loues delight, with sweet concent:
After whom marcht a jolly company,
In manner of a maske, enranged orderly.

The whiles a most delitious harmony,
In full straunge notes was sweetly heard to sound,
That the rare sweetnesse of the melody
The feeble senses wholly did confound,
And the fraile soule in deepe delight nigh dround:
And when it ceast, shrill trompets loud did bray,
That their report did farre away rebound,
And when they ceast, it gan againe to play,
The whiles the maskers marched forth in trim aray.

The first was *Fancy*, like a louely boy,
Of rare aspect, and beautie without peare....'

After him followed Desyre, Doubt, Feare, etc., then the great winged God of Love, and behind him *Reproch*, *Repentance*, etc.

'There were full many moe like maladies,
Whose names and natures I note readen well;
So many moe, as there be phantasies
In wauering wemens wit, that none can tell,
Or paines in loue, or punishments in hell;
All which disguized marcht in masking wise,
About the chamber with that Damozell,
And then returned, hauing marched thrise,
Into the inner roome, from whence they first did rise.'[1]

The Faerie Queene is full of processional entries; the riding of the Seven Deadly Sins, the assembly of the Rivers, when the Thames and the Medway celebrate their marriage in the banqueting hall of Proteus, the muster of seasons, months, day and night, life and death, at the trial by Nature to decide the justice of Mutability's claim to be sovereign of gods and men. These episodes are to all intents and purposes masques, although the word is not actually used. The animal-headed creatures, who assault the castle of Temperance in troops of twelve, remind one of the old ludi in Edward III's reign and of later grotesque masques.

[1] Bk III, cant. 12, st. 3 ff.

Sometimes the masque-like episodes have for their central movement not a procession but a ring-dance, such as the dance of the graces witnessed by Calidore[1] and the rescue of Una by the 'Wyld Wood Gods.'[2]

Not merely did the masque supply Spenser with imagery, it influenced the structure of his greatest poem. *The Faerie Queene* is not an epic. This is due partly to his weakness as a story-teller, partly to the fact that he had for his model not an epic-writer, but the romantic poet Ariosto, and partly also to the fact that his imagination was deeply affected by the influence of masque and pageantry. Spenser presented the life of his time not as a series of events, but as a series of pageants, a gorgeous procession filing past to slow music.

Although Spenser has not produced an epic, he belongs to that small and honourable company of poets who not only give worthy embodiment to the ideals of a whole age, but also create new imaginative worlds, new poetic symbols, available for those who come after. This of course is no light task, and the poet can hardly achieve it unless he has considerable help from contemporaries and predecessors, unless he can fall back upon a strong literary tradition, or upon contemporary social customs which are already in part aesthetic. It would, for instance, be most difficult for a modern poet to write an epic on the last war, for he would have no traditions of minstrelsy behind him, no audience prepared for a certain method of poetic heightening, for the kenning, the stock epithet, the introductory ejaculation: 'Lo we have heard tell how in days of old, etc.' The modern poet would have to create everything afresh: form, diction, and above all the poetic appetite of his audience. It was, therefore, an immense advantage to Spenser that, for the purpose of embodying the ideals of the Elizabethan age, he could make use of material which was already deeply impregnated with the influence of social custom and pageantry. Behind *The Faerie Queene* lay the customs of chivalry, seen through the ironic eyes of Ariosto, and steeped in all the sensuous beauty of the Italian Renaissance; and

[1] Bk VI, cant. 10, st. 10 ff.
[2] Bk I, cant. 6, st. 7 ff.

behind the work both of Ariosto and Spenser lay the romances of chivalry, which were idealised versions of actual social customs, particularly of those tournaments which, in the fourteenth and fifteenth centuries, were becoming aesthetic and spectacular even in real life. And not only was Spenser able to make use of material which was already a poetic version of social custom, but he was able to present his work to an audience who, through the frequency of masquing and pageantry, were already well prepared for the aesthetic presentment of contemporary life, and so were ready to enter the poet's mind and accept his method of dealing with his subject-matter.

> 'Right well I wote most mighty Soueraine,
> That all this famous antique history,
> Of some th'aboundance of an idle braine
> Will judged be, and painted forgery,
> Rather then matter of just memory,
> Sith none, that breatheth liuing aire, does know,
> Where is that happy land of Faery,
> Which I so much do vaunt, yet no where show,
> But vouch antiquities, which no body can know....
>
> Of Faerie lond yet if he more inquire,
> By certaine signes here set in sundry place
> He may it find;...
> And thou, O fairest Princesse vnder sky,
> In this faire mirrhour maist behold thy face,
> And thine owne realmes in lond of Faery,
> And in this antique Image thy great auncestry.
>
> The which O pardon me thus to enfold
> In couert vele, and wrap in shadowes light.'[1]

An Elizabethan audience would have no difficulty in accepting this apology; for when Spenser represented Elizabeth as Queen of Fairyland, when he set forth the national ideal by means of processional entries of vices and virtues, dressed up as knights and ladies, moving across a charming but conventional background, he was merely translating the doings at Kenilworth, Eltham, Norwich, and Bristol into a more interesting and imaginative language.

---

[1] Bk II, cant. I, st. I, 4, 5.

Just as the early masques were taken by Lyly and transposed into
the key of romantic comedy, so they were taken by Spenser and
transposed into the key of poetic romance. Spenser seized upon
all that was best in the ephemeral masque and pageant, and used
it as a medium for the setting forth of a golden world which has
never ceased to influence English poetry.

All poets who were influenced by Spenser were necessarily
indirectly influenced by the masques and pageants which he
transmuted into poetry. This is particularly true of Milton, who
absorbed all the masque-like characteristics of his predecessor,
and was also directly influenced by the elaborate Court masque
as developed by Ben Jonson and Inigo Jones.

Milton was well acquainted with the masques of Ben Jonson.
Comus is reminiscent of *Pleasure Reconciled to Virtue*, and also in
other poems of Milton there are echoes of Ben Jonson. For
instance *Il Penseroso* adjures Melancholy to

> 'Entice the dewy-feather'd Sleep;
> And let som strange mysterious dream,
> Wave at his Wings in Airy stream,
> Of lively portrature display'd,
> Softly on my eye-lids laid.
> And as I wake, sweet musick breath
> Above, about, or underneath,
> Sent by som spirit to mortals good,
> Or th'unseen Genius of the Wood.'

This seems to be a vague reminiscence of the *Vision of Delight*
where Night hovering over the place sang:

> 'Break, Phant'sie, from thy cave of cloud,
>   And spread thy purple wings;
> Now all thy figures are allowed,
>   And various shapes of things;
> Create of airy forms a stream,
> It must have blood, and nought of phlegm;
> And though it be a waking dream.
>
> CHO. Yet let it like an odour rise
>   To all the Senses here,
> And fall like sleep upon their eyes,
>   Or music in their ear.'

Again, the *Epitaph on the Marchioness of Winchester* contains what is probably an allusion to an actual masque:

> 'The Virgin quire for her request
> The God that sits at marriage feast;
> He at their invoking came
> But with a scarce-wel-lighted flame;
> And in his Garland as he stood,
> Ye might discern a Cipress bud.'

The most curious allusion to the masque comes in the poem on the *Passion*, in a stanza dealing with the Incarnation of our Lord, where the very unsuitability of the metaphor shows how readily thoughts of the masque came into the poet's mind:

> 'He sov'ran Priest stooping his regall head
> That dropt with odorous oil down his fair eyes,
> Poor fleshly Tabernacle entered,
> His starry front low-rooft beneath the skies;
> O what a Mask was there, what a disguise!'

Milton's early poetry is full of personifications which move and dance:

> 'Haste thee nymph, and bring with thee
> Jest and youthful Jollity,
> Quips and Cranks, and wanton Wiles,
> Nods, and Becks, and Wreathed Smiles...
> Sport that wrincled Care derides,
> And Laughter holding both his sides.
> Com, and trip it as ye go
> On the light fantastick toe.'

We are reminded of the beginning of Jonson's *Vision of Delight* when 'DELIGHT is seen to come as afar off, accompanied with GRACE, LOVE, HARMONY, REVEL, SPORT, LAUGHTER...' or of Cupid bringing in to dance the antimasque 'the Sports, and pretty Lightnesses that accompany Love, under the titles of Joci and Risus....'[1]

In Milton's poetry it is not only abstractions and fairies who dance, but dancing is one of the joys of the saints and angels in Heaven:

---

[1] *The Hue and Cry after Cupid.*

'That day, as other solem dayes, they spent
In song and dance about the sacred Hill,
Mystical dance, which yonder starrie Spheare
Of Planets and of fixt in all her Wheeles
Resembles nearest, mazes intricate,
Eccentric, intervolv'd, yet regular
Then most, when most irregular they seem:
And in thir motions harmonie Divine
So smooths her charming tones, that Gods own ear
Listens delighted.'[1]

In fact they danced the figured ballet which was one of the chief attractions of the masque all over Europe.

Like most Elizabethans Milton was in love with music, and for the most part music to him meant singing. *Upon the Circumcision, At a Solemn Music,* and many passages in *Paradise Lost* describe the triumph song of the Heavenly Host, and often the song is a dancing song:

'So spake the Eternal Father, and all Heaven
Admiring stood a space, then into Hymns
Burst forth, and in Celestial measures mov'd,
Circling the Throne and Singing, *while the hand
Sung with the voice....*'[2]

'There entertain him all the Saints above,
In solemn troops, and sweet Societies
That sing, and singing in their glory move....'[3]

The dance rhythm never got inside Milton's poetry, never informed his metre as it did the metre of Campion. But in *L'Allegro* Milton has described the lyric in terms suggestive of the dance, and the context suggests that the thought of the masque brought the dancing song, that most beautiful adornment of the masque, into his mind. After speaking of 'Mask and antique Pageantry,' of 'Jonson's learned sock' and the 'woodnotes wild' of Shakespeare he proceeds:

'And ever against eating Cares,
Lap me in soft Lydian Aires,
Married to immortal verse
Such as the meeting soul may pierce

---

[1] *Paradise Lost*, bk v, ll. 616 ff.
[2] *Paradise Regained*, bk i, ll. 168 ff.   [3] *Lycidas*, ll. 178–180.

> In notes, with many a winding bout
> Of lincked sweetnes long drawn out,
> With wanton heed, and giddy cunning,
> The melting voice through mazes running;
> Untwisting all the chains that ty
> The hidden soul of harmony.'

Milton was as deeply affected by the spectacular as by the musical side of the masque, and he draws his imagery with surprising frequency from the machinery and devices of the stage architect, particularly from the ascending and descending of divine beings in clouds:

> 'Or wert thou that sweet smiling Youth!
> Or that c[r]owned Matron sage white-robed Truth?
> Or any other of that heav'nly brood
> Let down in clowdie throne to do the world some good.'[1]

> 'But he her fears to cease,
> Sent down the meek-eyd Peace,
>   She crown'd with Olive green, came softly sliding
> Down through the turning sphear
> His ready Harbinger,
>   With Turtle wing the amorous clouds dividing,
> And waving wide her mirtle wand,
> She strikes a universall Peace through Sea and Land....

> For if such holy Song
> Enwrap our fancy long,
>   Time will run back, and fetch the age of gold,
> And speckl'd vanity
> Will sicken soon and die....

> Yea Truth, and Justice then
> Will down return to men,
>   Th'enameld *Arras* of the Rain-bow wearing,
> And Mercy set between,
> Thron'd in Celestiall sheen,
>   With radiant feet the tissued clouds down stearing,
> And Heav'n as at som festivall,
> Will open wide the Gates of her high Palace Hall.'[2]

We may compare with these verses various passages from Ben Jonson's masques:

[1] *On the Death of a fair Infant dying of a Cough*, st. 8.
[2] *On the Morning of Christ's Nativity.*

'Here one of the HOURS descending, the whole scene changed to the bower of ZEPHYRUS, whilst PEACE sung as followeth:

PEACE. Why look you so, and all turn dumb,
    To see the opener of the New Year come?'[1]

'PALLAS. Descend, you long, long wished and wanted pair,
    And as your softer times divide the air,
    So shake all clouds off with your golden hair;
    For Spite is spent: the Iron Age is fled,
    And with her power on earth, her name is dead.

ASTRAEA and the GOLDEN AGE descending with A SONG.'[2]

'JUNO, sitting in a throne...beneath her the rainbow IRIS, and on the two sides eight ladies, attired richly and alike, in the most celestial colours....Their descent was made in two great clouds, that put forth themselves severally, and, with one measure of time, were seen to stoop; and fall gently down upon the earth....'[3]

In *Paradise Lost* as in the *Nativity Ode* there are passages which may have been suggested to Milton by his memories of spectacular effects of the masque. The landscape of Eden, where the 'verdurous wall of Paradise' crowns a hill with trees ascending in ranks, 'a woodie Theatre, Of stateliest view' where 'Universal Pan, Knit with the Graces and the Hours in dance, Led on the Eternall Spring,'[4] is reminiscent of many a masque setting, especially of the scene in Shirley's *Triumph of Peace*, where the 'Masquers appear sitting on the ascent of a hill, cut out like the degrees of a theatre; and over them a delicious arbour...and then the Hours and Chori...move towards the state and sing.' The descriptions of Messiah going out to war with 'Eagle-winged... Victorie' sitting beside him in his chariot[5]; or riding out to create new worlds in a chariot surrounded by the numberless hosts of celestial spirits, while

'Heav'n open'd wide
Her ever-during Gates, Harmonious sound
On golden Hinges moving,'[6]

[1] *The Vision of Delight.*
[2] *The Golden Age Restored.*   [3] *Hymenaei.*
[4] Cf. *Paradise Lost*, bk IV, ll. 130 ff., 246 ff., 257 ff.
[5] *Ibid.* bk VI, ll. 749 ff.
[6] *Ibid.* bk VII, ll. 205 ff. The opening out of great palace doors was a favourite masque device and a favourite image of Milton's. Cf. *Nativ. Ode,* st. 15; *Comus,* ll. 13, 14; *Paradise Lost,* bk II, ll. 871 ff.; bk V, ll. 253 ff.; *Paradise Regained,* bk I, ll. 79 ff.

read like idealised versions of masque triumphs, and resemble in particular the scene where the great gate of Oberon's Palace opens to the sound of music, and out of it issues a procession accompanying the chariot of the Fairy Prince.

Most striking of all is the account of the building of Pandemonium:

'Anon out of the earth a Fabrick huge
Rose like an Exhalation, with the sound
Of Dulcet Symphonies and voices sweet,
Built like a Temple, where *Pilasters* round
Were set, and Doric pillars overlaid
With Golden Architrave; nor did there want
Cornice or Freeze, with bossy Sculptures grav'n,
The Roof was fretted Gold.... Th' ascending pile
Stood fixt her stately highth, and strait the dores
Op'ning thir brazen foulds discover wide
Within, her ample spaces, o're the smooth
And level pavement: from the arched roof
Pendant by suttle Magic many a row
Of Starry Lamps and blazing Cressets fed
With *Naphtha* and *Asphaltus* yeilded light
As from a sky. The hasty multitude
Admiring enter'd, and the work some praise
And some the Architect: his hand was known
In Heav'n by many a Towred structure high,
Where Scepter'd Angels held thir residence....
Nor was his name unheard or unador'd
In ancient *Greece*; and in Ausonian land
Men called him *Mulciber*....'[1]

It has been very generally recognised that Milton was thinking of Inigo Jones, when he described the work of Mulciber, for our English architect's hand was known 'by many a towered structure high' and moreover he devised for the masque *Britannia Triumphans* a golden palace shaped like a temple, which rose up from the ground and had great doors, which opened as soon as it reached its full height[2].

There is, of course, a strong family likeness between all the landscapes of Renaissance poets, painters and masque writers, and I do not mean to suggest that Milton borrowed directly (except

---

[1] *Paradise Lost*, bk I, ll. 670 ff.   [2] Cf. *supra*, p. 234.

in the case of the Pandemonium episode) from any of these passages; but only that masque episodes lived in his memory and coloured his imagination. Also, apart from any question of borrowing, it is interesting to notice that Milton, like Spenser, could employ a mode of poetic heightening, closely resembling stage-effects that had delighted audiences of quite ordinary men and women. It is not the nature of the debt, but the fact of the likeness that is interesting[1].

The Fall of Man was a theme which could very easily be treated in the imaginative mode of the masque [2]. The divine and angelic persons, with their ascendings and descendings and their symbolic dance movements; the transformation scenes, inaugurations of golden eras, the clear-cut scenery of cave and mount, grove, palace, and floating cloud, the plots hinging on deeds with magical and symbolical significance, all these familiar masque devices lay ready to the hand of the epic poet, as a means of giving understandable shape to the story of creation.

In most epics the movement is that of a cinematograph. The characters move along and with them the scenery, and, in proportion to the power of the poet and the strength of our imagination, we move along too, and wander through an ever-changing country. In *Paradise Lost*, however, the whole scene is set out clearly in front of us like a scene upon the stage. Down below is the vault of Hell with its gates, then the cloudy sea of Chaos, then up above the glittering battlements of the Empyreal Heavens

> 'And fast by, hanging in a Golden Chain
> This pendant world, in bigness as a Starr
> Of smallest Magnitude close by the Moon.'[3]

Inside the 'pendant world,' enclosed in the sphere which protects

---

[1] Compare the description of the eastern gate of Paradise, 'a Rock Of Alablaster, pil'd up to the Clouds,' where Gabriel sat between 'rockie Pillars,' where Uriel descended on a sunbeam, where the youth of Heaven 'exercis'd Heroic Games,' and where there was a 'Celestial Armourie, Shields, Helmes, and Speares' (*Paradise Lost*, bk IV, ll. 540 ff.), with, for instance, the steep, red cliff, 'before which...were erected two pilasters, charged with spoils and trophies of Love,' where Venus alighted, coming to look for Cupid and grace the wedding masque of Lord Haddington. (*The Hue and Cry after Cupid*.)

[2] Milton did, of course, at one time intend to treat the theme as a lyrical religious drama, in which at least one masque was to be introduced.

[3] *Paradise Lost*, bk II, ll. 1047 ff.; cf. also bk II, ll. 890 ff.

it from 'ever-threatning storms of chaos blustring round,' is the universe of sky, sun, moon and stars and earth, with the Garden of Eden planted upon a prominent hill. This interior of the sphere is what we should see if the whole scene opened. Thus, the characters of the epic move about in a setting which can very easily be visualised as a whole. One can almost imagine the poem arranged as a masque, either with multiple setting, or (better still) with one or two scene-changes. First the 'horrid hell' with its central mountain crowned by the palace of Pandemonium, a scene which turns to the cloud and confusion of chaos, then, when the smoke and mist have cleared away, the main scene is discovered, divided into an upper and a lower portion, a very common masque arrangement. In the upper part are the glittering, bejewelled palaces of Heaven encompassed with clouds and connected by a golden chain and ladder with the lower half of the scene, a great shining sphere which at the critical moment opens and reveals the Garden of Eden. Only the retrospective and prophetic parts of the narrative would fall outside this scheme. It is at least a curious coincidence that *The Faerie Queene* was written when the masque was still usually processional in form, and that *Paradise Lost* was written after the masque, and its offspring the opera, had come to be performed upon a picture stage.

So far we have been considering the influence of the masque upon the form and structure of Milton's poetry, and have suggested that his knowledge of the elaborate Court masque helped him to give to his great poem on the Fall of Man a shape that could be readily appreciated by his readers. If we are to go further and inquire how far Milton was influenced by the mood, as well as by the structure, of the masque it will be necessary to inquire into the true character of *Comus*.

Milton's debt to Ben Jonson has been on the whole under-estimated[1], for *Comus* owes at least as much to *Pleasure Reconciled to Virtue* as it does to Peele's crude romantic play *The Old*

---

[1] These words (like the rest of this book) were written before the publication of Professor Herford and Mr Simpson's *Ben Jonson*. Professor Herford does full justice to Milton's debt to Jonson. Cf. *op. cit.* pp. 307 ff.

Wives Tale. Jonson like Milton uses his masque to teach the
supremacy of virtue, and shows

> 'The voluptuous Comus, God of cheer,
> Beat from his grove....'

And even the notion of a temporary

> '...cessation of all jars,
> 'Twixt Virtue and her noted opposite,
> Pleasure'

may have led Milton to emphasise his own more austere conception of pleasure overcome by virtue. In both poems the
references to virtue are very many. The errand of the Attendant
Spirit in *Comus* is to those who are not

> 'Unmindfull of the crown that Vertue gives
> After this mortal change, to her true Servants....'

In Jonson's masque, Hercules, 'the active friend of Virtue,' is
invited to rest

> 'Whilst Virtue, for whose sake
> Thou dost this godlike travail take
> May of the choicest herbage make,
>   Here on this mountain bred,
>   A crown, a crown
>   For thy immortal head.'

Both poems end in verses in praise of virtue.

> 'She, she it is in darkness shines,
> 'Tis she that still herself refines,
> By her own light to every eye;
> More seen, more known, when vice stands by:
> And though a stranger here on earth,
> In heaven she hath her right of birth.
> There, there is Virtue's seat:
> Strive to keep her your own;
> 'Tis only she can make you great,
> Though place here make you known.'[1]

This reminds one not only of the closing song of the Attendant
Spirit, but of the words of the Elder Brother:

> 'Vertue could see to do what vertue would
> By her own radiant light, though Sun and Moon
> Were in the flat Sea sunk.'[2]

---

[1] *Pleasure Reconciled to Virtue.*   [2] *Comus*, ll. 373 ff.

In both *Comus* and *Pleasure Reconciled to Virtue* children are presented to their parents, by means of dances which celebrate the happy result of youthful training in virtue. The Prince and his companions having been bred

> 'Within the hill
> Of skill,
> May safely tread
> What path they will,
> No ground of good is hollow.'

Their dances are conducted by Daedalus the Wise. Similarly in *Comus*, the Attendant Spirit announces:

> 'Noble Lord, and Lady bright,
> I have brought ye new delight,
> Here behold so goodly grown
> Three fair branches of your own,
> Heav'n hath timely tri'd their youth,
> Their faith, their patience, and their truth.
> And sent them here through hard assays
> With a crown of deathless Praise,
>   To triumph in victorious dance
> O're sensual Folly, and Intemperance.'

Undoubtedly Milton owes a great deal to *Pleasure Reconciled to Virtue*, yet there is a difficulty in placing the two works in the same category. The question whether *Comus* is or is not a masque is not a matter of mere words, not a matter of attaching a correct label, but rather a matter of understanding the spirit of the poem, and defining its real relationship with those revels which culminated in the work of Ben Jonson and Inigo Jones.

It is hardly necessary to say once more that the central moment of the masque was the moment of the discovery of the masquers; that the essential movement of the masque was the masque dance and the revels; that the poetry was a mere explanation or adornment of the dancing, a method of providing a motive for the appearance of the masquers. *Comus* of course is not devoid of dancing. The entry of Comus and his rout is followed by 'The Measure.' Country dancers appear in the last scene, and their dances are dispersed by the Spirit, so that he may present the Lady and her two brothers to dance before their parents.

Is not this the usual masque construction: poetic induction, two antimasques, main masque and epilogue? The difficulty is that there are no masquers, for the Lady and her two brothers appear at the outset and take the most important speaking parts of the performance. It is true that the masquers in Jonson's *Gipsies Metamorphosed* have speaking parts, but these speeches are merely complimentary remarks addressed to the audience, and are obviously just a development of the gallant conversation which was supposed to take place during the revels. But the speeches of the sister and brothers do not refer to the audience, and are part of a real, though slight, dramatic action which reaches its fitting conclusion in the deliverance of the Lady from the enchantment of Comus. The concluding speeches and dances form a beautiful, but inessential, epilogue, the omission of which would in no way affect the unity and intelligibility of the piece.

Then again the position of the dance in *Comus* is very different from its position in an ordinary Court masque. It is possible to read *Comus* and hardly realise that there are dances; it is possible to act *Comus* without introducing any dances at all; but it is impossible to read Ben Jonson's masque without remembering that the dance was the main point of the whole performance. In *Pleasure Reconciled to Virtue* the quelling, first of Comus and then of the pigmies, by 'Hercules, the active friend of Virtue,' was only a prelude to the great event of the evening, which was the arrival of twelve masquers and their performance of dances symbolising the relationship between virtue and reason, love and beauty.

Similarly, in Browne's *Inner Temple Masque* the romantic tale of Circe, the Sirens, and Ulysses, is made to lead up to the moment when Ulysses takes Circe's wand and awakens his comrades that they may dance and revel with the ladies. If the masque dances and their accompanying songs were omitted, the whole point of the masques both of Browne and Jonson would be gone, for the literary part of their masque was devised solely to provide a motive for the appearance and movement of the masquers. Browne's masque as we have seen is unusually independent of its occasion, it certainly influenced the rhythm and imaginative quality of Milton's work, and in style it is much nearer to *Comus* than to *Pleasure Reconciled to Virtue*. Yet in the vital matter of structure Browne and Jonson are nearer to each other than either of them is to Milton. For in *Comus* the essential moment is not the presentation of the young people to their parents, but it is the steadfast refusal of the Lady to partake of the enchanted cup. The hinge therefore on which *Comus* turns is not the solution of a riddle, not a sudden metamorphosis or revelation, but an act of free choice. This is most important, for it shows that difference in structure corresponds to a difference in spirit between *Comus* and the Court masque; the masque is a dramatised dance, *Comus* is a dramatised debate.

In the same way the atmosphere of *Comus* is different from that of an ordinary masque. Although the majority of masques are full of references to woods, groves, and gardens, songs of birds and the scattering of spring flowers, yet it is never difficult to imagine them being performed indoors, even the best of them are touched with artificiality, they suggest torchlight and the ball-room, and therein lies much of their charm. But Milton's masque makes such a very different impression on the imagination that many have been deceived into supposing that it was intended for out-of-door performance, although it is expressly stated that it was performed at Ludlow Castle *by night* and although the stage directions make it clear that there were three scene-changes. Mr Ronald Bayne in his chapter on masque and pastoral in the *Cambridge History of English Literature*[1] falls into the trap and tells us that 'Peele's *Araygnement of Paris* comes before the development of the masque, as Milton's *Comus* comes after it, to suggest to us that in the method of the out-of-door entertainment or pastoral there is inherent a truer breath of poetry than is to be found in that of the indoor masque, in which scenery and carpentry and music and dance were always tending to smother and suppress the poetical soul.'[2] Mr Bayne cannot mean that *Comus* and *The Arraignment* are written merely in the spirit of outdoor poetry, for he distinctly states of *Comus*: 'It is a species of outdoor

[1] Vol. VI, chap. XIII.
[2] *Camb. Hist. of Eng. Lit.* vol. VI, p. 337.

entertainment, and, therefore, akin to pastoral,'[1] and again: 'These three plays (i.e. *The Faithful Shepherdess, The Sad Shepherd,* and *Amyntas*) are alike attempts by dramatists to put pastoral poetry upon the boards. They are not like Milton's *Comus,* written for outdoor presentation.'[2] The mistake is a tribute to the power of Milton's poetry.

Milton has freed *Comus* not only from the atmosphere and background of the banqueting hall, but also from the tone of compliment and gallantry which pervaded the Court masque. Jonson's poetry is only too often marred by flattery, but Milton does not break the illusion and spoil his fairy play by making it turn upon some tasteless unedifying compliment. The aesthetic gain was great, but unfortunately Milton substituted a harsh vein of moralising for the spirit of courtly gallantry. It is unpleasantly startling when the exquisite lyric speech of Comus is followed by the Lady's tart remarks:

> 'This way the noise was, if mine ear be true,
> My best guide now, me thought it was the sound
> Of Riot, and ill manag'd Merriment,
> Such as the jocond Flute, or gamesom Pipe
> Stirs up among the loose unleter'd Hinds,
> When for their teeming Flocks, and granges full
> In wanton dance they praise the bounteous *Pan*,
> And thank the gods amiss. I should be loath
> To meet the rudenesse, and swill'd insolence
> Of such late Wassailers.'

In this respect William Browne's *Circe* is more attractive than Milton's *Comus*. Both poets emptied their masques of compliment and filled them with poetry. Both poets translate us from reality into a land of magic, but they work this wizardry with very different ends in view. For Browne the supernatural beings, haunted woods, and enchantments make fittingly lovely surroundings for the eternal Dance of Youth, for Milton they are just imaginative expressions of the eternal debate between Good and Evil. There was of course no inherent incongruity between the masque form and the didactic spirit; both Spenser and Ben Jonson conveyed ethical teaching through the masque, and there

[1] *Ibid.* p. 363.   [2] *Ibid.* p. 366.

was, from first to last, an affinity between the masque and the morality play. But there is in *Comus* a subtle incongruity between the symbolism and the idea that it is meant to symbolise, and of this incongruity Milton seems to be entirely unaware. He could not see that the masque, whose presiding deity was Hymen, was a most unsuitable vehicle for the unfolding of the 'sage and serious doctrine of virginity'; he could not see that the ideal of self-righteous asceticism, which he expounds through the mouths of the virtuous characters, is incompatible with the ideal of the golden world of beauty which pervades so much of his poetry, and yet apparently has for him no special affinity with moral goodness, for, strangely enough, it is the heritage of saved and reprobate alike, and it is puzzling that Milton could love both beauty and goodness so well, and yet keep the two ideas so apart from one another[1].

The full beauty of this world becomes apparent when *Comus* is acted, for if the actors speak their lines clearly and well, image after image of loveliness rises up in 'airy stream' like a cloud of incense made of the quintessence of all that was best in all the masques and entertainments and pastorals of the Renaissance. At the heart of this golden world is the primeval ritual of life and of the spring. It is the world of Greek mythology idealised by pastoral poets, changed into a kind of romantic wonderland by writers of the late Middle Ages and Renaissance, set to music and motion by the composers of masque and ballet, humanised by Shakespeare, ennobled by Spenser and Jonson.

This golden world, with its graceful figures engaged in mystic dance, was a perfectly fitting symbol for the catholicism of a Dante, for the neo-platonism of a Politian or a Spenser, for the aristocratic romanticism of Shakespeare, Fletcher and Jonson. For, in all these modes of thought goodness is identified with harmony, order, and at bottom with self-expressive love, and in them there is no real contradiction between Hymen as leader of the Dance of Youth, and Hymen as the Good Principle of

[1] For instance in *Paradise Regained*, bk IV, ll. 236 ff., the poet's sincere love and admiration for Greece are voiced by Satan, and receive from the Messiah a most unconvincing reply.

the Universe, the vanquisher of all the forces of unreason and unrest.

But the golden world ruled by Hymen is emphatically not the right symbol for Milton's harsh creed, in which goodness is identified with power rather than with love, and evil is identified with sensuality rather than with cruelty or selfishness[1], and in which the Universe rests not upon self-expressive love but upon an everlasting antagonism, an ultimately insoluble dualism[2].

Fortunately, Milton's poetic morality was a wider, richer thing than his religious ethic. Though the idea of the golden world was a symbol fitted for a philosophy larger and sweeter than his own, he yet allows it to colour his imagination and soften the asperity of his judgments. Milton tells us again and again that Comus was evil, but there is very little in his presentment of him to suggest it—at any rate, he shows that the wizard and the good Attendant Spirit had tastes in common:

> 'We that are of purer fire
> Imitate the Starry Quire,
> Who in their nightly watchfull Sphears,
> Lead in swift round the Months and Years.'

> 'To the Ocean now I fly,
> And those happy climes that ly
> Where day never shuts his eye,
> Up in the broad fields of the sky:
> There I suck the liquid ayr
> All amidst the Gardens fair
> Of *Hesperus*, and his daughters three
> That sing about the golden tree.'

And to our great comfort Milton's Hell has alleviations unknown to Dante's Inferno:

> 'Others more milde,
> Retreated in a silent valley, sing
> With notes Angelical to many a Harp.'[3]

[1] This is strikingly exemplified in *Paradise Regained*, for it is only the first of our Lord's temptations that Milton seems at all capable of understanding.

[2]   'But evil on itself shall back recoyl,
       And mix no more with goodness, when at last
       Gather'd like scum, and setl'd to it self
       It shall be in eternal restless change
       Self-fed, and self-consum'd.'   *Comus*, ll. 593 ff.

[3] *Paradise Lost*, bk II, ll. 546 ff.

Their palace of Pandemonium

> 'Rose like an Exhalation, with the sound
> Of Dulcet Symphonies and voices sweet,'[1]

and they themselves appeared like

> 'Faerie Elves,
> Whose midnight Revels, by a Forrest side
> Or Fountain some belated Peasant sees,
> Or dreams he sees, while over head the Moon
> Sits Arbitress, and neerer to the Earth
> Wheels her pale course, they on thir mirth and dance
> Intent, with jocond Music charm his ear.'[2]

If Milton was not greatly skilled in the understanding of love, he was totally incapable of understanding or expressing ugliness, and the golden world never quite fades away from the hearts of his fallen angels.

But love of the golden world, with its dance and song and revel, did gradually fade away from the heart of Milton himself, driven out, not by religious asceticism, but by that political passion which had always been its rival. In *Paradise Lost* it makes even Heaven and Eden lovely, even Hell tolerable, and its worth is never questioned. In *Paradise Regained*, however, though it sheds a certain glamour on the wilderness, it appears chiefly as a visionary temptation, and its only advocate is Satan. Finally in *Samson Agonistes* it is degraded into a festival of Philistines, and disappears for ever in the ruinous *coup d'état* engineered by the great Leader of the Opposition.

The golden world and the spirit of the dance however died away in English literature even earlier than in Milton's poetry. Even in the masque itself the lyrics at last ceased to be dancing songs, and the spirit of the social ritual was sacrificed to operatic and spectacular effect. At the Restoration Davenant and Charles II tried to bring back the revels; but they only succeeded in reinaugurating the Philistine festival; there was no descent of Astraea, no revival of the golden world—only a few

---

[1] *Paradise Lost*, bk I, ll. 710 ff.
[2] *Ibid.* bk I, ll. 780 ff.

lingering memories of it surviving in opera and pantomime. For Puritanism broke up the dance of the Hours and Graces, as finally as Medusa's cold glance interrupted the banquet of Phineus and his guests. When the old gods ceased to move they ceased to live, they stiffened and shrivelled, grew harder and more abstract, and ended at last as cold figures of speech in a lifeless poetic diction.

CHAPTER XII

The Masque Transmuted

'From their gross matter she abstracts their forms,
And draws a kind of quintessence from things;
Which to her proper nature she transforms
To bear them, light, on her celestial wings.'

SIR JOHN DAVIES.

IN the last chapter I suggested that certain qualities in the poetry of Spenser and Milton were the result of the close relationship between masquing and poetry. In this chapter I shall make a special study of *A Midsummer Night's Dream* and *The Tempest*, two masque-like plays which are particularly happy examples of the transformation of the masque by the creative imagination of the poet. For the question as to the relation between *A Midsummer Night's Dream*, *The Tempest*, and the Court masque, is not merely a matter of classification: behind it lies the vital question as to how far the art of a nation is dependent on the quantity and quality of its recreation, and how far the individual genius is dependent upon the artistic talent diffused throughout society.

The suggestion that *A Midsummer Night's Dream* and *The Tempest* should be regarded as masques has little to recommend it. In all probability both plays were written for the celebration of Court weddings, but they are not masques, because there are no masquers, because they are independent of their occasion, because their plots are not mere inductions leading up to masque dances, because there is nothing in them corresponding to the sudden failure of detachment which occurs at the end of Peele's *Arraignment of Paris*, and even to a lesser extent in the final scene of Milton's *Comus*. On the other hand, if they are further removed from the masque form, they are much closer to its spirit than is *Comus*. For Shakespeare perceived, or at any rate acted upon, the principle that the masque must die to live. Ben Jonson failed nobly in his effort to exalt the soul of the masque, because he was for ever hampered by its body, but Shakespeare, being a playwright, not a masque poet, was able to disregard the masque body altogether, and instead of having to supply the place of music,

carpentry, and dancing by inadequate prose description, he transmuted all these things into poetry, and wove them into the very
texture of his plays.

The scenic element is almost as important in *A Midsummer
Night's Dream* as in the masque, but it is treated in a very
different way. The wood near Athens is not dependent upon,
rather it is antagonistic to, the art of the scene painter. Even if
A Midsummer Night's Dream was well-staged at Court, still
Oberon's description of his surroundings could hardly be translated into terms of paint and canvas, for what scene painter would
be quite equal to the 'bank where the wild thyme blows,' or,
indeed, what human actor could obey Titania's stage direction:

> 'Come, now a roundel and a fairy song;
> Then, for the third part of a minute, hence'?

The feeling of the countryside, the romantic fairy-haunted earth
has affected the very details of language.

> 'Your eyes are lode-stars; and your tongue's sweet air
> More tuneable than lark to shepherd's ear,
> When wheat is green, when hawthorn buds appear.'

When Bottom appears with his ass's head:

> 'As wild geese that the creeping fowler eye,
> Or russet-pated choughs, many in sort,
> Rising and cawing at the gun's report,
> Sever themselves and madly sweep the sky;
> So, at his sight, away his fellows fly.'

Titania winds Bottom in her arms:

> 'So doth the woodbine the sweet honeysuckle
> Gently entwist; the female ivy so
> Enrings the barky fingers of the elm.'

'Acorn,' 'canker-blossom,' 'hindering knot grass,' are epithets
flung at each other by the quarrelsome lovers.

When Duke Theseus has left the lovers to themselves,
Demetrius, still dazed and only half awake, murmurs:

> 'These things seem small and undistinguishable,
> Like far off mountains turned into clouds.'

It is a fine image, giving just that suggestion of awe and uncertainty which was needed to soften the transition from dream

to waking life. The magic of the phrase lies in the words 'small' and 'undistinguishable.' A lesser poet would probably have given the abstract idea in the first line and in the second its concrete illustration. But the word 'small' (instead of 'strange,' 'vague' or some other word of that kind) at once sets the imagination to work and suggests the picture which the next line expands, and the sound of the word 'undistinguishable,' with its accumulated syllables trailing off into silence, does for the ear what the word 'small' does for the eye, suggests the shimmering atmosphere, the blurred outline and the gradual vanishing of the distant mountains on the horizon.

Shakespeare has absorbed the scenic splendour of the masque, not only in description and picturesque language, but also in a blending of tones, a harmony of colours, which the poet has attained by a most delicate and subtle handling of the laws of resemblance and contrast. The play opens in the daylight, first in the Court, then in the cottage, and brings us into the presence of the two sets of characters who most emphatically belong to daylight and the solid earth, the genial cultivated rulers, the simple-minded artisans, the former serving as a framework, the latter as a foil to the poetry and moonshine of the dream. The excellence of the workmanship lies in the fact that the framework is organically connected with the picture, for Theseus and Hippolyta are accompanied by Philostrate the Master of the Revels. We are in the world of men, but men are in holiday mood. Ordinary workaday business is set aside, pomp, triumph, and revelling are in the air. Anything may happen. The moon is at once made the topic of conversation:

> 'Four days will quickly steep themselves in night;
> Four nights will quickly dream away the time;
> And then the moon, like to a silver bow
> New-bent in heaven, shall behold the night
> Of our solemnities.'[1]

By the end of the first act our minds are full of the wood where Helena and Hermia used to lie 'upon faint primrose beds,' where the young people used to meet 'to do observance to a morn of

[1] Act I, sc. I, ll. 7-11.

May,' and where very shortly lovers and workmen are to assemble by moonlight for diverse purposes. Moonshine is almost as real a personage in Shakespeare's as in Bottom's play. Her presence permeates the action, a delicate compliment to the maiden Queen, and Titania is merely a glancing beam of her light. Even the workmen help to make her presence felt:

'QUIN. Well, it shall be so. But there is two hard things, that is, to bring the moonlight into a chamber; for, you know, Pyramus and Thisby meet by moonlight.

SNOUT. Doth the moon shine that night we play our play?

BOT. A calendar, a calendar! look in the almanac; find out moonshine, find out moonshine.

QUIN. Yes, it doth shine that night.

BOT. Why, then may you leave a casement of the great chamberwindow, where we play, open; and the moon may shine in at the casement.

QUIN. Ay; or else one must come in with a bush of thorns and a lanthorne and say he comes to disfigure, or to present, the person of Moonshine.'

But if the transition from daylight to moonlight is delicately wrought, it is far surpassed by the gradual oncoming of the dawn in acts III and IV.

The first hint comes when Oberon commands Puck to cover the starry welkin with fog, the better to mislead the angry lovers. The latter replies:

'My fairy Lord, this must be done with haste,
For night's swift dragons cut the clouds full fast,
And yonder shines Aurora's harbinger.'

Then in comes Lysander vainly hunting for Demetrius. Thwarted by the darkness he lies down to rest:

'Come, thou gentle day!
For if but once thou show me thy grey light,
I'll find Demetrius and revenge this spite.'

In comes Demetrius in similar mood:

'Thou shalt buy this dear,
If ever I thy face by daylight see:
Now, go thy way. Faintness constraineth me
To measure out my length on this cold bed:
By day's approach look to be visited.'

But the women are suffering even more than the men from that exhaustion and bedraggledness, which is so oppressive in the small hours after a sleepless night:

'*Re-enter* HELENA

HEL.   O weary night! O long and tedious night,
    Abate thy hours! Shine, comforts, from the east!
    That I may back to Athens by daylight....

Re-enter HERMIA

HER.   Never so weary, never so in woe,
    Bedabbled with the dew and torn with briers,
    I can no further crawl, no further go;
    My legs can keep no pace with my desires.
    Here will I rest me till the break of day.
    Heavens shield Lysander, if they mean a fray!'

The lovers are all asleep on the flowery bank, when they are joined by Titania, Bottom and the fairies. Bottom has 'an exposition of sleep' come upon him and, as he and the Fairy Queen rest together, Oberon and Puck arrive and conquer Cupid's flower by Dian's bud. Titania wakes, freed from the spell, takes hands with Oberon, and the day dawns.

'PUCK.   Fairy king, attend, and mark:
    I do hear the morning lark.

OBE.   Then, my queen, in silence sad,
    Trip we after the night's shade;
    We the globe can compass soon,
    Swifter than the wandering moon.'

The fairies vanish, a horn winds, Theseus, Hippolyta, and the rest break in with a clatter of horses and hounds, the day breaks and the shadows flee away. But the broad sunlight is not suited to the Midsummer Night's Dream, the day soon passes and gives place to torchlight. It would have been a simple plan to leave the fairy part in the centre of the play as a dream interval in the waking workaday world, but Shakespeare knew better than that. There is nothing more disappointing to a child than to find that the fairy tale was only a dream after all, and children know best how a fairy tale should be conducted.

'The iron tongue of midnight hath tolled twelve;
    Lovers, to bed; 'tis almost fairy time.'

Once more the colouring changes. The mortals are gone, the bright festal lights are dimmed, 'now the wasted brands do glow,' now the fire is dead and drowsy, and very quietly, very lightly, the fairies come in; dreamland has invaded reality, and who shall say which is which, for Puck left behind with his broom and his parting word sweeps the whole thing away, like the leaves of yester-year.

To compare a very great with a very small thing, the imaginative effect of this kind of plot-weaving is like that of the transformation scenes in ballet or pantomime, where groups of dancers come in like waves of colour, melting one into another. The effect is attractive even when crudely and unbeautifully designed. Transmuted into poetry it is of surpassing charm. It could only have been so transmuted at a time when pageantry was part of the people's life, when beauty was an element in all their recreations and 'they drew it in as simply as their breath.'

Music in the Court masque was even more important than scenery. Again and again, in the accounts of Elizabethan and Jacobean revels, we are told of the entrancing quality of the music. Robert Laneham told his merchant friend how Elizabeth stood by night on the bridge at Kenilworth and listened to the music sounding from barges on the quiet water. The music which accompanied the show of the *Lady of the Lake* moved him to ecstasy:

'Noow, Syr, the ditty in mitter so aptly endighted to the matter, and after by voys so deliciously deliver'd...every instrument agayn in hiz kind so excellently tunabl; and this in the eeving of the day, resoounding from the calm waters, whear prezens of her Majesty, and longing to listen, had utterly damped all noyz and dyn; the hole armony conveyd in tyme, tune, and temper thus incomparably melodious; with what pleazure, Master Martyn, with what sharpnes of conceyt, with what lyvely delighte, this moought pears [pierce] into the heerers harts; I pray ye imagin yoorself az ye may; for, so God judge me, by all the wit and cunning I have, I cannot express, I promis yoo....Muzik iz a nobl art!'[1]

This music Shakespeare has transmuted into his poetry, as he

---

[1] Laneham's *Account of the Queen's Entertainment at Killingworth Castle*, 1575, reprinted in *Prog. Eliz.* vol. I, pp. 458, 459.

has transmuted the spectacular element of pageantry. Laneham's emotion still vibrates in the words of Oberon:

> 'My gentle Puck, come hither. Thou remember'st
> Since once I sat upon a promontory,
> And heard a mermaid on a dolphin's back
> Uttering such dulcet and harmonious breath,
> That the rude sea grew civil at her song,
> And certain stars shot madly from their spheres,
> To hear the sea-maid's music.'

The whole play is musically written. It is interesting to compare Milton's famous *Sabrina* lyric with any of the fairy songs in *A Midsummer Night's Dream* and *The Tempest*. In *Sabrina* each word is exquisitely right, each word is an entity with its own peculiar value. In Shakespeare's songs the words melt into one another, and sometimes meaning is almost lost in melody and emotion. There is the same musical quality in the flowing blank verse of *A Midsummer Night's Dream*, verse which is lyrical rather than dramatic; liquid clear, never checked in its course by some sudden, sharp, projecting thought. Milton's dialogue has the terse, stichomythic quality of Greek or Senecan drama, Shakespeare's is a part-song[1].

The real soul of the masque, however, was the rhythmic movement of living bodies. It is owing to this fact that *A Midsummer Night's Dream* is more nearly related to the genuine masque than is *Comus*. In *Comus*, as we have seen, though dances occur, they are merely incidental, and the play would be scarcely altered by their omission. In *A Midsummer Night's Dream* most—not all—of the dances are vitally connected with the plot. For instance, Titania's awakening in act IV, sc. I is an important point in the play, for it is the point where the ravel begins to be untangled, and the occasion is celebrated by a dance of reunion between Fairy King and Fairy Queen:

> 'OBE. Sound, music! Come, my queen, take hands with me,
> And rock the ground whereon these sleepers be.
> Now thou and I are new in amity,
> And will to-morrow midnight solemnly

---

[1] Cf. *A Midsummer Night's Dream*, act I, sc. I, ll. 132 ff., with *Comus*, ll. 271 ff.

Dance in Duke Theseus' house triumphantly,
And bless it to all fair prosperity.
There shall the pairs of faithful lovers be
Wedded, with Theseus, all in jollity.'

The rhythm of the poetry is a dance rhythm, the lines rock
and sway with the movement of the fairies. Even more closely
in the last scene does the verse echo the light pattering steps of
the elves. There is nothing like this in *Comus*. The lyrics there
are exquisite, melodious, but they are not dance-songs. Even the
entry of Comus is poetry of the *Il Penseroso* order, imaginative,
intellectual, reminiscent, while Shakespeare's lines are alive with
movement, and suggest the repeat and turn and rhythmic beat of
dancing. In a word, in *Comus* we have thought turned to poetry,
while in *A Midsummer Night's Dream* we have sound and
movement turned to poetry.

The influence of the dance has affected not merely isolated
songs and speeches, but the whole structure of *A Midsummer
Night's Dream*. Again a comparison with *Comus* is helpful. The
difference in style between *Comus* and *A Midsummer Night's Dream*
depends upon a difference of spirit. *Comus* is a criticism of life, it
springs from an abstract idea: *A Midsummer Night's Dream* is a
dance, a movement of bodies. The plot is a pattern, a figure,
rather than a series of events occasioned by human character and
passion, and this pattern, especially in the moonlight parts of the
play, is the pattern of a dance.

'Enter a Fairie at one doore, and Robin Goodfellow at another....
Enter the King of Fairies, at one doore, with his traine; and the Queene,
at another with hers.'

The appearance and disappearance and reappearance of the various
lovers, the will-o'-the-wisp movement of the elusive Puck, form
a kind of figured ballet. The lovers quarrel in a dance pattern:
first, there are two men to one woman and the other woman alone,
then for a brief space a circular movement, each one pursuing
and pursued, then a return to the first figure with the position of
the women reversed, then a cross-movement, man quarrelling
with man and woman with woman, and then, as finale, a general

setting to partners, including not only lovers but fairies and royal personages as well.

This dance-like structure makes it inevitable that the lovers should be almost as devoid of character as masquers or masque-presenters. The harmony and grace of the action would have been spoilt by convincing passion.

The only character study in *A Midsummer Night's Dream* is to be found in the portrayal of Bottom, Theseus, and perhaps Hippolyta. Even in drawing these characters Shakespeare was evidently influenced by the memory of pageants, complimentary speeches and entertainments addressed by townspeople and humble folk to the Queen or to the nobility. A glance through Nichols' *Public Progresses* shows what innumerable lengthy speeches, what innumerable disguisings and shows, Elizabeth was obliged to bear with gracious demeanour. Her experiences were similar to those of Theseus:

> 'Where I have come, great clerks have purposed
> To greet me with premeditated welcomes;
> Where I have seen them shiver and look pale,
> Make periods in the midst of sentences,
> Throttle their practis'd accent in their fears,
> And, in conclusion, dumbly have broke off,
> Not paying me a welcome.'

One Sunday afternoon, at Kenilworth Castle, Elizabeth and her Court whiled away the time by watching the country-people at a Brideale and Morris Dance. Their amused kindly tolerance is just that of Theseus and the lovers towards the Athenian workmen. So that even in the most solid and dramatic parts of his play Shakespeare is only giving an idealised version of courtly and country revels and of the people that played a part in them.

In *A Midsummer Night's Dream* Bottom and his companions serve the same purpose as the antimasque in the courtly revels. It is true that Shakespeare's play was written before Ben Jonson had elaborated and defined the antimasque, but from the first grotesque dances were popular, and the principle of contrast was always latent in the masque. There is, however, a great difference between Jonson's and Shakespeare's management of foil and relief. In the antimasque the transition is sudden and the contrast complete[1], a method of composition effective enough in spectacle and ballet. But in a play, as Shakespeare well knew, the greatest beauty is gained through contrast when the difference is obvious and striking, but rises out of a deep though unobtrusive resemblance. This could not be better illustrated than by the picture of Titania winding the ass-headed Bottom in her arms. Why is it that this is a pleasing picture, why is it that the rude mechanicals do not, as a matter of fact, disturb or sully Titania's 'close and consecrated bower'? Malvolio in Bottom's place would be repellent, yet Malvolio, regarded superficially, is less violently contrasted to the Fairy Queen than is Nick Bottom. Bottom with his ass's head is grotesquely hideous, and in ordinary life he is crude, raw, and very stupid. We have no reason to suppose that Malvolio was anything but a well set-up, proper-looking man, spruce, well-dressed, the perfect family butler. His mentality too is of a distinctly higher order than Bottom's. He fills a responsible position with credit, he follows a reasoned line of conduct, he thinks nobly of the soul. Two things alone he lacks (and that is why no self-respecting fay could ever kiss him) —humour and imagination. Malvolio is, therefore, the only character who cannot be included in the final harmony of *Twelfth Night*. Bottom and his fellows did perhaps lack humour (though the interview with the fairies suggests that Bottom had a smack of it), but in its place they possessed unreason. Imagination they did have, of the most simple, primal, childlike kind. It is their artistic ambition that lifts them out of the humdrum world and turns them into Midsummer Dreamers, and we have seen how cunningly Shakespeare extracts from their very stupidity romance and moonshine. But, indeed, grotesqueness and stupidity (of a certain kind) have a kinship with beauty. For these qualities usually imply a measure of spiritual freedom, they lead to at least a temporary relief from the tyranny of reason and from the pressure of the external world. In *A Midsummer Night's Dream* the dominance of the Lord of Misrule is not marked by coarse parody, but by the partial repeal of the laws of cause and effect. By

---

[1] Cf. *The Masque of Queens*, and *supra*, pp. 183, 267.

delicate beauty, gentle mockery, and simple romantic foolishness our freedom is gained.

If Shakespeare's play had, like *Comus*, been based upon an abstract idea, he might have found in Malvolio, not in Bottom, the most effective contrast to the Fairy Queen. The contrast between the prosaic man of business and the pierrot or elfin type of creature is a recurrent theme in literature. The amusement lies in putting the prosy people in charming or unconventional surroundings and laughing at their inadequacy and confusion—

> 'Big fat woman whom nobody loves,
> Why do you walk through the fields with gloves,
> Missing so much and so much?'

But either gloves or yellow stockings and cross garters would shatter Shakespeare's dream. For his play is not a criticism of life but a dance, and a dance of which the underlying motif is harmony. The contrast may be sharp as you please, but the unity must be deeper than the divergence. For, after all, the presiding deity is Hymen. His functions are performed by the fairies who are, indeed, emanations from him. Deeply rooted in folk-lore is the connection between the fairies and fertility, and Shakespeare had a happy inspiration when he substituted them for the Ceres, Dianas, and Junos of pageantry, and also turned them into an expression of the harmony and concord which was the keynote of most Elizabethan revels.

If the descriptions do not mislead us, civic and courtly entertainments must always have been tantalising those who witnessed them with suggestions of loveliness that were never quite realised. Just when the great gardens were about to turn into Fairyland, the poet would spoil everything with some clumsy allegory or compliment. These suggestions seem to have sunk down into Shakespeare's mind, and thence to have emerged transformed and perfected, moulded into final and satisfactory shape, a revelation of that world 'where music and moonlight and feeling are one.'

When Shakespeare wrote *A Midsummer Night's Dream*, the Court masque was less developed than the out-of-doors entertainment. At first Shakespeare, like Spenser, was influenced, not so much by the actual Court masque, as by open-air revelling, although, on the other hand, his early work is inspired more by the dance than by the old-fashioned processional momerie which informs so much of the work of Spenser.

By the time Shakespeare came to write *The Tempest* very great changes had taken place in the Court revels: on the one hand, Ben Jonson had dramatised the masque and used it as a vehicle for serious criticism of life; on the other hand, Inigo Jones had increased its sensuous attraction.

This difference between early and late revels is reflected in a difference of style and content between *A Midsummer Night's Dream* and *The Tempest*, a difference particularly obvious in the treatment of the background, which in both plays is of great importance.

In *A Midsummer Night's Dream* the action takes place in a domestic wood close to the town, which is reminiscent both of the pleasant Warwickshire countryside and of the pleasure grounds of great noblemen. In *The Tempest* the landscape has expanded. Prospero's Isle is a remote mysterious place. Never is it exactly described: only from Ariel and Caliban and the Duke himself we get allusions that give us a feeling of sea and wood, odd nooks, stagnant pools, and tall pines, vast stretches of shining sands. A sudden word from Ariel as to the 'still vexed Bermoothes,' a mention of Tunis 'ten leagues beyond man's life,' and new vistas open. The only thing in *A Midsummer Night's Dream* at all like this is the Fairy Queen's description of herself and her votaress, sitting by night on the shore, breathing the spiced Indian air, and watching the traders with their big-bellied sails. But this sense of spaciousness and mystery is exceptional in *A Midsummer Night's Dream*, whereas in *The Tempest* it pervades the play. This difference of background is due partly to difference of subject, but also, perhaps, to the influence of the developed masque. The gardens of Kenilworth and Eltham suggested an ordinary world, transformed and begetting fairies; but, in Whitehall, Inigo and Ben set imagination to work and suggested worlds, remote from reality, 'ten leagues beyond man's life.'

Again, it may be due to the influence of the developed masque, that in *The Tempest* both nature and the fairies are controlled by Prospero, whereas in *A Midsummer Night's Dream* the mortals are at the mercy of Oberon and Puck. The entertainments that influenced *A Midsummer Night's Dream* were the productions of many collaborators, and did not as a rule give an irresistible impression of a controlling mind. But to an artist the Court masques at Whitehall must always have brought the thought of the designing mind behind them. Of course I do not mean that Shakespeare meant Prospero to stand for the poet or architect, and the fairies and the background for his poetic achievement; but merely that the prominence of design and creative thought in the Court masque made an impression, and led him, perhaps unconsciously, to write a play in which the action was dominated by one purposeful spirit.

The Tempest was influenced not only by the masque in general, but by certain masques in particular. The resemblances between the inserted masque and Jonson's *Hymenaei* have often been pointed out, and it has been suggested that Shakespeare, when he conceived Ariel, had in his mind those musicians who in Ben Jonson's masque *Hymenaei* were seated upon the rainbow 'figuring airy spirits, their habits various, and resembling the several colours caused in that part of the air by reflection,' chief among whom was the famous Alphonso Ferrabosco, 'a man planted by himself in that divine sphere, and mastering all the spirits of music.' The setting of the play also bears some resemblance to the scenery of Jonson's masques of *Blackness* and *Beauty*. The wonderful sea-scape and sea-pageant of the former masque have already been described[1]. *The Masque of Beauty* is a sequel to *The Masque of Blackness*, and tells us how the black daughters of Niger journeyed by sea to Britania to be cured of their blackness and so excited the envy of Night who tossed them at sea

'Till on an island they by chance arrived,
That floated in the main....'

The scene, which showed 'an island floating on a calm water... in the midst thereof...the Throne of Beauty...shot itself to the land,' and 'the musicians, which were placed in the arbors, came

[1] Cf. *supra*, pp. 177, 178.

PLATE XI

1 'A LANDSCIPT AND A CALME SEA'
Design by Inigo Jones for Davenant's *Tempe Restored*

2 DESIGN
By Inigo Jones for an unidentified masque. See pp. 239, 240, and 240, n. 4
Copyright of His Grace the Duke of Devonshire

forth through the mazes to the other land; singing this full song, iterated in the closes by two Echoes, rising out of the fountains.' It is easy to see how these or similar masques, sinking down into the mind of the poet, might produce the fairy isle haunted by monstrous shapes, by spirits, by dancing and singing elves.

The Tempest, far more than A Midsummer Night's Dream, is pervaded by music. It is by music that the evil-doers are first convinced of their guilt and spell-bound, and then released from enchantment. It is by music that Ariel lures on Ferdinand, and decoys Caliban and his fellow-conspirators:

> 'I beat my tabor;
> At which, like unback'd colts, they prick'd their ears,
> Advanc'd their eyelids, lifted up their noses
> As they smelt music....'

In The Tempest, as in the masque, music and dancing are closely associated. The mock banquet is accompanied by dancing and pantomime. The first song by which Ariel lures Ferdinand into Prospero's power is written on a dance pattern. With Ariel's first words, 'Come unto these yellow sands,' we imagine the fairies running in from all sides, they take hands in a ring, then turn to one another, curtseying and kissing, or, in the time-honoured phrase of the country-dance, they honour their partners. At this act of elfin grace and courtesy there is a momentary pause in the dance, a momentary lull in the accompaniment of sea music, 'the wild waves whist.' Then the music and dancing break out afresh with renewed vigour, and those familiar with country dancing will recognise the to-and-fro movement, the setting to partners, which separates the different dance figures: 'foot it featly here and there, and, sweet sprites, the burden bear.' This is a perfect instance of the poetical transmutation of revelling. From innumerable intermixed dances of town and country, but chiefly from the figured ballet of the Court, rises up this ethereal, ghostly dance which is danced (for Ariel is invisible) solely in the mind, and yet transforms the mind into a spacious, lonely, mystic place, where elves may play by 'perilous seas in faery lands forlorn.'

Although dances and masque-like episodes penetrate into *The Tempest* and are occasionally transmuted into exquisite poetry, the action is not founded upon a dance movement but upon an idea. For instance, the principle of the antimasque is embodied in both this play and in *A Midsummer Night's Dream*; but the contrast between Titania and Bottom is a picturesque contrast, the contrast between Ariel and Caliban appeals both to eye and mind, and seems in some way to embody the contrast between flesh and spirit, earth and air, good and evil.

Not that the play is an allegory. It would seem that at the end of his working life Shakespeare liked to set down his thoughts without troubling to embody them in a story adjusted to ordinary probabilities; so he followed the example of the masque writers and adopted that convenient hypothesis of the omnipotence of magic, which has rescued many an inexpert story-teller in the nursery. Jonson's *Masque of Blackness* is not an allegory but a mythological fairy-tale, and it seems to have influenced not only the setting but also the content and structure of *The Tempest*.

In *The Winter's Tale* and *The Tempest* Shakespeare shows the sins of the fathers absolved in the happiness of the children. It is an attractive, but slow-moving theme, and its dramatisation presents grave difficulties as regards the treatment of character, almost insuperable difficulties as regards the treatment of time[1]. In *The Tempest* the latter difficulty is met by observance of the rules and by dramatising only the final phase of the story. Nevertheless, in spite of this superficial conformity, *The Tempest* is not a classical play; and if Shakespeare is following Ben Jonson, he is following, not his theories as a classicist, but his practice as a writer of masques; he is, indeed, overcoming a difficult dramatic problem by making skilful use of a typical masque construction.

We have seen how the masque libretto grew out of the need to explain the arrival of masquers at Court, and how this was

[1] Sir Arthur Quiller-Couch draws attention to this in his Introduction to *The Tempest*, ed. Sir Arthur Quiller-Couch and John Dover Wilson (Cambridge, 1921), pp. l, li.

generally done by giving a lengthy account of their past wanderings, and by inventing some ingenious and fantastic motive for their anxiety to see the sovereign. This is the principle which underlies the literary portions of *Blackness* and *Beauty*. In the journey of the nymphs across the sea, their final arrival at the Island of Albion and the long explanatory speeches of Niger and Boreas, these masques have points in common with the arrangement of *The Tempest*. After the introduction of the Italian picture stage, the masquers were usually 'discovered,' instead of entering in procession, so that it became the duty of the masque poet to explain how and why the masquers had been released from their concealment. The usual explanation was that the masquers had been hidden as a result of adverse spells, and had been freed from enchantment by the beneficent power of the sovereign. In the *Masque of Beauty* Jonson combines the wandering motif with the disenchantment motif, and Shakespeare in *The Tempest* follows his example. Only in Shakespeare's play the power who works the magic is no longer a royal spectator, but a character within the drama; and the story that lies behind his action is a story of human deeds and passions, not a mere fantastic mythological invention, such as the visionary appearance of the Ethiopian Moon goddess. Nevertheless, it is the story behind the play, rather than the play itself, which is dramatic; and the second scene of *The Tempest* has affinities with the masque induction rather than with the Greek prologue. For classical drama, whether Greek or French, is concerned with the final phase of a conflict, and the interest is concentrated upon the last few hours of uncertainty which must soon be terminated by irrevocable choice and decisive action: but the masque deals, not with the last phase of a conflict, but with a moment of transformation; it expresses, not uncertainty, ended by final success or failure, but expectancy, crowned by sudden revelation; and even when the opposition of good and evil is symbolised by masque and antimasque, this opposition is shown as a contrast rather than as a conflict. It is in this respect that *The Tempest* is more masquelike than dramatic, for Prospero addresses Miranda in the tone of a masque presenter and, throughout the play, he manipulates the human characters as surely as he manipulates the spirit masquers.

> 'Now does my project gather to a head:
> My charms crack not; my spirits obey; and time
> Goes upright with his carriage.'[1]

As the masque induction leads up to that moment of transformation, when the solution of difficulty, the conquest of adverse powers, is marked by the sudden appearance of the masquers; so the plot of *The Tempest* leads up, without hesitation or uncertainty, to that moment when Prospero gathers his forgiven enemies around him, draws back the curtain from before the inner stage, and 'discovers Ferdinand and Miranda playing at chess.'

The part played by Prospero makes *The Tempest* more masque-like than *Comus*, although both plays are founded on an idea rather than on a dance movement. Though *Comus* as a whole is undramatic, there is at the centre of it a dramatic clash of wills, a dramatic moment of uncertainty, as to whether or no Comus will overcome the resistance of the Lady; but there is never in *The Tempest* any serious fear that Caliban's conspiracy may succeed, and the only potent will is the will of Prospero. So far from being founded upon a conflict, the play does not even contain a debate. The whole plot of *The Tempest* is not very much more dramatic than that loud trumpet blast at whose sound the witches vanish and the House of Fame appears; nevertheless, it is just a little more dramatic than Jonson's *Masque of Queens*, because the miracles wrought by Prospero are only outward signs of an inward self-conquest, and behind *The Tempest* lie that conflict between two opposing parties and that conflict within the soul of the hero which was always the subject of Shakespearian tragedy. Only Shakespeare is now hymning the victory instead of describing the battle, the lyrical element has almost usurped the place of drama, time has almost disappeared into eternity.

Again, the spirit of *The Tempest* is far nearer to the spirit of the masque than is *Comus*. All through his life Milton used his poetic gift to deliver two quite different, and even contradictory

[1] Act v, sc. 1, ll. 1 ff.

messages. He spoke of the golden world, but he also spoke of a terrific, eternal conflict between the spirit and the flesh, and demanded an inhuman, arrogant detachment from pleasure, which was completely incompatible with the ideal expressed in the Court masque. What is it that Shakespeare is saying to us through his fairy tales? In *A Midsummer Night's Dream* he spoke, like Spenser and Milton, and many another Renaissance poet, of a delightful world of harmony and external beauty; but in *The Tempest* he seems to be saying something darker, and more profound.

The literary masque offered a criticism of life which was very simple and definite, it presented society as a harmony of unequal parts, a living organism. This ideal of harmony can be regarded as embodied in the person of Hymen, for in the Court masque marriage was treated as an event of social significance.

In *A Midsummer Night's Dream*, as we have seen, Hymen's part is played by the fairies, but Hymen in the larger sense, Hymen as the spirit of order and unity, only makes himself felt in the blending of plots, in the technique of the play. There is no suggestion of allegory and very little criticism of life.

In *The Tempest* the part of Hymen is played by Prospero. The feeling that Prospero's words have a mystical meaning becomes particularly strong during his meditation on the masque, which occurs immediately after the betrothal, and immediately before the defeat of Caliban. It is interesting that, in both *The Tempest* and *A Midsummer Night's Dream*, there is a moment when the influence of pageantry is felt with peculiar strength, and that this same moment marks a turning-point in the action.

Oberon relates his vision to Puck immediately before despatching him on that errand which sets in motion all the complications of the plot. The vision is divided into two parts. First of all, there is the description of what both Oberon and Puck saw, and that is simply an idealised account of a typical Court entertainment, possibly reminiscent of the shows at Kenilworth or Eltham. Then there is the account of what Oberon alone could see, and that is the allegorical meaning of the performance, a meaning which is expressed in clear-cut pictorial imagery, which has a complimentary reference to Queen Elizabeth, and is possibly connected with a definite piece of Court intrigue. Oberon's vision is no mere isolated compliment, but an ingenious device for turning the main theme of the play into a piece of subtle flattery, and connecting the potency of Cupid's flower as well as of Dian's bud with the charm and chastity of the Virgin Queen.

Prospero's meditation has a deeper and more universal meaning than Oberon's vision, and in it the influence of the revels is felt in a more subtle way, and has sunk down into the very texture of the language.

It has long been recognised that some of the imagery of this passage is reminiscent of the coronation festivities of James I. In order to grace the King's solemn progress through London, seven gates or arches were erected; over the first was represented the true likeness of all the notable houses, towers, steeples, within the city of London; on the sixth the globe of the world was seen to move; at Temple Bar a seventh arch or gate was erected, the forefront being proportioned in every respect like a temple[1]. But Prospero appears to have been thinking of the theatrical staging as well as of the pageantry of the streets.

The word 'rack' has caused considerable trouble to the commentators. Whiter and Staunton connect the word with the stage-craft of the time. Whiter applies it to 'a body of "clouds in motion" *when considered as a constituent part in the machinery of a* PAGEANT,' and cites Jonson's *Masque of Hymen*:

'Here the upper part of the scene, which was all of clouds, and made artificially to swell, and ride like the RACK, began to open; and the air clearing, from the top thereof was discovered Juno....'

Staunton follows Whiter and remarks:

'While it is evident that by "rack" was understood the drifting vapour or *scud*, as it is now termed, it would appear that Shakespeare ...was thinking not more of the actual clouds than of those gauzy semblances, which, in the pageants of his day, as in the stage spectacles of ours, were often used, partly or totally, to obscure the scene behind. Ben Jonson, in the description of his masques, very frequently mentions

[1] Cf. *Prog. James*, vol. I, pp. 339 ff.

this scenic contrivance....The evanishing of the actors, then, in Prospero's pageant...was doubtless effected by the agency of filmy curtains, which, being drawn one over another to resemble the flying mists, gave to the scene an appearance of gradual dissolution; when the objects were totally hidden, the drapery was withdrawn in the same manner, veil by veil, till at length even that had disappeared, and there was left, then, not even a *rack* behind.'[1]

Does this connection with theatrical trappings and street decorations drag the poetry down to earth? Surely not. Shakespeare has been thinking of the evanescence of art and of our human life, of which art is but a reflection. The masque suggests to his mind the most thin and perishable part of the machinery by means of which art finds expression. These things seem trivial and temporary—are they much more so than art itself? But the poet's thought travels swiftly from the mock scenic vapours to the scudding clouds of heaven, real and lovely, but even less permanent than their feeble imitations; and these same clouds, most fleeting of fleeting things, are but fitting images of the life of man. The revels are ended, the spirits are melted into air—a pause of pondering thought at the queerness of it—into thin air; and then the verse surges up in sudden illumination: 'and like the baseless fabric of this vision....' The word *baseless* lifts us gently from the earth; *fabric* goes back to the thin air, the unsubstantial stuff of which the solid seeming world is made; the *cloud-capp'd towers* carry us up to a soaring height; *the gorgeous palaces* display a spreading splendour of pinnacles; *the solemn temples* suggest the appearance of majesty, linked to all that we hope to be enduring in the hearts of men; and then, finally, *the great globe itself* offers a comprehensive vision of the world and all that is upon it. For one moment the vision stands, for one moment it hangs before us, rounded, definite, complete, then it wavers, it becomes unreal as a theatre scene, then light and filmy as a cloud, and then it vanishes. The underlying impression is of great masses of cloud, piled up in the sky, which seems to have generated them, which encompasses and will again absorb them. Lit up by the sunlight, they look like great snow mountains, yet as we look they change,

---

[1] *The Tempest*, in *A New Variorum Edition of Shakespeare*, ed. H. H Furness, vol. IX, pp. 215–217.

they become a moving scud, they dissolve and finally disappear, vanishing clean away, even down to the last light film of flying vapour. Then, with the picture of the unfathomed depth of the sky round the clouds still in the mind, the thought moves from the outer world to the inner life of man, that life which is encompassed by the mystery of silence, rises out of it, and returns to it as a dream rises out of, and vanishes into, a dreamless sleep. Our thoughts return again to the thin gauzy substance of the theatre—more shadowy still—'we are such stuff as dreams are made on.' The sense of encompassing mystery does not exclude the idea of sleep coming as a completion and crown to life.

The philosophy of this passage has been very variously judged, it has been taken as a proof that Shakespeare was an atheist, a materialist, an idealist, and so on. If it is taken at its face value it certainly seems an utterance of pessimism, but it should be borne in mind that Prospero's utterance is not only dramatic[1], it is incomplete and cannot be fully interpreted apart from later passages, and, in particular, it should be connected with the speech in the first scene of the fifth act. Prospero has mastered the forces arrayed against him; at a hint from Ariel he has decided that 'the rarer action is in virtue than in vengeance.' He summons all the powers and arts at his command, to execute this, his final and noblest purpose, and then the solemn moment of forgiveness comes. His enemies enter as madmen into his charmed circle and remain there spell-bound, until Prospero calls for a heavenly air, and solemn music is played to restore their senses. At the breath of evil, the beauteous forms of art vanished away, and left behind a vision of the fading of the whole earth into its original nothingness. Now there is a gradual restoration of reason to maddened creatures; Prospero attacks unreason, and at each step of the ground gained the goodness of Gonzalo seems something to hold fast by:

> 'A solemn air and the best comforter
> To an unsettled fancy, cure thy brains,
> Now useless, boil'd within thy skull!...

[1] For the *dramatic* significance of this pessimistic utterance and its connection with the preceding masque see Professor A. C. Bradley, *Shakespearean Tragedy* (London, 1911), pp. 328 ff.

> Holy Gonzalo, honourable man,
> Mine eyes, even sociable to the show of thine,
> Fall fellowly drops. The charm dissolves apace;
> And as the morning steals upon the night,
> Melting the darkness, so their rising senses
> Begin to chase the ignorant fumes that mantle
> Their clearer reason.—O good Gonzalo!
> My true preserver, and a loyal sir
> To him thou follow'st, I will pay thy graces
> Home, both in word and deed....
>
>   Their understanding
> Begins to swell, and the approaching tide
> Will shortly fill the reasonable shores
> That now lie foul and muddy.'

Though the poetry is far less lovely than in the more famous lines, this speech also must be remembered if we are to understand the latest mood of Shakespeare.

In *A Midsummer Night's Dream,* as in other romantic comedies, Hymen comes into his kingdom easily, because the characters are easily malleable, and because our eyes are averted from the serious side of life. But in these later plays Shakespeare has shown sorrow and joy, good and ill, mingled together as in real life they are mingled, so if Hymen is to reign at all it must be through conquests, through reconciliations and absolutions. The lovers win our sympathy, but our chief interest is focussed on the healing of ancient troubles, by which alone the wedding can be brought about. In *The Winter's Tale* and *The Tempest* peace and harmony are achieved by long and far-sighted suffering, but they are only consummated when out of them there suddenly springs a new birth of joy. It is significant that whereas in *A Midsummer Night's Dream* the part of Hymen is played by the fairies, in *The Tempest* it is played by Prospero, the man who hopes, who looks forward.

But if *The Tempest* is not a proof of Shakespeare's pessimism, still less is it an outburst of facile optimism, and those critics are right who call attention to the harsher side of Shakespeare's outlook, his recognition of apparently insoluble problems, hopeless disasters, incurable evils. Shakespeare, like Milton, perceived that there was much in life which could not be included in the glibly harmonious scheme of the masquers; which, even in its most idealised form, could not be made part of the dance of the Hours and Graces. But Shakespeare dealt with these anomalies in a very different spirit from that of the great Puritan. For Milton there was an imaginative world, clear cut, harmonious, entirely free from ugliness or darkness; there was also a perfectly straight fight between the utterly opposed forces of good and evil, and these two conceptions co-existed in his mind, but had apparently very little connection with one another. But increasing years brought to Shakespeare an ever-increasing profundity, and a decreasing clarity of thought. Good and evil are infinitely unlike each other and yet, paradoxically enough, they are not always completely separable; even Fairyland is composed of vice and virtue, beauty and ugliness. And always the hard edges of things are softened by changing shadows.

For Milton viewed the world from the classical standpoint, but Shakespeare was a romantic, and his romanticism was greatest at the end of his working life. The difference between *A Midsummer Night's Dream* and *The Tempest* may be partly due to the development of the masque, but it is also due to a change from the classical to the romantic method of creation. In *A Midsummer Night's Dream* Shakespeare moulds his vague memories of revels into the precise, clear-cut images of Oberon and Puck sitting on the promontory, the mermaid on the dolphin's back, the flying Cupid. In *The Tempest* Shakespeare meditates upon the masque and dissolves it.

> 'These our actors,
> As I foretold you, were all spirits and
> Are melted into air, into thin air.'

Omnia exeunt in mysterium. Prospero's great speech is an utterance neither of pessimism nor of ennui but of awe, and his ponderings are perhaps not so much the meditations of a philosopher as the expression of a mood, a mood which was often produced by the influence of the masque.

One of the strongest feelings evoked by the masque was a sense of transitoriness and illusion. This feeling is perfectly understandable, for it arises naturally at theatres, balls, solemn processions, gay social functions, which are always apt to arouse thoughts of the swift and irrecoverable flight of time. This sense of illusion and transience is (I can only speak of course from my own experience) very far from being depressing. It has nothing to do with the dull philosophy of the Preacher, and his tiresome reiteration that all is vanity and vexation of spirit. Rather it arouses a sense of dilation, of opening vistas, of life regarded *sub specie aeternitatis*. For a moment the world becomes thin as a theatre curtain, a cloudy veil about to be withdrawn.

This surely is the dominant mood of *The Tempest*. I have compared its plot with the masque induction, and suggested that it is founded upon an idea rather than upon an action. But the word *idea* is not quite the right one; *The Tempest*, like the masque, presents a moment of revelation, but the revelation is made by way of the emotions rather than the understanding, and our play is founded, not upon a concept, but upon an intuition.

A study of sources and influences is chiefly valuable in so far as it illuminates the process of poetic creation. The masque supplied Shakespeare with much of his material for *A Midsummer Night's Dream* and *The Tempest*, but in return he immortalised in those masterpieces much of the grace and beauty of a Court function.

The Renaissance differed from our own age not so much in that it was a time of great artistic fecundity, but in that it was a time when social life was itself aesthetically beautiful, so beautiful indeed that it seemed unbearable that it should be doomed to die.

Through *A Midsummer Night's Dream* and *The Tempest* the loveliness of the masque is still accessible to us. How did Shakespeare bring this about? Not by imitating any one masque, not by indulging in vague rhapsodies on the beauties of the revels, but by taking his floating recollections of Court festivities and moulding them into a new, definite, concrete form. We have already seen this shaping process at work in the case of Oberon's vision, and it is particularly obvious also in the case of the fairies of *A Midsummer Night's Dream*. There they stand, clearly outlined in the moonlight, shapely, attractive, positive little creatures, but behind them, stretching back and back into the darkness, are innumerable forms, ill-defined, shifting, transitory, northern elves, haunters of burial mounds, Greek nymphs of standing lakes and groves, witches, fates, norns, gnomes, and hobgoblins of the folk, mediaeval fairy kings and queens, all the thoughts and fancies of the generations, crossing and re-crossing, branching off, combining, coalescing—no wonder that in this play Shakespeare cannot refrain from speaking of the arduous process of creation:

> 'The poet's eye, in a fine frenzy rolling,
> Doth glance from heaven to earth, from earth to heaven;
> And, as imagination bodies forth
> The forms of things unknown, the poet's pen
> Turns them to shapes, and gives to airy nothing
> A local habitation and a name.'

This shaping process is most obviously at work in poetry written in the classical spirit, but it is part of all poetic creation. In poems which are pervaded by the sense of mystery, this sense of mystery is still expressed by the definite story or image or rhythm. In *The Tempest*, for instance, free play is given to all those mystical feelings which were so often evoked by the masque, but these feelings are expressed by means of one particular story, one particular background. Many travellers' tales, and many scenic splendours, have gone to the making of the Fairy Isle, vague mediaeval theories as to elemental spirits, half-memories of disguised musicians, seated in stage clouds, have taken individual shape in Ariel, many rumours and inaccurate yarns of Elizabethan sailors have become concrete in Caliban with his ancient and fish-like smell. The poet's pen turns them to shape.

Creation, then, is a higher kind of definition. The poet, like the theologian, is a dogmatist, for he puts into words, and so limits and preserves, the thoughts of himself and his generation and of all those whose minds are akin to his own. And by so doing he not only immortalises the life of his time, he makes it dynamic. It is not unusual to draw a contrast between the living spirit and the dead form. But in art certainly the dynamic quality of a masterpiece is usually in direct proportion to its concreteness and comely outline. Shakespeare, by making his fairies definite, also made them fruitful, and ever since he created them, they have never ceased to influence literature and the nursery. As soon as the vague idea, or fluid revel, has been moulded into definite form, it is re-absorbed into the general consciousness, which is raised to a higher level. *A Midsummer Night's Dream* was the product of many earlier masques and entertainments, it was afterwards used to enrich the libretti of Ben Jonson. Spenser embodied a whole era of social life in his poem; his poem then proceeded to colour, not only the social life of his time, but a very great deal of the literature of his own and subsequent ages, and if his *Faerie Queene* does not quite rank with the greatest poems of the world, it is chiefly because it is too fluid. For the poet's definition is not merely conservative, it is also creative. Through *A Midsummer Night's Dream* and *The Tempest* we experience not only what the masque was, but what it might have been.

CHAPTER XIII

Mumming

'If the grey dust is over all,
And stars and leaves and wings forgot,
And your blood holds no festival—
Go out from us; we need you not.

But if you are immoderate men,
Zealots of joy, the salt and sting
And savour of life upon you—then
We call you to our counselling.'

JOHN DRINKWATER, *Epilogue.*

So far I have dealt with the history and influence of the masque; in these last chapters I shall try to gather up results and to put down certain thoughts about the function of art and its relation to ordinary life, which have been suggested to me by my study of the subject. I give my conclusions for what they are worth, realising all the time how tentative such conclusions are bound to be. Though I cannot always show it by the turn of my sentences, yet this section is written throughout in the interrogative rather than the indicative mood.

The masque should be interesting to students of aesthetics, because it does not fit into any of the ordinary categories: it is doubtful whether it should be regarded as art or play or ritual, or as an elaborate composition of all the arts. It will be well, therefore, to begin by clearing up this ambiguity.

The cricketer on the playing-field, the actor on the stage, the priest celebrating Mass, all resemble one another in exhibiting a lack of practical purpose, an intentional loss of contact with ordinary life. To which, if any of them, is the masquer most akin? Let us look more closely at their doings.

The cricketer has set aside a portion of space and time within which he may perform activities that are to be unimpeded by, and to have no effect upon, ordinary life. Within these limits he pursues a purpose as strenuously as any worker can do; only the difference is that the worker acts in order to gain his ends, whereas the player proposes to himself an end in order to set himself in motion; the worker's acts are related to the rest of life, the player's acts are ordered so that they may safely be performed for their own sake alone.

Obviously the masquer is still further removed from the worker than is the cricketer, for not only his aim, but his whole action is characterised by lack of struggle and practical purpose. The game can be lost or won; not so the masque.

The loss of practical intention is still more plainly seen when we turn from the cricketer to the actor. The actor has also set aside a portion of space and time within which he may perform actions unrelated to ordinary life; but the deeds done upon the stage have not even a momentary earnestness. The actor does not seriously try to achieve an object which has only a temporary and pretended importance; he pretends the whole time to be performing a serious action. Moreover, he pretends not to himself but to others. Spectators may or may not stand round a playing-field: the stage is useless apart from the auditorium. Since the actor is carrying out a pretence, it follows that he is acting in accordance with a preconceived plan, that he has a playwright behind him as well as an audience in front of him. But the existence of the artist with his plan makes the actor less secure than the cricketer, the drama more permanent than the cricket-match. The same match cannot be repeated, a drama can be performed any number of times, in any number of places, or it need never be performed at all, but pass straight from the mind of the playwright to the mind of the audience by means of the written word; and when this happens the actor vanishes, or retains at most a ghostly, potential existence in the imagination. Of course, I do not mean that book and theatre are simply interchangeable. A good play, as Shakespearian critics now realise, must be judged as a stage play; yet it can be enjoyed in the library, and this enjoyment does not depend upon the power to visualise the acting, as enjoyment of a musical score depends upon the reader's power of making the performance audible to himself. Moreover, to the reader there is no formal difference between the libretto of a stage play and a literary drama incapable of theatrical production   Nor is there any hard and fast distinction between poetic and theatrical drama; but plays that are only effective when acted merge into plays more or less easily detachable or wholly detached from the theatre.

The disappearance of actor and theatre completes the process of detaching art from ordinary life. If we want games we must provide holidays and playing-fields, but no special time or place need be left free for the poet, because his 'game' involves not only the minimum interference with, but the minimum displacement of ordinary life.

The masquer appears disguised upon a stage, with an audience in front of him, artists behind him, and he is taking part in a kind of drama. So far he resembles the actor, but he is in a much stronger position. First of all, his actions are done as much for his own pleasure as for the pleasure of the audience, and indeed he cannot be sharply distinguished from a spectator, for he remains quite silent until he has descended from the stage to chat and dance with the ladies of the company. Again, the masquer is no mere mouthpiece of the artist; rather artists and actors are co-operating in order to introduce, explain, and extol him. Of course the importance of the masquer is due to his noble birth; but a man of noble birth can be a masquer only because the masque is no mere pretence, no action unrelated to the rest of life, but rather a celebration of an event with which he himself may be intimately concerned, and which may even be of international importance. 'The dancing courtiers' had good reason to behave 'as if poetry were made to set out their activity,' but their attitude was naturally disconcerting to a dramatist accustomed to regarding actor and theatre as a medium, and a medium whose solidity was —in a sense—dependent upon his own will. The playwright sold his play to the company; yet when, as at a wave of a wand, the robustious periwig-pated fellows of the Globe had melted into thin air, there remained behind a work of magic invisible and everlasting. But when the wretched Ben waved his wand at Court, the masquers, so far from melting into air, hustled their magician from the banqueting hall. And this happened because the masque was not quite a work of art but still part of the actual life of society.

The social importance and possible pagan origin of the masque suggest that the masquer may be akin, not to the actor or the athlete, but to the priest.

If we open the door of a cathedral on Sunday morning we see something not unlike a theatrical performance. The altar and choir correspond to the stage, the nave and aisles to the auditorium, and the action that is going forward has something of the mimetic character of the drama, none of the struggle, effort, and risk of failure proper to the athletic game or to ordinary work. Yet the priest is not merely a religious actor performing an edifying play. In the first place he has no audience, for the congregation— partly in fact, wholly in intention—associate themselves with his deeds, or, rather, he acts as their representative. Then, again, he is not engaged in a pretence, but is performing an action which he believes to be of the utmost importance and to have the most far-reaching effects. If we go on to ask what is the nature of that strange *opus operatum*, that work worked at the altar, we shall find ourselves involved in a storm of controversy, but at least everyone would agree that priest and congregation are renewing their corporate consciousness by re-enacting a supposedly historical episode in the life of the Founder of their society, and are expressing the significance of this re-enactment by speech, song, and symbolical action. The underlying intention of this, as of all ritual, is, by expressive acts performed in common, to promote consciousness of the unity and continuity of the group, and it is therefore natural that the action should be stereotyped and the spectator and the artist not differentiated from the actor.

The masquer differs from the priest in that he has no serious purpose and no fixed plan; he comes to amuse himself and others, his coming is unexpected, his actions spontaneous. Even after the masque had developed into an imposing Court function the element of spontaneity was retained in the revels, each fresh occasion required a fresh piece, and in theory the masque was always a surprise.

What, then, is the masque if it is neither a rite nor a game nor a drama? It is, I believe, just a peculiarly elaborate example of a rudimentary form of art, of which the first stirrings are seen whenever people express an emotional attitude to life by means

of their own bodies. The obvious instance of this rudimentary
art is, of course, the dance, but the term may be applied to any
direct emotional expression by rhythmic or imitative movement,
by dance or song or dressing up. There is no adequate word in
our language for this protoplasmic art, but examples of it are all
around us, every day and everywhere. When children dance
round a barrel organ, when soldiers sing on the march, when
people dine in fancy dress, art is welling up straight out of the
needs and instincts and pleasures of the moment. Art is not a thing
that is developed once for all, it is a 'spontaneous overflow of
powerful feelings,' which may occur at any moment, and which
is constantly recurring.

There is a scene which is impressed on my memory. In the
middle of one of the fruit farms near Wisbech there is an en-
campment. Round a colossal dustbin are grouped a number of
old sheds and railway carriages, where the pickers from London
are housed during the fruiting season. It is a London slum
planted in a dreary waste of country. Beyond the railway
carriages there is a large marquee tent, partly open to the evening
sun and air, and inside it a crowd of noisy dirty pickers closely
packed together. They are mostly responsible for their own
entertainment; they shout out choruses or whole songs, they
stamp and sway to the rhythm of the music. Just now someone
is singing one of Chevalier's songs, 'Come along o' me o' Saturday night,' which has a pronounced and haunting rhythm,
especially in the refrain:

> 'Fair Flo, to watch 'er's a treat,
> Can't keep me eyes off yer feet,
> And you're as nice as you're neat,
> I'm dead nuts on your dancing.'

The words and the tune and the circumstances are all in harmony,
and express the very essence of poetry, rising up from squalid
London streets, the primal, instinctive, unquenchable love of
rhythm, of 'patterned language' and of 'patterned life.' In the
fruit pickers' camp there is no communal creation of folk-song;
the pickers sing music-hall songs, bits and snatches of anything
they have happened to pick up. Their taste is not good; it is not the

simple taste of unlettered folk, but the bad taste of the dregs of a civilisation. Yet, in spite of all that, and although there is, in a sense, nothing creative about their performance, it still shows most unmistakably how deep and how natural is the human need for some kind of artistic expression. Whether that instinct or need leads to original production, or satisfies itself by using the work of others, or finds an outlet in activities almost indistinguishable from play, is just a question of intensity. The difference between the East Ender shouting out the latest popular song and Coleridge composing *Kubla Khan* is, in the main, a difference not of kind but of degree. And if even the artist is hardly necessary for the production of the most rudimentary art, the audience is most certainly not indispensable. The primal impulse is the impulse to dance or sing or dress up, regardless of whether there is anybody to look on or not, although no doubt the impulse is most apt to arise at convivial gatherings, and is usually the result of a transient group consciousness.

In trying to find a category for the masque, I have been forced to use the clumsy expression 'rudimentary art,' because there is no word in current use adequate to describe that form of art which occurs when those who feel the aesthetic emotion translate that emotion into immediate bodily action. Perhaps the word 'revelling' might be adopted as a term for this activity which is, I believe, very nearly identical with what is meant by 'revelry,' though that word itself conveys too much suggestion of noise and bluster to serve the purpose. But I think that anyone who compares the ideas conjured up by the words 'ritual' and 'revelry' will see why I would equate my rudimentary art with the latter rather than with the former activity. There is, of course, a good deal in common between them. In both ritual and revelry there is bodily movement, excited emotion, the sense of a special occasion; both ritual and revelry are group activities, and often have a social meal for their central action. Ritual may easily melt into revelry, revelry may harden into ritual. But the difference between them becomes very apparent when the singular instead of the collective nouns are used. The word 'rite' is heavy with monotonous procedure and the sense of obligation; the

word 'revel' suggests spontaneity, light-heartedness, and irre-
sponsibility. These are precisely the differences and similarities
which we discerned between ritual and that rudimentary art of
which the masque is the most striking example. Moreover, there
is historical justification for this use of the word 'revelling.'

From the reign of Edward III to the fall of Charles I (i.e.
the period of the mumming and the masque) revelry and art
were in peculiarly close contact, and aesthetic revelry played
such an important part in social life that it was organised into
a kind of Government Department, and the Master of the
Revels became an important and powerful Court official. The
different shades of meaning given during the above mentioned
period to the term 'revel' are instructive. The word comes from
France, where its original meaning seems to have been 'rebellion,'
'insurrection' (from Latin *rebellare*) and its secondary meaning
'merrymaking,' which latter meaning it must have acquired
through the notion of tumult and noisy activity characteristic
both of times of rebellion and of times of revelry. The root
meaning of 'revel' is therefore bodily movements made by a set
of people owing to their state of excitement, but the word very
soon acquired a more aesthetic significance. In 1400, for instance,
Christine de Pisan represents her goddess of loyalty as singing
par grant revel Hault et cler un motet nouvel[1]. In the Authorised
Version of the Bible revellings are among the works of the flesh
condemned by St Paul[2], and the word is used to translate the
Greek κῶμοι, a term applied to the torchlight processions
held in honour of Bacchus or of the victors of the Olympic
games; ritual turned into revelry, in fact. But the most interesting
variations of meaning occur when the word 'revels' is used in
connection with courtly entertainments of the Tudor and Stuart
periods. It is used first of all for the merrymakings which took
place in celebration of some important social event or festive
season such as Christmas or Shrovetide. On such occasions plays
were quite as much in request as were masques or tourneys or
morris-dances, so that in this case the revels include works of art,
and the work of art is regarded as a revel in so far as it is regarded

[1] Cf. *supra*, p. 75. [2] Galatians, v. 21.

as part of a social function. Then, again, the word 'revel' serves to distinguish between that part of the masque in which masquers took partners from among the audience and danced the ordinary ballroom dances of the time from that part which was occupied with speeches and grotesque dances performed by professionals. In this case, though the whole masque is a revel, the word 'revel' is felt to apply peculiarly to that part of the masque which is most obviously a social function or amusement. Sometimes the words 'revel' and 'reveller' are almost equivalent to 'dance' and 'dancer.'[1] In Elizabethan and Stuart times the words 'revel,' 'revellers,' etc., were applied to games or social practices that had an aesthetic quality, to art that was hardly distinguishable from play, and it is often found that those activities which are described as revels arose in fact from the débris of ancient ritual and folk-custom. There is, therefore, historical justification for applying the term 'revelling' to that rudimentary art which is akin to, but not identical with, ritual, and of which the masque is the classical example. And now that we are in possession of a more or less adequate term, it becomes easier to study the relationship between art and revelling, for indeed the process of seeking and defining a sufficiently descriptive word has already suggested the difference between them.

The artist differs from the reveller in that he feels the creative impulse, the emotional attitude towards life, so passionately that he wants to give it lasting expression, to make it independent of the transitory movements of mortal bodies. It is in order to achieve permanence that the artist seeks detachment. He steals away from the Pont d'Avignon, 'tout le monde y danse en ronde,' but his share of the common emotion is too intense to need the bodily presence of his fellows as a stimulus to expression, is too precious to be lost when the circle is broken and the dancers

---

[1] Cf. the use of the word in connection with the Christmas games of the Inns of Court, *Prog. Eliz.* vol. I, pp. 131 ff. 'And that nothing might be wanting for their encouragement in this excellent study, they have very antiently had *dancings* for their recreation and delight, commonly called *Revels*, allowed at certain seasons; and that by special order of the Society as appeareth in 9 Hen. VI....Nor were these exercises of dancing merely permitted; but thought very necessary (as it seems) and much conducing to the making of gentlemen more fit for their books at other times.'—*Op. cit.* vol. I, p. 251.

have dispersed. He will so record, so imitate, so body forth the spirit of that dance in sound or word or stone, that it, or the emotion behind it, may be revived at any time, in any place, by anybody. So, in days of old, Caedmon rose up from the table and went home when it was his turn to make mirth for the assembly by singing poetry to the harp. But at night time when he was alone he sang in his sleep 'the beginning of created things,' and awaking, 'he remembered all he had sung while sleeping, and soon added much more.... But he, keeping in mind all that he had been able to learn by hearing, and as it were chewing the cud, converted it into a most sweet song, and singing it still more sweetly made his teachers in their turn his hearers.'[1] Did this or anything like this ever actually happen? Possibly not. But the story of Caedmon may serve as a symbol, if not of the historic development of art, at least of the essential relationship between art and revelling[2].

It is possible, however, to find historical evidence for the artist as a strayed reveller. Take, for instance, the Prince des Sots or Lord of Misrule. Originally, perhaps, he was a sacrificial victim; in the later Middle Ages he was the leader of a riotous band of revellers, chiefly ecclesiastical; in the earlier Renaissance he was not only the central figure of the revels, but an organiser or even a composer of masques, soties, and comedies. Pierre Gringoire and George Ferrars are historical instances of leaders of the revels who found that the proper discharge of their functions necessitated artistic creation. If it is objected that the Feast of Fools is too late a phenomenon to throw any light on the origin of art, I would reply that origin means a spring, a starting-point, a cause, but it does not necessarily imply remoteness. Indeed, the history of the masque is particularly interesting just because it suggests that the origin of art must not be sought solely in a distant past. The masque is not prior in time, but it is more rudimentary in nature than the drama, because it is not an art that has emerged but an art that is emerging from life. I use the word *emerging*

---

[1] Bede, *Eccl. Hist.* IV, 24.
[2] See, however, the life of Suso, which is a concrete example of what I mean. Cf. *supra*, pp. 76, 77.

instead of *evolving* because a step in evolution is only retraced when decay and disintegration have set in, and the end of that process is death; but art does not spring out of the womb of circumstance and return no more; it is continually being born again, and its movement is more like breathing than the flowing of a stream. If revelling may lead up to art, art may enrich revelling, and both have their own intrinsic worth.

It is a more or less familiar idea that art springs from the dance, but it is less widely recognised that art may and should sometimes return to its source and enrich revelling. Take the case of the drama. I have suggested that the composition of a dramatic poem marks the completion of a process that begins with the first stirrings of the reveller. Is this to depreciate the theatre? Far from it. It is a sound instinct that makes many people regard a flourishing national theatre as wholesome both for art and for social life. What does this mean? It means firstly that the vitalising influence of art should circulate in society like blood in the body, and secondly that, if art is to circulate freely, there must be some channel by which the art that sprang from bodily movement should return to bodily movement, some way of bringing back the artist into the rude presence of his fellows. The return movement, however, should not end in the theatre, it should end in social ritual and recreation. This flux and reflux, which happened continually during the Renaissance, happens but rarely now, with the result—so I believe—that there is an almost complete cleavage in taste between different sections of society, and that comparatively few people care for art at all. It was at a time when the greatest poets and painters used an idiom readily translatable into ballroom dancing and street pageantry that Heminge and Condell were able to offer their edition of Shakespeare to the whole body of readers 'from the most able to him that can but spell.'

So far I have been suggesting that art and revelling are different ways of reacting to the same impulse—an impulse which I have described rather vaguely as a desire to express an emotional attitude to life. What is this impulse, this emotional attitude? The masque, I believe, suggests an answer to this question.

When we compared the cricket-match with the drama we noticed that in the latter performance the loss of practical purpose had spread over the whole course of the action, and that the play was intended to please not the actors but the spectators. Taken by itself, this fact suggests that at least one of the impulses behind art is the impulse to escape from life, to enjoy the pleasure of action without its responsibility. But this fact cannot be taken by itself. An athletic team-game devoid of risk and purpose would look more like a figured dance than a drama[1]; but the actor is not moving in a dance pattern, he is pretending to be serious, and his imitative acts are meant to remind his audience of the real world. It may be, however, that the actor's imitation of life is a faith-aiding device required by spectators, who find it pleasant but difficult to believe in a world that makes no demands upon them. If this is so, the presence of imitation, like the absence of practical purpose, shows that art is an attempt to escape from reality, and to fulfil those desires that life cannot satisfy. This is an interpretation of art which constantly recurs, and which is particularly prevalent at the present day. The theory is bound up with the theory implicit in much of modern thought, that religion and art are entirely subjective; that inspiration, even when the word is used in its vaguest possible sense, is an impossibility; that artist and worshipper are ministering to their inner and primarily physical needs, rather than expressing what they feel to be the truth of a reality outside themselves. We may, for instance, compare the utterances of Marlowe, the man of the Renaissance, with those of Robert Graves, the man of the twentieth century. To Marlowe the poet is a man who strives to catch an elusive and incomprehensible beauty which is not only greater than himself, but greater than all the pens that all the poets held, and all the feelings that inspired their minds; but to Mr Graves the poet is a man who has inherited various strong but conflicting impulses, and poetry is his solution of the interior conflict, and part at least of its healing power lies in the hypnotic effect of the

[1] Examples of this kind of performance actually occurred in Renaissance Italy. See, for example, Callot's illustrations (nos. 630–632) of the Florentine tournaments of 1615 and 1616. Cf. *supra*, pp. 100, 232.

rhythm[1]. Therefore in discussing whether art and revelling spring mainly from unsatisfied desire, I am not using the expression in its widest sense as equivalent to the impulse to progress, to move to an unknown goal, to create a new world, but I am asking whether art and revelling spring from anxiety, fear, from desire for physical benefits which has not found immediate satisfaction, and, at a higher level, desire for relief from the fear of consequences, the strain of conflicting thoughts and emotions. In a word, is art mainly a movement of response or a movement of flight?

The theory that art springs from unsatisfied desire is sometimes thought to be supported by the results of historical and anthropological inquiries. Hoping that they might analyse art more easily if they could catch it before it had had time to grow complicated, scholars have looked out into remote regions and back into pre-history, and have discovered the beginnings of art (or, at least, of some forms of it) among savages and untaught peasants dancing those magical dances which were discussed in the first chapter of this book. What impulses do they find stirring in those simple-minded mummers? Partly—so we are told—the dancers are engaged in a wrong-headed attempt to achieve practical ends, partly they are venting their feelings, chiefly those feelings of anxious desire that arise so naturally at critical moments in the agricultural year. 'The savage utters his will to live, his intense desire for food; but it should be noted, it is desire and will and longing, not certainty and satisfaction

---

[1] 'When conflicting issues disturb his mind, which in its conscious state is unable to reconcile them logically, the poet acquires the habit of self-hypnotism, as practised by the witch doctors, his ancestors in poetry. He learns in self-protection to take pen and paper and let the pen solve the hitherto insoluble problem which has caused the disturbance.'—Robert Graves, *On English Poetry*, VI. 'Inspiration' (Heinemann, 1922). The drawback to this theory is that it reduces poetry to a form of mental medicine which has no reason for existing apart from an unsatisfactory, regrettable condition of the mind, or of the external world. Mr I. A. Richards holds much the same view, and has worked it out in his most stimulating book, *Principles of Literary Criticism*. He regards the sense of 'revelation' that comes from reading a poem as a sign that a balance or equilibrium has been established between impulses which are usually discordant. Speaking of Tragedy, he says: 'The joy which is so strangely the heart of the experience is not an indication that "all's right with the world" or that "somewhere, somehow, there is Justice"; it is an indication that all is right here and now in the nervous system.' (p. 246.)

that he utters.'[1] When a girl from East Russia leaps through a hoop crying, '"Flax, grow"...she *does* what she *wants done,*' and anyone who has watched a game with keen interest can understand why her longings lead to imitative movements[2]. 'Art and religion, though perhaps not wholly ritual, spring from the incomplete cycle, from unsatisfied desire, from perception and emotion that have somehow not found immediate outlet in practical action.'[3]

This may well be true, but I doubt if it is the whole truth. Is it not probable that at least sometimes the savage uttered not only his will to live, but also his feeling that life is well worth living, precisely as a child jumps for joy? In her interesting account of the folk-music and dancing of the Faroese Islanders Mrs H. M. Chadwick tells us how 'after a whale hunt the men sometimes dance in their wet, bloody clothes, singing the popular ballad of the ca'ing whale with the refrain:

> To us bold men great joy it is
> To slay a whale!'[4]

The excitement which so often accompanies mumming and masking, especially those masked dances which are connected with belief in 'possession,' surely marks an increase of vitality which would be caused more naturally by satisfied than by unsatisfied desire. The dance is akin to play, and play is possible because the 'well-fed and well-rested animal, especially the young animal, has a surplus of nervous energy which works through the channels of the various motor mechanisms....It is the primal *libido* or vital energy flowing not in the channels of instinct, but overflowing, generating a vague appetite for movement and finding outlet in any or all of the motor mechanisms in turn.'[5] Durkheim has pointed out how art may arise from the high spirits, the 'effervescence' which prevails at social festivals[6].

[1] J. Harrison, *Ancient Art and Ritual*, p. 65.
[2] *Ibid.* p. 33.   [3] *Ibid.* p. 41.
[4] N. Kershaw (Mrs Chadwick), *Stories and Ballads of the Far Past* (Cambridge, 1921), p. 161.
[5] W. McDougall, *An Outline of Psychology* (London, 1922), pp. 171, 172.
[6] *Les formes élémentaires de la vie religieuse,* pp. 542–645.

To understand the motives of the artist it is surely well to take into account the unmistakable gladness of the masquer as well as the conjectural yearnings of the savage mummer. It is true that the masque is elaborate and sophisticated, but, as I have already suggested, there is no need to go far back or far afield to find the origin of art. Not only in the wilderness but in the ball-room and the public-house we can catch people moved by the first stirrings of the aesthetic impulse, and we catch them there as revellers. Revelling, or at least revelry, is essentially an expression of attainment and satisfaction; it occurs at the banquet, after the victory, on the anniversary. It is a result rather of fulness than of appetite, it can be deprecated as a work of the flesh, and it is an activity of the fat rather than of the lean year. 'To revel in' is an expression which implies not mere liking or appreciation, but possession or experience causing mental enjoyment. Revelling, in fact, springs from joy which it both expresses and enhances; events are significant, life is rich and full, and ordinary activities are raised to a higher power. The reveller does not talk, he sings; he does not walk, he dances; he throws off his ordinary clothes and dresses up; he throws off his ordinary personality and becomes a god or an incarnate virtue. His very surroundings are affected by the glories of the time, trees are lit up, houses are garlanded, Inigo Jones is called to Whitehall. The dramatist might depict life as sorrowful or ridiculous or contemptible, but in the masque absurd or malevolent beings appeared only to be put to flight by the entry of the noble joyous and joy-bringing masquers.

But if art and revelling cannot be *wholly* explained as expressions of unsatisfied desire, neither can they be *wholly* explained as the result of social effervescence. As soon as we get an activity which contains even the germ of art or religion, we find that rhythmic movements are so ordered that they express and induce a certain attitude to the life of the tribe or to the external world[1].

---

[1] I do not want to be misunderstood. I do *not* mean to deny that activities and objects which we regard as aesthetic may be at the outset purely practical. Nor am I in the least concerned with *when* the change takes place. But I do mean to say that art originates at the moment when the purely practical motive begins to be supplanted or supplemented by a different motive which

PLATE XII

THE TEMPLE OF APOLLO

Design for Davenant's *The Triumphs of the Prince d'Amour*, probably by Inigo Jones

Copyright of His Grace the Duke of Devonshire

The life of the tribe is valued for its own sake; the external world is conceived, however dimly, as something more than a means of satisfying instinct. 'Art and religion...spring from the incomplete cycle, from unsatisfied desire, from perception and emotion that have somehow not found immediate outlet in practical action.'[1] These clauses are not all synonymous, and it seems to me to be the last that is the truest. I think I can make my meaning clearest by a somewhat simple example. Let us imagine, for instance, that an apple hangs upon a tree and excites in the man standing underneath it the instinct of food-seeking. If he can reach it, he eats and his instinct is satisfied, but if it hangs too high his desire must, for a time at least, remain unfulfilled; and this interval of hunger will probably bring into play all his resourcefulness and ingenuity, but it is not clear that it will lead to religious or aesthetic activities. He may try to bring the apple down by magic, but that will only be a mistaken effort to use applied science; he may pray for the apple, but that means he has already accepted a creed. What he will hardly do is to make an imitation of the apple and pretend to eat it. Surely the apple could never become the object of worship or of aesthetic imitation unless it were possible to fix attention upon it, even when it does not excite the instinct of food-seeking. But when the man looks at the apple with his hunger allayed, he can become aware of the apple as something whose meaning is not exhausted when it is considered as food; he can become aware both of more energy in himself and more significance and attractive power in the apple than could be used up in satisfying his normal instinctive needs. He can become aware of the apple as of something with intrinsic value, which is independent of his appetite and yet is of concern to him, for it holds his attention and rouses emotion, gives him at least a dim and passing consciousness of a life that is more than meat; stirs in him at least a faint desire to express that sense of more abundant life, to retain it, to increase it. This lively aware-

is of such and such a kind. Also art ceases to be at the moment when the practical motive once more predominates. Didactic art is a contradiction in terms, though a work may be both didactic *and* artistic.

[1] Harrison, *Ancient Art and Ritual*, p. 41.

ness of extra meaning is the *sine qua non* of art. Other motives, other perceptions, may be at work, must be at work, but that must not be absent. It is the fact of this awareness which makes the difference between revelling and revelry and between revelling and the purposeless activities of the most rudimentary kind of play, or purely practical magic. This awareness always produces excitement and usually joy. When our awareness of the extra meaning of an object causes us joy, we say that the object is beautiful. But whether or no the awareness causes us joy, it is made possible, not by the slip between the cup and the lip, but by the possession of superabundant vitality, by the previous satisfaction or control of our instinctive desires.

But here I am anxious not to be misunderstood. It is possible that by describing the aesthetic experience as awareness of the extra meaning, I may seem to imply that it is awareness of that bit of the apple, so to speak, which may be left over after all its useful properties, its power of satisfying our instinctive needs, have been abstracted. But the extra meaning that I am trying to describe is inclusive. Superabundant would have been a better word for my purpose, had it not suggested superfluity, overflow, ideas which are as misleading as the idea of exclusiveness, which is unfortunately suggested by the word extra. But awareness of the extra meaning comes from contemplating an object as a whole with its own intrinsic value independent of our desires. The savage might be contemplating the apple simply and solely as food (and usually the idea of the apple as a food would form a part of his contemplation of it), but if he were contemplating it as *food*[1], not just as stuff which could satisfy an instinctive and temporary craving, he would be making aesthetic experience possible for himself.

This will become clearer perhaps if we consider a more advanced kind of aesthetic contemplation. Take, for instance, the case of a keen historian who comes into an old library in search

---

[1] Here I may seem to be describing, not the capacity for aesthetic experience, but the capacity for forming general ideas, but I guard myself by using the word *contemplating*, instead of *examining, trying to understand*. Moreover, I am describing a process of *feeling* something as *a whole*, not primarily of analysing something with the understanding.

of a highly important piece of information. Until he has found what he seeks, he is unable to gain any aesthetic experience from the books; to him they are simply possible sources of knowledge about certain facts. Then suddenly he comes upon the right passage, and it tells him all that he wanted to know and more than he could have hoped. In the delight of discovery he pauses and looks up at the invaluable book, and as he looks he becomes aware, not only of that book, but of its surroundings. It is in a small alcove, the walls of which are lined with big volumes in fine old leather bindings, and a shaft of light strikes across them, bringing out their rich mellow colours. He notices that with pleasure, and if he were not a student his aesthetic experience might end there, but being what he is, to him a book is always more than a binding. The sun illumines more than the outside of the volumes. There they stand, musty old tomes, and inside one of them perhaps the key to a fresh wisdom. Most of them indeed lost their meaning hundreds of years ago. Yet what hours of labour, what thought, what hope, what deathless curiosity they enshrine. To what purpose? Yes, and that startling, that revolutionary discovery of his own, shall time stale that, shall that too lie with the dead theologies? Our historian moves about restlessly; he is no poet, but he longs to write a poem.

I think it will be obvious that our historian could not contemplate the books aesthetically until he had first either forgotten or satisfied his intense thirst for a particular piece of information; but also it is equally clear that the books' property of imparting knowledge was part of his aesthetic contemplation of it, and moreover, as soon as he could regard this property with detachment, he could use it to enrich and broaden his aesthetic contemplation, until this contemplation widened out into an emotional awareness, not only of the individual book, but of its surroundings, and of all the books in all the world of whose making there is no end. And moreover, not only the external book, but the internal desire for knowledge, could be an object of aesthetic contemplation, but only after it had been objectified and regarded with detachment.

As soon as we contemplate an object without appetite, and so become aware of its wholeness and intrinsic value, we necessarily become aware at the same time that this intrinsic value, though recognised, is uncomprehended. I do not mean that this conception is actually formulated in our minds; it is a matter of emotion rather than of reason; but I do mean that there is always a strangeness about any object that is contemplated aesthetically, and that this strangeness lures us on, makes us long to penetrate it, to appropriate it. The man whose hunger is already appeased looks at his apple with new eyes, but as he looks, a new kind of hunger awakes in him; he becomes not aloof, but queerly excited. For art springs from vitality, from joy, from the sense of value, but by nature it is an insatiable desire, for it is with beauty as with wisdom; 'they that eat me shall yet be hungry, and they that drink me shall yet be thirsty.' In *The Story of my Heart*, Richard Jefferies has given passionate expression to this form of experience which lies behind art and religion. First there is the joy and ecstatic sense of value roused through contemplating external nature, and so far is he from regarding this nature as a creation of his mind that he looks upon even the animals as utterly alien from humanity and outside human understanding. Still, though there is no understanding, there is joy, and from the joy springs desire, desire for more joy, desire to expand the personality by appropriating all the meaning of the external world, and then to move forward into the unknown.

'After the sensuous enjoyment always came the thought, the desire: That I might be like this; that I might have the inner meaning of the sun, the light, the earth, the trees and grass, translated into some growth of excellence in myself....Not all that the stars could have given, had they been destinies, could have satiated me. This, all this, and more, I wanted to myself....Full to the brim of the wondrous past, I felt the wondrous present....Now, this moment was the wonder and the glory. Now, this moment was exceedingly wonderful. Now, this moment give me all the thought, all the idea, all the soul expressed in the cosmos around me. Give me still more.'[1]

But why should the feeling of overflowing vitality, the awareness of extra significance, express itself in imitative action? We

---

[1] *The Story of my Heart*, pp. 56, 57, 14.

can understand from experience that intense desire may issue in eager anticipatory movement; but why should joy lead to imitation?

Is it not possible that imitative acts are naïve expressions of sympathy and admiration, and that sometimes the peasant dances like the growing crops, and the artist copies the figures of the dancers, just as a child will express his delight and interest in a dog by imitating its bark. This kind of imitation is an attempt to enlarge our personality, to bring within our experience something that was originally outside it. The vocation of a child may be 'endless imitation,' but the well-worn childish formula is not 'let us copy,' but 'let us *pretend*.' The whole fun of the business lies in the fact that, knowing quite well that you are yourself, you become somebody else at the same time. Since we naturally try to experience that part of reality which interests us, it follows that aesthetic imitation being primarily an act of appropriation is secondarily a means of defining the nature of that which we have appropriated and the character of the emotion it has evoked. It is in favour of this interpretation that it can be applied to all kinds of aesthetic imitation, and that shows the connection between representative and non-representative art.

Here, again, the masque is particularly instructive. It starts with a given fact, an event that has just happened or is still happening. There has been, for instance, a fashionable wedding and the *Masque of Hymen* imitates this wedding, or rather it represents it in its ideal aspect. Again, Charles I is endeavouring to check certain Puritanic tendencies in the nation, the masque *Salmacida Spolia* imitates the political struggle, that is to say, it represents it in such a way as to portray its essence from the point of view of the Court. 'A curtain flying up, a horrid scene appeared of storm and tempest; no glimpse of the sun was seen, as if darkness, confusion, and deformity, had possesst the world.' The reason of this is that Discord, 'malicious fury,' is invoking evil spirits who vent their malevolence in an antimasque, until they 'on a sudden are surprised and stopped in their motion by a secret power whose wisdom they tremble at, and depart as foreknowing that Wisdom will change all their malicious hope of these disorders into a sudden calm.' The scene then changed to the prospect of a fruitful country, on to which descended Concord and the Good Genius of Great Britain, who, having alighted from their chariot, departed on their several ways to incite 'the beloved people to honest pleasures and recreations which have ever been peculiar to this nation.' After more antimasques the scene changed to craggy rocks, the top of which reached the clouds; the midmost rock was hollow, and inside it was the Throne of Honour, the ascent to which 'was steep and difficult.' Then the secret Wisdom, whose influence had been felt in the quieting of the storm, was revealed to sight 'in the person of the King attended by his nobles and under the name of Philogenes, or Lover of his People, hath his appearance prepared by a chorus representing the beloved people, and is instantly discovered environed with these nobles on the Throne of Honour.'

Such was the essence of the political situation according to the views prevalent at Court in the middle of the seventeenth century; and for us that Whitehall stage is an instance of dramatic irony as great and striking as any Sophoclean tragedy; for to poor Charles the way to the Throne of Honour was to prove steep and difficult indeed. But for the moment Charles interests us not as the predestined tragic victim, but as the central figure of the masque. For the hero of *Salmacida Spolia* is not imitated; he is there in actual fact, and the plot of the piece only draws out and emphasises the significance of that royal presence. To us certainly the masque seems to express desires that were to be utterly and for ever unsatisfied, but to the composers and performers it merely stated in symbolic form and action the truth of an actual political situation.

From this point of view the masque forms a link between decorative and imitative art. The craftsman who gives a graceful but unnecessary curve to his table-leg shows by so doing that to him a table is more than a piece of wood raised from the ground so that objects may be conveniently placed upon it. As the craftsman expresses by decoration his sense of the intrinsic value of an object, so the masque writer employs imitation as a means of expressing the significance of present events, and in so doing he differs from the dramatist and other imitative artists, although the difference is one of degree rather than of kind. The masque emphasises quite simply the joyous meaning of the present. Art may be very far from joyous, and it must have a certain detachment from the present, yet at the root of it there is a joy, or at least an ecstatic sense of value, and it imitates life in order that it may express the significance of life. Perhaps it would be better to say that the artist imitates reality so that he may enter into its very heart and conquer it. This is well brought out by Dr Bosanquet who illustrates the meaning of aesthetic imitation by an example drawn from Homer.

'It is—I am shamelessly quoting from myself—perhaps the earliest aesthetic judgment which Western literature contains. It is in the Homeric description of the metal-working deity's craftsmanship in the shield of Achilles. He has made upon it the representation of a deep fallow field with the ploughmen driving their furrows on it; and the poet observes, "And behind the plough the earth went black, and looked like ploughed ground, though it was made of gold; that was a very miracle of his craft." Now what was the miracle here, that made Homer cry out at it with delight? It was not, surely, that when you have one bit of ploughed land you can make another like it. That goes on all day when a man ploughs a field....Surely the miracle lies in what Homer accents when he says, "Though it was made of gold." It lies here; that without the heavy matter and whole natural process of the reality, man's mind possesses a magic by which it can extract the soul of the actual thing or event, and confer it on any medium which is convenient to him....And when these great poets insist on the likeness of the imitation, I take it that the real underlying interest is in the conquest of the difference of the medium. So that really, in the naïve praise of successful imitation, we have, if we read it rightly, the germ of the fundamental doctrine of aesthetic semblance. That is to say, what matters is not the thing, but the appearance which you can carry off, and deal with apart from it, and recreate. And the real sting of even the crudest glorification of copying is this wonder that you can carry off with you a thing's soul, and leave its body behind.'[1]

[1] Bernard Bosanquet, *Three Lectures on Aesthetic* (London, 1915), pp. 49 ff.

And to this I would add that the poet's cry of delight is due not only to the appreciation of the power of carrying off the soul of reality, but to the appreciation of the fact that reality has a soul worth conquering. Never would even Vulcan have accomplished that miracle of his art had he not first contemplated the ploughed field as a god, and as a god pronounced the god-like judgment, 'Behold it is very good.'

And yet, though religion and art are rooted in the sense of value, though the masque which is so very near to the mumming dance, so close to the simple essence of both imitative and decorative art, is just an expression of enjoyment, yet still there is something in us that responds when Miss Harrison speaks of art as arising from the incomplete cycle from unsatisfied desire. Nothing was wanting from the solemnities at Whitehall, neither 'delicacy of the dances, magnificence of the scene, or divine rapture of music. Only the envy was that it lasted not still....' There is indeed often a peculiar note of wistfulness in the passages of Elizabethan drama which are most influenced by Court masque and pageantry. 'Our revels now are ended....' How splendid life is, but how transitory.

ἡμεῖς δ' οἷά τε φύλλα φύει πολυάνθεμος ὥρη
ἔαρος, ὅτ' αἶψ' αὐγῇσ' αὔξεται ἠελίου,
τοῖσ' ἴκελοι πήχυιον ἐπὶ χρόνον ἄνθεσιν ἥβης
τερπόμεθα, πρὸς θεῶν εἰδότες οὔτε κακὸν
οὔτ' ἀγαθόν· Κῆρες δὲ παρεστήκασι μέλαιναι,
ἡ μὲν ἔχουσα τέλος γήραος ἀργαλέου,
ἡ δ' ἑτέρη θανάτοιο...[1]

That is the classic sadness, the regret for comely form that must dissolve at last; the unsatisfied desire for an everlasting spring. But the spirit behind Elizabethan masque and pageantry, the spirit of the Renaissance, even of Renaissance melancholy, is different. It is the spirit of life, fierce, defiant, triumphant, playing out its play against a sombre background, of which it is never wholly unconscious, but to whose ultimate dominance it will never wholly submit.

[1] Mimnermus, *Eleg.* 2, 1 ff.

'Hey nonny no!
Men are fools that wish to die!
Is 't not fine to dance and sing
When the bells of death do ring?
Is 't not fine to swim in wine,
And turn upon the toe,
And sing hey nonny no!
When the winds blow and the seas flow?
Hey nonny no!'[1]

'Man does not yield himself to the angels, nor to death utterly, save hrough the weakness of his feeble will.'[2]

[1] Anon.   [2] Glanvill.

CHAPTER XIV

Misrule

'I must have liberty
Withal, as large a charter as the wind,
To blow on whom I please; for so fools have.'
As You Like It.

'"What think you of this fool, Malvolio? doth he not mend?"
"Yes, and shall do till the pangs of death shake him."'
Twelfth Night.

ONE CHRISTMAS time when the Court was seated the jolly Season himself appeared on the scene: 'Why, gentlemen, do you know what you do? ha! would you have kept me out? CHRISTMAS, old Christmas, Christmas of London, and Captain Christmas?...The truth is, I have brought a Masque here out o' the city, of my own making, and do present it by a set of my sons, that come out of the lanes of London, good dancing boys all.'[1] These children of his, led on a string by Cupid, are: Misrule, Carol, Mince-pie, Gambol, Post and Pair, New-Year's-Gift, Mumming, Wassail, Offering, and Baby-Cake. Each one of these is probably a true offspring of the ancient festivals that became absorbed in old Father Christmas; but the most important members of the family are 'Mumming, in a masquing pied suit, with a vizor,' 'Misrule, in a velvet cap, with a sprig, a short cloak, great yellow ruff, like a reveller....'

Holy days are always apt to turn into holidays. Licence and disorder seem to be the exact opposite of solemn ritual, yet both often appear together at festival time. So far I have been concerned with Mumming, i.e. revelling in its more orderly rhythmic aspect; it remains to look at the reverse side of the picture and inquire into the character of the Lord of Misrule. The customs connected with the masque are mostly reducible to two kinds of activity: the dance movements with processions of disguised persons or mummers, and the buffoonery of disguisers who behave as though possessed or lunatic, and who often create a general topsy-turvydom in which all ordinary social laws are in suspense, social distinctions disregarded, and some low-born clownish fellow

[1] Jonson, *Christmas his Masque.*

is set up as the fool or the mock king. Misrule springs merely from the simple need of reaction and recreation. I have often heard fruit-pickers from East London summing up their comments on the actions of their refractory children or neighbours in the forlorn appeal 'Do be different.' Humanity has always made the same request of life, and at intervals taken the affair into its own hands. The mediaeval clergy, for instance, used the Christmas and New Year holidays to bring about a most violent and astonishing interruption in the ordinary ecclesiastical round, and their attitude is probably quite justly described in a letter of protest against the Feast of Fools addressed by the University of Paris to the bishops and chapters of France:

'Les Tonneaux de vin créveroient, si on ne leur ouvroit quelquefois la bonde ou le fosset, pour leur donner de l'air. Or nous sommes de vieux vaisseaux & des tonneaux mal reliéz, que le vin de la sagesse feroit rompre, si nous le laissions bouillir ainsi par une dévotion continuelle au service Divin....C'est pour cela que nous donnons quelques jours aux jeux & aux bouffonneries, afin de retourner ensuite avec plus de joye & de ferveur, à l'étude & aux exercices de la Religion.'[1]

The conservative clerics have anticipated Lamb's defence of Restoration Comedy, and have given us a clue to the respectable English family enjoying the innuendoes of musical comedy, and the frank improprieties of *The Beggar's Opera*.

The Feast of Fools was probably a survival of the Kalends. It was, as Dr Chambers points out, 'an ebullition of the natural lout beneath the cassock'; only the riotous clergy did things for fun rather than for luck, and the holiday needs of clerk and peasant were very different. The farm labourers needed relief from monotony, the clerks, living together in colleges, choir schools, etc., where the bounds of community life were tightly drawn, needed a temporary freedom from the pressure of social arrangements, a temporary permission to 'take but degree away, untune that string.' Even to-day in schools and colleges there is a certain relaxation of convention on speech days and commemorations; masters and scholars meet almost on terms of

---

[1] Du Tilliot, *Mém. pour servir à l'Hist. de la Fête des Fous* (1741), p. 30. For original Latin see Migne, *P.L.* vol. CCVII, col. 1171.

equality, and by their toasts and speeches seem to suggest that their usual relationship is half-fictitious. In the Middle Ages this kind of relaxation went very far; too far, indeed, according to the views of the higher authorities of the Church.

But however morally dubious, the turn taken by the ecclesiastical Feast of Fools was certainly favourable to the aesthetic development of the revels, for the clerics seized upon and elaborated festival customs, such as the inversion of status, which afforded delightful opportunities for satire and parody, and had considerable dramatic possibilities.

The aesthetic development of misrule was carried a stage further when the Feast of Fools, suppressed in the churches, began to flourish in the streets. The difference is clear. In its earlier ecclesiastical form the festival was a periodical and traditional event, and the fools were clergy who for the time being were allowing themselves a somewhat startling freedom from ordinary duty and decorum. The fools of the later sociétés joyeuses were young men banded together in mock guilds for the purpose of continuing to hold the Feast of Fools after it had been banned by ecclesiastical authority, and although they kept up the tradition they also went beyond it. They did not merely allow themselves periodic breaks in the ordinary routine of life, but in their own special feasts, their initiation ceremonies, their charivaris, etc., they kept up a running commentary on the events of the hour and the social life of their town. The ecclesiastical fools contented themselves with a brief periodic holiday, in which they refreshed their spirits by turning everything topsy-turvy, but the secular fools or 'sots' formed a permanent association which they made into an expression of the idea that life itself was a perpetual Feast of Fools, that in ordinary society there was a lasting inversion of status, and that for those who had eyes to see the first were always last and the last first. Naturally the 'sots' sometimes got into trouble, but on the whole they were popular because they kept the public plentifully supplied with spectacular masquerades and dramatised scandal[1]. That peculiar form of French comedy known as the 'sotie' is a direct outcome

[1] Cf. Julleville, *Les Comédiens en France au Moyen Age*, pp. 200–221.

of their activities; for, as M. Petit de Julleville points out, it is played by fools, and it is based on the idea of 'parodie universelle, de bouleversement de la hiérarchie établie.' The idea which inspired the sotie also inspires a whole body of Fool literature, of which Erasmus's *Praise of Folly* and Sebastian Brandt's *Narren-Schiff* are the most famous examples. How far this idea also inspired the masque is a question that will be more profitably considered when we have looked more closely at the fool as conceived by the sociétés joyeuses.

It was the humour of the sociétés joyeuses to depict the world by their feasts and ceremonies and soties as a great stage of fools, but for them the fool meant more than the merely unwise man; it was a semi-technical term, and stood for an odd figure clothed in motley, coxcomb, cap and bells, clothes which bear witness to the strange mixed feeling of disgust, amusement, and awe which madmen have always roused in the breasts of their fellow-men. For the fool is a madman, his coxcomb and his cap and bells are sophistications of the old ominous sacrificial tokens; they have also become symbols of a spirit of laughter and comedy, that most variable and elusive human gesture. Indeed, as the sociétés joyeuses never tired of pointing out, the spirit of folly is a very Proteus. If with Jaques we were to cry 'ducdame,' what a large ill-assorted company would be drawn into the magic circle at our summons: the possessed slave fleeing off into the jungle, the beribboned whitened clown belabouring the rustics with his tongue and bladder whip, the dwarf and jester mopping and mowing about Renaissance palaces, the spirited young reveller of Paris or the Inns of Court, Harlequin, Pierrot, Punch, the comic devil: they are all akin, they are all different, and both by their likeness and their difference they reveal the true meaning of Misrule, the inmost essence of comedy. For the spirit of the fool changes but does not die. It grows and varies, and the measure of its growth is the measure of the growth of the human spirit.

'Numerus stultorum est infinitus' and it is difficult to determine what precise kind of fool it was that the members of the sociétés joyeuses had in their mind. The Lord of Misrule or

Prince des Sots is almost certainly a descendant of the sacrificial victim and a more cultivated brother of the rustic mock king; but the behaviour of the sots, their topical jokes and personal allusions, seem rather modelled on the behaviour of the Court jester, the man who was kept in most great houses to amuse his betters by real or pretended madness. There is some evidence (though it is inconclusive) that the official livery of this Court jester was very similar to the uniform of the sociétés joyeuses; at any rate it seems pretty clear that jesters, sots, and village clowns all wore the sacrificial exuviae. If we may believe Lodge, there was a marked resemblance between the domestic jester and the rustic Lord of Misrule[1].

For our purpose, however, the precise distinction between the clown and the jester is not very important, because by the fifteenth century even the traditional grotesques had lost most of their *special* magical character, and on the other hand *vague* memories of ancient taboos still hung around all fools and clowns, as indeed they do to this day. For the notion that there is a queer sanctity about a fool is a belief not only of great antiquity but of great tenacity. Even now uneducated people are apt to regard a natural with some affection. People will say of an idiot that he is 'not all there,' and by that expressive phrase they conjure up the old uncanny feeling that we only see a lunatic in part, that the rest of him is off and away in dim communion with Unknown Powers, or worse still, that part of him has been pushed out to make room for an alien spirit, and this irrational awe can and does co-exist with the cruel notion that madness is a ludicrous deformity comparable to a pigmy frame or a hump back.

The idiot and the dwarf excite laughter simply by being themselves. That is the lowest stage of comedy, the laughter provoked

---

[1] 'Lodge, in his *Wits Miserie*, 1596, p. 84, speaking of *a jeaster*, says, "This fellow in person is comely, in apparel courtly, but in behaviour a very ape, and no man; his studye is to coine bitter jeastes, or to show antique motions, or to sing baudie sonnets and ballads: give him a little wine in his head, he is continually flearing and making of mouths; he laughs intemperately at every little occasion, and dances about the house, leaps over tables, outskips men's heads, trips up his companions' heeles, burns sacke with a candle, and hath *all the feates of a Lord of Missrule in the countrie*. It is a special marke of him at table, he sits and makes faces." '—Brand, *op. cit.* vol. I, p. 503.

by sheer incongruity, grotesqueness, abnormality. Tilt your hat on one side, or make any sudden unexpected movement, and a baby will bubble with laughter. It is the lowest stage of comedy but it is never outgrown. Let any man come in with a miniature top-hat poised at a slight angle on a shiny bald head and he will be greeted with roars of applause. It is the sudden glory at the sight of an inferior described by Hobbes, although there is a certain civilised maliciousness about his definition, which is by no means always a just description of the emotion. It is the stage of comedy which corresponds to the rowdier forms of Misrule, the buffoonery and horseplay of the folk-festival, the undisciplined antimasque, and of a good deal of the comic business in pantomimes and at music halls.

The Court fool, as is well known, develops into the all-licensed 'Jester'; he becomes a professional, a man 'who assumes his folly as a stalking horse and under it he shoots his wit.' This professional jester is no longer a mere butt or foil to the normal members of the community, but his detachment enables him to be their critic. The laughter becomes more subtle. It is no longer caused by the mere juxtaposition of normal and abnormal; it is caused by the incongruity of the servant being in reality stronger than the master, the madman wiser than the man of sense. Shakespeare's fools are detached critics of society; Feste sees through the affectation of the Duke and Olivia, Touchstone brings out the insincerity of fashionable cravings for the simple life; when Jaques met the fool in the forest and delighted in him, the real humour of the situation lay in the fact that all the time when Jaques was patronisingly appreciating the fool, the fool was parodying Jaques. It is at this point in his evolution that the fool becomes the patron saint of sociétés joyeuses, the lord of a misrule which has developed beyond mere high spirits and licentiousness and has become a parody of the social order.

But it would be a grave injustice to the wearer of motley to regard him as a critic and nothing more. If that were a sufficient description of him, he would be more at home in the intellectual comedy of Meredith's definition than in our English Romantic comedy. The sanity of Shakespeare's fools is doubtful; their criticisms and comments, shrewd as they are, may be due to that power of keen sharp observation which children often possess rather than to any faculty for sustained reasoning.

> 'And in his brain,—
> Which is as dry as the remainder biscuit
> After a voyage,—he hath strange places cramm'd
> With observation, the which he vents
> In mangled forms.'[1]

The fool is the person whose speech whether natural or affected is impulsive, disconnected, disregarding all the usual laws of thought and logical sequence. This makes him an object of ridicule, this sets him apart from ordinary folk. Even when the entertainment he affords is of a higher kind than the loathsome amusement caused by mere deformity of mind or body, it is the idea that he is irresponsible, childish, and innocent, that lends piquancy to his shrewd criticism. The point of the jest is gone if the fool is regarded as other men; it is his business at least to appear a pariah. But there is always a tendency in art, and perhaps in life too, for the centre of gravity to shift, for sympathy to desert well-regulated society and veer round to the outcasts, the fools and the knaves and the scapegraces.

'I will confess a truth to thee, reader,' says Charles Lamb, 'I love a *Fool*—as naturally as if I were of kith and kin to him. When a child... I had more yearnings towards that simple architect that built his house upon the sand than I entertained for his more cautious neighbour. I grudged at the hard censure pronounced upon the quiet soul that kept his talent; and—prizing their simplicity beyond the more provident, and, to my apprehension, somewhat *unfeminine* wariness of their competitors—I felt a kindliness, that almost amounted to a *tendre*, for those five thoughtless virgins. I have never made an acquaintance since that lasted, or a friendship that answered, with any that had not some tincture of the absurd in their characters.'[2]

So the fool is neither mocked nor pitied for his folly, he is loved for it. Pierrot and Harlequin are attractive, even lovable figures, but not as a rule exemplars of the social virtues. The greatest and fattest of Shakespeare's fools has always been able to win hearts, even the hearts of those he gulls. We blame Malvolio

---

[1] *As You Like It*, act II, sc. 6, ll. 38–42.   [2] *All Fools' Day.*

for trying to disturb the uncivil rule in Olivia's household; we applaud the Jolly Men of Feckenham when, in defiance of common-sense, they build a stack not of hay but of blossom.

> 'And was not this I tell to you
> A fiery-hearted thing to do?'[1]

The fool is no longer a mere butt, he is no longer a grotesque living symbol of the baser side of human nature, he is no longer a walking sneer, he is becoming a delightful, if not a venerable figure. 'Blossom stacks are not good for trade' says the Puritan; 'What of it?' says the fool, and he speaks once more as the ancient mouthpiece of the gods. The Puritan, of course, is right; the stacked-up blossoms have no market value, and they injure the fruit harvest. If left to himself the fool will do a great deal of harm in the real world. He is a menace. But since we cannot do without him we take him up out of reality and plant him in the temporary holiday world of misrule or the permanent imaginary world of comedy, a world where he and his brother knave can do their worst against society and no hurt done. This indeed seems to be the true meaning of comedy; it is the kind of drama that provides a safe environment for the fool, a primrose world in which the virtuous man may lie down with the knave because nothing is of any real consequence. Without a touch of misrule a play may be a most brilliantly witty tract or satire but hardly a successful comedy.

This point of view is brought out by Charles Lamb in his famous defence of Restoration Comedy. He found in the Comedy of Manners that 'escape from the pressure of reality' which almost everybody needs, and which is the foundation of the cult of the fool.

'I confess for myself that (with no great delinquencies to answer for) I am glad for a season to take an airing beyond the diocese of the strict conscience, not to live always in the precincts of the law courts, but now and then, for a dream-while or so, to imagine a world with no meddling restrictions, to get into recesses whither the hunter cannot follow me.... I wear my shackles more contentedly for having respired the breath of an imaginary freedom.'[2]

---

[1] John Drinkwater, *The Feckenham Men.*
[2] *On the Artificial Comedy of the Last Century.*

This apology of Lamb's is only a more subtle form of the argument that had been used at Paris in defence of the Feast of Fools. The divines, of course, had the harder task, for they were defending a Misrule which really did interfere with the business of life, and Lamb is emphatic that his Misrule has no sort of connection with reality. Both, however, dwell on the value of a temporary escape from law. Lamb, indeed, is speaking of an aesthetic escape from the laws of morality, but his argument serves equally well as a justification of the shrewd but half-witted fool who, by engaging our sympathy for himself, enables us to escape from sympathy with the laws of reason. It comes to much the same thing. In both cases the real desire is for escape from fact, from actuality, from the remorseless law of cause and effect, of irrevocable consequence, whether this actuality manifest itself through the cold reasonings of the logician—the Caledonian intellect which Lamb describes so feelingly[1]—or through the weight of senseless matter which at any moment may crash down upon us and wipe out all our fancies, all our loves, all our life. There is no escape from these things except by way of laughter and inattention. Like Falstaff, we must be afflicted with 'the disease of not listening, the malady of not marking' when the Lord Chief Justice approaches. And here the fool can help us. We love and need him because his very absurdity seems to render him invulnerable, he cannot make a plan himself, and almost he persuades us that no plan need ever be made. As Lord of Misrule the fool leads us away for a time from the ordinary working world, and plunges us into revelry and forgetfulness; but in his higher capacity as Abbot of Unreason he draws the sting out of the workaday world and suggests that we have only to shift our point of view ever so slightly and we shall see it for the illusory, insubstantial pageant that it is.

The fool then is applauded because he is the person to whom nothing really matters, because he is the great foe of fact, of fact at least as defined by the Puritan and the business man. He appears again and again in Shakespeare's plays, not always in the cap and bells. Falstaff, the apotheosis of the stage-clown, defies

[1] *Imperfect Sympathies.*

social law by the force of his personality and the genius behind
his humour. He shakes himself free of fact with a jest, and goes
on his way rejoicing. But he is tripped up in the end. One fact
cannot be evaded: the fool can persuade us that wisdom is not
wise, that goodness is not good; he can hardly persuade us that
we are not to die.

So pathos makes its way into comedy. The opponent of fact is
fighting a losing battle. Into the midst of the pageantry and mummings of the Middle Ages and Renaissance, steals the sinister
danse macabre. It is a recessional of all society. Emperor, Pope,
peasant, one after another they come on as in a review, and one
after another the skeleton death beckons them away. One of the
stock figures in the danse macabre is the fool. He laughs in death's
face but his laughter cannot save him. But although predestined
to defeat, the fool is apt to be regarded as the particular foe of
death, the most troublesome of all his victims. The Duke in
Measure for Measure desires the miserable Claudio to reason
thus with life:

> 'Merely, thou art death's fool;
> For him thou labour'st by thy flight to shun,
> And yet run'st toward him still.'

And Douce thinks that the reference is to 'the fool in the old
dumb shows exhibited at fairs and perhaps at inns, in which he
was generally engaged in a struggle with Death.'[1] In engravings
of capital letters illustrating the danse macabre the fight between
death and the fool is represented. Douce had in his possession one
of these letters in which 'the *Fool* is engaged in a very stout combat
with his adversary, and is actually buffeting him with a bladder
filled with peas or small pebbles, an instrument yet in fashion
among *Merry Andrews*.'[2] Douce, moreover, told Steevens that
when he was a young man he had seen a figure disguised as a
skeleton sitting in the booth of a fair, and Steevens also relates in
this connection an anecdote told him by an old clergyman:

'He told me that he very well remembered to have met with such

[1] Francis Douce, *Illustrations of Shakespeare* (London, 1807), vol. II,
p. 305; cf. also vol. I, pp. 129 ff., vol. II, pp. 129 ff.
[2] *Shakespeare*, ed. Johnson and Steevens (London, 1793), vol. XIII, p. 498,
note 2 on *Pericles*, act III, sc. 2, ll. 40, 41.

another figure, above fifty years ago, at Salisbury. Being there during the time of some publick meeting, he happened to call on a surgeon at the very instant when the representative of *Death* was brought in to be let blood on account of a tumble he had had on the stage, while in pursuit of his antagonist, a *Merry Andrew*, who very anxiously attended him (dressed also in character) to the phlebotomist's house. The same gentleman's curiosity a few days afterwards, prevailed on him to be a spectator of the dance in which our emblem of mortality was a performer. This dance, he says, entirely consisted of *Death's* contrivances to surprize the *Merry Andrew*, and of the *Merry Andrew's* efforts to elude the stratagems of *Death*, by whom at last he was overpowered; his *finale* being attended with such circumstances as mark the exit of the Dragon of Wantley.'[1]

No stress, of course, can be laid on a single incident of this kind, for knowledge of which we depend on Steevens' good faith and an old man's memory. But I mention it not as a proof of any theory, but as an illustration of a mood which is constantly recurring, and which may find expression in crude revel or in subtle art. It was a mood which coloured French and English literature in the Middle Ages, especially in the fifteenth century; and we can trace the same kind of mingling of the macabre and fool spirit during the Romantic period. Heine's work is full of it. Charles Lamb is a living embodiment of it. It finds fascinating expression in the illustrated anecdotes of *Pauvre Pierrot*, with which Willette adorned the walls of the Café du Chat Noir. His Pierrot is an ambiguous figure. Is he an accomplished rascal or an innocent child? It is difficult to decide, because his very presence reduces both this world and the next to nonsense. He jests the world away, but he jests with death dogging him at his heels. He makes love to a rose by moonlight, and the moon has the face of a skull. He plays at cards, and the result is a forgone conclusion. 'Elles sont si jolies, les cartes, leurs couleurs si vives et si gaies,...Il joue, il joue avec la Mort, qui gagne toujours la partie, mais elle du moins n'a pas triché.' The last picture of all represents the Plague, a terrible figure with a scythe, rushing through a landscape swept clean of Pierrots and Columbines. 'Enfin voilà le choléra....Bim-Boum, Zoum-Zim. Toujours

[1] *Loc. cit.* p. 498.

comme ça.' The joy of escaping from fact only increases the terror of that last fact from which there is no escape.

Sometimes, however, the relationship between the adversaries is ambiguous. Is death the great final fact, or is he himself one of those serious things that do not matter? Sometimes death and the fool seem to be regarded not as enemies but as allies united in antagonism to the world: they are represented in some old engravings as sitting together amicably enough, mocking at the miser and his money bag. Shakespeare must refer to some drawing of this kind when he makes Cerimon prefer to practise physic

> 'Than to be thirsty after tottering honour,
> Or tie my treasure up in silken bags
> To please the fool and death.'[1]

In the danse macabre death himself sometimes appears in the cap and bells.

Ambiguity and escape is then the keynote of the fool and of his festival. Misrule offers us a safety-valve for superfluous energies, a contrast to the normal, a temporary holiday from restraint, an opportunity for satirising the social order, but above and beyond all this it induces in us a suspension of belief in law. The fool is not a rebel; he does not revolt against circumstance, but he suggests a doubt as to the finality of circumstance. He offers us a momentary freedom and an undefined hope. He confronts the solidity of things with a note of interrogation.

Desire for freedom lies at the bottom of all the various manifestations of the fool, but it expresses itself in many different forms among different classes of people, and it is satisfied by many different kinds of revelling and art from rough Saturnalian riots to the subtle imaginative freedom of Romantic comedy. What kind of freedom do we find in the masque? It is, as we have seen, closely connected with misrule and the Lord of Misrule, and we should expect it to stand in some well-defined relation to the sotie, which is the direct outcome of the Feast of Fools described by M. Petit de Julleville as a pure masquerade.

However, at first sight, the sotie as analysed by M. Petit de

[1] *Pericles*, act III, sc. 2, ll. 40–43.

Julleville[1] seems to be the direct antithesis of the masque. In Pierre Gringoire's sotie Mère Eglise arrives from Italy to stir up sedition against the good Prince des Sots (i.e. Louis XII). Can it indeed be holy Mother Church who does such wrong? But no. Look at her a little more closely. After all, it is only the old Mère Sotte at her tricks again[2]. Look, on the other hand, at the procession of radiant beings, Oberons, Fairy Queens and what not, who haunt our courtly masques. What are they but feeble shadows and pale reflections of the Royal Family of England?

> 'Melt earth to sea, sea flow to air,
> And air fly into fire,
> Whilst we in tunes to Arthur's chair
> Bear Oberon's desire;
> Than which there's nothing can be higher,
> Save James to whom it flies:
> But he the wonder is of tongues, of ears, of eyes.'[3]

What connection can there be between the noble masquers, glories of the spring, famous queens of antiquity, and the sots who symbolise 'l'homme en général et les grands en particulier, abandonnés à la bêtise et au vice qui sont au fond de nos instincts'?[4] The contrast, however, is more striking than real. It is true that masque is the opposite of satire, the one a compliment to life, the other an insult; but unless our research into the nature of the fool has been in vain, the satirical side of the sotie must be regarded as almost accidental. The Feast of Fools afforded a grand opportunity for making fun of opponents, but though satire was often the outcome, it was not the essence of the foolery. Fundamentally the sotie does not satirise reality but escapes from it.

This becomes clear if we compare the sotie with other forms of comedy less directly influenced by the fool motif. Ben Jonson in his Comedy of Humours, for instance, lashes out at the vices and follies of the time, and excites his readers either to sympathetic moral indignation or to an angry repelling of his attacks. But

---

[1] *Les Comédiens en France au Moyen Age*, pp. 32, 33, 144–146.
[2] *Le Jeu du Prince des Sotz et Mère Sotte*, reprinted in *Œuvres Complètes de Gringore*, ed. Ch. d'Héricault, A. de Montaiglon (Paris, 1858), vol. I, pp. 198 ff.
[3] *The Masque of Oberon*.
[4] Petit de Julleville, *Les Comédiens en France au Moyen Age*, p. 32.

the sotie and other forms of Fool literature divert earnest hatred
into appreciative laughter, and leave one with a half-pleasant,
half-melancholy sense that all life is nothing but vanity and
illusion. Perhaps it was because the ironic temperament of
Erasmus led him to regard the church life of his day as a kind of
huge sotie, that he was so powerless to bring about the reformation he so sincerely desired. Like Meredith's 'Spirit of Comedy,'
he sought to lead the erring into the paths of moderation by
means of intellectual laughter, but perhaps all unwittingly he
merely helped them to outjest the grim realities of the situation
until they were rudely awakened by the thunders of Genevan
conventicles, which closed up all the channels of escape, and proclaimed the good news of a universe in which there was no
kindly Feast of Fools, no truce from the remorseless vigilance of
the 'great Taskmaster's eye.'

In spite of all the Court etiquette, the Lord of Misrule left his
mark on the masque as well as the sotie. Over the Court masque
too there lay the veil of illusion and unreality. Even at Whitehall
expression was given to the desire for freedom and for flight.
For the escape from our dread world where fact cannot be over-
ridden, and where causes must have consequences, can be made
through two small gates, the gate of humour and the gate of magic.
The artist who would relieve us from the oppressive reality of
potentates and politicians may gain his ends either by adorning
the grave creatures with the motley and the coxcomb or by blur-
ring their outlines in a bright unearthly radiance. The poet,
musician and scene painter put their heads together, and that
Court, where the decision as to whether an ambassador should
sit on a chair or a stool might be connected with the fate of nations
and of Churches, was transformed into a fairy land, where Time
was vindicated, Pleasure reconciled to Virtue, and the Golden Age
restored. To those around her Queen Elizabeth's frown might
mean loss of money or loss of life. But at Hertford this was the
Fairies' song:
　　　　　　　　'Elisa is the fairest Quene,
　　　　　　　　That ever trod upon this greene.
　　　　　　　　Elisaes eyes are blessed starres,
　　　　　　　　Inducing peace, subduing warres.

Elisaes hand is christal bright,
Her wordes are balme, her lookes are light.
Elisaes brest is that faire hill,
Where Vertue dwels, and sacred skill,
O blessed bee each day and houre,
Where sweet Elisa builds her bowre.'[1]

To treat the terrible lady in this playful lovesick fashion must have been almost as satisfying as to discover that the Church was only the old Mère Sotte after all.

But although through its courtly environment the masque tended to become very conventional, it was not always nor essentially a mere vehicle for pompous flattery. The early Florentine masquerades were, as we have seen, parodies of folk-festivals, the French ballet de Cour was often merely a collection of bouffonneries, and however resplendent the masque became it never quite lost its grotesque aspect, not even at the English Court.

Grotesque masques abounded in the two years of Edward VI's reign, when George Ferrars came to Court as the mock monarch, bringing with him a whole bevy of fools, all wearing a motley coat.

When the grotesque dance, instead of being an independent entertainment, was a prelude to the main masque, its development was inevitably restricted. The theme of the Court masque was always the same at bottom; it was the theme of social harmony, the glorification of marriage as a social function, the idealisation of a united nation under a strong centralised government. The antimasque afforded relief from all this high seriousness, but the poet who desired to achieve artistic unity and at the same time to gratify his employers, had to keep his foolery in strict bounds. Misrule had to be shown as the foe and moreover the vanquished foe of Hymen. So the she-follies are represented as the wicked servants of the Sphinx from whom love is freed; the misshapen creatures of the alchemists disappeared on the arrival of the beautiful masquers. It was through methods such as these that Ben Jonson managed to preserve the unity of action by keeping the comic element in a subordinate position. And even he in his

[1] *Prog. Eliz.* vol. III, p. 119.

later masques had to give undue prominence to the antimasque. Most of the poets, however, were not overburdened with artistic conscience, and supplied without demur the grotesque dances that the public demanded. In consequence, the vitality of the masque passed from the main dance to the antimasque, which expanded and multiplied itself, and too often had little enough connection with the true theme, all that the spectators required being strangeness, variety, and buffoonery. The stately Court masque was on its way to becoming a mere phantasmagoria.

In spite, however, of the encroachments of the antimasque, it never developed the subtler traits of fool comedy. The instinct of escape was satisfied, as it was in folk-festivals, by eccentric gestures, absurdity, and abnormality. But that society itself was fantastic, that the courtier and fool might well change places, that was a suggestion not to be breathed in the banqueting hall.

If the masque had little of the freedom of the sotie, it had still less of the grim irony of the danse macabre. Death, who was such a common figure in the art and drama of the fifteenth century, seldom appeared in the courtly revels of Renaissance England. But as if there was something sinister in his very absence, the masque seems often to have suggested the thought of death and the brevity and insignificance of life to the writers of the time. The antimasque, for instance, took on a macabre colouring in the mind of Sir Thomas Browne: 'The World to me is but a dream or mock-show, and we all therein but Pantalones and Anticks to my severer contemplations.'[1]

There is no doubt that aesthetically the masque suffered greatly from the inevitable suppression of the comic and macabre spirit. The poets might have done great things with the masque if sometimes they could have turned the antimasque into a sly criticism or parody of the main masque, or if they had dared to mingle romance and irony. As it was, however, even apart from the ambitions of Inigo Jones and the tastes of the Philistine courtiers, it was almost inevitable that the main masque should develop into a series of elaborate transformation scenes and the antimasque into a variety entertainment; for there was no other

[1] *Religio Medici*, Part I.

permissible way of relieving the sameness and conventionality of the performance. And it was not only from the aesthetic point of view that this was regrettable. Unfortunately, the development of the masque meant not only a decrease of poetic value, but an increase of expense.

During the last years of King Charles' unquestioned reign the Court masque grew continually in splendour and magnificence, and all the time, unknown to the performers, death and the fool were haunting Whitehall, invisible spectators of the revels, waiting in silence for the danse macabre to be danced in bitter earnest:

> 'Within the hollow crown
> That rounds the mortal temples of a king
> Keeps Death his court, and there the antick sits,
> Scoffing his state and grinning at his pomp.'[1]

In the last chapter I suggested that art springs from revelling; that the man who makes a poem, the mummer who dances in the spring, the housemaid who croons over her work, are all moved by one and the same impulse, and that is the impulse to express the joy and value of existence. The masque was chosen as the theme of this book because by its peculiar position it is a demonstration of the fact that art is no looking-glass land, no pale reflection of life, but the inevitable outcome of intense living, of passionate faith in life for life's sake. The turbulent high spirits of the mummer are indeed rarefied and transmuted into the artist's more subtle sense of value, but both express the same fundamental loyalty to existence.

In this chapter I have been dealing with a complementary aspect of revelling, and have endeavoured to show that when misrule is present, revelling is used as a means of escape, not indeed from life, but from those grim realities that hang over life and force men to lose their grip of joy, and 'propter vitam vivendi perdere causas.' In its crudest form this misrule is a mere outburst of high spirits and physical energy, a violent departure from normal conduct; but in its higher manifestations it is an attempt—though possibly an unconscious one—to attain a sense

[1] *Richard II*, act III, sc. 2, ll. 160–163.

of freedom from circumstance by a slight adjustment of the point of view. In a very subtle form this higher kind of misrule, this sense of the ambiguity of things, impregnates not only the revels but all art.

Every successful work of art brings home to the emotions—though not necessarily to the reason—the fact that, deeply considered, all human experience is mysterious, all human consciousness consciousness of the unknown. Every landscape painting, for instance, is ambiguous. Why was it done? Was the painter imitating something outside himself that he had seen, or expressing something within himself that he had felt? And then we realise that the ambiguity is not so much in the landscape painting as in the landscape. The very word scenery indicates that for us nature is only an extension of art, a background for the human drama.

> 'O Lady, we receive but what we give,
> And in our life alone does Nature live.'

Yes, but if it is *all* there in our minds, why can we not enjoy it directly without having to receive it back again at Nature's hand? Most works of art record a moment when the mind of a man was in conscious emotional contact with an unknown something that came to him from outside through his senses or memory; it is an expression of the felt value of that contact, but it is not and it cannot be a full elucidation of the *nature* of that contact, for even the acutest philosophers have so far failed to give a wholly acceptable decision as to how much the mind gives and how much the mind receives from the external world, and how far our consciousness is a faithful mirror of reality.

The poet and the philosopher have always been inclined to look askance at each other, probably because they are both concerned with the same mystery but with very different ends in view. The philosopher seeks to understand, to elucidate, to destroy mystery by explanation, and because it is the greatest of all obstacles to explanation, he tries to do away with the dualism of mind and matter, existence and value. Sometimes he tries to simplify his problem by demonstrating either that mind is matter, or that matter is mind. Neither of these simplifications has ever been accepted by the average man; both of them are implicitly rejected by the artist as such, whatever his conscious philosophy may be.

The materialist, as such, is antipathetic both to the artist and the fool, for both of them consciously or unconsciously bear witness to a possible spiritual freedom, the fool by escaping from the real, the artist by creating a new reality.

There is, however, possibly a certain affinity between the Lord of Misrule and the idealistic philosopher. The antics of the fool and the beautiful syllogisms of the idealist both give us the same sense of escape from circumstance, and both break down in the same way. The arguments of the idealist may seem unanswerable, his system beautifully complete; but just as we are exulting in the nothingness of matter and the omnipotence of mind, there rises up in us our one stubborn unshakable piece of knowledge, and we cry in the old human way,

> 'Ay, but to die, and go we know not where;
> To lie in cold obstruction and to rot;
> This sensible warm motion to become
> A kneaded clod.'

Death has defeated the Merry Andrew. Or is it perhaps that death and the fool, together, watch the philosopher elaborating arguments as they watch the miser heaping gold, with the same sly malice and the same ambiguous amusement?

For pure idealism is really hardly less fatal to art than is pure materialism. Surely, for instance, we should miss much of the significance of the drama if we regarded the dramatist as an arbitrary creator instead of as a man brooding upon a reality common to him and to us. It is not the coherence of art but the incoherence of dream which is the result of mental activity uncontrolled by anything outside itself.

But in truth it is not so much either idealism or materialism, but full logical explanation which is antipathetic both to misrule and to art. The fool, as we have seen, is always suggesting that there is no finality, no certainty, perhaps no reality. The artist, whether he knows it or not, is constantly putting his reason to St Paul's sanctuary, constantly losing himself in an 'O altitudo.'

The poet as poet delights in the dualism, ambiguity and mystery, that the philosopher longs to explain away. Nevertheless, the poet is a help rather than a hindrance to the philosopher, for his constant assertion of value, wholeness, and mystery is an incentive and a challenge. The poet is always producing something that eludes logical analysis and so acts as a solvent of the closed system, the perfect synthesis, the full explanation, which must always be sought, and yet, being found, would cause intellectual stagnation, the decay of philosophical effort. The poet is not an obscurantist; he delights in the mysterious dualism of mind and matter, not because he loves ignorance, but because he loves life. For the interest both of life and art does seem to depend on the idea that man is neither a mere helpless machine nor a spiritual being moving in a world that offers no resistance, no opportunity for real work or real effort. Inner liberty and external necessity have been called the poles of the Shakespearian tragic conflict, but they are also the poles of all valiant human endeavour, and the poet by his very existence both resists and stimulates the philosopher's effort to deny either the one or the other. The philosopher would unite the soul and the world for the sake of understanding, the poet would divide them for the sake of love.

Poetry can no more be explained or explained away by the philosopher than Socrates could be buried by his friends.

> 'Under the arch of Life, where love and death,
>> Terror and mystery, guard her shrine, I saw
>> Beauty enthroned; and though her gaze struck awe,
> I drew it in as simply as my breath....
> This is that Lady Beauty, in whose praise
>> Thy voice and hand shake still,—long known to thee
>> By flying hair and fluttering hem,—the beat
>> Following her daily of thy heart and feet,
>> How passionately and irretrievably,
> In what fond flight, how many ways and days!'[1]

The poet rejoices in the elusive nature of his art and of that which his art expresses, not indeed because he wishes to end the quest for knowledge, but because he fervently desires that it

---

[1] D. G. Rossetti, *Soul's Beauty* in *The House of Life*, Sonnet CXXVII.

should last for ever He sees reality as an unknown angel with whom mankind must wrestle till the breaking of the day. 'I pray thee tell me thy name.' There is no answer. But the result of the strange ambiguous conflict is a blessing and a wound.

CHAPTER XV

Hymen

'This motion was of Love begot,
It was so airy, light, and good,
His wings into their feet he shot,
Or else himself into their blood.
But ask not how: the end will prove
That Love's in them, or they're in Love.'

JONSON.

ONE of the most familiar figures in the masque was Hymen, Hymen, regarded not merely as 'the god who sits at wedding feasts' but also as the god of marriage regarded as a social function, and even as a mystic symbol of national unity or of the harmony of all men with one another.

Harmony, particularly social harmony, is the underlying theme of most of the masquing and pageantry of our period. The civic pageants were planned as representations of various aspects of civic life displayed in visible form to the honour of the community and the glory of the sovereign, who was himself a kind of embodiment of national unity. The compliment which was essential to the Court masque was inspired by the same motive, and occasionally the poets make this quite clear.

'LOVE. 'Tis done! 'tis done! I've found it out—
Britain's the world, the world without.
The King's the eye, as we do call
The sun the eye of this great all....
The contraries which time till now
Nor fate knew where to join, or how,
Are Majesty and Love; which there,
And nowhere else, have their true sphere.'[1]

'Now move united, and in gait,
As you in pairs do front the state,
With grateful honours thank his grace
That hath so glorified the place:
And as in circle you depart,
Linked hand in hand, so heart in heart
May all those bodies still remain
Whom he with so much sacred pain

[1] Jonson, *Love freed from Ignorance and Folly.*

No less hath bound within his realms
Than they are with the ocean's streams.
Long may his Union find increase,
As he to ours hath deigned his peace!'[1]

These lines are poor but they are explicit, they indicate the social value of revelling, and they help us to understand why revelling attained its fullest development during the Tudor and Stuart régime.

The mediaeval thinker not only regarded Christendom as one living body, he regarded the whole universe as a single organism, made of diverse and unequal members, and created to satisfy the craving of Divine Love for expression and response[2]. This idea might be most satisfying to a certain type of temperament, but the drawback to it was that it left little room for the idea of progress, that the individual was encouraged to fulfil his vocation rather than express his personality or improve his position, and that institutions were apt to be accepted as the unalterable expressions of the Divine Will.

The humanists disturbed but they did not wholly abolish the mediaeval attitude of mind. Their interest in the city-states of antiquity helped to undermine the ideal of a united Christendom, but the idea of organic unity was still applied to the secular state, and was still a conservative ideal involving the principle of a fixed and rigid classification of society. When this ideal was applied to the state instead of to the whole of Christendom, its religious character was naturally weakened. There was a tendency to value social organisation as a bulwark against anarchy rather than as a reflection of the divine order[3]; and the blasphemous flattering of princes, which was such a disagreeable characteristic of Renaissance literature and revelling, was not a mere fashion of speech but

[1] Jonson, *Hymenaei*.
[2] Cf. *Paradiso*, cant. I, ll. 103–120, where Dante expresses in brief, poetic form, the quintessence of the philosophy of St Thomas Aquinas.
[3] Cf. the 'Piccarda' incident in *Paradiso*, cant. III, ll. 34 ff., with the curious episode of Artegall and the Giant with the Ballance in *Faerie Queene*, bk v, cant. 2. Both Piccarda and Artegall defend permanent inequality of status, as an expression of divine order, but Artegall dwells on the perils of anarchy, Piccarda on the blessedness of love—'E la sua volontade è nostra pace.' Cf. also Ulysses' powerful plea for the maintenance of degree as the only defence against universal chaos in *Troilus and Cressida*.

a sign that the state was being regarded as an end in itself. At the Renaissance the state was regarded as a work of art to be enjoyed for its own sake, quite apart from any assumptions as to the nature of the universe[1].

These political ideas of the Renaissance found a fitting vehicle of expression in revelling and pageantry. The reveller glories in an existing situation; like the sportsman he is usually one of a group, but unlike the sportsman he lacks the competitive motive; he is full of the enhanced vitality that comes from shared enjoyment, he is pleasantly conscious of the presence of his fellows, and so, when he becomes aware of his group, he becomes aware of it, not as *his* party to be upheld in opposition to the *other man's* party, but as something to be enjoyed without ulterior motive, something that lifts him out of himself. Revelling springs from high spirits, and when it develops into a solemn social function it naturally represents the community, not as an association founded through fear, not as a necessary or unnecessary evil to be perpetually attacked or changed, but as a society of which the essential principle is harmony and the chief object the supplying of the individual with a fuller draught of life and experience. Undue conservatism is not inherent in this view of society, but it is the exaggeration into which it is most likely to fall, especially when the circumstances of the time are such as to distort love of harmony into fear of chaos.

The Tudor and Stuart masque was bound up with creeds and institutions that the staunchest modern Tory would hardly wish to revive, yet the essential virtue of the masque lay not in its conservative character but in its capacity for expressing the value of fellowship. It strengthened not only the will to live but the will to live in society.

In the last two chapters I took two figures from Jonson's *Masque of Christmas*, Mumming and Misrule, and used them as symbols of the two aspects of revelling. Mumming presides over the revels in so far as they express joie-de-vivre, Misrule lords it

---

[1] See Jacob Burckhardt on 'The State as a work of Art' in *The Civilization of the Renaissance in Italy*. Cf. also the political discussion of Exeter and Canterbury in *Henry V*, act I, sc. 2, ll. 180 ff.

at Christmas time because the revels offer change and freedom; and there is no conflict between the two potentates, because revellers seek to escape not from life but from law and from all those circumstances that threaten their vitality and joy. I also suggested that, in a sublimated and rarefied form, the influence of Mumming and Misrule pervades the whole of art. In this chapter I have tried to show that when revelling develops into a Court function, it owns the sway of a third sovereign; and Hymen begins to preside over the masque as the god of marriage and of social unity. Does Hymen, like Mumming and Misrule, have some influence upon art as well as upon the revels? Is the reveller's praise of human fellowship merely a naïve treatment of the central theme of art? The drama suggests an affirmative answer, but can the drama be taken as the representative art?

When in order to demonstrate the difference between art and revelling I contrasted the drama with the masque, I chose the drama because the survival of the actor makes it more suitable than the other arts for purposes of comparison: the desirability of the actor linking drama to athletic games, ritual and revelling; the fact that the actor can be dispensed with, linking drama to other arts such as music, poetry, and painting. This suggests that the drama occupies a central position amid the non-utilitarian activities; that the masque, the stage play, and the dramatic poem are different stages in the process of disengaging art from actuality; that the drama is the starting-point of the arts; that as the drama can escape from dependence upon bodily movement and current events, so the other arts can escape from drama and find fresh embodiment outside the walls of the theatre. The musician, for instance, can isolate the emotion, the painter record the episodes and elaborate the background, the sculptor can immortalise the gestures, poets and novelists can stretch out the plot, vivisect the actors, expand the utterances, distil the quintessence of the play.

When art is cut loose from actuality, its content as well as its form begins to change. To the ritualist fellowship is a stable possession, to the reveller a source of immediate enjoyment, but to the dramatist it is a difficult achievement, often endangered and disturbed, sometimes destroyed. For when the dramatist steps outside the circle of revellers, he glances at their environment and loses the blithe assurance of the 'dancing courtiers.' He sees that conflict, the threat to harmony, is inseparable from drama, and conflict is set in motion not only by faults of character but also by circumstances over which the human will has no control. Sometimes, indeed, he gazes so fixedly at the environment that his vision grows too large for presentation upon a stage, and he writes a dramatic poem such as *The Dynasts* or *Prometheus Unbound*; or his vision may even grow too large and too elusive not only for presentation upon a stage, but for presentation to the reason, and be expressible only in the emotional language of music. But always the dramatist looks to see how the environment affects the drama.

Needless to say, I do not mean that all forms of art have sprung from some form of drama, although that is a process that can and often does occur[1], but I mean that art is primarily dramatic and appeals mainly to our interest in human intercourse[2].

To say that human intercourse is the central theme of art is not the equivalent of saying that art expresses the worth of that intercourse, and even though it must be admitted that artists generally assume that love is a valuable experience, and that to achieve right relationship with others is an unquestionable good, still they may be using their art to express their wishes rather than their beliefs. That seems to bring us back to the theory that art springs from unsatisfied desire. Mr Sacheverell Sitwell defends baroque art from the attacks of the realists by a curious argument:

'I know that the subjects of my choice are arraigned, in the earnest tones of the learned, because they possessed an entirely scenic conception of life, but the camera should have taught us by now how elusive a quarry is realism. Life, in its human aspect, is very ugly, and has always been so, it being the duty of Art to improve and select, transmuting for our own eyes that which we know to have been sordid into what we can

[1] It is difficult to avoid temporal metaphors, but throughout this section I am trying to trace relationships rather than to describe temporal processes.

[2] The artist may, of course, express his awareness of the external non-human world, cf. *supra*, p. 367; but usually, I think, this awareness includes awareness of a relationship between the non-human and the human, or at least of the fact that the latter may be affected by the former.

be persuaded was beautiful. Let not our generation, then, who are painfully learning to distil once more these forgotten vapours, blame their near ancestors for the density of their smoke-cloud—there are many things still with us that are better hidden!'[1]

This is surely to deliver art up to the iconoclasts, to play into the hands of those who in all ages complain that poetry is useless and the mother of lies. Mr Sitwell is not speaking of origins, yet his remarks help one to understand that the logical consequence of the theory that art is rooted in unsatisfied desire is the further theory that art is nothing more or less than a hypnotic drug which works by means of false and insincere suggestion.

Yet is not the theory that art is rooted in the sense of value open to still graver objections? Does it not force us to regard the artist as a blind optimist, an unconscious if not a conscious hypocrite? The masque, regarded as a social function ruled by Hymen, does, I believe, suggest an answer to this objection.

If it is mainly the human drama that evokes the artist's sense of value, then there is no need for his art to express an easy hopefulness, for human drama and human destiny are two very different things. The artist knows that 'love is a great and thorough good,' his primary concern is with human intercourse and usually with the very simplest aspects of it: love and hatred, meeting and parting, success and failure. But human beings converse with one another 'against a tremendous background of natural happening,'[2] and it is difficult to evade the question as to what is the nature of that background and how it affects the human drama. To some it is the ultimate home of the spirit, to others the realm of Chaos and Old Night. The artist may take either of these views, or he may completely ignore the background, but the one thing which as artist he cannot do is to allow the background to swallow up the drama, until it has 'dwarfed human life to imaginative extinction,'[3] to interpret the human actors in terms of dust and darkness. There is all the difference in the world between the passionate utterance of a despair that comes

[1] *Southern Baroque Art* (London, 1924), pp. 11, 12.
[2] Cf. on the subject of the encroachment of the background in modern art a very fine passage in Miss Harrison's *Ancient Art and Ritual*, pp. 199 ff.
[3] *Loc. cit.*

from finding that the universe as a whole does not correspond to our sense of value, and the utterance which either relieves or drugs the feeling that human life is so worthless that all that we can do is to cheat ourselves into a momentary persuasion that the sordid is beautiful. The artist may travel far into darkness, but his work must surely retain a last flicker of faith, if not in the universe as a whole, at least in the spirit of man as a wild and inexplicable exception to the general scheme of things.

Whether in the long run the humanist attitude can be maintained in the face of a supposedly hostile or indifferent universe I do not know[1]—but humanism is the typical attitude of the artist. The scientist may properly treat men as things, and pick personality to pieces to discover of what it is made. But the artist, as artist, resists the encroachment of the background, he checks the tendency not only to dwarf but to disintegrate human life to imaginative extinction, he takes for granted the mysterious wholeness of personality, and focusses attention upon the moving figures in the foreground rather than upon the scene that lies behind. And in so doing he helps to keep us sane.

In these last chapters I have tried to show that in the masquing-hall we can watch art emerging, not among remote savages, but among people very like ourselves, a sight that naturally encourages us to reflect anew on the nature of art and its function in society. Do these reflections lead to any conclusion as to the worth of the revels? Is study of the masque merely a matter of antiquarian interest or does it revive the memory of something whose loss is to be regretted?

The study of the masque suggests, I believe, that art is essentially the expression of an emotional awareness, firstly of a worth

[1] This question is examined and answered in the affirmative by Mr I. A. Richards in *Science and Poetry* (London, 1926). He points out that a difficult and dangerous mental situation has been created by the predominance of the scientific outlook and the disappearance of religion, which he assumes to be inevitable and complete. He hopes that we may be saved by poetry if poetry can be cut loose from 'beliefs,' a term which for him includes far more than religious dogmas. With ruthless courage and logic Mr Richards shows how many of our apparently secular ideas and institutions are dependent upon the religious attitude, but, to my mind at least, he does not furnish any convincing reason for hoping that poetry will be able to survive the loss of these 'beliefs' and the ideas and institutions dependent upon them.

which is not synonymous with utility, and secondly and perhaps less essentially of an apparent tendency in things to withdraw themselves and to keep on the further side of our powers of critical analysis, of an element in our experience which is not amenable to logical statement. Anything whatsoever may excite this awareness of value and mysteriousness, but the most secure, the most recurrent, the most fundamental theme of the artist is the worth of the human soul, the inexhaustible finality of human love. Elsewhere the artist may have to retreat before the man of science, the philosopher, or the moralist; here he is on the firmer ground of an immediate and universal human experience. His art could not long survive the surrender of this position.

It was, I believe, because the masque emphasised very simply the value of human fellowship, because—in spite of Inigo Jones—it was a drama without a background, that it could be made to serve a useful social purpose, and that it exerted in the main a wholesome influence upon literature. For in the part played by Hymen we have a clue to the connection between the social utility and the aesthetic value of a work of art.

The masque poet was kept close to the fundamental theme, because the masque was still so close to the original source of art, and this fact must be borne in mind by those who would judge rightly of the worth of the masque, or of the possibility of producing a harmony of all the arts. In attacking this problem critics are apt, first to assume that the arts in their most highly developed forms are to be adjusted to one another, and then to show that this adjustment is undesirable if not impossible. But they disregard the possibility that the arts may be combined *at low pressure*, and that there may be a peculiar beauty in the combination, which compensates for the fact that each art has had to sacrifice something of its own proper excellence. The masque shows how this may happen, and under what conditions it is desirable. The arts draw nearer to each other as they draw nearer to life, nearer to their rudimentary function as an enhancement of ordinary social activities. The libretto, the stage design, and the musical composition might be mediocre; but the

masque itself was electric with the mirth and vitality of the ballroom.

But does this really settle the question of the worth of the
masque, of the developed aesthetic revel? If we can enjoy the
artist's subtle experiences of value and mystery and love, why
should we recall him to adorn the leapings of the mummer, the
irrational buffooneries of the Lord of Misrule, the complacent
postures of Hymen? Is he to be recalled for his own sake or
only for the sake of those who cannot digest the highest forms
of art?

If the artist is to express the full worth of love, if he is to
create a space for the meeting of human personalities possessed
of the most complete integrity and of the fullest possible awareness of themselves and their surroundings, he cannot confine his
attention to the village green or the dancing floor at Whitehall.
The impulse that moves the revellers' limbs sometimes drives
the thoughts of the artist to the very verge of the mind, that
abyss to which all extremes of thought or emotion lead at last.
This is as it should be, because this experience is part of a full
human consciousness; but this experience is peculiarly perilous
to the artist. He always uses a language which is inevitably more
emotional, fluid, and private than that of the philosopher;
confronted with the abyss he may be tempted to express his
feelings in an inarticulate stammer significant to no one but himself. There is also a danger that the original impulse may fail,
and that the tired and giddy artist may turn to those other
mental adventurers who stand with him by the precipice, and
may allow his art to be converted into an inexact science or an
ineffectual religion. Or dazzled by the rich and varied contents
of consciousness he may lose faith in the integrity of personality.

Threatened by these dangers the artist needs an occasional
reminder that he is not a philosopher but a strayed reveller, he
needs to be recalled to his fellows, to be encouraged to stop
thinking and begin once more to dance. This recall is perhaps
particularly needed now, but it is particularly difficult to bring
about, because the modern artist has so far outdistanced the
revellers that he is out of earshot. But at a time like the

Renaissance, when the revels had developed an art of their own, this recall was frequent but almost unnecessary, because the revellers were so close behind that even on the verge of the abyss the artist could hardly help thinking in time to the bells, the waving torches and moving feet of the spring-dancers.

As a work of art, then, the masque could be good though perhaps not excellent. As an influence upon art it might be of the greatest value, firstly, because it encouraged sanity of outlook and technique by concentrating upon the fundamental theme, and secondly, because through its closeness to real life it vitalised art and supplied the poet with an ever fresh source of fervent, yet tantalising, inspiration. This is admirably illustrated by Fuller's description of a court-lady watching the masque with a prim yet wistful pleasure[1]:

'*Though pleasantly affected, she is not transported with Court-delights:* as in their statelie Masques and Pageants....He is no friend to the tree, that strips it of the bark; neither do they mean well to majestie, which would deprive it of outward shews, and State-solemnities...however, our Lady by degrees is brought from delighting in such Masques, onely to be contented to see them, and at last (perchance) could desire to be excused from that also.

*Yet in her reduced thoughts she makes all the sport she hath seen earnest to her self....*When she remembreth how suddenly the Scene in the Masque was altered (almost before moment it self could take notice of it) she considereth, how quickly mutable all things are in this world.... The lively representing of things so curiously, that Nature her self might grow jealous of Art, in outdoing her, minds our Lady to make sure work with her own soul, seeing hypocrisie may be so like to sincerity. But, O what a wealthy exchequer of beauties did she there behold, severall faces most different, most excellent, (so great is the variety even in bests) what a rich mine of jewels above ground, all so brave, so costly! To give Court-masques their due, of all the bubbles in this world, they have the greatest variety of fine colours. But all is quickly ended: this is the spight of the world, if ever she affordeth fine ware, she always pincheth it in the measure, and it lasts not long: But oh, thinks our Lady, how glorious a place is Heaven, *where there are joyes for evermore.*'

This, coming from an unworldly divine, is a remarkable

[1] *The Holy State*, bk IV, chap. XIII.

tribute to the attractiveness of these entertainments. Fuller's meditation has only to be transposed from the ethical to the aesthetic key to become an admirable account of the poetic imagination at work upon the masque, as half-disdainful yet wholly charmed by the glowing, joyous festivities, it makes them the starting-point for its own subtler regrets and musings.